THE ERA
1947-1957

When the Yankees,

the Giants, and

the Dodgers

Ruled the World

◆

ROGER KAHN

WITH A NEW AFTERWORD BY THE AUTHOR

UNIVERSITY OF NEBRASKA PRESS
LINCOLN AND LONDON

First Bison Books printing: 2002
The Chesterfield advertisement on page 287 is reprinted by permission of Eve
Holdings Inc.

Library of Congress Cataloging-in-Publication Data
Kahn, Roger.
The era, 1947–1957: when the Yankees, the Giants, and the Dodgers ruled the
world / Roger Kahn; with a new afterword by the author.
p. cm.
Originally published: New York: Ticknor & Fields, 1993.
Includes bibliographical references (p.   ) and index.
ISBN 0-8032-7805-5 (pbk: alk. paper)
1. New York Yankees (Baseball team)—History—20th century. 2. New York
Giants (Baseball team)—History—20th century. 3. Brooklyn Dodgers (Baseball
team)—History—20th century. 4. Baseball—United States—History—20th
century. 5. United States—History—1945–   I. Title.
GV875.N4 K34 2002
796.357'64'097471—dc21
2001052240

To Katy

Contents

◆

THE ERA

◆

Prologue

◆

ISTORY, LIKE WAR AND LOVE, is seldom neat, and I want to set down right here that *The Era* is not a story about ten years. Not a nice round number. *The Era* covers eleven seasons. These were, I believe, equally the most important and the most exciting years in the history of sport. But the time span remains eleven seasons, rather than ten. That small accuracy invalidates such phrases as "Baseball's Golden Decade," an effect that is not entirely unfortunate.

The Era centers on the three great baseball teams that played in New York City from 1947 through 1957, when New York was the capital of the world. I don't mean that in the conventional, jargonistic way: media capital, financial capital, whatever. New York was those things, but more than that New York was where everyone wanted to come to write or compose or dance or toot the oboe or make a fortune or find a lover or play baseball. The city was affordable and, barring nuclear war, safe for human habitation. It wasn't a local stop, New York,

New York. It was the closest we have seen to a cosmic town. New York, USA; New York, Solar System; New York, Milky Way; New York, Universe. Well, come on in.

Following publication of *The Boys of Summer,* which centers on the years 1952 and 1953 in the borough of Brooklyn, journalists and academics jumped into the Era with a vengeance. The subsequent orgy produced at least twenty-eight books that touch aspects of the Era. Unfortunately, as spruce forests fell in the service of literature, errata mounted. On the most basic level I find myself like the person who has been on the scene of an incident of some kind that makes the newspapers. Perhaps you have been in that situation yourself. Reading the paper the next day, you shake your head and say, "That isn't quite right. The paper has it wrong. That's not the way it was. Worst of all, they misspelled cousin Sulinda's middle name." I am a graduate of the Era and susceptible to the wrongly-spelled-middle-name syndrome.

Each specific error may appear minor, but each is disquieting. If you set down small details incorrectly, the picture at large appears false, or at least unbelievable. Such is the stuff of the writing seminars that occupy so many summer days on so many summer hills, so far from big-town ballparks. Put more succinctly, if you can't get the third baseman's name right, if you lose track of the count, what else have you gotten wrong?

One purpose here is to set down the Era as it was. For that, for accuracy, an author can offer up nine parts research and one intense muttered prayer.

To seek accuracy is not to surrender one's prejudices. Accordingly, this work reflects some.

I think the Jackie Robinson experience is enormous, both in intensity and in significance, and it earns a great deal of space. The Stengel phenomenon of 1949 — entering the Bronx as a comedian and exiting as a field marshal — is another kind of triumph. Larry MacPhail's public nervous breakdown in 1947 was a memorable disaster, and Leo Durocher's '47 collision with the commissioner of baseball and the Roman Catholic Church is bruising and extraordinary.

Joe DiMaggio encountering old baseball age and Willie Mays joining us from Olympus are irresistible sagas. Accordingly, I have more to say in these pages about the years from 1947 to 1951, when these things happened, than I do about the seasons from 1952 to 1957.

Do not expect silence about Don Larsen's perfect game, or his court date that followed. I knew Walter O'Malley for more than fifty years and I don't look at his uprooting the Dodgers to California with bland acceptance. But in sum, I give the most acreage to those who were Founding Fathers to the Era.

It is regularly written that Jackie Robinson, the first black major leaguer of this century, was a boon to attendance at Ebbets Field. In 1946, the all-white Brooklyn Dodgers drew 1,796,824 at home. With Jackie Robinson in 1947, the integrated Dodgers drew 1,807,526. The difference, about 11,000 spectators, works out to 150 fans a game. That is not a significant number. Good, winning baseball, not integration, put good Brooklyn bottoms onto the green-slatted seats at Ebbets Field. Robinson was a winning ballplayer, a great winning ballplayer, but the impact of his hue on local gate receipts has been wildly exaggerated.

Integration did have a most powerful effect in focusing attention on baseball and, more important, on racism. Would Robinson make it? Who was the Giants' new kid Mays and did he really call his manager "Mistuh Leo"? Would the Yankees ever allow a black to wear the hallowed pinstripes? How dare the Giants field an all-black outfield? These questions led to challenging talk. I don't think baseball talk ever again has been quite so passionate, quite so unselfconsciously sociological.

But here is a curious thing. From the start of the Era to the end, attendance declined sharply at all three New York ballparks. In 1947, about 5.5 million tickets were sold for New York baseball. In 1957, the total was 3.2 million. If the talk was as rich as I say, the baseball so compelling, the interest so fervid, where on earth were all the people?

Some were packing for a move to the suburbs. Others, most of the others, were watching television. In a practical sense, television was born during the Era. As people from Brooklyn to Baghdad are forever discovering, television changes the world.

We stood on a Brooklyn street, Washington Avenue, birth-place of Aaron Copland, one warm June night in 1947. The Boston Braves had just swapped pitchers with the Giants, Mort Cooper for Bill Voiselle, plus cash. We massed outside Roy's Radio Store, staring at a large wooden box, within which glowed a small, round, grayish, snowy screen. Joe Hatten was pitching to Willard Marshall ten blocks away. That was the ballgame. Roy's snowy screen — baseball *live* on television — was magic.

Two of the various men who owned significant parts of New York ballclubs during most of the Era can fairly be described as (1) a drunk and (2) a dilettante. But another, Branch Rickey in Brooklyn, may have been a genius, and his successor, Walter O'Malley, was a daring, dazzling businessman. Still, none of these people, from the drunk to the dazzler, knew how to cope with television. (At the end of his life, disappointed with the look of televised baseball, Rickey was seriously suggesting that engineers get to work developing a pyramidal screen.)

The owners first regarded television simply as a new reve-nue source and grabbed. Business 101. Greed without fore-sight. By 1950 or so, every home game played by every New York ballclub was televised, without fee to the viewer. Cable tele-vision was not yet practicable. The first thing that changed was the skyline of New York. Scrawny forests of antennas sprang up on rooftops from Canarsie by the sea to Woodlawn Cemetery in the trackless north Bronx. Beneath these iron branches, patterns were redone.

Watch Milton Berle. He's dressed up like a *yenta*. Uncle Miltie. Too much. He's wearing a dress!

Hey, Jackie Gleason. Hah! His upper lip is twitching! He's clenched his fist. He's gonna punch that pretty wife of his to the moon!

Screens grew. It stopped snowing in July. Jewish grand-mothers noticed that Pee Wee Reese was a fine-looking boy. (Too bad he's married already.) Italian housewives saw the scooting speed of Phil Rizzuto. But he's so little. *Mangia*, Phillie. *Mangia*. Not the least of the changes that modified baseball during the Era was this. As second base moved into everybody's parlor, rooting went coed.

Coincidentally and independently, baseball flowered. As start-ers, we had integration. Then the loudest, crudest, and one of the best managers since the dawn of time was booted from the game. The somewhat blurry charges against him included loose living, easy gambling, offending the Roman Catholic Church, and fornication. Thus beset, the manager grabbed the pretty movie actress he had just married, probably illegally, and told the sporting press he was taking her straight to bed. The game brimmed with satyrs and artists and rogues and emperors and clowns.

Robinson and Durocher, of course, and Casey Stengel and Jolting Joe DiMaggio, who would not speak to one another, and Willie, Mickey, and the Duke, who never felt the rivalry that legend lately has created. Mantle was playing out from under DiMaggio's shadow. Snider was upset mostly when com-pared to matchless Stan Musial. Willie played wholly in his own space, at the crest of Mount Olympus.

We watched the Barber, Big Newk, and the Superchief; Yogi and Campy and Nappy Westrum, stout catchers three; Hoss, Preach, Oisk, and Skoonj; Mandrake and Ol' Reliable and the Royal Scots Express. Those rapscallion owners were variously the Roarin' Redhead, Mahatma, the Big Oom. We did not lack for nicknames in the Era.

Broadcasters then were professional announcers, schooled first in the glorious gabbiness of radio. These were Mel Allen, Red Barber, kind Ernie Harwell, Russ Hodges, and Vin Scully, boy baritone. When Scully spoke in conversation, his voice sounded a pleasing tenor. Turn on a microphone and the Scully pitch dropped several registers down to light operatic baritone. Egos flowered among the tonsils of the broadcast booths. Nor were egos alien to press boxes.

The Power Columnists, Red Smith of the elegant *Herald Tribune* and Jimmy Cannon of the passionate *Post,* expressed discreet disdain for one another. Cannon conceded that Smith wrote well-formed sentences but felt him too clinical, too arch. "You get the feeling," Cannon said, "that the guy is writing for a restricted audience. Three English teachers up at Columbia." Smith insisted that he liked Cannon's stuff, "except that when Jimmy sits down to write a column, he feels he has to leave the English language there for dead." Cannon and Smith did hold hands in horror when the first Pulitzer Prize for sportswriting went to neither. Arthur Daley, a soul of geniality, won it for a few quite ordinary pieces, "conversations around the batting cage," published in the *New York Times.*

I moved through the Era on several levels. At the beginning I was a collegian, enthralled by baseball, like my father before me, rooting for the Dodgers, again like my father, and most especially for Jackie Robinson to succeed in the major leagues. That issue was said to be in doubt, even though Robinson had batted .349 in the International League the season before. "He hit a *soft* .349," insisted one old scout.

My next persona was as a newspaperman, a sportswriter employed by the *Herald Tribune* when it was famous as the best-written paper in the country. My salary advanced from $48 a week as a cub reporter to $10,000 a year as a baseball writer, a flattering newspaper wage for the time. I covered the

Dodgers for two seasons and the Giants and Yankees after that. Jackie Robinson hired me to help him compose a monthly column. Leo Durocher promised scoop after scoop if I would meet certain conditions. Whitey Ford pounded on my hotel room door and roared: "This is the house detective. Get that woman out of there!"

For four years I covered a ballgame pretty much every day from spring training through the World Series, about 750 major league games in all. Since the *Tribune* published a variety of editions, each requiring fresh material, I wrote 2,000 baseball stories for the paper. I moved on after a squabble with Durocher. The daily baseball beat was grinding down my fingers and my nerves. I was ready to proceed to something else.

That turned out to be a $14,000 position as sports editor of *Newsweek*. There one went to story conferences, composed interoffice memoranda, and bought martinis for pretty research assistants who Wanted to Write. The job was no better than a mixed bag, but it had the salubrious effect of giving me distance from the fervid New York baseball scene. When the Dodgers and the Giants abandoned ship, I was saddened, but not devastated. I continued to cover Carl Furillo and Willie Mays in their new California locales.

Things end. Dramas, wars, reigns, lives, loves. I know two reasons why the Era remains magnificent in our memories. The first is simple. The Era was magnificent. The second is more complex. The Era came to a dramatically proper finale.

It ended when the time was right; its end was sad but suitable. The drama was played out. By the time the ballclubs moved West, the great Dodger team was waning. Pee Wee Reese, the immortal shortstop, had moved to third base. Jackie Robinson was working for a chain of lunch counters. The Giants had fired Leo Durocher. The Yankee decline took longer, but eventually even the Yankees collapsed. Along that route, someone finally fired Casey Stengel.

The Era possesses an inevitability and a rightness. It begins with Jackie Robinson arriving and ends with Walter O'Malley departing. Hero and brigand, who despised each other.

As actors say, you have to know when to get off the stage. But it was the most exciting time for baseball.

You should have been there.

I mean to take you.

1

Leo, Larry, and Jackie or Notes from the Hookworm Belt

♦

W E REMEMBER CERTAIN ballgames, certain players, certain plays on vanished fields.

Willie Mays is rushing out from under his cap in mad pursuit of a line-drive, ticketed three-base hit . . . until Willie outspeeds the baseball. The sizzling liner settles in the dark mitt at his belt. "Willie's glove," the witty Vin Scully says, "is where triples go to die."

Stan Musial coils at home plate, slope-shouldered, balanced, taut as the bow of a stout archer. The pitch comes hurtling and Musial uncoils, his swing a mix of grace and violence. A long high drive sails out of Flatbush toward Crown Heights. "The man," mutters a Dodger fan. "Stan the Man. He's killing us again. But you can't root *against* a guy that hits that great."

The funny-looking catcher works the Bronx. Thick body. Baggy knickers. Shirt puffing at the waist. Absolutely the shortest neck in town. Yogi Berra doesn't look like an athlete until he poles a buzzing fastball all the way into the third tier behind right field, the topmost deck of the old Yankee Stadium, the biggest, grandest ballpark in the world.

The old center fielder . . . no one ever looked *more* like a ballplayer than broad-shouldered Joe DiMaggio. He covered center with a long gliding stride and he punished pitchers. At bat, he did not stride; he didn't need to. The punishing power flowed up from ankle, leg, and hip. "Every job has drawbacks," said the great right-hander Early Wynn. "The drawback of my job is that I gotta pitch to Joe DiMaggio."

The memories crowd together, quickly now. Allie Reynolds throws a fastball at the head of Roy Campanella and the sturdy catcher has to dive for mother earth. Nothing personal. Nothing personal, perhaps. Reynolds is staking out his territory. Carl Furillo playing a carom off the right field wall and making a throw, a Carl Furillo throw. The runners stand still, each frozen to a base. Don Mueller spots a hole in the defense and pokes a base hit there. Mickey Mantle, the uptown strongboy, beats out a surprise bunt. Sal Maglie throws at Jackie Robinson. Jackie steals home. The Yankees overshift on Ted Williams, throttling him. Al Dark sprawls awkwardly but makes a play he has to make. The Duke leaps. Preacher throws his spitter. Bobby Thomson swings . . .

Memory revives the vanished ballfields. You see the fields; you see the ball and bat. Yet, as the Era begins, with two overwhelming stories, the fields are secondary, or seem to be. The passion of Leo Durocher and the ordeal of Jackie Robinson lead us very far from second base.

But without second base, without the ballfields in the background, neither story could ever have played out.

◆

THE *HERALD TRIBUNE* entombed the story on page 24. It was the sports scoop of the century, but in 1947 managing editors confined sports stories to the back of the newspaper. Blacks rode in the back of the bus. Sports ran in the back of the paper. That was the way things were, the way they'd always been, everyone said, although of course nothing was really the way it had always been anymore.

It was a time of thunder and tectonic change. All at once people were trying to adjust to peace and television and something called "the emerging backward areas." At last the sun was setting on the British Empire. (Hitler and Mussolini were only two years dead.) But we were also trying to comprehend virulent Stalinism, thermonuclear bombs, a brushfire conflict in Indochina, and the unspeakable revelations of the Holocaust. What was this anyway, peace or war? Had Christianity failed? we asked portentously at campfires beside a cedar-dark summer lake.

In the words of A. A. Milne, we were very young. The heavy world was lightened by dreams of goldfields and pretty girls, and those were things you could consider without furrowing a youthful brow. Assuming the Russians or the right-wingers didn't blow up the planet, what was more important, we wondered, big bucks that could buy you a Packard convertible or a Saturday night date with blonde Cookie Bernstein, who strutted so prettily in her two-piece Lastex bathing suit, which almost but did not quite reveal the navel?

"Easy," said Harvey Katz, handsome and bespectacled like Clark Kent, and very worldly-wise. Harvey was six months older than the rest of us, which meant that he had served a tour with the occupying army in Germany. "Make money and the pretty girls will come. In Europe, I got any woman I wanted for a tin of coffee."

We'd heard that before. We were virgins mostly and we were tired of hearing about European women, all appealing as Eleanor of Aquitaine, all instantly available to Harvey Katz, the white slaver from Empire Boulevard, which ran east-west, just south of Ebbets Field.

We lit our cigarettes, Chesterfields and Camels and Virginia Rounds. We hit the jukebox. For a nickel Frank Sinatra sang:

> In dreams I kiss your hand, Mam'selle,
> Your dainty fingertips . . .

"And there was this French one," Katz continued. "What a time I had one night in Paris . . ."

"Shut up, Harv," we said, our envy turning into anger.

The temperature in New York City dropped to 39 degrees on May 8, 1947. That, decreed George Anthony Cornish, managing editor of the *Herald Tribune*, was front-page news.

"I think the baseball story should go outside, too," said Rufus Stanley Woodward, a huge, volcanic, bespectacled sports editor and classicist who insisted on being called "Coach." The men were arrayed for a story conference in Cornish's office, five stories above West 41st Street. A bust of Adolf Hitler glowered near a window. Or maybe winced. Bullets from a dozen Garand rifles had pierced the bronze.

"I think not, Stanley," Cornish said. He was a courtly Alabaman who enjoyed being called "Mister."

"The baseball story is more important than the weather."

"I think not," Cornish repeated in a refined and gelid way.

Cornish controlled the front page; the issue was settled.

The strike against Jackie Robinson, racist and hateful and newsworthy as hell, would have to go inside the paper, twenty-four pages behind the front-pager on the weather.

That chilly May, veterans were saying they could not remember a baseball year like this one, and here we were still in the middle of spring. They could not remember a baseball year like this one for an excellent reason. There had not been a season like 1947 before. It was exciting even in January, four months before feisty, gabby Harry Truman, who was sixty-two, threw out the first ball at Griffith Stadium in Washington.

Leo Durocher, a lifetime .247 hitter, was the loudest .247 hitter in the annals. In a time of ornate nicknames — the Wild Horse of the Osage, the Sultan of Swat — Durocher was simply the Lip. He was a slick shortstop for four different teams and after that a slick manager across twenty-four seasons. He possessed charm and fire and a gambler's wits, but cruelty marred his character. He is the only person I've heard seriously knocked by the knightly Stan Musial of St. Louis.

The cruelty ran strong and deep. Up top Durocher offered flash and glitter, which created a powerfully appealing manner, just the sort of fellow you would love to shoot pool with, even though he'd take your shirt and pants and wallet.

When 1947 began, Durocher was manager of the Dodgers, who had narrowly missed the pennant in '46. The Dodgers tied the St. Louis Cardinals across the 154 games of the season but lost two straight in a special playoff and had to go home. Durocher fled West to Hollywood for consolation and presently recovered sufficiently to seduce the popular hazel-eyed movie star Laraine Day. When Joe DiMaggio married Marilyn Monroe in 1954, the mating of a ballplayer with an actress so aroused gossip columnists that some called the tortured couple Mr. and Mrs. America. (That marriage lasted nine months, no more.)

The Leo-Laraine affair differed in significant ways. Unlike Marilyn, Laraine was a high-neckline sort of girl, comfortable playing a prim and lovely nurse in lightweight movies about young Dr. Kildare. There was a sweetness to Laraine onscreen and a sense of churchly propriety, characteristics not commonly associated with Monroe. But Laraine was steamy enough to win the heart of Cary Grant in a film called *Mr. Lucky*, where Grant played a dissolute gambler and Laraine played a noble society lady with what the Freudians might call intense suppressed sexuality. Press releases described her as a devout Mormon who neither drank nor smoked.

Now, incredibly, the Lip, Loud Leo, had seduced the upright, or formerly upright, Mormon beauty. Someone, possibly Leo, said he had consummated the act for the first time with Laraine on her living room piano bench.

An additional consideration further piqued national interest. Laraine was married to somebody else, one J. Ray Hendricks, who ran the Santa Monica airport and who, Laraine charged, drank too much. As the Hendrickses' marriage staggered toward divorce, the husband went public with his troubles. He'd welcomed Leo Durocher into his home as a friend, Hendricks insisted. Served him food and drink. Now his house guest had seduced his wife. The *Los Angeles Examiner* summed up Hendricks's complaints in a clear headline: DUROCHER BRANDED LOVE THIEF.

On January 20, 1947, Laraine Day divorced J. Ray Hendricks in California. On January 21, she married Leo Ernest Durocher in Mexico. A predecessor of Kitty Kelley named Florabelle Muir reviewed matters for the New York *Daily News:*

> Leo (The Lip) Durocher is what they call dynamic, which means that you can't tell which direction he's going to explode in. People like that act first and pick up the pieces afterward.
>
> As a result of his dynamism, Durocher and his bride Laraine Day are nervously sitting out their honeymoon while platoons of legal authorities decide whether they are man and wife, parties to bigamy or just very dear friends who have been hasty.
>
> Superior Court Judge George Dockweiler gave Laraine her divorce last Monday. The judge, ordinarily an easy-going fellow, was considerably upset when he heard Laraine had gone to Mexico the next day for another divorce and had then married Lippy in Texas.
>
> "They imposed themselves on the court," Judge Dockweiler said. "She begged for a decree and then was not willing to abide by the terms: a one year wait before the decree becomes final, a one year wait before she could re-marry."
>
> The judge now wants to set aside the divorce. . . .

Old baseball hands grumbled. Who needed all this gossip stuff, issues of lust and lawyers?

But the stuff was weightier than gossip. Once Judge Dockweiler calmed down, Durocher and his wife would stay out of prison, but Durocher was riding toward a debacle that profoundly affected the next decade in baseball and, in a sense, the nature of the nation.

Back East, up in the Bronx, and around his ornate offices in the Squibb Building on Fifth Avenue, Larry MacPhail, the president of the Yankees, was drinking too much. Flat-faced, hyperactive Leland Stanford MacPhail had rescued the Dodgers from bankruptcy during the dolorous 1930s. MacPhail signed on to work in Brooklyn when the Dodgers were drawing fewer than 500,000 fans a season. Only 6,500 fans a game in a sports-happy borough of 2 million people within a city of 8 million souls.

Legend insists that the Dodgers were a beloved band of comics during the Depression. "Hey," yelps the fan in a Flatbush Avenue saloon, according to one story. "The Dodgers got three men on base."

"Oh, yeah?" says his companion. "Which base?"

My father, a solid college third baseman who smacked rocketing line drives, took me to Ebbets Field as a special treat on spring and autumn days in the 1930s. During that period, afternoon games began at 3:15 and sometimes my father could not make it to the ballpark until three o'clock. No matter. We sat behind third base, first base, or home plate. Plenty of seats. Ebbets Field was never crowded, fortunate for my father and myself, disastrous for the owners, the feuding descendants of old Charley Ebbets and Steve McKeever. The feuding paralyzed the franchise until the Brooklyn Trust Company, which held Dodger mortgages and Dodger paper, demanded — on the threat of foreclosing on Ebbets Field — that competent management be hired. Unlike the Yankees and the Giants, the Dodgers had to spend decades crawling out of debt, which worked mightily on the shape of things to come.

Nor is it accurate to maintain that the few customers in Ebbets Field enjoyed themselves in tolerant merriment while staring at losing pitchers. No Dodger fan was amused in 1937 when the team lost 91 times and finished 33½ games behind the pennant-winning Giants (whose home attendance was 926,887).

A particularly hollow substory holds that "Dem Bums" was a local term of affection. Fantasy portrays Brooklynites washing down flagons of Trommer's beer while regaling one another with stories of "Our Beloved Bums" hitting doubles that turned into double plays.

Trommer's beer was brewed in Brooklyn, all right, and there was a fine beer garden serving German food alongside the brewery. But "beloved Bums"? Never happened.

"Them stinking bums" was what you heard among the ball fans, as in "I'm never gonna buy a ticket to see them stinking bums again."

My father, courtly and elegant, disliked imprecise speech and vulgarisms such as "stinking." Further, he explained, "bum," a term of uncertain origin, wasn't much of a word, and if it was intended to suggest incompetence, that usage was not appropriate. There were no incompetent ballplayers in the major leagues, none at all. Every major leaguer was at least a good ballplayer, else how would he have reached the majors? If a few looked bad, that was because they were coming up against some great ones. "Pay attention now. Let's watch Van Lingle Mungo spot his fastball. Good pitch. Good pitch. Right up around the shoulders. They call that the high hard one, son. Say, Mungo's almost as fast as Dazzy Vance."

Robert Creamer, the author and critic, once began a baseball essay: "Spaniards have the gift for patient melancholy." My father was sprung from cheerful Alsatian stock, but when I conjure up his face as he sat beside me at Ebbets Field long ago, that's just what I see, patient melancholy. (Creamer was writing about Al Lopez, a skillful catcher, whose job it was

during the 1930s to get Van Lingle Mungo to throw strikes.
Patient, melancholy work.)

MacPhail came East from Cincinnati, a whirlwind blowing
away dust and apathy. Before he arrived in Brooklyn, in January
1938, he had been promised a "free untrammeled hand" in
running the club (and an unlimited expense account). Quickly,
he broke New York's long-standing radio blackout. In collective
ignorance, the ballclubs believed that radio broadcasts would
reduce attendance. "Hell," said whirlwind, tradition-breaking
Leland Stanford MacPhail. "There's nothing to reduce. What
was our attendance in Brooklyn last year?"

Precisely 482,481 for seventy-six home games.

"Then what have we got to lose, goddammit? We're broadcasting." And MacPhail brought Red Barber into Brooklyn. In
person, Walter Lanier Barber was rather stiff. Small talk made
him impatient or uncomfortable.* But turn on a microphone
and the Ol' Redhead became the loving, witty, quietly learned
uncle you always wished had sprouted on the southern side of
the family. No better baseball broadcaster (or baseball ticket
salesman) ever lived.

Next MacPhail ordered lights installed at Ebbets Field. On
June 15, 1938, at the first major league night game in the
history of New York City, Johnny Vander Meer of the Cincinnati Reds pitched a no-hit game. It was Vander Meer's second consecutive no-hitter. No other pitcher has accomplished
that, to this moment. And the day after *that*, MacPhail hired
a new first base coach, George Herman Ruth. From time to
time at Ebbets Field the Great Man stepped up during batting practice and showed some earnest, geriatric, belly-jiggling
swings.

Baseball the sport and baseball the business proceed ulti-

---

*Leaving a St. Louis hotel with Barber once, I was struck with 95-degree heat
and said one word: "Hot." Barber's response: "You have to expect heat in St.
Louis if you want to be a baseball writer, young man."

mately from those columns of numbers headed Won and Lost.
What MacPhail could do as well as anyone who ever lived was
assemble a winning ballclub in a hurry. He brought Durocher
in from St. Louis to play shortstop and later to manage. (Babe
Ruth, who wanted to manage the Dodgers, was released, dismissed like aged Falstaff.) MacPhail spent and dealt for such
splendid players as Dolph Camilli, a strong, graceful first baseman; Dixie Walker, a good right fielder and a superb batsman;
and Billy Herman, the best second baseman extant. MacPhail
stole Pee Wee Reese from a Boston Red Sox farm and bought
fine pitchers Whit Wyatt and Kirby Higbe. Quite suddenly the
Dodgers rose out of the lower depths and won the 1941 pennant.

They attracted 1,214,910 fans to their small ballpark, a quarter million more than the champion Yankees drew in the cav-
ernous Bronx stadium. (The Giants, slumping to fifth place,
fell yet another quarter million back.) In the brevity of four
seasons Larry MacPhail had won a pennant and almost tripled
home attendance. When someone said of the Dodgers, "It
looks at last as though the worms have turned," even my father
smiled.

War came. MacPhail enlisted in the army and that prince of
parsons, Wesley Branch Rickey, came in from St. Louis as the
new Dodger president. He meant to stay.

On MacPhail's military discharge in 1945, his old Brooklyn job was taken. No matter. MacPhail decided to buy the
New York Giants, who had collapsed into last place in 1943.
Larry MacPhail was a great seafarer. His passion was salvaging
wrecks.

But the Giants were not for sale, even to a certified redheaded genius.

That left only one team in New York City, the Yankees,
owned in 1945 by the estate of Colonel Jacob Ruppert, a beer
baron and a bachelor. According to Larry MacPhail's son Lee,
later president of the American League, "My father offered a
flat three million dollars and the Ruppert lawyers were de-

lighted. But of course my father didn't have three million dollars. He never was able to hold on to money. He did have a backer. But then that fell through. The backer was too close to racetrack people, too close to gambling. So Dad had this great deal with Colonel Ruppert's estate. All he was lacking was the cash."

MacPhail took his grief to the bar of "21," at 21 West 52nd Street, a long way from the raucous beer bars along Flatbush Avenue. There he encountered Dan Topping, a sports buff and an heir to Anaconda Copper, a great American fortune. The swizzle-stick financing was magic. Topping instantly was interested "for a third." He had a friend, a contractor in Arizona, who would surely take another third. That turned out to be Del Webb, a cold-eyed man who boasted of the efficiency with which his firm erected concentration camps imprisoning Japanese Americans during World War II.

MacPhail put the package together with his two new partners and commandeered the Yankees for a final price of $2.8 million. For $2.8 million, MacPhail and his rich associates obtained the New York American League team — a monarch of franchises — plus Yankee Stadium (which was later sold), plus the land under Yankee Stadium (later sold in a separate deal), plus signed contracts from people named Rizzuto, Henrich, Keller, and DiMaggio.

It was as good a business deal as anybody in baseball could remember, and it was recognized as a great deal at the time. Why, then, was Larry MacPhail drinking so much so often?

His partners wondered about that, too. Two millionaires and the Whirlwind Promoter, the Yankee troika, soon were moving unevenly toward a World Series, a memorable collision, and fistfights. Not fistfights among the ballplayers. Ballplayer brawls are common as grass. These fistfights broke out among the owners.

Horace Stoneham, the president of the Giants, *always* drank too much. He had inherited the New York ballclub with the oldest traditions in town, and perhaps the grandest traditions as well. There was no reason in the world for Horace to sell his heirloom.

The Giants had been playing in New York since May 1, 1883, when an early version opened the National League season by defeating Boston, 7 to 5. John McGraw came to manage in 1902 and ran the team for thirty years. He won ten pennants and finished high in the first division twenty-seven times, twenty-seven times out of thirty. Even today the name McGraw speaks banners.

Christy Mathewson, out of Bucknell, was surely the first ballplayer worshiped as a superhero. Tall, fair-haired, handsome as a god, Mathewson affected a cape for his entrance to the playing field on days when he was to pitch at the Polo Grounds. He looked Apollonian and he may have been the best pitcher who ever lived. The one book my father saved from his own early boyhood, and handed down to me, is *Pitching in a Pinch* by Christy Mathewson, in the Every Boy's Library Boy Scout Edition of 1912. I still have it. I still read it, and with awe.

Charles Stoneham, a freewheeling broker from the old Curb Exchange, bought the Giants in 1918. He was a financial wizard or a shady operator or both. During the stock market crash of 1929, Charley Stoneham lost scores of millions of dollars, a family member recalls. "He had been very wealthy, but the crash wiped him out. Wiped out everything but the Giants. That was his jewel, the one possession above all others, he would not part with, whatever the cost."

Keep the Giants Charles A. Stoneham did, for his son Horace to inherit in 1935. The team succeeded for a while under McGraw's successor, the very gifted, very dour Memphis Bill Terry, winning pennants in 1933, '36, and '37. But Terry got on everybody's nerves and he antagonized the sporting press, which had loved old John McGraw. When someone criticized a pitching choice, Terry told a half dozen writers, "I don't know who you guys think you are. No goddamn forty-buck-a-week reporter tells me what to do."

Harold Ross of *The New Yorker* asked the wonderfully talented John Lardner to compose a profile on Bill Terry. Most would have been flattered. Memphis Bill demanded a fee.

"Where were you born, Mr. Terry?" Lardner asked, innocently enough.

"The answer to that question is worth plenty of money to me," Terry said.

(Atlanta. Memphis Bill was born in Atlanta. He also batted .401 in 1930. Lardner never wrote the profile.)

Terry stayed on everybody's nerves and after he finished fifth in 1941, he was fired in favor of the genial, stumpy home run hitter Mel Ott. Since Ott had made the Giant squad when he was seventeen years old, he drew the nickname Master Melvin.

Although he became the greatest five-foot, nine-inch left-hand-hitting slugger on earth, Master Melvin couldn't manage much. But the residual loyalty of the old Giant fans was so strong that in 1946, when the team finished last, attendance at the Polo Grounds reached 1,219,873.*

Why in the world would Horace Stoneham *want* to sell the team? He was reaping major profits in the cellar. Horace had a porky face, fleshy and soft. His baseball intelligence seemed reasonably developed when he was sober, but Stoneham's drinking bouts were legend.

Back of center field at the Polo Grounds rose a stately blockhouse. Within, one found the clubhouses and, one level higher, a dining room for sportswriters and celebrities. At the very top of the blockhouse, which was painted green, four stories above the deepest center field anywhere, 505 feet distant from home plate, Stoneham maintained an apartment. As far as I can learn, no teetotaler ever crossed that threshold.

---

*This may indicate that the Giants, rather than the Dodgers, were truly the beloved bums.

One night in the spring of 1947, Horace invited Jim Mc-Culley, who covered the Giants for the *Daily News*, to imbibe. "C'mon, pally. A few El Beltos."

They proceeded from the press dining room to Stoneham's apartment. Toward two A.M. McCulley decided he'd had enough.

"Stay with me, pally," Stoneham said. "I doan wanna drink alone."

McCulley moved toward the door. Stoneham had locked it.

"I got the key, pally," said the president of the New York Giants. "I'm keeping it, pally. You gotta stay with me."

McCulley came to on the living room floor, hearing "the damnedest hammering."

Rap.

Rap.

Rap.

McCulley's head hurt. He crawled to a window and pulled himself erect.

Rap.

It wasn't hammering at all.

Rap.

It was one o'clock the next afternoon. It was the damn next day. The Giants were taking batting practice.

Rap.

That was Big Jawn Mize, slashing his mighty swings.

Line drive. Line drive. Line drive.

Rapraprapraprap.

As the Era dawned, all three New York ballclubs looked like problem areas. Branch Rickey, master of the Dodger house, was also a master of tergiversation, as he demonstrated with his comment on the sorrows of Durocher. "Leo," Rickey said genially, "has an infinite capacity for going into a bad situation and making it worse." In truth, following the Laraine Day affair, the Durocher and Dodger situations were more grave than Rickey admitted.

The Giants were lost in Harlem. In 1946, Stoneham soberly appointed his nephew Charles (Chub) Feeney executive vice president. Feeney was bright and decisive, a graduate of Dartmouth and Fordham Law School. He told a few, but not many, friends a story which is a paradigm for the perfect New York Giant background. "As a baby," Feeney said, "I was rocked to sleep by John McGraw." Feeney was the brightest kid in the family, but still a kid. The Giants finished fifth, fifth and last, going into 1947. The kid was young and John McGraw was dead.

Joe McCarthy had managed the Yankees since 1931. Efficient, sour, arrogant, McCarthy won eight championships (helped by supporting players named Ruth, Gehrig, and DiMaggio). After MacPhail asserted his presidency in 1946, McCarthy managed for just thirty-five games more. Then he quit. That season the Yankees employed three different managers. Suddenly they looked as stable as the kingdom of Freedonia, whose ruler was Groucho Marx.

The season of 1946 ended when a wonderful young St. Louis Cardinal team defeated the Boston Red Sox, 4 to 3, in the seventh game of the World Series. Damnedest Series. Stan Musial hit .222. Ted Williams hit .200. They were a .400 hitter, all right, *between the two of them!* It was tough, as the Era began, to make sense out of what was going on.

Were the Yankees going to collapse into anarchy? Could MacPhail, truly a Dodger, a *daffy* Dodger, turn into a button-down success in limousine country north of the Flatbush subway line called the BMT? The Polo Grounds stood half a mile from Yankee Stadium. You could walk from one to the other in fifteen minutes. But would old Giant fans continue to populate their hallowed horseshoe and watch a squat left-handed pitcher named Dave Koslo, born George Bernard Koslowski, lead the National League in losing ballgames with nineteen? The nearby, chaotic Yankees played better ball. All this was uptown stuff. The major story was developing somewhere else, in Brooklyn. Until that day in May 1947, where we began, the papers mostly missed it.

Long, long afterward, I find myself, in the approximate present, at the village of Fallbrook, California. It isn't hard to make your way to Fallbrook. You simply drive to Bonsall and turn right. (Actually, Fallbrook lies an hour north and east of San Diego.) Once this was avocado country. Now developments have overrun the avocado fields, but a sense of spaciousness persists and the air is clear and dry.

Duke Snider sits at his ease in a tasteful, conservative living room. A picture window looks down across tee, fairway, and green. Snider says, "The nicest thing about the view is that I don't have to mow the grass." He tosses a rubber ball to his puppy. A leaping, rolling snag. "You know," Snider says, "I'd only have a dog who could catch."

Snider went to New Zealand with his firstborn, Kevin, a few years ago to spend time together, father and son. Half a world from home, he suffered a heart attack. "No pain. The only symptom was I coughed up a little blood."

After that Duke, one of the five or six best center fielders since the dawn of man, had to have a coronary bypass. He doesn't complain, but I suspect the Duke can now spell forwards and backwards the word *cholesterol*.

"A lot of the big writers never wanted to come over to Brooklyn to see us play. They'd only catch us when they had to in the World Series. Then they'd tell us what we were doing wrong.

"We resented it. Pee Wee and Jackie and all the rest of us. We didn't say it out loud. You don't want to fight all the New York press. But we resented it. We were pretty good ballplayers, and they wouldn't come to watch, and when they did they said what we were doin' wrong."

"Red Smith . . ." I began.

"He didn't go to Dodger games," Snider said. "You were there. He wasn't with you."

"Jimmy Cannon wrote that Jackie Robinson was the loneliest man he ever saw in sport."

Snider was wearing eyeglasses. He, who could see a baseball flicking a bat 350 feet away, see it and react in microseconds, was wearing steel-rimmed spectacles.

"I liked Jimmy," Snider said. "And I liked Jackie. I learned so much from Jack . . ."

"Such as?"

"And I hope he learned a bit from me."

"Such as?"

"How did Cannon know that Jack was lonely? Did Jack wear his loneliness on the outside?"

Duke lost twenty-five pounds after the coronary bypass. He wears a blue baseball cap marked "Cooperstown" and, with just a little imagination, I see Duke playing ball tomorrow, adding to his 407 home runs. But on this California morning, Snider is sixty-five, beyond ball playing and approaching wisdom. Two presidents, Ronald Reagan and George Bush, have sought his autograph. That thrills Snider, but also leads him to wonder about fame.

"Playing in Brooklyn once or twice I didn't go down to first as hard as I should have. I started hard and then pulled up. Jackie called me aside, just the two of us. This wasn't black and white. This was two ballplayers.

"'Duke,' Jack said. 'Home to first base. That's ninety feet. Not seventy-five . . .'

"I used to watch Robinson get into uniform. Jack could joke and kid and talk about the racetrack. But as he pulled on the Brooklyn shirt and the blue Brooklyn stirrups, and the Brooklyn pants and the blue Brooklyn cap, he just got more and more serious. He was putting on his game face. Jack had a helluva game face. Take no prisoners.

"How did Jimmy Cannon know what he was seeing? A lonely athlete or the best game face in the world?"

*

Robinson played for the Dodger farm team at Montreal in 1946. "The beanballs kept coming and coming," says Homer Elliott "Dixie" Howell, a Kentuckian who caught for Montreal that season. "The pitchers kept throwing fastballs at Robinson's head, trying to get the black guy out of baseball forever, maybe clear out of this world. It was about the worst thing I've ever seen."

"I was at Montreal for a while in '46," says George "Shotgun" Shuba, who later pinch hit a home run in the 1953 World Series. "It was something the way the other players went at Robinson with their spikes. Looking back, I'm amazed that he wasn't maimed."

You did not learn such things from the press at that time. "It probably isn't fair to say that the sportswriters and the newspaper editors then were downright bigoted against Robinson," Al Parsley, an excellent Montreal newspaperman, once said. "Let me put it this way. When it came to Jackie Robinson, they were belligerently neutral."

Robinson played his first game for Montreal at Roosevelt Stadium in Jersey City on April 18, 1946. He hit a home run, went four for five, and stole two bases. Beat writers, men regularly assigned to the Montreal Royals and the Jersey City Giants, covered the game. So did three reporters from the black press, papers such as the *Baltimore Afro-American*. None of the major New York newspapers thought to send a man twenty miles to note Jackie Robinson's spectacular debut. The first appearance by a black in organized baseball since 1891 was overlooked, with belligerent neutrality. Montreal defeated Jersey City, 14 to 1.

Robinson batted .349 that year, stole forty bases, and led the International League in scoring runs. After one triumphant late-season ballgame in Canada, a swarm of white fans pressed toward Robinson on the street outside Montreal Stadium. Unnerved, Robinson began to run. The crowd ran after him. Before outdistancing his pursuers, Robinson was weeping.

"These people," he said years later, "wanted to pat me on the back. There was no menace in them. When I was running, I started to think, here I am a black man and these people are running after me, not to lynch me. These white people are running after me to shake my hand. When I thought that, how wonderful that was, I started to cry."

Such episodes went unreported at the time.

To judge by the papers in 1947, Leo the Lip was the biggest news story in all sport. While Judge Dockweiler was considering whether to charge Laraine Day Durocher with bigamy, Durocher telephoned the judge in chambers. "Your Honor," said the Lip to the judge, "the least you can do is give me and my wife an opportunity to come to your office [*sic*] and explain."

Dockweiler acceded and a few hours later the judge found himself being treated like an incompetent umpire. "The position of the court," Dockweiler said, "is that by marrying before Miss Day's divorce was final, just the act of getting married constitutes adultery, whatever else you people did or did not do."

"Lemme ask you somethin'," Durocher said. "Would you be makin' this damn fuss if our names were Sarah Zilch and Joe Blow?"

"Obviously not. I'm not a watchdog. The court cannot watch everyone. But there's one thing I can do. I can make an example of you two."

"Oooh," Durocher said, "you condone what you say is adultery in other people, but you're not gonna condone it in us. Maybe the only thing you're interested in, Judge, is publicity for yourself."

"My concern," Dockweiler said, "is the dignity of my court and you people have made my court look very undignified."

Durocher began to shout. Then he and Laraine stalked out of the chambers to a crush of waiting reporters and a blur of photographers. "That judge," Durocher told the assemblage, "is nothing more than a pious, Bible-reading hypocrite." Then Leo fled California.

Within baseball, charges against Durocher had been accumulating for some time. He was playing high-stakes card games with ballplayers, and the games were rigged. He was cleaning out his own team, taking serious money from farm boys. In Hollywood he ran with George Raft, possibly the worst actor ever to sustain a career as a leading man. Raft was said to be close to mobsters Owney Madden and Bugsy Siegel, and it was a mobster, specifically Arnold Rothstein, who rigged the 1919 World Series. Rumor — and there was apparently no evidence to back it up — cried that Durocher deliberately mishandled Dodger pitching in 1946 and handed the pennant to the Cardinals in a gambling coup.

Durocher told me in 1990 that the rumor was outrageous. No one ever wanted to win more than he did. But Durocher loved to play cards, shoot craps, make bets, and run up debts, and he was at the very least careless in choosing associates. That was all the pulp that the rumor mills needed.

In two hundred newspapers, Westbrook Pegler, the famous right-wing columnist, described Durocher as "a moral delinquent." Against this background, Durocher announced to the world that Judge George Dockweiler was a Bible-reading hypocrite.

Durocher had been raised in a devoutly Roman Catholic neighborhood in West Springfield, Massachusetts. His mother, Clara Provost, was born near Montreal. Hard as it is to believe, Durocher the child wore a surplice and served as an altar boy with his oldest brother, Clarence.

By 1947 Durocher, then forty-two, was expanding the definition of lapsed Catholicism. He had been divorced twice. He flouted the dogmas of his youth with swaggering, practically public fornication. He had lost the right to receive communion and have his confession heard. As he put it, he didn't give a damn. Princes of the Church were not amused.

A popular promotion throughout the major leagues brought

youngsters into ballparks free on slow afternoons. Small boys admitted without charge may mature into ticket-buying adults. The Brooklyn version was a heavily promoted venture called the Knothole Gang, from the distant days when children watched ballgames free through the knotholes of wooden outfield fences. The leading single participant in the Dodger Knothole Gang was the Brooklyn Catholic Youth Organization, directed by a zealous priest named Vincent J. Powell and supervised by Monsignor Edward Lodge Curran.

Father Powell gained an audience with Branch Rickey and said that Durocher was a bad example for Catholic youngsters, and indeed for youngsters of all faiths.

"Doesn't your church," Rickey said, "still dispense mercy and forgiveness?"

Vincent Powell had not traveled to the Dodger office at 215 Montague Street near Brooklyn Heights to discuss comparative religion with a Methodist. If Durocher remained as manager of the Dodgers, the priest said, he would have no choice but to withdraw the Catholic Youth Organization from the Knothole Gang. He stopped barely short of threatening a Catholic boycott of the Dodgers.

Another matter was dominating Rickey's thoughts. The integration of baseball. When the young priest left, Rickey summoned the Dodger lawyer, a Roman Catholic, to deal with what he assumed to be a single rigid cleric. The club lawyer, stout, bespectacled, cigar-smoking — caricature of a Tammany Hall sachem — was named Walter Francis O'Malley.

Walter O'Malley was a political creature, and activity in the Catholic Church, as in the Democratic party, was part of his public presentation of himself. Actually he was not prominent in either. Outside of baseball O'Malley was simply a collection lawyer for a bank.

O'Malley spoke to Father Powell in Durocher's behalf but had no more success than Rickey. On March 1, 1947, Powell issued an announcement: "The Brooklyn Catholic Youth Organization is withdrawing from the Dodgers' Knothole Club."

Leo Durocher "is undermining the moral training of Brooklyn's Roman Catholic Youth. The C.Y.O. cannot continue to have our youngsters associated with a man who represents an example in complete contradiction to our moral teachings."

It may seem surprising to have Walter O'Malley, the Big Oom, the most overpowering baseball executive in history, enter the story losing his first case.

"It doesn't surprise me," said William Shea, the late Manhattan lawyer and power broker for whom the Mets' ballpark would be named. "Walter was one lousy lawyer."

We were walking toward Gage and Tollner's, a gaslight restaurant in downtown Brooklyn, on a spring evening after a meeting at the Brooklyn Historical Society.

"How can you say that, Bill? O'Malley made more money out of baseball than anyone in history."

"That's right," Shea said, "but he was one lousy lawyer. O'Malley was the most brilliant businessman I've ever met, but we were talking law here, weren't we?

"Of course he lost when he tried to plead Durocher's case to that priest. He wasn't *trying* to lose to embarrass Rickey. He just lost.

"I wouldn't have let O'Malley plead a parking ticket for me."

We move, in our time warp, back to the approximate present, at La Jolla, California, where Emil J. "Buzzie" Bavasi, a man who kept the secrets, has retired to a towering hill. From his living room, Bavasi watches migrating whales stir the surface of the metallic blue Pacific Ocean. "Of course I'm comfortable," Bavasi says in his affluence. "Always have been. But I worked in baseball for forty-six years and now that it's over I don't get a pension. Not a dime. Did you ever hear of anybody else in baseball forty-six years without a pension? Assistant trainers get pensions. Not me."

Bavasi is bitching without malice, comfortable bitching to someone he first befriended in 1952. "I'm gonna tell you something nobody knows," Bavasi says. He is heavier than he should be — thirty-five pounds too heavy, he complains — but his eyes flicker with youthful amusement. "You've gotta get it right. Well, maybe you won't, but you gotta try. Agreed? You know Ford Frick brought me into baseball, in the Brooklyn organization, right after the war. So I was there, I was working there, when the idea to integrate baseball hatched.

"This is what *really* happened. For damn near half a century, Branch Rickey has gotten all the credit and that isn't right. Rickey owned a quarter of the Dodgers. Twenty-five percent. The other partners were John Smith, who owned Pfizer Chemical; Jim Mulvey, a power at Metro-Goldwyn-Mayer, and our buddy Walter O'Malley.

"There was no way we [the Dodgers] were going to hire a black player without all four partners agreeing. We knew it would be something like a revolution. You had to have the four partners standing together, standing tall. And they did. Give them credit. Give all of them credit, not just Rickey.

"Now, we'd been scouting numbers of black players. There was never a plan to integrate the major leagues with more than one, but to find the right one we scouted all over the old colored leagues.

"I remember the meeting. Lem Jones. Fresco Thompson. A lot of solid baseball people. The scouts agreed that the one best prospect in colored ball was Don Newcombe. Six feet four. Two hundred twenty pounds. A good hitter. Intelligent. And, of course, just an overpowering right-handed pitcher.

"Rickey went with the scouts. He hadn't seen any of the prospects personally. Practically speaking, at that time, the president of the Dodgers could not go to a Negro League game himself.

"He was accepting the scouts' recommendation until he got to the entry for Newcombe's age. Newk was only nineteen. Too young for what he'd have to take, Rickey reasoned. No nineteen-year-old could survive the racist garbage.

"That's why we integrated the major leagues with Jackie Robinson. He was in his middle twenties. But from a strict baseball viewpoint, Jackie was our second choice."*

Rickey had been spending many days with a variety of clerical people. He intended to put Robinson on the Dodger roster by Opening Day 1947. That would attract black fans to Ebbets Field and Rickey was concerned about their behavior. He sought out ministers from Brooklyn's black churches and told them individually what he thought. "Not only will Jackie Robinson, a lone colored man, be on trial next season. So will the entire black community. I want to urge you to impress that on your parishioners. We welcome colored fans, we surely do, but, please, no drinking in my ballpark, no rowdy behavior, no switchblades. If the colored fans act up, it will work to the disadvantage of them and to my team and to my colored ballplayer." Rickey spoke to seventeen black ministers. Every one agreed to spread his message from the pulpit.

In 1946 Robinson had trained with the Montreal Royals in Florida. One day in Daytona Beach an armed sheriff walked on the field during an exhibition game. "Down here," he said, "we don't have nigras mixing with whites. Not marrying with whites. Not playing ball with whites. Now, nigra, git!" Robinson had to leave the game.

Rather than train his athletes in Florida again, Rickey moved both his Montreal and Brooklyn players to Havana for the spring of 1947. The racial climate of Cuba was less charged. He put the Dodgers and the New York sportswriters into the Hotel Nacional, which in those pre-Castro days was enlivened by

---

*The Brooklyn organization did sign Newcombe and Roy Campanella, but both were sent to play under circumstances of obscurity and minimal confrontation with the Nashua ballclub of the old New England League in the summer of 1946. Bavasi went to Nashua to oversee a sensitive situation and run the club. On one road trip, a rival general manager refused to turn over the Nashua team's share of the gate receipts "because you're just dirtying up our town with your two niggers." Thus exposed to the peaceful tolerance of New England, Bavasi decked the other man. He got his money.

roulette wheels, dice tables, and prostitutes from several continents. No ballplayer or journalist protested.

White Montreal players were quartered in cadet barracks at the Havana Military Academy. Campanella and Newcombe had been promoted to the Montreal roster. Along with Robinson, they were sequestered in a drab hotel fifteen miles from the Royals' practice field. Robinson's anger flared. "I thought we left Florida so we could get away from Jim Crow. What the hell is this, sticking us all out here, segregating us in the middle of a colored country, Cuba?"

Neither the Cuban government of Fulgencio Batista nor the Havana hotels demanded segregation. The idea of segregation inside Cuba sprang directly from Branch Rickey. He was concerned that fights might break out between the black players and the white players if the integrated Montreal squad was billeted together. Someone explained that to Robinson.

"I don't like it," Robinson said. "I don't like it at all. But I'll go along with Mr. Rickey's judgment. He's been right so far."

Exported segregation was not Branch Rickey's only curious idea. Another simply seems ingenuous. Rickey believed that Dodger players, seeing how gifted Robinson was, would clamor, petition, insist, demand that he move Robinson to the big squad. "Ballplayers love money," Rickey told several votaries. "They love World Series checks. When they see how good this colored boy is, when they realize he can get them into the World Series, they'll force me to make him a Dodger. After the players do that, one problem — Robinson's acceptance by his fellows — will solve itself."

During the seven exhibition games between the Montreal Royals and the Brooklyn Dodgers — most played on a giddy tour through the Canal Zone — Robinson stole seven bases. He batted .625.

Sartre defined bigotry as passion; and passion is, of course, irrational. That is its nature, like lust and avarice. The core of veteran Dodger players was not roused by Jackie Robinson's success. The veteran core felt passionate outrage. Bigoted ballplayers would hate Jackie Robinson even if he batted 1.000, which he damn near did. "How dare a colored fella be that good!"

In Panama the Dodgers were billeted briefly in an army barracks at Fort Gulick. There Clyde Sukeforth, called Sukey, a Maine man, went to Durocher with disturbing news. Sukeforth had been the primary scout assigned to watch Robinson in the Negro American League. Now, Sukey told Durocher, he had found out about a petition. A simple petition, really. The signers swore that they would never play on the same team as Jackie Robinson.

Fred "Dixie" Walker, the right fielder who was so popular that Manhattan sportswriters, making fun of Brooklyn speech, called him "the Pee-pul's Cherce," prepared the document. A native of Villa Rica, Georgia, who lived in Birmingham, Walker recently had led the National League in batting. Now thirty-six years old, he was the leader of the team. Walker did not glower in solitude. Hugh Casey of Atlanta, the best relief pitcher in baseball, supported the petition. So did a character named Bobby Bragan, from Birmingham, a third-string catcher but an influence because of his loud and caustic manner.

Confederates started the petition. Union forces did not lack for representation. Harry "Cookie" Lavagetto, the third baseman from Oakland who was almost as popular in Brooklyn as Dixie Walker, hurried to sign. Others who also signed included the kid center fielder Carl Furillo of Reading, Pennsylvania, and a fine second baseman out of Philadelphia, Eddie Stanky.

Harold "Pee Wee" Reese, of Louisville, underwent a crisis. He had grown up in a segregated community. Indeed, he remembered his father, a detective for the Louisville and Nashville Railroad, taking him to a tree with strong, low branches. "This is the hanging tree," the father said. "When a nigger gets out of line, we hang him here."

In a quiet, non-evangelical way, Pee Wee Reese was a Christian. Now, he wondered, as a Christian, how could he deny Robinson the right to inherit a small portion of the earth? He

could not and he would not. Reese was not comfortable opening his heart to Dixie Walker. Instead he said, "Look, Dix.
This thing might rebound. I can't take the chance of signing it.
I just got out of the navy. I got no money. I have a wife and
baby to support. Skip me, Dixie."*

Although a few other Dodgers declined to sign, Reese's
statement was as close as any ballplayer came to challenging
the preeminent establishment racists, Walker† and Casey.

Leo Durocher was approaching what was probably the finest
hour of his life. He could not sleep on the cot in the barracks
at Fort Gulick in the Canal Zone. At one o'clock in the morning,
Durocher decided that there was no reason why he should
sleep. No reason at all. The petition was going to rip apart the
ballclub. *Get the hell up!* In pajamas, Durocher roused his
coaches and told them to bring all the players into a big empty
kitchen behind an army mess.

The team assembled in night clothing and underwear. "Boys,"
Durocher began, in the raspy, brassy voice that rattled spinal
disks. "I hear some of you don't want to play with Robinson.
Some of you have drawn up a petition."

The players sat on chopping blocks. They leaned against
stoves.

---

*Reese says today, "People tell me that I helped Jackie. But knowing my
background and the progress I've made, I have to say he helped me as much as
I helped him."

†In 1976, Walker approached me at Dodger Stadium in Los Angeles and asked
if we could drink wine together after a game. He was working as a Dodger coach
and had just finished giving batting tips to Steve Yeager, a white catcher, and
Dusty Baker, a black outfielder. Walker turned out to be an oenophile and we
sipped a marvelous Margaux. He told me of a recent trip to England to search
for ancestral roots, and he spoke of Salisbury Cathedral and Devonshire gardens.
Then Walker got to his point. "I organized that petition in 1947, not because I
had anything against Robinson personally or against Negroes generally. I had a
wholesale hardware business in Birmingham and people told me I'd lose my
business if I played ball with a black man. That's why I started the petition. It
was the dumbest thing I did in all my life. If you ever get a chance, sometime,
please write that I am deeply sorry." Walker died in Birmingham on May 17,
1982.

"Well, boys, you know what you can use that petition for.
"Yeah, you know.
"You're not that fucking dumb.
"Take the petition and, you know, wipe your ass."
The Brooklyn Dodgers suddenly were awake.

"I'm the manager and I'm paid to win and I'd play an elephant if he could win for me and this fellow Robinson is no elephant. You can't throw him out on the bases and you can't get him out at the plate. This fellow is a great player. He's gonna win pennants. He's gonna put money in your pockets and mine.

"And here's something else. He's only the first, boys, only the first! There's many more colored ballplayers coming right behind him and they're hungry, boys. They're scratching and diving.

"Unless you wake up, these colored ballplayers are gonna run you right out of the park.

"I don't want to see your petition. I don't want to hear anything about it. Fuck your petition.

"The meeting is over. Go back to bed."

A few days later, the precise March date in 1947 is unknown, Frank Murphy of Michigan, an associate justice on the U.S. Supreme Court, telephoned Albert Benjamin "Happy" Chandler, the commissioner of baseball. Murphy left no record of the conversation. He died in 1949, after nine years on the bench. Chandler, who died in 1991 at age ninety-two, offered a brief account. "Murphy was an honorable and honored man," Chandler told the sports journalist John Underwood. Chandler reported this conversation:

MURPHY: Commissioner, you are a man of character. You must do something to stop this fellow Durocher.
CHANDLER: I will.
MURPHY: If you don't I'm going to advise the [national] Catholic Youth Organization to prohibit its youngsters from going to ballgames this year.

Murphy was a pro-labor Democratic senator until President Roosevelt appointed him to the Supreme Court in 1940, moving toward a liberal, some said New Deal, Court. On the bench Murphy wrote few interesting opinions but he did assume a position newspapermen described as "the leading lay Catholic in the United States." When Murphy spoke to Chandler, he brought to his words the full authority of a militant Church.

Unless Durocher were punished severely, twenty million Catholic children would be forbidden to go to ballgames during 1947. After Frank Murphy's phone call, Happy Chandler had one thing he had to do. Find an excuse to throw Durocher out of baseball.

Morals? Perhaps. Business? Certainly. The business of the commissioner of baseball is business.

Articles, chapters, entire books have been written about Chandler v. Durocher, 1947. (Chandler's own contribution is a book entitled *Heroes, Plain Folks and Skunks.*) The focus centers on specific episodes of that spring, which is naive. After the warning from the Catholic Church, Chandler was going to throw Durocher out of baseball. If the worst infraction Chandler found was jaywalking, so be it. Durocher was gone.

Chandler, himself a former senator, was country-slick. He knew that if he gave Durocher a chance, just a little time, Leo would walk into trouble, jaywalk into trouble along a road that now led nowhere.

Durocher lent his name to a column in the *Brooklyn Eagle* written by a smallish, rabbit-toothed newspaperman, Harold Parrott. "Shoulda been Harold Rabbitt," everybody said. Parrott liked to whisper, giving what he said a suggestion of confidentiality and importance.*

---

*In 1948 Parrott quit journalism and became traveling secretary for the Dodgers. In time, he moved up to ticket manager, a position that provides a limitless opportunity for private profit, through off-the-book deals on tickets to sold-out games. O'Malley fired Parrott, who by this time owned a yacht, at Los Angeles in 1968. Parrott spent his remaining years firing salvos toward O'Malley.

The *Eagle* column was called "Durocher Says." Durocher
claimed that he had nothing to do with writing the material
and "I didn't always read it either."

Larry MacPhail may or may not have asked Durocher to
leave Brooklyn and manage the Yankees as the Era began. Durocher claims that MacPhail made the offer in 1946 and he
turned it down. MacPhail did hire a gabby little coach, Charlie
Dressen, who had been Durocher's chief assistant. (As a Yankee, Dressen antagonized Joe DiMaggio with record speed.)

Durocher stayed in Brooklyn for 1947, but MacPhail had
"stolen" a Dodger coach. Under the heading "Durocher Says,"
Harold Parrott wrote:

> This is a declaration of war. I want to beat the Yankees because
> of MacPhail and Dressen. MacPhail tried to drive a wedge
> between myself and all these things I hold dear. When MacPhail
> found I couldn't be induced to manage the Yankees . . . he
> resolved to knock me and make life as hard as possible for
> me. . . . Surely people recognize it is the same old MacPhail.

"Just a little friendly controversy," Durocher maintained later.
"Just stirring some stuff up to sell some tickets."

MacPhail disagreed. He wrote Commissioner Chandler in
rage. "The New York Yankees request a hearing to determine
responsibility for these statements."

Then, just before a Dodger-Yankee exhibition game in Havana, an odd episode occurred. Larry MacPhail ordered his
publicity man, Arthur E. "Red" Patterson, to leave tickets for
a pair of gamblers, Max "Memphis" Engleberg, a bookmaker,
and Connie Immerman, a heavy roller who owned the Cotton
Club in New York. The two had been visiting the casino at the
Hotel Nacional and had met the notorious mobster Lucky Lu-
ciano for purposes unknown.

"Don't you know those guys?" Dick Young of the *Daily News*
asked Durocher in the Dodger dugout. He pointed to Engleberg and Immerman.

"Damn right," Durocher said, "but if I go near them, I'm dead. Where does MacPhail come off flaunting his company with gamblers right in the players' faces? They're sitting in his fucking box. If I even spoke to either one of them, MacPhail's guests, Chandler would have *me* fucking barred."

Young, a merciless reporter, printed a laundered version of Durocher's comment.

Early in April, Chandler summoned Branch Rickey to his home in Versailles, Kentucky. As commissioner, Chandler maintained an office in Carew Tower, an early Cincinnati skyscraper. He liked to point across the brown Ohio River toward the Kentucky hills beyond. "God's Country," Chandler said.

This meeting was too important for the office. Too private. Chandler led Rickey into his Kentucky study, paneled in walnut. On the desk sat signed photographs from Roosevelt, Churchill, David Ben-Gurion.

Rickey believed that the meeting was to consider integration of the major leagues, now less than a month away. He came prepared to discuss his plans for Robinson and to ask for Chandler's support. But integration was not on the agenda.

"Branch," Chandler began, "I'm going to have to sit [suspend] your manager."

"You can't do that," Rickey said.

"I have no choice."

On April 9, Chandler announced that Durocher was suspended for the balance of 1947 "for [unspecified] conduct detrimental to baseball."

The Brooklyn ballclub was fined $2,000.

The Yankee ballclub was fined $2,000.

Harold Parrott was fined $500.

By order of the commissioner, all parties were forbidden to discuss crimes, real or alleged, and punishment.

Durocher had been driven out of baseball. He looked at reporters outside a Manhattan hotel suite and told them he had only one thing to say: "Now is the time a man needs a woman." Then he led Laraine Day into the suite. The couple remained within for forty-eight hours.

On April 11, the Catholic Youth Organization rejoined the Dodger Knothole Gang.

Chandler had kept his promise to Frank Murphy. The Church forgave Baseball for having sinned.

On April 9, a press release announced that Jackie Robinson was being added to the Dodger roster. He would play first base, a new position. But with Durocher exiled, who would lead the team?

Rickey pleaded with the deposed Yankee manager Joe McCarthy to take over. McCarthy declined. Casey Stengel, managing the Oakland Oaks of the Pacific Coast League, said he hadn't been approached and wasn't really interested. He liked California. Of course, he did have some nice Brooklyn memories. Stengel was never asked.

Clyde Sukeforth ran the Dodgers on Opening Day. Robinson went hitless. The Dodgers defeated the Braves. Then Rickey brought in an old boy from Ohio whom Rickey had known for forty years. Burton Edwin "Barney" Shotton would manage from the dugout in civilian clothes. At sixty-two, Shotton said he was too old to put on a uniform.

The Dodgers started well. Robinson seemed quiet, poised, swift. The Yankees were playing good ball. The Giants looked improved. The weather was cold, but ahead lay a summer of promise.

Then the *Herald Tribune* broke its story. The St. Louis Cardinals, champions of the baseball world, were planning a strike. They were going to strike against Jackie Robinson themselves and they were going to enlist cohorts on every other team in the league.

The strike would last until Robinson was thrown out of baseball.

The boys from what Stanley Woodward called "the Hook-worm Belt" had one thing only against Robinson.

The color of his skin.

You see what you want to see, I suppose. The racists saw ominous black. To others, Jackie Robinson's color was something else.

Imperial Ebony.

2

Breakthrough at the Ballyards

◆

J ACKIE ROBINSON, who had begun his minor league career so gloriously in Jersey City, began his major league career slowly in Ebbets Field. Opening Day, against the Boston Braves, he grounded out, flied out, and hit into a double play. "Was I nervous?" Robinson said long afterward. "Yes, I was nervous. But it wasn't nerves that stopped me from getting any hits. Johnny Sain was pitching for the Braves. He threw just about the best curve ball I'd seen."

Press scrutiny was intense, though not terribly informed. Bob Feller, the great Cleveland pitcher, had done some barnstorming with Robinson. "Good field, no hit," Feller pronounced. Someone dredged that up after Robinson's hitless game. (The man batted .500 through a month of spring training; after one quiet game a columnist writes that he can't hit.)

That was Tuesday. On Wednesday it rained. On Thursday, again against the Braves, Robinson bunted toward third base and beat the throw. He had his first major league hit. Now things went the other way. "Robinson could bat .300 just bunting," someone claimed.

People were electric with anticipation and alarm. Bob Cooke, a witty, graceful baseball writer with the *Herald Tribune*, had been a hockey star at Yale. He was social by background but not a snob and certainly not a classic bigot.

"Branch Rickey," Cooke told two newspaper associates, "has done more to hurt baseball than anybody else in history."

"How's that, Cookie?"

Cooke was tall, lean, patrician, and normally quite gentle. "When I played hockey at Yale, I shot the puck harder than any of the Rangers. But I couldn't play in the National Hockey League. I couldn't skate with the Canadians. They had the legs. Now we have the same damn thing in baseball. The Negroes have the legs. It starts with Robinson but it doesn't end with Robinson. Negroes are going to run the white people out of baseball. They're going to take over our game."

The speed of blacks had threatened some whites, particularly after the 1936 Olympics in Berlin, when American blacks, led by Jesse Owens, won gold medals at 100 meters, 200 meters, 400 meters, and 800 meters. (Jackie Robinson's brother Mack finished second to Jesse Owens in the 200-meter sprint.) An anthropologist, whose name seems lost, claimed to have analyzed the skeletal structures of scores of black and white athletes and made a discovery. The heel bones of blacks were somewhat longer, the anthropologist said, giving them extra running power.*

Now on Friday, April 18, the Dodgers moved into the Polo Grounds to start a three-game series. Coming to bat for the first time against left-handed Montia Kennedy, Robinson lined a home run into the left field stands. The Polo Grounds resounded with cheering. Robinson had hit his first major league home run.

*The reasoning is mysterious. Sprinters run on the balls of their feet.

In the press box, behind home plate, Heywood Hale Broun, covering the ballgame for the vanished newspaper *PM*, turned to Bob Cooke and said solemnly: "That's because their heels are longer."

Baseball integration proceeds from the passion of a white Methodist Republican, the foresight of a conservative governor, and a Jewish counterstrike at anti-Semitism. That is not popular with some of today's revisionist black historians, but it is so. Jews put the law on the side of Jackie Robinson.

For a significant part of the twentieth century, organized medicine — the American Medical Association and governing bodies at medical schools — limited the number of Jews allowed into the lucrative business of doctoring. The situation was particularly dramatic in New York City, where thousands of outstanding Jewish science students were routinely denied admission to medical school. Jews made up about a third of the voters in New York City, and that was a wedge that various Jewish groups, led by the famous Reform rabbi Stephen Wise, used to persuade the state legislature to hold hearings.

These proved a disaster for the establishment reactionaries. One dean at Cornell Medical School testified that a quota was indeed enforced at Cornell Med. No matter how many qualified Jews applied, no more than five percent of a freshman class could be Jewish. The dean defended the quota with such arrogance that some heard Hitlerism in his response. Out of that, in 1944, came the drafting of the so-called Ives-Quinn law, which made job discrimination a crime in New York State. (Journalists and others soon were calling this new law FEP, for Fair Employment Practices.)

Governor Thomas E. Dewey signed the FEP bill on March 12, 1945, using twenty-two pens in a crowded ceremony at the Red Room of the State Capitol in Albany. Westbrook Pegler attacked the new law as "pernicious heresy against the ancient privilege of human beings to hate." But the American Jewish Congress, the Federal Council of (Protestant) Churches, Archbishop Richard J. Cushing of Boston, and Thurgood Marshall of the NAACP figuratively cheered.

A prominent black news photographer, Chick Solomon, covered the twenty-two-pen signing and drove at high (and probably illegal) speed 150 miles from Albany to the Hotel Theresa in Harlem, where officials of the Negro National Baseball League were meeting. Solomon was exultant. He brought copies of the new law with him. "Listen, everybody," he said. "The law is on our side now. Doesn't mean we're gonna make Christians out of the bastards who run the major leagues. But at least there's nothing now that can stop a black ballplayer from going up and demanding a tryout."*

Wesley Branch Rickey, the devout Methodist who ran the Dodgers, traced his decision to integrate baseball to an episode in 1903 when he was student-coach of baseball at Ohio Wesleyan University in Delaware, Ohio. (His salary was $15 a month.) The Ohio Wesleyan team included one black player, first baseman Charles "Cha" Thomas, later a successful dentist who settled in Albuquerque. When the Ohio Wesleyan team traveled to South Bend to play Notre Dame in April, a desk clerk at the Hotel Oliver said Thomas could not stay there. "We provide accommodations only for white people." Voices were raised. Thomas volunteered to leave. Rickey raged and cajoled. Finally the hotel manager agreed that Thomas could spend the night, on a cot in Rickey's room.

---

*Solomon's view of the power of the law was optimistic. Nine years later, in 1954, the New York Yankees still employed no black players. They shipped an excellent first base prospect, Victor Pellot Power, a black Puerto Rican, to the Philadelphia Athletics, explaining to several trusted baseball writers: "Power is not the Yankee type. He's a good ballplayer, but he's always chasing white women." It was not until 1955, ten years after passage of the FEP act, that the Yankees hired a black player, Elston Howard. "The truth," George Weiss, the general manager, told me in 1954, "is that our box seat customers from Westchester County don't want to sit with a lot of colored fans from Harlem." Like Jackie Robinson, Weiss, who died in 1972, is a member of the Baseball Hall of Fame.

Upstairs, Thomas began to weep. As Rickey recounted the scene, "His shoulders heaved, and he rubbed one great hand over the other with all the power of his body, muttering, 'Black skin . . . black skin. If I could only make it white.' He was trying literally to claw the black skin off his bones."

When Rickey told me this story, tears appeared in *his* eyes. Signing Jackie Robinson, he said, was a way of trying to make things right for his old and wounded Wesleyan friend, Cha Thomas. That was Rickey, crusader and thespian. He was also a graduate of the University of Michigan Law School. Baseball lured him away from practice, but when Rickey learned something of the law, he remembered it.

New York was the only one of the forty-eight states with a fair employment act. Without question, Rickey's decision to sign Robinson proceeded from a sense of justice. But before Rickey acted, job discrimination had been made illegal in his venue.

Rickey read the Bible regularly and never attended baseball games on Sundays. "A promise to my wonderful mother, Emily," he said. He was not comfortable with radicals of the left or of the right. He respected institutions. He paid his parking tickets.

"Having the law on my side when I signed Robinson," he told me, "was a comfort, during some dark days. A comfort like religion. You can understand what I mean. I'm an institutional kind of man."

On April 22, a clear, cold day — the temperature never rose above 45 degrees — the Philadelphia Phillies came to Ebbets Field to start a three-game series. Ben Chapman, born in Tennessee and raised in Alabama, was the manager of the Phillies, a thick-browed, volatile character with a tumultuous history. He played outfield for the Yankees during the early 1930s, batting as high as .316 and stealing sixty-one bases in a single season. Like anyone else, he made bad plays from time to time and when he did, the fans at Yankee Stadium sometimes jeered. Most ballplayers ignore hoots. Chapman took a different route. Jeered by Yankee fans in the Bronx one day in 1932, he turned to the grandstand and shouted: "Fucking Jew bastards."

His intemperance persisted. Fans complained to the Yankee management, and at length, in 1936, the Yankees traded Chapman to Washington for another outfielder, Alvin "Jake" Powell.* Chapman went from Washington to the Red Sox to the Indians to the White Sox, before dropping out of the major leagues. Late in World War II, when the military had claimed the best ballplayers — Greenberg, DiMaggio, Musial, Williams — Chapman signed with a weak Dodger team as a backup outfielder and sometime pitcher. The Phillies hired him to manage in 1945.

If Chapman disliked Jews, and he did dislike Jews, he *hated* "nigras." As the Dodger-Phillies game began, Chapman's strong, carrying drawl rose from the visiting dugout.

"Hey you, there. Snowflake. Yeah, you. You heah me. When did they let you outa the jungle . . .

"Hey, we doan need no niggers here . . .

"Hey, black boy. You like white poontang, black boy? You like white pussy? Which one o' the white boys' wives are you fucking tonight?"

Usually in baseball, even crude assaults give rise to back and forth banter. None was forthcoming in Ebbets Field that chilly April day. The Dodgers, southern and northern Dodgers, Dixie Walker and Carl Furillo, Pee Wee Reese and Spider Jorgensen, were shocked. Like Robinson, they sat in silence.

Lee Handley, Ben Chapman's third baseman, later made it a point to seek out Robinson. He said quietly, "I'm sorry. I want you to know that stuff doesn't go for me." Handley was the first opposing major leaguer to treat Robinson as a man.

---

*Powell himself was no peony. Off season, he told reporters at his first Yankee press conference, he worked as a cop in Toledo, Ohio. When asked specifically what he did on the Toledo police force, Powell told the New York press: "I hit niggers over the head with my nightstick."

Robinson remembered Lee Handley, out of Clarion, Iowa, for the rest of his life. But he could no more respond to Handley at the time than he could respond to Ben Chapman. He thought of the many times he had been told that he *had* to turn the other cheek. But, Robinson asked himself, do I really have to live a sermon?

Years later, when we were working up a story on bigotry for *Our Sports,* a magazine in which he had invested, Robinson recalled his reactions to Ben Chapman in the Golgotha of that clear, cold April day.

"I don't remember everything they shouted. Probably just as well. My wife, Rae, she's into psychology. She says that some things that are too upsetting, you make yourself forget."

Although Robinson could not or would not recount all that he heard, he vividly remembered his emotions. "All my life I've been a proud guy. I won't sit in the back of a bus. If you call me nigger or boy, I want to tear your throat out. I'm a proud guy.

"So there I am in Brooklyn, which is supposed to be the Promised Land, and I'm hearing the worst garbage I ever heard in my whole life, counting the streets, counting the army, but I've sworn to Mr. Rickey that I won't fight back.

"It's Chapman and some of the Phillies ballplayers, and I set my face and I say goddamn, I'm supposed to ignore 'em and just play ball.

"So I play ball. but they don't stop. Jungle bunny. Snowflake. I start breathing hard. I'm just playing ball. I'm doing my job. I'm a good ballplayer. Deep down, I've been thinking, people will see I'm a good ballplayer and they'll see I'm black and they'll put that together. A black guy's a good ballplayer. A black guy can be a good guy.

"But that's not happening. What do the Phillies want from me? What did I ever do to them? What does Mr. Rickey want? I'm in great shape. I'm playing hard. I'm not sassing anybody. What the hell does everybody want from me?

"All of a sudden I thought, the hell with this. This isn't me.

They're making me be some crazy pacifist black freak. Hell, no. Hell, no. I'm going back to being myself. Right now. I'm going into the Phillie dugout and grab one of those white sons of bitches and smash his fucking teeth and walk away. Walk away from this ballpark. Walk away from baseball.

"I thought some more. This didn't take as long in my head as it takes to tell you, Rog. I thought of Mr. Rickey and Rae and my baby son. Standing on that ballfield in Brooklyn, standing still, I had come to a crossroads.

"For a second I felt, this is it. I'm cracking up.

"But wait, wait, wait. Am I gonna give Ben Chapman that satisfaction . . ."

In the eighth inning Robinson singled up the middle. Then he stole second base. When Andy Seminick's throw bounced into center field, Robinson ran on to third. Gene Hermanski singled to right. That was the run. There weren't any more. The Dodgers defeated the Phillies, 1 to 0, on Robinson's run.

Robinson took the subway back to the McAlpin Hotel on 34th Street in Manhattan, where he lived while looking for an apartment. Rachel cooked dinner on an electric hotplate. The baby, Jack Roosevelt Robinson, Jr., had a cold and the couple stayed up much of the night trying to help their child sleep.

At Ebbets Field the next day, Robinson walked up to bat in the first inning feeling better than he had the day before.

"Hey, Jungle Bunny," Ben Chapman shouted. "You go out and get yo-sef some white pussy last night?"

Stanky and a few other ballplayers told newspapermen what was going on. Branch Rickey, informed by his new manager, Burt Shotton, telephoned the commissioner, Happy Chandler. Something had to be done, Rickey said, in the name of decency.

Chandler had suspended Leo Durocher for a year, ostensibly for living loosely. What punishment, then, would be appropriate for William Benjamin Chapman, Klansman without a hood?

Chandler considered at length. Then he ordered Chapman to grant an interview to Wendell Smith, a congenial black sportswriter for the black newspaper the *Pittsburgh Courier.*

No suspension. Not even a fine. Just a suggestion that Chapman ease up and an order that he spend one hour in civil conversation with a Negro.

Dan Parker wrote a column in the *Daily Mirror* criticizing Chapman's "guttersnipe" language. But generally the press persisted in its belligerent neutrality. This account, from *The Sporting News* of May 7, 1947, is characteristic:

> Jackie Robinson's position in the major leagues and the manner in which he will be treated by the Philadelphia Phillies was clarified in a straight from the shoulder interview from Ben Chapman. . . .
>
> "We treat Robinson the same as we do Hank Greenberg of the Pirates, Clint Hartung of the Giants, Connie Ryan of the Braves," Chapman said.
>
> "When I came into the big leagues, pitchers threw at me, dusted me off, pegged at my head, my legs. I was dangerous.
>
> "Robinson can run. He can bunt. He's dangerous.
>
> "When I came into the league, they wanted to see if I would lose my temper and forget to play ball. They tried to break my morale. They played baseball for keeps. That's the way we're going to play with Robinson.
>
> "If Robinson has the stuff, he'll be accepted in baseball, the same as the Sullivans and the Grodzickis. All I expect him to do is prove it. Let's get the chips off our shoulders and play ball."

I mean to suggest that at this point, early in the 1947 season, the issue of Robinson's success — the question of integrated baseball — was seriously in doubt. (So, indeed, was Robinson's mental health.) Oddly, his most vociferous ballfield supporter at that time was Eddie Stanky, the second baseman from Philadelphia who had moved to Mobile and who years later himself needled Robinson in unpleasant ways. But in May 1947 something deep and good was touched within Eddie Stanky, a combative, thin-lipped, verbal ballplayer with limited physical skills and limitless fire. "Those guys [the Phillies] are a disgrace," Stanky told the New York newspapermen. "They know Robinson can't fight back. There isn't one of them who has the guts of a louse." After Chapman's behavior moved Stanky to Jackie Robinson's side, other Dodgers, notably Pee Wee Reese, quickly followed. Some — Bobby Bragan, Hugh Casey, Cookie Lavagetto, and Dixie Walker — did not.

The issue still was in doubt. Herb Pennock, the general manager of the Phillies, had been the leading left-handed pitcher on the 1927 New York Yankees, a team that remains the benchmark of baseball excellence. Tall, lean, dignified, Pennock was nicknamed "The Squire of Kennett Square," after the Pennsylvania town where he was born.

The Dodgers were scheduled to begin a series in Philadelphia on May 9 and Pennock telephoned Branch Rickey to impose conditions. "You just can't bring the nigger here with the rest of your team, Branch," Pennock said. "We're not ready for that sort of thing yet in Philadelphia. We won't be able to take the field [at Shibe Park] against your Brooklyn team, if that boy is in uniform."

Major league rules require that both sides field a team for every scheduled game. Should one side fail to appear, the other team is awarded victory by forfeit. The score of a forfeit is recorded as 9 to 0.

"Very well, Herbert," Rickey said, "if you don't field a team and we must claim the game, 9 to 0, we will do just that, I assure you."

Rickey hung up. Pennock was not through making mischief. When the Dodgers arrived at the 30th Street Station in Philadelphia and took taxis to the Benjamin Franklin Hotel on the morning of May 9, they were turned away in the lobby. Pennock and his employers had spoken to the hotel owners. The hotel would take "no ballclub nigras." Harold Parrott, the Dodgers' toothy traveling secretary, had to shuttle about Philadelphia for hours before he found a hotel — the Warwick — willing to accommodate the team. Until then, the Dodgers were considering commuting for the series. Recalling that Philadelphia story, Parrott summed up: "Talk about brotherly love."

Rickey, not satisfied with Ben Chapman's feathery reprimand, continued to press Commissioner Chandler for significant action. Chandler responded by hiring Jack Demoise, a former FBI agent, to travel the National League "and look for troublemakers." Then, finally, the commissioner telephoned Pennock. "If you move in on Robinson," Chandler said, "I'll move in on you."

Chapman himself was slow recognizing the new thrust of things. Gene Hermanski, a Dodger outfielder for seven seasons, is white-haired now, but so vigorous and feisty in his seventies that someone describes him as a "walking advertisement *against* Grecian Formula" (a popular over-the-counter product that turns white hair dark). Hermanski, who was born in Pittsfield, Massachusetts, and resides in central New Jersey, says, as so many old Dodgers do, "Jackie Robinson was a great man."

"Philadelphia, Gene," I say. "Do you remember Philadelphia, 1947?"

Hermanski's eyes light. "That bastard Chapman." Hermanski moves backwards on wings of memory. His eyes are burning now.

In Philadelphia, first game there, during pregame warmups, Chapman started shouting again. But not at Robinson this time. "Hey, Pee Wee," Chapman yelled. "Yeah, you. Reese. How ya like playin' with a fuckin' nigger?"

Reese ignored Chapman, who shouted the question again. And yet a third time.

Reese stopped picking up ground balls and jogged over to Robinson at first base. Then, staring into the Philadelphia dugout, Reese put an arm around Jackie Robinson's shoulders.

"Pee Wee didn't say a word," Gene Hermanski remembers. "But Chapman had his answer."

Later that day or early the next, someone prominent in baseball placed a long-distance telephone call to Chapman. (Commissioner Chandler took credit for the call three or four decades later, but Chandler was a frightfully unreliable source.) The telephone call to Chapman probably came from Ford Frick, the president of the National League, or from one of Frick's assistants.

The sense of the call was this: Chapman's behavior was out of line. It had to stop. On moral grounds and on *practical* grounds as well.

Walter Winchell, the famous gossip columnist, had picked up reports on Chapman's conduct. He was telling flunkies at the Stork Club in New York that he was going to "use the column to get Chapman out of baseball. I'll nail him on my radio show, too. I'm gonna make a *big hit* on that *bigot.*"

The caller told Ben Chapman that organized baseball would not tolerate syndicated embarrassment. If Chapman intended to keep his job, he had better curb his tongue immediately. An apology would not be out of line.

Cornered, Chapman sent word to Robinson before the next day's ballgame. He would like to start fresh. Maybe he *had* been kinda loud. Would Robinson pose with him for newspaper photographers?

In a remarkably forgiving mood, Robinson agreed. The surviving prints show each man looking as though he'd like to be ten thousand miles away, but after that Chapman never again dared to bait Jackie Robinson or Pee Wee Reese or any others among the athletes Branch Rickey proudly called in subsequent years "my ferocious gentlemen."*

The final spasm of baseball racism, hurled forth against Robinson, quite the most serious, comes down to us in several versions. As I write these pages early in the 1990s, some of the

---

*Herb Pennock died in 1948 at the age of fifty-three. Subsequently, he was voted into the Baseball Hall of Fame, obviously not the only racist so honored. The Phillies fired Ben Chapman midway through 1948, when he was thirty-nine years old. Chapman never again managed in the major leagues. Two years later, under Eddie Sawyer, the Phillies won a pennant.

principals from 1947 survive. But their memories, even the memories of those who want passionately to be honest, have grown blurry. Unlike the Christopher Isherwood heroine, an old ballplayer, an old newspaperman, is not a camera. Besides, not all *want* to be honest.

During the 1940s, the St. Louis Cardinals were the closest thing in the major leagues to a team representing the Old South. Born in another time, Jefferson Davis would have been a St. Louis Cardinal fan.

St. Louis, the "Mound City," is mostly flat. It sits on the western bank of the Mississippi River, a major manufacturer of aircraft today and a colossal brewer of beer, no more racially troubled or racially tranquil than New York or Boston. But in the 1940s, St. Louis was militantly southern. *All* the hotels were segregated. (Robinson was not permitted to join his Dodger teammates at the Hotel Chase until 1953.) The stands at Sportsman's Park were segregated until 1946. St. Louis newspapers, from the conservative *Globe Democrat* to the more liberal *Post-Dispatch*, routinely identified individuals in news stories as Negro. "John Walters, 58, Negro, was injured when fire swept through his residence. . . ."

Playing amid this white-supremacist climate in the southwestern corner of the major leagues, the Cardinals evolved into a team of fire and primitive élan. Branch Rickey, vice president and business manager for twenty-one years, devised baseball's first farm system, and soon strings of minor league teams in Rochester, Columbus, Houston, and smaller towns were developing young players for the big club. Rickey's boss, Sam Breadon, had eastern roots. He began as a garage mechanic, worked hard, saved his money, and somehow acquired a Rolls-Royce dealership. Breadon obtained a controlling interest in the Cardinals for $20,000 in 1920. Like so many old-time baseball owners, Breadon was a flinty businessman, but he was also capable of small kindnesses, and the old garage mechanic was shrewd enough to let Rickey run his baseball team.

The famous Gashouse Gang, performing in St. Louis dur-

ing the 1930s, included such uninhibited characters as Jay
"Dizzy" Dean, Johnny Leonard Roosevelt "Pepper" Martin,
and "Lippy" Leo Durocher. The manager, Frank Frisch, was a
Fordham graduate, but the slant of the team was hillbilly and
southern. During the 1934 World Series, which the Gashouse
Gang won from Detroit, Dean and some others shouted nasty
stuff at Hank Greenberg, whom Dean insisted on calling "Mo."
The Cards for decades were the Ku Klux Klan's favorite team,
an image that changed only slowly and grudgingly over many
years with the ascent of Stan Musial, the greatest hitter I have
ever seen — and a liberal Democrat.

The Cardinals won pennants in 1942, 1943, 1944, and 1946
and won three of those four World Series. The Cards were
strong and tough and raucous and dominant. Before leaving St.
Louis for Brooklyn, Branch Rickey had put together a dynasty
in the Mississippi Valley. Mickey Mantle remembers rooting
for the Cardinals as a child, sitting beside a radio in Oklahoma.
Fans came to Sportsman's Park from Arkansas and Tennessee.
The Cardinals were an absolute down-home triumph.

But in 1947 Sam Breadon felt beset. Rickey was gone. A pair
of Mexican banditos — actually oil megamillionaires — Jorge
and Alfonso Pasquel, were starting an "outlaw" league south of
the Rio Grande. They had "stolen" the fine left-handed pitcher
Max Lanier. Breadon worried obsessively about money. St.
Louis, he told friends, really wasn't big enough to support two
major league teams, his Cardinals and the Browns. He talked
of moving the Cardinals to Los Angeles.

The Cardinals of 1947, defending world champions, were a
gifted group, but not a happy one. Almost everyone on the
team felt underpaid. Cliques were developing. Some players
were drinking heavily. The world champion Cardinals lost nine
of eleven games in April and played no better than .500 ball in
May.

Except for Musial and the bibulous third baseman, George
"Whitey" Kurowski, the team had a Confederate cast. Shortstop Marty Marion, captain and center fielder Terry Moore,

and right fielder Enos Slaughter were all southerners. The manager, Eddie Dyer, was a native of Louisiana. The promising young catcher, Joe Garagiola, raised on "Dago Hill" in St. Louis, was not as enlightened as he would become.

These were the '47 Cardinals: losing, underpaid. They did not seem able to do much about either. What they *could* do was conspire. Several did.

"I heard talk," Stan Musial says. "It was rough and racial and I can tell you a few things about that." Musial is seventy as we speak at breakfast in St. Louis. He has been grand marshal of a parade in Tennessee the day before and is traveling to Washington tomorrow, but he has rearranged his schedule to make time to talk about something significant that makes him uncomfortable.

"First of all, everybody has racial feelings. We don't admit it. We aren't proud of it. But it's there. And this is big league baseball, not an English tea, and ballplayers make noise. So I heard the words and I knew there was some feelings behind the words, but I didn't take it seriously. That was baseball.

"I had no trouble myself with integration. I'd played with a black kid in high school,* for one thing. Second, I knew that integration was overdue.

"I make jokes now and then about being Polish. Actually my father, Lukas, was born in Poland but my mother, Mary Lancos, was Czech. They both came to America for the same reason. They wanted economic opportunity. Dad worked in a steel mill and he sweated but he made a decent living. I knew these things. My parents came to America for economic opportunity. That was the first thing Jackie Robinson was asking for, it seemed to me. An economic opportunity. That's something of what America is about.

"For me at that time — I was twenty-six — saying all that would have been a speech and I didn't know how to make

---

*The grandfather of Ken Griffey, Jr., the 1990s young star outfielder.

speeches. Saying it to older players, that was beyond me. Besides, I thought the racial talk was just hot air."

The leaders of the anti-Robinson movement on the Cardinals did not take Musial — who was in pain much of the time from appendicitis — into their confidence. They did talk to several Dodgers, including Dixie Walker. Some later claimed that Walker developed the idea of a general strike throughout the league. At first the Cardinals thought of striking on May 6, when the team was scheduled to play at Ebbets Field.

But Brooklyn was, after all, Robinson's home turf. It made more sense, the conspirators decided, to wait until May 20 when the Dodgers played their opening game at Sportsman's Park in St. Louis. Walker said he might go on strike himself then and enlist some other Dodgers to join. It began to look as though on the sixth of May seven Cardinals and several key Dodgers would refuse to take the field with Jackie Robinson.

Nor did the scheme stop there. Some Phillies might join the strike. Ben Chapman did not stand alone. The best pitcher in baseball, Ewell "the Whip" Blackwell of Cincinnati, didn't care for integration. He could be recruited. As the Cardinals traveled about the circuit, the redneck ballplayers began loosely to organize a league-wide strike.

The Cardinals' team physician, a doctor named Robert Hyland, liked to hear himself described as the surgeon general of baseball. Like most team physicians, Hyland was a ball fan and he enjoyed the camaraderie of major league athletes. Someone, no one remembers who, told Hyland of the strike plan. Hyland sought out Terry Moore, the St. Louis captain, called "the greatest center fielder I ever saw" by Joe DiMaggio. Moore was thirty-five years old, approaching the end of an outstanding career.

Hyland told Moore that he had heard about the strike and that the players ought to be pretty damn careful. He wasn't saying anybody had to like "nigras." He just wanted to tell them they were heading for trouble.

Moore is hazy about his end of the conversation. (I found him in Collinsville, in southern Illinois, on a simmering summer day made lively by the wails of a tornado warning siren. Moore was seventy-nine and undergoing treatment for prostate cancer. He recalled Doc Hyland speaking to him "about the Robinson thing" forty-four years before; he said he was not sure what he told Hyland.)

The conspiring ballplayers recognized that secrecy was essential. They believed wildly that a surprise strike, bringing baseball to a stop one day in May, would drive the nigger from the game before his supporters could counterattack. The press, which, as I say, had not been notably friendly to Robinson, was nonetheless an enemy of secrecy. The conspiring players agreed no words, no hints, no nothin' to the sportswriters.

Once two people know a secret, as the saying is, it ceases to be a secret. Dr. Hyland felt honor bound to report what he knew to his employer, flinty old Sam Breadon, who was now planning to sell the Cardinals to secure himself a pecunious, quiet old age. Breadon was no social activist, but as a businessman he recognized that the strike could tear down the value of his franchise. Who wanted to buy into the Civil War? Breadon flew to New York. There, as he later said, "I talked things over with some of the men" at the New Yorker hotel. He heard enough to fill him with dread. He took a taxi to the Rockefeller Center building that housed the office of Ford C. Frick, the president of the National League.

Frick listened thoughtfully, heavily. He was not a confrontational man, nor even, over the years, a very strong one. But Breadon's report stirred Frick as nothing in baseball ever had or would again. He proceeded to Ebbets Field at once — it was early in the afternoon of May 6 — and commandeered a small office high up, behind home plate, adjacent to the press room and the bar, where some hours later sportswriters would be drinking free whiskey, supplied by the teetotaling Branch Rickey. The office was secure because no sportswriter would be coming to work at Ebbets Field for several hours.

Frick called up seven Cardinals, individually. He did not want to address a group. He would divide the strikers before conquering them. Musial was not summoned.*

The message Frick delivered to each player was unyielding. It went like this:

> If you strike, you will be suspended from the league. You will find the friends you think you have in the press box will not support you. You will be outcasts. I do not care if half the league strikes. Those who do will encounter quick retribution. All will be suspended. I don't care if it wrecks the National League for five years. This is the United States of America and one citizen has as much right to play as another. . . . You will find if you go through with your intention that you will have been guilty of complete madness.

And there amid shafts of spring sunlight the strike withered. Was there ever a more glorious moment in sport?

A version of these events reached the ubiquitous Dr. Robert Hyland. Among the surgeon's avocations was singing in a barbershop quartet. Good whiskey and nighttime crooning pleased the soul. One good friend, with whom Hyland sang, was a Canadian native named Cecil Rutherford Rennie, who wrote baseball for the *Herald Tribune* under the name of Rud Rennie.

By the time I came to know Rennie, in 1953, he had suffered a heart attack and had covered too many ballgames. He was noted then for the speed with which he composed his stories rather than for their excellence. But the somewhat younger Rennie was a fine newspaperman.

Rennie came to St. Louis with the Yankees early in May, and Hyland, in his cups, provided a version of the strike story. Rennie, not entirely sober himself, slipped away from the quar-

---

*"Ford," says Buzzie Bavasi, a close friend, "knew Stan had too much sense and class to be associated with a harebrained strike. The only ones he talked to were the troublemakers."

tet and telephoned his sports editor, Stanley Woodward. "I can't write this myself, Coach. It would trace back to Doc Hyland. Maybe you can do something with it."

Woodward telephoned Frick, who would not speak on the record. In fact, he did not want to talk at all.

"In that case," Woodward said, "I'm going with what I have. What I have makes the National League look bad."

"Now, Stanley," Frick said, in his accustomed conciliatory way.

"Now nothing, Ford. What the hell happened?"

Frick grudgingly began to re-create events. He didn't care for this; he didn't care for this at all. He was giving a major story exclusively to the *Herald Tribune* which, despite editorial excellence, was neither as powerful as the *Times* nor as popular as the *Daily News*.

But if he held his tongue . . . Frick had been a newspaperman himself, rather an establishment character, a ghostwriter for Babe Ruth, and he was literate. He knew that a roused Stanley Woodward could write up a storm.

Some details were garbled in the long telephone conversation between Frick and Woodward. But on May 9, 1947, the *Herald Tribune* published what remains the sports scoop of the century, the story that did not make page one.

"A National League players' strike," Woodward began, under an eight-column headline,

> instigated by some of the St. Louis Cardinals against the presence in the league of Jackie Robinson, Negro first baseman, has been averted temporarily and perhaps permanently quashed. . . .
>
> In recent days Ford Frick, president of the National League, and Sam Breadon, president of the St. Louis club, have been conferring with St. Louis players. Mr. Breadon flew east when he heard of the projected strike. The story that he came to consult with Eddie Dyer, manager, about the lowly state of the St. Louis club was fictitious. He came on a much more serious errand.

The strike, formulated by certain St. Louis players, was instigated by a member of the Brooklyn Dodgers, who has since recanted. . . .

It is understood that the players involved — and the recalcitrants are not all Cardinals — will say that their objective is to gain the right to have a say on who shall be eligible to play in the major leagues. . . .

This story is factually and thoroughly substantiated. The St. Louis players involved will unquestionably deny it. We doubt, however, Frick and Breadon, will go that far. A return of no comment from either or both will serve.

Breadon, reported Bob Broeg in the *St. Louis Post-Dispatch,* "emphatically denied that there had been a movement to stage a protest strike." Broeg quoted Breadon as saying, "The whole thing is ridiculous."

Over the years, careful disinformation has been developed. Breadon came to New York suddenly to see why his team was losing ballgames. He spoke to Terry Moore and Marty Marion about drinking on the ballclub and about possibly replacing the manager, Eddie Dyer. Broeg himself still claims that there was never a strike threat. He adds that Woodward, who scooped him, was "guilty of barnyard journalism."

One man who did not deny the story was Ford Frick. He never elaborated and seemed embarrassed to take credit for his own decisive action. A few days later he told a reporter for *The Sporting News:* "The National League stands firmly behind Jackie Robinson."

Was there a strike threat? the reporter asked.

Frick said: "Any player who tries to strike will leave me no recourse but to suspend him indefinitely."

Stanley Woodward wrote in triumph:

The blast of publicity which followed . . . the revelation that the Cardinals were promoting a players' strike against the presence of Jackie Robinson, Brooklyn's Negro first baseman, will serve to squash further strolls down Tobacco Road.

In other words it can now be honestly doubted that the boys

from the Hookworm Belt will have the nerve to foist their quaint sectional folklore on the rest of the country.

The denial by Sam Breadon is so spurious as to be beneath notice. [The statement by Ford Frick] obviously is the most noble ever made by a baseball man.

That autumn Woodward's article won the E. P. Dutton Award as the best sports reporting job of the year. (The Pulitzer Committee had not yet found the sports page.) By that time, of course, Robinson's success was assured and the course of American history had been changed.

3

A Guy Named Joe

◆

WHILE INTEGRATION was stirring souls in Brooklyn, Philadelphia, and St. Louis, Larry MacPhail was looking at a baseball problem in the Bronx. The Yankees of 1946 were mediocre. They finished third, seventeen games behind the champion Red Sox. No Yankee batted .300 in 1946. The team attracted 2.3 million customers, a Yankee record, but that was the heady wine of peace as much as Yankee baseball. Finishing last in the National League, the Giants drew an imposing 1.2 million. The postwar Yankee story in 1946 centered on Joe DiMaggio.

Larry MacPhail wanted Yankee baseball to resound with carnival noises. He offered nylon stockings as gifts on Ladies Day. He booked the team on airlines in an era when train travel was both efficient and luxurious. He dispensed immoderate quantities of liquor to the press. But the ballclub did not win. On May 9, 1946, in a game against the Browns, DiMaggio dropped a routine fly ball. Two plays later, trying to take a single on one bounce, he misread the hop and the ball skipped past him. Two errors in a single inning. The Browns won, 6 to 1. In the press room later, MacPhail drank hard. After three bourbons he announced, "Looks like DiMaggio came out of service too damn soon. Biggest disappointment of my life. That guy may be all washed up."

Sober the following day, MacPhail called Clark Griffith, the penurious old pitcher who owned the Washington Senators. According to one Washington sportswriter, MacPhail offered DiMaggio for Mickey Vernon, a rangy left-handed first baseman who had never hit as many as ten home runs in a season. Griffith turned down the deal.

The idea of that trade brings a denial from Lee MacPhail ("My father would have mentioned it. He never did") and occasions shudders of horror in the Bronx ("Vernun fuh DiMaj? Whadaya? Nuts?"). MacPhail may have been drinking when he propositioned Griffith. That would explain his memory loss around the house. Or he may have felt embarrassed. Anyway, the deal was not as ridiculous as it seems. DiMaggio might have been through in 1946, an athlete dying very, very young. Vernon, while no superstar, was competent* and durable. He was also four years younger than DiMaggio and, in fact, played major league ball until 1960, nine seasons after DiMaggio's retirement.

MacPhail's next attempt to discard his somber center fielder showed the man at his roarin' redheaded best. He invited Tom Yawkey, the multimillionaire bon vivant who owned the Red Sox, to join him for a night of talk and drink at Toots Shor's. Yawkey kept his distance from the press, in the manner of many monied men, but Shor's was a safe saloon for public drinking. By unwritten rule, what went on at Shor's was off the record, unless a specific exception was made.[†]

---

*And sometimes more than that. He won the 1946 American League batting championship at .353. But two years later he hit under .250.

†This rule was demanded by Shor himself, a loud, beefy, softhearted character. I saw one of America's most famous columnists drink himself into a stupor at Shor's. The proprietor hired a limousine with driver to take the man home to Connecticut and had a headwaiter ride along and pour the columnist into bed.

MacPhail steered Yawkey to a banquette in a corner and told him rollicking stories. How he had built a winner in Cincinnati. How he had patched together a champion for Brooklyn. What he had needed to create a winner there in 1941, MacPhail told Yawkey, was Billy Herman, the great second baseman of the Chicago Cubs. Philip K. Wrigley, the chewing gum manufacturer who owned the Cubs, hadn't wanted to give up Herman, but MacPhail induced Wrigley to drink with him in a hotel suite. In four hours, MacPhail's Dodgers had Billy Herman. "I *poured* drink for drink with Wrigley, but I didn't swallow the stuff," MacPhail explained. "I kept excusing myself to go to the bathroom. Then I'd throw my drink down the sink. After a while I was a helluva lot more sober than Wrigley. I pulled out some papers and he signed them. I got Herman for a coupla second-raters and some cash and won the pennant in Brooklyn. Some guys say we won it on the ballfield, around second base. Sure. But we also won it when I was filling a sink hole with good booze."

MacPhail threw out no booze at Shor's. He knocked back drinks, and Yawkey joined him. MacPhail got to his idea. "I have this big dago in center field. He hits the hell out of the ball, but to left center. We got a spot out there that's four hundred seventy feet from home. He hits these tremendous drives, home runs anywhere else, and in my ballpark they're just damn long outs."

"That's the way this game is," Yawkey said. "I got this skinny kid, pulls everything left-handed, hits these long balls to right and right center. In my ballpark, right center reaches four hundred twenty feet from home."

The men drank some more. Yawkey wanted to know what

That indiscretion stayed off record. My former wife, a pretty Pennsylvania girl, arrived one night noticeably pregnant. Shor pointed a finger at her navel and said, "You been doing that thing again." After the baby was born a few weeks later, Shor sent two dozen red roses to the hospital room. I found it impossible to *stay* offended by blustery, gauche Toots Shor.

MacPhail thought about Rickey's plan to bring "nigras" into baseball. Shor later recalled the conversation for me.

"Gonna kill our business," MacPhail said.

Yawkey nodded. (Yawkey's Red Sox did not employ a black ballplayer until 1959, fully *twelve* years after Robinson's major league debut.)

They were both drinking hard and they were getting along very well. After a while, at two in the morning, MacPhail proposed his trade.

The Big Dago for the Skinny Kid.

No cash. No other ballplayers.

Even up, Joe DiMaggio for Ted Williams.

"Helluvan idea," Yawkey said.

"Put the Dago up there with your close-in left field wall," MacPhail said, "and he'll hit sixty homers."

"Right," Yawkey said. "Put the Kid in the Stadium, with the right field stands so close, and he'll hit seventy!"

"We gotta deal?"

"We gotta deal!!"

"Shake."

"Skoal."

"Let's have another."

"There's got to be a morning after . . ."

Maureen McGovern, who was not born until 1949, sang that hangover lyric decades later. When this particular 1946 morning after struck, Yawkey telephoned. "I can't do it, Larry."

"I thought we had a deal."

"We did. I'm not denying that. But I can't do it. They let Babe Ruth out of Boston. If I let Williams go, the fans will crucify me."

"You'll make new fans. Every Italian in New England will pay to see my guy."

"No deal," Yawkey said. "Excuse me. I've got to go and get a Bromo-Seltzer."

*

As World War II had moved toward its mushroom-cloud conclusion, DiMaggio was out of shape, plagued by stomach ul-
cers, beset by arthritis, and brooding about the breakup of his
marriage to a blonde starlet named Dorothy Arnold, whom
someone has described as "spring training for Marilyn Monroe."

After the 1942 season, with the draft closing in, DiMaggio
enlisted in the air force. DiMaggio claims he never asked for
special treatment, but the air force cast him as a celebrity
soldier. His tours of duty took him no closer to a battlefield
than the New Jersey pine flats, and DiMaggio, an enlisted
man, was not your basic grunt. He found GI uniforms "a little
skimpy" and hired a tailor to make alterations. Custom-tailored
olive drabs. He lent his name to a sports column some forgotten ghost tapped out for service publications. And, for the
entertainment of generals and admirals, he was required to
play baseball.

First, Staff Sergeant Joe DiMaggio played center field for a
team at the Santa Ana Army Air Base in southern California.
"Our pitching was so bad," he complained, "I once had to
spend forty-five minutes chasing base hits around the outfield."
(Sherman was right. War *is* hell.) Later, transferred to Hawaii,
DiMaggio starred for the Seventh Air Force team, a Pacific
powerhouse packed with conscripted major leaguers and managed by a tall lieutenant named Long Tom Winsett, who had
flopped as a Dodger outfielder across three seasons. Under
manager Winsett, a lifetime .237 hitter, DiMaggio played ninety
games and batted .401.

Viewed from Guadalcanal or Remagen Bridge, DiMaggio's
wartime hitch was a Sunday afternoon stroll beside the lily
pond in southeast Central Park. But DiMaggio was not a Sun-
day-strolling character. In the best of times, he was high-
strung, intense, chain-smoking. Wired, people say today. The
older, milder term was "He's a worrier." Now as an enlisted
man, the Wired Worried Clipper had real reason for concern.
How long would the war last? Afterwards, whenever after-

wards began, how much of his baseball skills would remain? There was no pension, much less job security, for major league ballplayers, and the war was robbing DiMaggio, as it robbed Bob Feller and Hank Greenberg, of prime earning years.*

Beyond that endemic insecurity, Dorothy Arnold's decision to divorce DiMaggio troubled him in ways he did not fully understand. He was something of a roué, as famous among New York showgirls as he was among New York ball fans. But he was also the son of devout Roman Catholics. The Church, not prominent in his everyday life, asserted itself when DiMaggio married, as loudly as a bass organ chord.

DiMaggio insisted on a church wedding, which meant that Dorothy had to agree that their children would be raised as Roman Catholic. (She was nominally Lutheran.) She then decided to take instruction in the Catholic faith, although her conversion turned out to be less permanent than a cathedral. After the marriage, on November 19, 1939, in a huge ceremony at St. Peter and St. Paul's, a San Francisco columnist reported that the DiMaggios' wedding guests were so numerous and hungry that they consumed twelve turkeys, eight hams, fifteen chickens, and four sides of beef. This very gaudy, very crowded Italian Catholic wedding made front-page news for the tabloids.

Now, less than four years later, Dorothy was suing for divorce. The DiMaggio family was shocked. Divorce was unknown on the island near Sicily where the parents were born. How could that little blondie from Minnesota divorce their beloved Joe? The family felt scandalized and DiMaggio himself became a very angry man. He was a big, broad-shouldered character and on several occasions threatened to punch out people who asked about the divorce.

Dorothy was less inclined toward silence. She told reporters

---

*But only DiMaggio was so graceless as to complain about the relative rigors of service. Greenberg, who never complained, did hard duty, rising from private to captain, with a fighting unit in South China.

that her home life as Mrs. DiMaggio was dull. Joe went out a lot, leaving her alone. He liked to have fun with the boys. At least she hoped it was the boys. She herself liked to entertain and found nice apartments, even a penthouse on Central Park West, in New York, but Joe didn't seem to want to be the host at parties. He liked to go out with the boys. At least, she hoped it was the boys. She thought the arrival of their son, Joe Di-Maggio Junior, would secure their marriage. But the baby, she complained, couldn't compete with Joe's other interests, the boys he loved to talk and drink with at Toots Shor's. At least, Dorothy concluded, raising one carefully plucked brow, "I *hope* it was the boys." Subsequently, on instructions from her attorney, Joseph P. Haller, Dorothy shut up. Early in 1944, she divorced DiMaggio following, as *Time* magazine put it, "four and a half years of marriage, two trips to Reno and one child."

Like very few — Charles Augustus Lindbergh comes to mind — Joe DiMaggio is a neurotically private public man. In a memorable observation that appeared in *The Aspirin Age*, John Lardner wrote: "Lindbergh was deliberately responsible for his continuing fame and notoriety [after the solo flight to Paris in 1927]. Loathing the blatant contactual phases of publicity, he showed nonetheless one of the truest gifts ever seen on this planet for attracting it. . . . It appeared that he needed fame to subsist, to support his confidence in the role he had won. Here is the paradox that engrosses his analyzers: a man supernormally ingrown and aloof becoming with sure instincts a chronic public figure."

If we substitute DiMaggio's 56-game hitting streak in 1941 for Lindbergh's historic flight — and I don't mean to diminish either accomplishment — we have a splendid parallel. Later Di-Maggio would celebrate or compensate for his retirement from baseball by marrying Marilyn Monroe. Then, having plighted his troth with the most famous blonde on earth, DiMaggio faulted the press and public for intruding on his privacy. If

Colonel Lindbergh noticed, he would have offered a steely but approving smile.

DiMaggio was born in the Bay Area village of Martinez, California, on November 25, 1914, the eighth child of a couple who emigrated from Isola delle Femmine, a small, impoverished island off Palermo. All the boys — Thomas, Michael, Vincent, Joseph, and Dominic — were given the middle name Paul. It was impossible in the cabin household where Joe DiMaggio began life to forget that Paul was his father's favorite saint. Giuseppe Paolo DiMaggio, Sr., never learned to read English. The household language was Italian.

In 1915 the family moved to a ground-floor apartment at 2047 Taylor Street on the slope of Russian Hill in the North Beach section of San Francisco, about a quarter mile from the dock. Giuseppe had bought a fishing boat that he named for his devout wife. In a phenomenon astonishing not only to baseball enthusiasts but to geneticists, the three youngest children of Giuseppe and Rosalie — Vince, Joe, and Dom DiMaggio — grew up to become major league center fielders.*

DiMaggio has not been expansive about his early years, but he says, "My parents told me I was knock-kneed and I had to wear some kind of braces. After that I had weak ankles. When I was seven or eight I picked up a broken paddle and started swinging. My sister Frances liked to pitch to me. They tell me I hit my sister's stuff pretty hard."

DiMaggio attended Hancock Grammar School and San Francisco Junior High before entering Galileo High School. He neither achieved nor aspired to distinction on school teams or in the classroom. After a while he quit school and went to work

---

*Vince was a gifted defensive player, but he led the National League in strikeouts six times. Dom, who wore spectacles, played eleven seasons for the Boston Red Sox. Fenway Park rooters made him the hero of a song Harvard men and others chanted to the tune of "O Tannenbaum":

Oh, Dominic DiMaggio!
He's better than his brother Joe.

in an orange juice cannery. He peeled oranges eight hours a day. "I used to wonder," said his sister Marie, "if Joe was backward. Not quick." She was suggesting retardation. "I mean, I wondered what was the matter with Joe. Then I decided it was mostly that he was so shy."

The baseball talent bloomed on rocky sandlots for teams called the Salesian Boys and the Jolly Knights, and then we find an oft-told and still lovely story. A shy and lonely boy, a social wallflower, steps onto a ballfield and suddenly assumes great grace and strength and beauty. "Joe," said his brother Tom, "could always hit like hell." At eighteen DiMaggio played 187 games for the San Francisco Seals of the Pacific Coast League. He batted safely in sixty-one straight games and knocked in 169 runs. That was in 1933. After that, someone else had to peel the oranges in the cannery. The Yankees signed DiMaggio two seasons later.

With some urging from the Yankee front office, two California veterans, Frank Crosetti and Tony Lazzeri, agreed to take DiMaggio with them to his first major league spring training in 1936. Lazzeri and Crosetti shared the driving and then — it may have been in Texas, it may have been in Alabama — Lazzeri turned to DiMaggio and said: "Okay, champ. It's your turn to drive."

"I don't know how to drive a car," said twenty-one-year-old Joe DiMaggio.

After watching DiMaggio take batting practice on March 2, 1936 — just batting practice, no 95-mile-an-hour fastballs, no shooting, hissing, snapping curves — Dan M. Daniel wrote in the New York *World-Telegram:* "Here is the replacement for Babe Ruth." That was the first fusillade in the DiMaggio publicity barrage that continues into the present.

The three New York ballclubs underwrote New York baseball journalism years ago, and promotional copy — that is what Daniel actually wrote — was the return. The teams paid expenses for baseball writers on the road: hotel, Pullman berths, a weekly meal allowance. "Loans" were common. The teams served (and still serve) free meals and drinks to sportswriters before and after every home game. Favored journalists, who wrote with scarlet passion, drew special rewards, say a free trip to Florida for the wife and children during spring training. In this climate, most New York baseball writers were not in fact reporters. They were hairy-legged cheerleaders sans pom-poms.*

Stanley Woodward, whose integrity eventually cost him his job at the *Herald Tribune,* visited the Yankee camp on DiMaggio's first day and reported that during a half dozen turns at batting practice DiMaggio hit three balls over the left field fence. "But the question still exists," Woodward wrote, "whether he can power the offerings of the American League brothers after they start cutting loose, whether he can go and get them in the outfield and whether he can throw as well as his enraptured ex manager, Lefty O'Doul, says he can."

Daniel dined out into the 1970s on his extravagant rhapsodic sentence from 1936. "I could tell at once," he liked to say in a raspy, not unpleasant voice, "DiMaggio was the apotheosis of poetry in motion. I knew he was a great one right away."

But Stanley Woodward, clearly, didn't know. Good sportswriters come with a healthy skepticism. They know the story of the rookie who hits hard across several weeks of batting practice. A few weeks later, the rookie dispatches a collect telegram:

Dear Ma:
Be home soon.
They're starting to throw curves.

DiMaggio never had to send that wire. In the seasons before he enlisted in the air force, decent Scotch sold for $2.50 a

*Editors and publishers allowed the baseball writers to live in indentured servitude because, bless my M.B.A., it saved money. Only after World War II did several nasty incidents prompt three newspapers to pay their own way. These were the *New York Times,* the *New York Herald Tribune,* and the *Daily News.*

fifth, and a new Plymouth, with safety steel body and hydraulic brakes, cost $510, sales tax extra in those few states that imposed sales taxes. DiMaggio's accomplishments in New York and a certain stubborn contentiousness brought him a salary of $43,750 by 1942. He was such a formidable businessman that the commissioner of baseball, hatchet-jawed, white-haired Kenesaw Mountain Landis, investigated a charge that Joe Gould, a tough little boxing manager, was DiMaggio's business agent.

"He's just a friend, Judge," DiMaggio told Landis. "He gives me advice on endorsements."

"We have no objection to that," Landis said, "but is Gould getting a percentage of your Yankee salary?"

"No, sir."

"Because if he is, DiMaggio, I'll suspend you. My job is to protect baseball. We can't have agents dirtying up the game. Suspend you. Maybe banish you for life."

In a sense, DiMaggio called Landis's bluff, as no other player ever did. He reported his chilling meeting to Bob Considine, a popular columnist for the Hearst newspapers.

"Why this heavy righteousness in Landis' office?" Considine wrote the next day. "If Gould dug up easy endorsement dough for DiMaggio, it's none of Landis' business.

"The lackadaying is a front. The big league bosses are afraid that the ball players will smarten up enough to hire tough agents to speak for them.

"And if that ever comes to pass, the ball clubs would have to pay the blokes what they're actually worth."*

DiMaggio, a strong, rangy slugger who rarely struck out, clearly was worth a great deal. Center field at Yankee Stadium was only slightly smaller than the state of Nebraska and DiMaggio roamed the Bronx prairie with great skill. When Hank Greenberg walloped a 460-foot drive in August of 1939, DiMaggio ran back and caught that formidable wallop. DiMaggio could throw and catch the ball and hit, and with remarkable

---

Mirabile dictu, it has come to pass.

quickness he learned to play the New York press as well as he
played the outfield.

Toots Shor's restaurant in the West Fifties had a special
appeal to athletes and celebrities. It was against house rules to
bother anyone for an autograph; ballplayers in Shor's were safe
from tourists and fans.

The place was a clubby kind of barn; a lady I took there once
said it had all the chic warmth of her boarding school gymna-
sium. Shor pampered the columnists and the ballplayers and
they reveled in hard-drinking, nonstop talking camaraderie. At
table one in Shor's, DiMaggio came to know Considine and
Jimmy Cannon and Bill Corum and Red Smith, and if any of
them ever wrote a critical sentence about him, it has escaped
my research. DiMaggio took the sports columnists into his
confidence. Leaving his shyness far behind, he learned to swap
stories until each important New York sports columnist regarded Joe DiMaggio as a personal buddy. Although this obviously was distinct from playing ball, it stands as a remarkable
accomplishment on its own. In time someone remarked of Cannon that he "romanced DiMaggio as if Joe were some broad."
DiMaggio has a poker player's feel for people, their strengths
and vulnerability. He treated Cannon like a friend and the
writer rewarded him with love poems in the shape of columns.
As sports editor, Woodward felt he had to reprimand Red
Smith only once.

"Walter," Woodward said, using Smith's baptismal name for
emphasis. "You are *not* writing about deities. Stop godding up
the athletes."

The reference was to DiMaggio.

If you had any doubts about the batting skills of Ted Williams,
you could get them cleared up by Williams himself, often in a
memorable way. Once, trying to understand the sudden stardom of one of Williams's teammates, the journeyman infielder
Billy Klaus, I asked if Williams could explain a man having a
very good year after experiencing a relatively bad one.

"Who ya askin'?" Williams said in a congenial bellow.

"You."

"Mister," Williams said, "I can see you don't know very much about baseball, if you're asking me about a bad year. See them bastards there." He indicated a semicircle of New England sports reporters auditing from a distance. "Every one of them would give their left nut to see me have a bad year. But, mister, it ain't gonna happen because ol' T.S.W. [Theodore Samuel Williams], he don't have bad years." Lest I miss the point, Williams bounced a bat off the grass with great force, caught it one-handed on the rebound, and walked away.*

Such extravagant behavior was alien to DiMaggio. Indeed, he took pride in keeping his emotions under rigid control. When questions annoyed him, DiMaggio glared through the questioner. He didn't boast. He was a more subtle artist than Williams and is perhaps more difficult to appreciate.

Fast as he was in his youth, DiMaggio never stole more than six bases in any major league season. As a rookie, stationed in left field, he threw out 22 base runners. By 1940, established in center, he threw out only 5. DiMaggio was an outstanding base runner on a team that did not steal, but there is no statistic for that. Rival base runners stopped taking chances when Joe DiMaggio was throwing from the outfield, and no statistic covers frozen base runners either. He twice led the league in home runs, batting average, and runs batted in, but he never led in all three columns during the same year. The vaunted "triple crown" eluded him.

Williams is most famous for hitting .406 in 1941. "You know," DiMaggio remarked as we sat with Hank Greenberg at a little table on an Old Timers' Day at Shea Stadium, "I wanted to hit .400 myself. One year, I really had a chance. That was 1939. On September 8, I think it was, I was hitting .408.

---

*The senior Boston baseball writer on this trip, Hy Hurwitz of the *Globe*, later told me: "I know Williams. We were in the Marines together. He staged that tantrum to get you to knock the Boston press in a national magazine. Whatever you asked him, he was going to end up knocking the Boston press."

"Then something went wrong with my left eye. Really wrong. It got sore as hell, all bloodshot and inflamed. I could hardly see out of it. Allergy? I don't know.

"But Joe McCarthy didn't believe in cheese champions [a boxing term, for champions of small worth]. He kept playing me every day. He had to know the agony I was going through, swinging at that tough pitching with a blurry eye. I'll never understand why he didn't give me a couple of days off. But he didn't. You played in those days with anything short of a broken leg." His vision reduced, DiMaggio finished the 1939 season with a batting average of .381.*

DiMaggio's most soaring accomplishment is generally said to be his great batting streak. In 1941, he hit safely in 56 games, swinging hard, not bunting, even when the streak was on the line. No one has come within a dozen games of matching that streak, but appreciating DiMaggio, even for 1941, requires a certain sophistication. During 1941, DiMaggio struck out 13 times. Swinging as hard as he could, clouting 30 home runs, against the best pitchers in baseball throwing him their best stuff at the corners, DiMaggio struck out once every two weeks. "He simply had no weakness," Bob Feller says. No one has ever gotten his bat on the ball with so much power so consistently as Joe DiMaggio, 1941.

He was not the same player after World War II. DiMaggio was a winner down to his last at bat — a two-base hit — but after the war his excellence came fitfully. He was not quite as fast a runner as he had been. His throwing arm weakened. Good inside fastballs bothered him. These foibles and slumps upset Larry MacPhail. Like Red Smith, MacPhail confused a star with a deity.

---

*The season of 1939 was not easy. In the grip of a fatal disease, Lou Gehrig had to stop playing for the Yankees after eight games. Subsequently, pulled muscles and inflamed corneas seemed less than serious. Still, McCarthy could safely have rested DiMaggio in September and protected the .400 average while the eye healed. The Yankees won the pennant by seventeen games.

Larry MacPhail discovered that he had a mortal playing center field. These pages may suggest that Leland Stanford MacPhail was a bit of a clown. He was not that. Increasingly he was a bit of a drunk. He could be petulant, petty, and, as on the issue of integration, as wrong-headed as a sinful Janus. But what saved MacPhail in baseball, at least for a little while, was inspired pragmatism. All right. We're stuck with DiMaggio. God is not available to play center field in the Bronx. Let's make the best of what we have.

DiMaggio had waged contract wars with the Yankees across many seasons. Some fault was his. Once he told San Francisco reporters that he threw a Yankee contract into the municipal dump. The story that followed infuriated the Yankees' feudal lords. But some fault traced to Yankee management, which was mean-spirited.

MacPhail, stuck with DiMaggio, called the star into his office at the Squibb Building immediately after the 1946 season. Aside from hitting under .300, DiMaggio had failed to bat in 100 runs for the first time in his major league career. His divorce was final now. Absolute. He wasn't hitting. He was alone. DiMaggio did not feel good about himself.

"We know what happened last summer, Joe," MacPhail began. "We're going to move on from there. We aren't going to brood about the past."

Brooding is an avocation with DiMaggio. He looked at Mac-Phail and exercised his right to remain silent.

"This yellow pad," MacPhail said. "*I'm* taking one sheet. I'm giving *you* one sheet. Do you have a pen?"

DiMaggio nodded.

"We're going to do numbers. Last year, Joe, coming out of the army you were paid $43,500. I want you to write down on that yellow paper what you think you should be paid for next year. I'm going to write down what I think. Then we'll compare numbers."

DiMaggio took his time. He didn't trust baseball people. He

wanted to be careful. But he wasn't a thief. He'd had a lousy year. He got $43,500 and gave the team a lousy year. They finished third. He wasn't worth another $43,500.

DiMaggio wrote down five numbers. The salary he proposed for himself, a significant cut, was $37,500.

MacPhail looked and nodded and said, "Now I want you to see *my* numbers, Joe." MacPhail had written $43,500.

"I guess," MacPhail said, "you'd rather play for my numbers than for yours."

DiMaggio smiled. The somber presence lightened.

A satisfied DiMaggio was nobody you wanted to pitch to when a game was on the line.

A few days later, October 19, MacPhail traded Joe Gordon, a splendid second baseman, to Cleveland for Allie Reynolds, a right-handed pitcher of great strength, who for mysterious reasons had not won consistently.

Reynolds, an Oklahoma Creek Indian, was reborn in the Bronx and nicknamed Superchief. He could start and relieve and overpower every batter in the league, including Theodore S. Williams.

Years later Casey Stengel talked to me about Reynolds's ability to win as a starter and win as a reliever with grammar unique to Stengel and, in the middle of all that crowded syntax, a quality of awe.

"Reynolds," Stengel said, "is the greatest two ways, which is startin' and relievin', the greatest ever, and I seen the great ones, Mathewson, and I seen Cy Young and I wondered who that fat old guy was, which tells you what a dumb young punk I was. You could look it up."

With a happy DiMaggio and a primed Superchief, the revived Yankees were ready to take over the world, come 1947 and the years that followed. MacPhail was an architect of that great team, which now awaited only a Second Coming, the arrival of Casey Stengel, ringed by light. But for that the Yankees would have to wait through another Christmas or two.

4

Birth of the Bombers

◆

We weren't a very subtle team. We didn't pull
a lot of squeeze plays. All we tried to do was
hit the ball so hard it broke in half.
— *Robert W. Brown,*
third baseman and M.D.,
looking back on his days with the Yankees

IN THE LAST WEEK of May 1947, the champion Red Sox
came to New York to play four games against the Yankees.
As the Reliable Jersey House* foretold, Detroit and Boston
were leading the league, with the Tigers out front of Boston
by half a game. Pat Mullin of Detroit was leading American
League batsmen at .355. Ted Williams was leading American
League sluggers with ten home runs in thirty games. The Yankees, playing under .500 ball, stuttered in sixth place and L. S.
MacPhail suddenly erupted.

He fined Joe DiMaggio $100 for refusing to pose for a special

---

*A mythic bookmaking establishment created by the *Herald Tribune*'s Stanley
Woodward. Real betting lines were available in the composing room of the
Tribune from a printer who was wired, so to speak, to what was then called the
Syndicate. Such activity, quoting odds and placing bets, was respectively im-
moral and illegal. Protecting the printer and other guilty parties, Woodward
invented a gambling house, safely across the extradition barrier of the Hudson
River. When a vice president of the newspaper protested Woodward's use of
odds in his column, the editor responded: "I'll stop running betting odds on the
day you stop running stock market tables."

promotional newsreel. "I've been with this team since 1936," DiMaggio said, "and this is the first damn time I was ever fined." He fined outfielder Johnny Lindell $50 for telling some young Yankees that they didn't really have to attend banquets arranged by the Yankee publicity department. MacPhail remained obsessed by his image of the high-flying (though sixth-place) Yankees, not all of whom trusted aircraft to retain their wings. "After May 31," MacPhail announced, "any Yankee who refuses to fly, except Frank Crosetti, who has always refused to fly, will pay his own fare for train transportation."

At the same time, with no publicity, MacPhail hauled in Phil Rizzuto and second baseman George Stirnweiss. "I know you two bastards met with Jorge Pasquel at the Concourse Plaza [a hotel a block away from Yankee Stadium]." Working outside the frame of organized baseball, Pasquel was scouting talent for his Mexican League and offering generous contracts.

"I thought it was a free country, Mr. MacPhail," Rizzuto said. "I thought I had a right to hear what the man had to say."

"Well, listen, you little bastard, and that goes for you too, Stirnweiss, if you guys talk to Pasquel again . . . just talk . . . you're goddamn suspended. Got that straight?"

Thus within three days MacPhail publicly fined two-thirds of his starting outfield and privately threatened to suspend half of his starting infield. Recollecting, Rizzuto, the greatest short-stop not yet chosen for the Hall of Fame, said, "Whoosh."

"What does that mean, Phil?" I asked.

"Nothing. Just thinking about MacPhail makes me go 'Whoosh.'"

Stanley "Bucky" Harris, the Yankee manager, told Rud Rennie that "all this stuff just before the Red Sox series is regrettable. I mean, I got some guys with low spirits who aren't hitting like they should. I'm afraid this will just depress them further."

The Yankees seemed in disarray. But it wasn't mere disarray at all. It was the first stage of labor. The Bronx Bombers were about to be born.

*

As far as most knew, it was a comfortable time. Anyone honorably discharged from the military could draw $20 a week in federal funds for one year. Loafing veterans said they were members of the 52–20 club. It wasn't a fortune, about equal to $125 a week today, but you could buy bottles of Rheingold beer for a dime, play pinball at a nickel a game, or, if your bent was more serious, take your girl to see that surprising smash movie *Gentleman's Agreement,* the first film in which Hollywood allowed itself a long look at anti-Semitism. (But you went at risk. Women found the male lead, Gregory Peck, irresistible. Peck played a Christian character named Green who changed his name to Greenberg to find out for reasons of journalism if anti-Semitism in America was real. As John Garfield — playing a cardboard serviceman named Captain Goldman with remarkable fire — explained to Mr. Green-Greenberg, anti-Semitism was "as real as perspiration.")

Still, it seemed to be a comfortable time. We loved our radios in 1947. Any typical Tuesday night, we heard on the large boxy Imperial Model Capehart Radio Phonograph (with Flip-o-Matic record changer) the *Bob Hope Show,* with Jerry Colonna and Vera Vague and, as special guest star, dancer-actor-singer Van Johnson. A little later came the *Milton Berle Show* and after that the *Red Skelton Show,* in which Red played the famous country bumpkin Clem Kadiddlehopper. That same Tuesday, live on WJZ New York and on the seventy-one other stations belonging to NBC's Blue Network, Serge Koussevitzky led the Boston Symphony in a program of works by J. S. Bach and Richard Strauss, who was still alive and busy explaining why he had not been — to put this charitably — more passionately anti-Nazi.

We comfortably read *Kingsblood Royal,* the novel in which Sinclair Lewis attacked phony charities in his increasingly shorthand but still commanding way. Or A. B. Guthrie's fine Montana novel *The Big Sky.* Nonfiction bestsellers included the always readable John Gunther turning his sights homeward in *Inside U.S.A.,* Toynbee's classic *Study of History,* the *Infor-*

mation Please Almanac, and a kind of consolation called *Peace of Mind*, written by a rabbi named Joshua Loth Liebman. Rabbi Liebman wrote of "the shock-proof balance achieved within a soul." A year later, in 1948, when he reached the age of forty-one, Liebman committed suicide.

Certain aspects of existence were uncomfortable. The mood was materialistic, like the mood of our own present, but at the Stork Club or El Morocco late in the 1940s, women did not look like women of today. Hair was lacquered. Cuts were severe. And women's bodies seemed to be shaped differently.

The corset salon at Tailored Woman on Fifth Avenue and 57th Street advertised a free-lift contour control corselette for a hefty $29.50. "Your bottom stays pocketed," said the advertisement in the *Herald Tribune*, "its natural curves sweetly rounded." Perhaps, but with all the corsetting and girdling, women's bottoms seemed unitary, so to speak, like the rearmost segment of a honeybee.

And, of course, no one knew that the national sense of comfort was a delusion. For all its silly, ingenuous, manic surface optimism, 1947 deeply was something darker and indeed terrifying.

The year 1947 was the gateway to the cold war.

On the last Friday night in May at Yankee Stadium, Allie Reynolds held the Red Sox to two hits. One was a grounder that took a bad hop off Bobby Brown's chest. The other, Billy Goodman's single to center in the sixth inning, was the one clean hit Boston made. Reynolds held Pesky, Dom DiMaggio, Ted Williams, Rudy York, and Bobby Doerr hitless. He started a big Yankee inning with a double. The Yankees won, 9 to 0, and afterward MacPhail told everyone who would listen, "Watching the big Indian [Reynolds] is a helluva lot more fun than watching some fucking seal with an oboe."*

---

*MacPhail was responding to Red Smith, who wrote tartly that MacPhail was more a circus promoter than a baseball man.

On Saturday, 42,219 fans paid their way into the Stadium, pushing attendance up over half a million after just seventeen home games. The Yankees started thirty-nine-year-old Spurgeon Ferdinand "Call Me Spud" Chandler, who supposedly had lost his fastball. Ol' Spud worked the corners, took a little off, and threw a wicked, dipping forkball. Across nine innings, the Red Sox were able to drive only seven pitches beyond the infield. Five were gentle fly balls. Once again, Dom DiMaggio, Doerr, Pesky, and Williams went hitless. Journeyman George McQuinn, a first baseman MacPhail had acquired, played brilliant defense and batted in two runs. The Yankees won this game, 5 to 0. The New York pitching staff had now flung back-to-back two-hitters into the faces and hearts of the Red Sox.

The Sunday punch was memorable. The Yankees assaulted three Boston pitchers for seventeen hits. They scored five runs in the first inning. After three innings, the Yankees led by ten. Joe DiMaggio, Billy Johnson, George Stirnweiss, and catcher Aaron Robinson hit doubles. Phil Rizzuto tripled. Charlie Keller and George McQuinn hit home runs. With two out in the ninth inning and a runner on first base, Ted Williams cracked a home run into the third tier in right field. He caught one of Bill Bevens's zapping fastballs just right. Just right, but nine innings too late. The Yankees won their third in a row from the champion Red Sox, this one by 17 to 2.

Not only were the Yankees suddenly awesome, the Red Sox were playing nervous baseball. Boston made five errors during the 17 to 2 rout. Bevens held them hitless into the seventh inning by which time the Yankees were ahead by eleven runs.

Williams hadn't hit in the World Series against the Cardinals. Now he wasn't hitting against the Yankees. He was taking a lot of bases on balls, but that, some said, was not leading a team as great sluggers, Ruth and Greenberg, had done. They led with their strength; they led with power.

Why all the walks when the Red Sox needed batting punch?

"If I swing at a pitch a half inch off home plate," Williams said, "then the next time I may swing at one an inch off, then two inches, then six inches. And that's no way to hit. You have to wait for your pitch."

But the Yankees were not giving him his pitch. Williams had been neutralized. Some baseball men suggested that the chatter about inches was mostly a diversion. DiMaggio and Henrich swung at bad pitches when the Yankees needed a big hit. Williams was less than the perfect team player.

"It's worse than that," said Moe Berg, a major league catcher for fifteen years, and after that a noted linguist. "The truth is Williams is a choker."

Berg's listener (myself) expressed shock. The Splendid Splinter, John Updike's Great WASP God, light on competitive fire, possessed of a heart of Jell-O?

"It's plain enough if you look," Moe Berg said. "For Christ's sake, the Red Sox don't win big ones, do they?"*

By Monday night nobody was talking about trained seals or circuses. New York and much of the country was galvanized by the hammer job the Yankees were beating on the team some writers called "the Crimson Hose." The sporting press, fickle as an April day, or a May night, began writing with great enthusiasm about the "rejuvenated Yankees." MacPhail himself was transmogrifying with incredible speed from clown to genius.

What turned out to be the largest crowd to see a single game in baseball annals up to the Era jammed subway and elevator lines to the Stadium. That Monday night, the twenty-sixth of May, 74,747 people paid their way into the Bronx ballyard (and 1,140 people who had bought standing room tickets demanded

---

*A countercomment on Berg's view is offered by the baseball scholar Bill Deane, senior research associate at the Hall of Fame. "Without Williams," Deane says, "the Red Sox wouldn't have been playing any big games in the first place." Another savvy sportsman, the noted attorney (and retired amateur shortstop) Charles Rembar, says Deane's point does not touch Berg's argument. "It only means Williams was good enough to get to the last round before losing." I report these remarks knowing that they may set in motion debates that will continue till sunup, when there's nothing left to drink but Aunt Ada's Apricot Liqueur.

and got their money back when it turned out there was no place left to stand). The seating capacity of the old triple-tiered Yankee Stadium was officially 67,000, a round number because the bleachers consisted of benches rather than individual seats. Something like 7,000 people stood through all nine innings on that long ago Monday night.

The Yankees started Frank "Spec" Shea, a strong right-handed rookie from John Brown's hometown in Connecticut, whom the Yankee publicist called "the Naugatuck Nugget."

The Nugget was dull. By the third inning, the Red Sox led, 3 to 1 — the first time they led any game in the series — and had runners on first and second with nobody out. The next three Red Sox batters were Ted Williams, Rudy York, and Bobby Doerr — a Hall of Famer, a home run champion, and another Hall of Famer. Not exactly a pitcher's dream of peace.

Bucky Harris lifted Shea for Joe Page, a strapping free spirit, of whom John Lardner said, "Joe had a lot of stuff. He drank a lot of stuff so he had a lot of stuff. He was a lefthanded pitcher, but a switch drinker. He could raise a glass with either hand."

Page roomed with DiMaggio for a time but when he came back to the hotel too late too loud too often, DiMaggio insisted that the Yankees room Page somewhere else. That Page's habits disturbed DiMaggio, himself a passionate night owl, power-fully testifies to the pitcher's dislike for rest in bed.

But he could throw. Hard, low sinking stuff and, some al-leged, a dipping spitball. Trying to balance talent and disci-pline, Bucky Harris decided that if the Red Sox pounded Page that Monday night, he was going to send the pitcher to Newark, forever.

So here came genial Joe Page jumping over the bullpen railing. The three-tiered stands were packed. The night rang with ballpark noise. Page's career swung in the balance. Wil-liams, York, and Doerr were coming to bat.

Williams bounced to first. George McQuinn fumbled the ball and the bases were loaded.

Page threw three wide fastballs to Rudy York. Bases loaded,

nobody out, and the count on a strong slugger three and nothing. "If he throws ball four," Harris said, "he goes to Newark. Now!"

York swung on three and nothing and missed a fastball. He swung and missed two more. Mighty Rudy had struck out.*

When the cheers died down, Page fell behind to Doerr, three balls and one strike. Then he struck out Doerr, on two low, tailing fastballs. Eddie Pellagrini, playing short ahead of Johnny Pesky, flied to right. Given a chance, the Red Sox had not been able to break open the ballgame. This night, like so many others, belonged to Joe Page.

Across his seven innings, Page held the Red Sox to two singles. He struck out eight. His buddy, but no longer roommate, Joe DiMaggio, played a big game with three hits, including a decisive three-run home run. The Yankees won their fourth straight game from Boston, 9 to 3.

In four games against the strongest team in the league, the Yankees scored forty runs. Forty Yankee runs. Five for the Red Sox. I cannot think of one contending team so trampling another and so humiliating them in clutch situations. It may be hyperbolic, but only mildly, to point out that after this incredible May series at Yankee Stadium, the Red Sox could not win an important ballgame for a generation.

On June 20 the Yankees took over first place and never relinquished it. In 1946, they had finished seventeen games behind the Red Sox and five behind Detroit. Now in 1947, enacting an astounding reversal, they would win the pennant by twelve games over the Tigers. Boston in third place finished fourteen games behind. The Yankees made up no fewer than thirty-one games on the Red Sox from 1946 to 1947.

Early in the summer the Yankees won nineteen in a row.

---

*York, himself a devout drinker, was coming apart at the age of thirty-three. That June the Red Sox traded him to Chicago. He was out of the major leagues by the next year.

Over a slightly longer span, they won thirty-one games out of thirty-four. Sportswriters began referring to the team as a juggernaut, after the Hindi *juggannath*, which Eastern religion describes as "a massive, inexorable force that crushes whatever is in its path."

Nice to have the sporting press citing Hindi — *pajama* and *thug* are better-known Hindi words — but not terribly accurate. For MacPhail's Bronx juggernaut was really less massive than it appeared. The Yankees constantly needed patching and repair.

The field leader, trim, soft-voiced former infielder Bucky Harris, had become famous in 1924 when he directed the Washington Senators to a pennant. He was twenty-seven and earned the nickname "the Boy Manager." He won again in 1925. After that, in seventeen seasons managing American League teams, Harris never finished higher than third. Thirteen times his teams at Washington, Detroit, and Philadelphia finished in the second division. By 1943, he dropped out of the major leagues. In the harsh charge of some journalists, Bucky Harris was a proven failure.

He was also well spoken, intelligent, and ingratiating. He went to work in Buffalo for a couple of years before MacPhail brought him back. Red Barber wrote: "Bucky ran a happy ball club in New York. He managed quietly and didn't raise his voice. He had a group of grown men and treated them as such." That was one way of looking at matters. Another way was less kind. Harris was no disciplinarian.

He was not notably familiar with the characters and talents of his players. He had to rely on MacPhail for constant guidance, but MacPhail amid all the drinking, and on the way to self-destruction, was putting together one final, brilliant year, an outstanding farewell to the game.

Early, to acquire Allie Reynolds, he had given up Joe Gordon to Cleveland, reasoning that the less talented infielder, George "Snuffy" Stirnweiss, could play second and hit well enough. Gordon smacked twenty-nine home runs for Cleve-

land, but the Indians finished just over .500. Snuffy Stirnweiss
was indeed good enough for a Bronx ballclub armored with
Reynolds.

As the Reliable Jersey House reported accurately, via Stanley Woodward, first base seemed a problem. Nick Etten, the
incumbent, couldn't hit much anymore and had not been distinguished for his work with a glove.* George McQuinn was a
journeyman who had spent eight seasons with the St. Louis
Browns, nobody's pantheon team. After employing McQuinn
for a year in Philadelphia, Connie Mack released him. MacPhail
acquired McQuinn for nothing, and suddenly as June arrived
with rare days and blossoming roses, old journeyman George
McQuinn was hitting better than Williams, DiMaggio, or Henrich. Ol' Journeyman George briefly was the leading American
League batsman at .381.

Yogi Berra could pound a baseball. In 1946 at Newark he
batted .314 and hit fifteen home runs in half a season. MacPhail
promptly promoted him. When the veteran catcher Aaron Robinson went down with a painful back, Berra became the starter.
He was marginal defensively but he learned fast and he covered
up for imperfections with consistently punishing swings. ("The
guy *fields* with his bat," Dick Young maintained.)

Charlie Keller, the beetle-browed veteran from Maryland,
"has the most powerful swing in baseball," MacPhail boasted
in a paid advertisement in the *Herald Tribune:* "King Kong
Keller slams out those home runs." Like Aaron Robinson and
unlike the super ape, Keller developed back miseries, which
would destroy a fine career. He was well enough to play in only
forty-five games in 1947. To replace him, MacPhail anointed
tall John Lindell, a converted pitcher and an off-season police-
man in the town of Acadia, California.

---

*Etten was famous for trying to batter Joe Trimble, a reporter for the *Daily
News.* When Etten signed for $17,500 to play in 1946, Trimble wrote: "The $500
is for Etten's fielding." Subsequently on a Yankee trip, Etten chased Trimble
through a number of Pullman cars with ferocious intent. Trimble escaped injury
by locking himself inside a women's lavatory.

Was ever a juggernaut such a thing of shreds and patches?

Pitching is the mystery within the enigma. "Pitchers," the other ballplayers say, "ain't athletes." They don't work every day. They are a mass of phobias, beyond understanding, and aches that not even that greatest of baseball liniments, Atomic Balm, can ameliorate. "Pitchers are like women," one old ballplayer says. "They're impossible." And like women they are singularly essential to the survival of a group. Pitchers are half-mad. Good baseball men know that. And knowing it, they resign themselves. As with women, the sensible way to deal with pitchers is to love 'em. An imperfect choice, but the best available.

MacPhail found a great jewel, a diamond stud, in Allie Reynolds. MacPhail and Harris more or less stumbled upon the excellence of lefty Joe Page. They had a grand veteran in Spud Chandler and fine young fireballers in Bill Bevens, a big right-hander from Oregon, and Frank Shea, the Nugget. But Bevens had wild, wild days and age suddenly overtook Spud Chandler and tough Frank Shea was wincing when he threw. Arm trouble.

MacPhail reached into the Yankee farm system and plucked Vic Raschi up from Portland in the Pacific Coast League. Big, glowering Raschi pitched ninety-seven complete games for the Yankees during the Era. A fine pitcher; a superb competitor.

Finally, in July, working under a theory that no team can have too much experienced pitching, MacPhail signed the swaggering veteran Louis Norman "Bobo" or "Buck" Newsom. A strong, imbibing right-hander who had come up with the Dodgers in 1929 and crashed before the stock market, Newsom became the most traded ballplayer in history. Here in order are the teams for which Bobo Newsom had pitched: the Dodgers, the Cubs, the St. Louis Browns, the Washington Senators, the Boston Red Sox, the Browns (again), the Tigers, the Senators (again), the Dodgers (again), the Browns (again, again), the Senators (again, again), the Philadelphia Athletics, the Senators (again, again, again), until on July 11, 1947, Washington released Newsom. MacPhail signed him forthwith. Newsom promptly won four ballgames in a row.

What was there about the Bronx, people wondered. The air? The water? The three-tiered Stadium? No one knew, so some composed essays on the Yankee mystique.

"We just had real tough players," Bobby Brown says. "Every day we thought we were gonna win. I don't want to get *too* psychological. You have to hit the ball and catch the ball and throw it. But beyond physical skills, emotions are terribly important. You will not succeed in the major leagues if you go to bat saying to yourself, 'I just hope I don't strike out.'

"And on this team, which didn't have all the skills in the world, people did not go to bat like that. People went to bat saying to themselves, 'Damn, I'm gonna hit a home run.'

"DiMaggio and Henrich, of course, but the rest of us, too. Lindell and myself and Billy Johnson. It seemed to flow from our best players. You knew DiMaggio and Henrich were watching and you wanted to look good in their eyes.

"I was a cardiologist, not a shrink, but can I give you a cross-disciplinary opinion?

"There was never a mentally tougher team than the 1947 Yankees."

I called him Bob; older people called him Brownie. He seemed to be the quintessential good scout. He was handsome, rangy, gray-eyed, soft-voiced, well bred, a little stiff, and he could hit. He was trying to balance a career in the major leagues and a career in medicine and some of the writers thought that was kinda funny. Some of the writers were most comfortable with simpletons.

Here was a cum laude science student, and whom did the Yankees room him with on the road? Yogi Berra. Lawrence Peter Berra. Cum laude only at hitting bad balls into the cheap seats.

One night, in a forgotten hotel room, Brown sat at the desk studying his pathology text. Berra lay supine with a comic book. After a while, Brown closed the text. Farewell for now to tissues of the dead.

"You finish your book?" Berra said. "I just finished mine."

Brown nodded. The pathology text had run 1,132 pages.

"Say," Berra asked, "how did *your* book come out?"*

Within the civility and the electric intelligence, Brown was a ferocious competitor. I remember a game in Boston when the opposing pitcher took a dust mote in the iris. The catcher tried to remove the speck and failed. An umpire tried. Finally the Red Sox trainer succeeded with a cotton swab. Through all this, the pitcher's discomfort was obvious. But the batter, Robert W. Brown, M.D., never moved to help.

"Bob," I said later over a beer. "The guy was suffering. What about the Hippocratic oath?"

"When I'm batting, and the pitcher is in trouble, fuck the Hippocratic oath." Brown spoke without malice and, given the context, with elegance.

He would bat 1.000 in the 1947 World Series. He pinch hit four times and walked and singled and hit two doubles and batted in three runs and scored two more. The way Oakland Raider football linemen ate cars, Bobby Brown devoured Dodger pitchers. "They had a lot of strong young fastball pitchers," he says. "Great strong young arms. As it happened, we were one hell of a fastball-hitting team."

In a subdued Park Avenue office, brightened by a mix of baseball photos, Bobby Brown, clutch hitter, cardiologist, and now president of the American League, permits himself a smile, remembering old wars that he has won. "I suppose the medicine took away a bit from my baseball career. I was always

---

*Actually, Berra, though unread, possesses significant intelligence. As a catcher, he had to call 120 pitches a day. He mixed them in shrewd, calculating ways. On trains he liked to play a version of gin rummy called Hollywood in which scores have to be computed in three columns simultaneously. Berra could keep perfect score for Hollywood gin without making notes. He used only his sometimes maligned head.

studying or working as an intern and showing up late for spring training. No manager really likes that. Down toward the end, as I was getting to be thirty, an excellent residency opened at Stanford. Right smack in the middle of a season. I told the professor I wanted to finish out the year. Figuring my baseball salary and a World Series share, I was looking at about $20,000 more, if I was allowed to keep playing for the Yankees and start the residency in October."

The professor, J. K. Lewis, a prosperous Bay Area cardiologist, was not intensely sympathetic. "The residency begins in June," he said. "That can't be changed. But about the $20,000 . . ."

"Yes, Dr. Lewis?" Bobby Brown said.

"In twenty years you'll never miss it."

Twenty years and many more had passed. Brown rose from behind his desk, eighteen stories above Park Avenue, and indicated an extraordinary montage photograph of the demolished shrine, the colossus of Brooklyn, Ebbets Field. Decades ago, in black and white, Brown has cracked a sharp drive to right field. "What's interesting about this picture," Brown says, "is not my hit, although that was plenty interesting to me, and still is. Rather, it's that in this one montage, you can see seven Hall of Famers on the field."

Joe DiMaggio and Berra are base runners. Considering the Dodger defense, a careful eye finds Roy Campanella, Jackie Robinson, Duke Snider, Pee Wee Reese. Coaching first base for the Yankees is Bill Dickey.

"I hit that ball good," says Dr. Bobby Brown, the ballplayer.

Aaron Robinson wouldn't fly. Neither would three others. And, of course, MacPhail relented and paid their train fare. DiMaggio's leadership was essentially subtle. He was having a much better experience than his dreariness of 1946. Not in any sense a great year. He batted .315, with twenty homers and 97 runs batted in. Williams in Boston would hit .343, with thirty-two homers and 114 runs knocked across the plate. But at Yankee Stadium that season, Williams went nine for thirty-six, .250. DiMaggio hit .388 against the Sox.

The Yankees' nineteen-game winning streak began on June 29 and when it ended on July 20, the pennant race was over. DiMaggio had ankle pain. Berra missed three weeks with a throat infection. Bone chips in the elbow finished Spud Chandler. Shea hurt his arm. Even Reynolds missed two weeks. But someone always picked up the slack and MacPhail always found the someone who could do that. For all the drinking and the tantrums, this was a bravura performance and on September 26, the last Friday of the season, MacPhail was asked to march to home plate before a game against the Senators.

"What for?"

"Just do it, will ya, Larry?" the broadcaster Mel Allen said.

DiMaggio and Rizzuto and Brown and the others stood silent as Allen handed MacPhail a seven-piece silver tea service. The players had gotten together for the inscription:

> TO LARRY MACPHAIL
> greatest executive in baseball,
> whose zealous efforts were a major factor
> in our 19-game streak and the winning
> of the American League pennant.
> *From his Yankees, 1947*

For once the Roaring Redhead was silent. But only briefly. Then he began to cry.

The Dodgers clinched their National League pennant on Monday, September 22, a day when they did not have to play ball. They were not scheduled. The Chicago Cubs split a doubleheader with the Cardinals in St. Louis that night. With the second game, the one the Cubs won, the Dodgers, as the saying is, backed in to the pennant. They stood seven and a half games out front, with seven left. The *Herald Tribune* reported:

> Although it was past midnight when the news flashed from the midwest, Brooklyn immediately started a celebration. Flatbush Avenue was jammed with a mob that milled about, going nowhere and having a wonderful time. Focal point of the hilarity was the bar and grill operated by Hugh Casey, the Dodgers' expert relief pitcher. Here most of the Dodgers players [but not Jackie Robinson or Pee Wee Reese] and their wives gathered to follow the progress of the Cardinal game by radio.
>
> Seated in one booth at the tavern were Pete Reiser, Hank Behrman, Harry Taylor, Bruce Edwards, Vic Lombardi, Johnny Jorgensen and Hugh Casey. "We did it, we did it," shouted Lombardi. "And we'll take the series too," yelled Taylor, outstanding rookie pitcher.
>
> "Naturally, I'll wire my congratulations," Cardinal manager Eddie Dyer said in St. Louis. "I'd better not say more. It would seem like an alibi."
>
> On hearing that several Dodger fans said, "Natch."

This was quite an extraordinary victory, only Brooklyn's second pennant since the year 1921. Two factors, above others, made it possible. Jackie Robinson broke in with a wonderful year. He led the team in hits and runs and stolen bases. He rose above abuse in a triumph that lifted men and women everywhere. Then, on the Cardinal side, Stan Musial was sick. His infected appendix plagued him for the entire season — it was removed in October — and he had a perfectly wretched time trying to hit in Brooklyn. Healthy, in his prime, Stan Musial at Ebbets Field was the greatest hitter in the history of baseball. That is not theory or adolescent enthusiasm. Consider a number or two.

In eleven games at Brooklyn in 1948, Musial batted .522. Twenty-four hits, four homers, and seventeen runs scored in eleven games. In his twelve games at Brooklyn in 1949, Musial improved. He batted .535, with twenty-three hits, six homers, and nineteen runs scored. That is better than anyone can possibly hit major league pitching. Dodger fans called Musial "the Man," as in "Uh-oh, two men on base and here comes the Man again." At Ebbets Field the Man was Superman.

Except in 1947. Then, wrenched by abdominal pains, Musial batted only .225 in Brooklyn. Double Musial's Brooklyn hits, have him bat, say, .450 at Ebbets Field, and the pennant race would have been a different story. Color it Cardinal red.

This was an interesting, not entirely attractive Dodger team. When Durocher was banished in April and Joe McCarthy turned down Branch Rickey's offer to step in, sixty-two-year-old Burt Shotton became manager. Plodding, slow, methodical, Shotton talked to Ed Stanky and Dixie Walker and Pee Wee Reese and Hugh Casey, the shrewdest Dodger veterans, and absorbed a crash course in players around the league. He insisted that he was too old to climb into uniform and, as I've noted, managed entirely from the dugout. There he kept a record of each play in scruffy scorebooks.

Scoring ballgames employs universal symbols, as many know. Each position is assigned a number so that, for example, 6 to 3 is a ground out, shortstop to first. Shotton had his own symbols, F for fly and O for making an out, hardly as precise as the accepted hieroglyphs. All game long, every day, Shotton made odd vague notes in his book. Dick Young was no admirer. "With that goofy scorebook," Young said, "no wonder the old bastard is always one out behind the other manager."

As Young suggested, Shotton was not as quick as Durocher nor as assertive as Durocher, for that matter. He walked away from episodes that a more forceful man would not have tolerated. He simply ignored the terrible racial tension tormenting Jackie Robinson.

On a train ride to Boston early in the season, Robinson was invited into a club car poker game. He accepted happily. Hugh Casey had been drinking and could not see his cards well enough to play them properly. Casey lost money on every deal for twenty minutes. Finally he said to Robinson:

"Jackie, man! Am I in lousy luck today! Got to change my luck, boy. Back home in Georgia when my poker luck ran bad, Jackie boy, I'd jes go out and rub me the tits of the biggest, blackest nigger woman I could find." Casey leaned forward and rubbed his teammate's head.

Robinson went into shock. His vision blurred. His throat parched. He felt a jumble of anger and hurt. No one else at that poker table said anything. Robinson recovered — the whole episode lasted perhaps twenty seconds — and shook his head. Then he said to Casey in an even voice: "Just deal, man. Just deal." Manager Shotton took no action, none at all.

In one game in May, Enos Slaughter ran across first base and planted spikes in Robinson's right foot. Slaughter later made a mini-career out of denying the deed, but Robinson said, "He denies it? I still feel his spikes. They hurt like hell." Indeed, in that same game, after the spiking, Robinson remarked to Stan Musial at first, "I wish I could punch the son of a bitch in the mouth."

"If you did," Musial said, "I wouldn't blame you."

Slaughter is not the only man who would rewrite history, as I learned when I tried to run down the charge that Joe Garagiola also tried to spike Robinson in 1947. "Let me tell you about *my* Robinson incident," Garagiola said grandly one morning in 1991 in his office at NBC. "I was hitting, like, .356 [for the Cardinals] at the end of May 1950. That year, 1950, is the only year I still wish I could have finished playing because everything that could happen right was happening right. I was hitting the ball hard at least twice every game.

"We're going to play the Dodgers and I figure I sit. You know I hit left-handed and Preacher Roe, that great old lefty, was going for Brooklyn. But all of a sudden Eddie Dyer has this meeting and says to me, 'Kid.' He didn't know my name. 'Kid, you're catching because you're hot.'

"First time I'm up we got runners on first and second and I

get the bunt sign. Don't believe it the way I'm hitting. But there it is.

"I make a lousy bunt. Robinson is playing second. He has to come over and cover first base. I have to bust my ass or else I bunt into a double play. It had been drizzling. Getting to first, Robinson fell. If you're beatin' a double play, you don't care if the guy is black, white, or polka dot.

"I tried to step over Jackie's legs. He lifted up and clipped me. I landed on my shoulder. I could never swing right after that. I had to have my shoulder wired. I still remember lying on the ground in terrible pain . . .

"I still get mail at the *Today* show. How could you have spiked Robinson in 1947? I didn't spike Robinson. The only contact I had with him was 1950. I busted my career *not* spiking him."

It is a risk to substitute memory for truth. Let me recount a picture caption from *The Sporting News* of September 24, 1947. (And let me repeat that I asked Garagiola about '47. Sidewinding to 1950 was his idea.)

The *Sporting News* caption reads:

QUICK THINKING by Umpire Beans Reardon broke up an incipient rhubarb between the Dodgers and the Cardinals at Sportsman's Park, [St. Louis] September 11. Jackie Robinson (left) and Joe Garagiola (right) exchanged words when the Brooklyn first baseman came to the plate in the third inning after the St. Louis catcher had stepped on Jackie's foot, ending a double play in the previous frame. Coach Clyde Sukeforth rushed from the bench to push Robinson away from Garagiola and, in turn, was vigorously pushed by Reardon who thus drew attention away from the Robinson-Garagiola flareup.

The Brooklyn bench gave Garagiola a going-over all night and members of both clubs stepped dangerously close to rivals' tootsies. But no toes were cut off, although Ed Stanky took off his shoe to make sure.

Above this caption is a picture. Garagiola is raging at the umpire, Beans Reardon, who has an uplifted hand that seems to say peace. Robinson is watching with his palms pressed together as though in church. Lest there be combat, his bat rests at the ready against one thigh.

This episode is literally unforgettable. Garagiola wants me, and you, to believe that at the very least he has forgotten it.

The Dodgers were one fine baseball team, with a manager who could not leave the dugout. Ralph Branca, twenty-one, won twenty-one games. He threw hard and his curve ball snapped like a flag in March. Joe Hatten was a pretty good left-hander. Vic Lombardi, a five-foot, seven-inch left-hander, could win some games, without throwing hard enough to dominate. Hard-drinking Hugh Casey was the best relief pitcher on earth.

As we've observed, the Cards started poorly. Boston was a good team, featuring, as Boston writers reminded everyone, Spahn and Sain and two days of rain.*

Mostly what happened was that the Dodgers got out front by seven games and held on. A tall right-hander, Ewell Blackwell at Cincinnati, became the best pitcher in the league. But his team was weak. Dixie Walker hurt a hand and a young outfielder replaced him. That enabled rookie Duke Snider, facing Blackwell, to strike out five times in a single game.

"This young man is going to be a great one," Rickey told Harold Rosenthal of the *Herald Tribune*.

"He just struck out five times," Rosenthal said.

"He has steel springs for legs."

"Five strikeouts."

"Harold, this young man, who will be a great one, has no idea of what the strike zone is. My solemn responsibility is to instruct him."

The Dodgers had a lot of talent. They learned to live with and to admire Robinson.

Pitchers hit Robinson with fastballs six times in his first thirty-

---

*Warren Spahn, the great left-hander, won twenty-one games. Johnny Sain, a right-hander with a fine sinker, won another twenty-one. The Braves' number three pitcher, Charles Henry "Red" Barrett, won eleven games and lost twelve.

seven games. Once a week he had to take a 90-mile-an-hour baseball in the ribs or in the arm. And he was agile. He was hard to hit.

If Robinson complained, no one heard him. He played the game.

The Boys of Summer, like the Bronx Bombers, were coming to birth.

On September 23 before a Giants game, the Dodger management staged Jackie Robinson Day at Ebbets Field. The park sold out. Ballplayers crowded to home plate.

Describing this, Robinson said, "There to honor me was Ralph Branca of New York and Joe Hatten of Iowa and Clint Hartung of Texas and even . . . Dixie Walker of Alabama.

"I looked at the Dodger box. It was all so beautiful. Democracy. Decency. Sanity. My wife, Rachel, in the Dodger box was crying."

Tears of joy in the bloodshot blue eyes of Larry MacPhail.

Tears of joy in the clear dark eyes of Rachel Robinson.

It was going to be quite a World Series.

5

The Greatest Ballgame
Ever Played

◆

It wasn't tough at all.
It was just like eatin' spaghetti.

— *Pinch hitter Harry Lavagetto,*
after delivering the most dramatic
pinch hit in history

THE CITY WAS THE CAPITAL of the world. The war-dimmed lights burned bright again from Coney Island clear to Westchester and the streets were safe and subway crime was less than deadly.

"Expectorating on Platform Prohibited!" warned signs in all the stations. "Violators Guilty of Misdemeanor!" Spitting in a subway station, like smoking in a subway station, drew a five-dollar fine in night court, if you were dumb enough to let matters go that far. Generally a spitter or a smoker got the cop to drop charges for a deuce. Two dollars cash. Indeed, police officers frequently approached subway smokers with the venal greeting: "Five bucks, buddy, or two?" Most of us, who spat and smoked, supported our local police.

The parks were tranquil. The word *mugging* had not yet entered the language. Roads and bridges were beautifully maintained. Infrastructure, as in today's jargon, "crumbling infrastructure," was still strictly a military term. We were safe and optimistic and prosperous and peaceful in our New York, the capital city of the world.

True, the new mayor was a crook. But few realized that. A glow, sometimes roseate, sometimes volcanic, lingered at City Hall in the wake of the great Fiorello H. La Guardia, mayor of New York from 1934 to 1945.

Pancreatic cancer killed La Guardia on September 20, 1947, and grief for this fiery part-Jewish, part-Italian American original was tangible and intense. *Herald Tribune* reporters recorded tributes to La Guardia from Herbert Hoover; George C. Marshall; Arturo Toscanini; Trygve Lie, secretary-general of the United Nations; Andrei Vishinsky, a customarily choleric Russian who was deputy foreign minister of the Soviet Union; and Eddie Rickenbacker, the old World War I fighter ace, now a devout right-winger and president of Eastern Airlines. Said Henry Agard Wallace, who would soon run for president from the left: "The people of the world have lost a friend when they needed him most. He was the most colorful, beloved figure in American politics and his loss is our greatest tragedy since April 12, 1945. First Roosevelt — now Fiorello. The fighters are taken from us when we need them most, but the fight must go on."

Everyone agreed with that, but there was significant confusion over what fight it was that Americans should be fighting. To Hoover and Rickenbacker we were up against "godless, atheistic communism," pronounced, by people like Rickenbacker and Hoover, "common-ism." The Russians did not develop an atomic bomb until 1949, and in 1947 some felt that a sane U.S. foreign policy would have us atom bomb the Soviet Union into history. Millions would die, but, the right-wingers said, what was so terrible about sending atheists to hell?

Henry Agard Wallace was talking about a different vision: a parliament of man, a federation of the nations, and food for the hungry everywhere. Harry Truman snapped that Wallace was naive. Besides, the Russians *always* broke their promises. Clare Boothe Luce, beautiful, shrill, and cutting as a shard of glass, derided aid for developing nations as "milk for every Hottentot." And that, said Mrs. Luce, was "Globaloney."

The United Nations met in temporary quarters, an old World's Fair building in Queens that has since evolved into a skating rink. Speaking with Gallic passion and remarkable foresight, Georges Bidault, the foreign minister of France, stood up in Queens and said that the developing conflict between the United States and Russia "imperils the very life of the United Nations." Bidault cited rancorous speeches on the Flushing Meadow floor, mouthed recently by Marshall and Vishinsky.

Bidault's comments were headlined on the front page of the *Sunday Herald Tribune* nine days before a great World Series began. Four columns to the right, a corollary *Tribune* headline announced:

43 FROM HOLLYWOOD SUBPOENAED
BY HOUSE UN-AMERICAN INQUIRY
COMMITTEE TO HEAR BOTH SIDES ON
COMMUNISM, PARNELL THOMAS SAYS;
*Gary Cooper, Goldwyn, Disney,
Eric Johnston Among Those Called*

So it was begun, the American witch-hunt, our very own, very homegrown Inquisition. Gary Cooper, Walt Disney, and Robert Taylor told tales of a red menace that curdled their true-blue Yankee Doodle blood. Eventually, it turned out that John Parnell Thomas, the chairman of the House Un-American Activities Committee, was less honest even than Mayor William O'Dwyer of New York. Thomas was jailed in 1950 for putting relatives who did no work, who never even visited Washington, on his personal, tax-supported payroll. But before this crass porky politician was locked up in the federal correctional institution at Danbury, Connecticut, he had broken good men and women, wounded others, and conducted the overture for Joe McCarthy.

Yet in the bright October of 1947, few dark thoughts clouded the New York skies or outlook. Red Barber wrote in a memoir that the 1947 World Series was "the greatest Series ever played." It was that, of course, and more. Along with the World Series of 1952 and the World Series of 1955 and the World Series of 1991 and, uh, oh yes, the World Series of 1905 and 1934 and . . .*

To call any Series, or any ballgame, the "greatest ever played" is sophomoric. None of us has seen every Series, much less every game, and even if we had, we'd still be adrift, trying to quantify words like *great* and *exciting.* So much depends not only on the game but on the viewpoint and criteria and possibly the digestion of the observer. Personally, I've seen the greatest ballgame ever played at least five times on five different occasions. The Greatest Series Ever is suitable for debating in sports bars but warrants no more sober consideration than the tabloid headline that it is. What one reasonably can say is this: The 1947 Series was very wonderful and very exciting. It kicks up controversy and rocks passions to this day.

Going to a ballgame was different more than half a lifetime ago. The Series of '47 was televised but camera lenses were primitive. Even if you owned an early television set by Admiral or DuMont, reception was chancy. Passing aircraft and electronic glitches troubled the picture. If you did own a television set, you could watch the Series at home, all right, but you'd see a lot of it through visual static, blur, and snow.

Some trekked to Yankee Stadium on the night of September 29, with jackets and blankets, prepared to camp out until morning. It would be an uncomfortable wait. The temperature that night dropped to 42. But queuing in the dark was the only way

---

*Barber was an exemplar of restraint when broadcasting, but a typewriter did funny things to his self-control. Writing on Jackie Robinson across the season of 1947, Barber not merely blows his own horn but blasts his own tuba: "I had the microphone at Brooklyn when Robinson came. It was the hottest microphone any announcer had to face." Working in liberal New Deal Brooklyn, where most people supported Robinson and where the corporation that hired Robinson also employed the announcers, all Barber had to do was watch his Confederate drawl. Hot mike? Barber held a piece of cake.

ordinary fans could be sure of getting into the Series. Reserved seats, sold only in strips for three or four games, ran to a whopping $24 a strip.

The Yankees opened the bleacher gates at nine A.M. Within twenty minutes every seat was filled. Later, in midmorning, 7,000 holders of standing room tickets swarmed into the park. The crowd would total 73,365, but sportswriters later complained that the grandstands, as opposed to the bleachers, were full of wealthy types, not ball fans. The Stadium crowd, they said, was rich and dull.

Ralph Branca started for the Dodgers. He was big, rangy, hawk-nosed, strong, and, at the age of twenty-one, coming off the season of his life. He had won twenty-one games, including several big ones. His fastball snarled, his big curve snapped. Still moving toward a baccalaureate at NYU, young Branca had the world before him. There was not a better youthful pitcher on earth.

"And I was confident," Branca remembers. "I was twenty-one and I was confident that I could beat the Yankees. I'd beaten all the good clubs in the National League. I'd struck out Stan Musial with the bases loaded. I wasn't afraid at all. And I went out there, big crowd and all, and I pitched four perfect innings."

Spec Shea of Naugatuck started for the Yankees and, after getting Eddie Stanky on a fly ball, walked Jackie Robinson. With Pistol Pete Reiser, the plagued and gifted center fielder, batting, Robinson stole second. "He didn't steal it off the pitcher," Berra says. "I didn't get rid of the ball good. Robinson stole that one off me." Reiser bounced slowly to the mound and Robinson fled for third.

He couldn't make it. You can't go from second base to third on a bounder back to the pitcher. Shea threw to Billy Johnson, the third baseman, and Robinson stopped short. No one could stop shorter than Jackie Robinson. Johnson chased Robinson toward second, where Phil Rizzuto waited. Another short and dusty stop. George Stirnweiss ran over from his second base spot to help. Spec Shea ran behind third to back up. Robinson dodged and lunged, dodged and lunged. By the time Rizzuto finally was able to tag out Robinson, Reiser had slid safely into second base.

Technically, Robinson had made a bad play. But he had shown the Yankees basepath magic. The Yankees, if not rattled, were impressed. Dixie Walker lined a hit to left, Reiser scored, and the Dodgers led, 1 to 0.

In Ring Lardner's phrase, the Yankees didn't molest Branca none. Soft flies, strikeouts, grounders. In the third inning, Robinson drew his second base on balls. He led far off first, making small, aggravating hops. Shea moved to pick him off first base with four straight throws. Then he balked.

Robinson had not made a hit but he was dominating. Pete Reiser flied to Tommy Henrich and the Dodgers failed to score. But they held their 1 to 0 lead and Branca was overwhelming. He struck out John Lindell. Rizzuto popped to left. Branca struck out Spec Shea. That was his third inning.

George Stirnweiss looked at a third strike, a big, snapping curveball. Henrich flied out. Berra struck out swinging. That was Branca's fourth inning. He was pitching perfect baseball. Branca says that he has replayed what happened next "maybe five hundred times.

"I knew I was dominating. I knew I had a perfect game and then in my youth — I'm a twenty-one-year-old kid from West-chester County pitching a perfect World Series game ten miles from home at Yankee Stadium — in my youth I get excited. I start pitching too fast, not taking enough breathing time between throws. I start overthrowing and with that I get a little wild . . ."

DiMaggio led off the fifth with a hard grounder to deep short-stop. Reese ranged far to his left and made a marvelous back-handed stop. But DiMaggio, who was thirty-two, still had fair speed. He beat the throw to first by a step. Base hit. Now a more experienced pitcher would have slowed his pace, deliberately. Losing a perfect game is a jolt. A man needs time to refocus.

Instead Branca remembers "just wanting to get the next guy out as quick as I could." He walked George McQuinn on four pitches. He wanted to start Billy Johnson with a fastball on the fists, but still working too quickly, Branca lost the edge of his control. A fastball nicked Johnson. Bases loaded.

Branca threw a strike to John Lindell, whom he had struck out in the third inning. Then Lindell cracked a fastball down the left field line for two bases. DiMaggio and McQuinn scored. The Yankees led, 2 to 1.

Branca was still working too fast. He walked Rizzuto on five pitches, loading the bases for a second time. Bucky Harris sent Bobby Brown up to bat for Shea. Branca threw two outside pitches to Brown and Burt Shotton sent a coach to lift his rattled starting pitcher. A journeyman named Hank Behrman replaced Branca and walked Brown, forcing home another run. Before the inning ended, the Yankees had scored 5 runs. Joe Page, the free spirit whom sportswriters were calling "the Gay Reliever," replaced Shea. "Page," Red Smith wrote, "had no romp, but the confident lefthander got by. His manner said, 'Gimme the ball and lemme at those Bums.'" The Yankees won the ballgame, 5 to 3.

Bucky Harris had outmanaged elderly Burt Shotton. Some Dodger players said as much. "That was a helluva move, lifting Shea and putting in Joe Page," Ed Stanky said. "That won the game."

Shea had been pitching adequately, against Branca's perfection, and when he was scheduled to bat in the fifth the Yankees had taken that 2 to 1 lead. Thus Harris lifted his starting pitcher for pinch hitter Bobby Brown when the starter was *ahead*. "Bucky Harris," Smith said, "had resolved to wring every last drop of blood out of his big inning." In later years Casey Stengel perfected this sort of managing. Go for it! Don't save pitchers and pinch hitters for the late innings. If a typhoon hits, we'll never play them anyway. Go For It Now!

That tactic in 1947 was just about unheard of.

"You got to hand it to Bucky Harris," Stanky repeated in the Dodger clubhouse.

"What about Shotton?" a reporter said to Pee Wee Reese. "Did he say anything before he let the writers in the clubhouse?"

"Yes, he did," Reese said. "He said there would be another game tomorrow."

Branca was the Dodgers' best pitcher through 1947. In winning twenty-one games, he'd pitched 280 innings with a fine earned run average of 2.67. He had overpowering stuff.

Now — there is simply no accounting for this — the Dodger high command, Shotton, Rickey, and the rest, went into panic. Branca, the ace, did not get another start in the World Series. The kid had one bad inning and they quit on him.* Panic does not usually win a World Series. The Reliable Jersey House was favoring the Yankees 2 to 9. In other words, nine dollars bet on the Yankees to win the Series would return two dollars. The gamblers were not impressed with the performance under pressure of elderly Burt Shotton.

Wednesday, October 1, came up cool and hazy and the Dodger team appeared to disintegrate. At the center, the embodiment of the Brooklyn collapse was Harold Patrick "Pistol Pete" Reiser, who was coming apart at the age of twenty-eight.

Sometimes Leo Durocher used to say that Willie Mays was the best ballplayer he ever saw. Then, if he were feeling even a little contemplative, Durocher added: "Willie was, but Pete Reiser coulda been."

In his first full season at Brooklyn, 1941, Reiser led the National League in doubles, triples, runs scored, slugging percentage, and batting average (.343). He could bat right-handed or

---

*"That was pretty bad for our ballclub," Branca says, "but not as bad as 1951, when the team was totally mismanaged by that piece of dreck Charlie Dressen."

left-handed and he could *throw* right-handed or left-handed. In full baseball uniform, wearing spikes, Reiser sprinted 100 yards in 9.8 seconds. Although he didn't compete at track, Reiser was probably the fastest man on earth. He had it all, everything, and he was tough.

That first year in Brooklyn, Reiser was beaned twice, cracked into the cement center field wall head first, and still led the league. Next year he ran into another wall head first. "We were in the twelfth inning, no score, two outs, and Enos Slaughter hit the ball at Sportsman's Park, St. Louis. I caught it and hit the wall and dropped the damn ball. I had the instinct to throw it to Pee Wee Reese, and we just missed gettin' Slaughter at the plate, and they won, 1 to 0.

"I made one step to start off the field and I woke up the next morning in St. John's Hospital. My head was bandaged. I had an awful headache." He would suffer dizzy spells for the rest of his days.

Playing for an army team in 1943, Reiser dove into a hedge running down a fly. Behind the hedge was a ten-foot ditch. He landed on his right shoulder. His throwing arm was never the same. When he came out of the service and returned to the Dodgers, Pistol Pete, dizzy spells, gimpy arm, and all, stole thirty-four bases, the best in the league by twelve. Among the thirty-four he stole home seven times. That was 1946, a year in which Reiser knocked himself out again trying for a diving catch, dislocated his left shoulder, ripped muscles in his left leg, and broke his left ankle. "Pete," Dixie Walker told me once, "was just the damnedest, son-of-a-bitchin' best ballplayer in the world. Or woulda been, if only he hadn't played so son-of-a-bitchin' hard."

On October 1, 1947, at hazy Yankee Stadium, Reiser suffered episodes of vertigo. He told nobody. It was not his way to complain. He wanted to play. The other center fielder was Joe DiMaggio. Maybe Pete felt he had something special to prove.

When autumn came, the outfield at the old Yankee Stadium posed harsh problems for the defenders. Autumn sunlight splashed into the fielders' eyes. The three-tiered stands behind the plate seemed dark and vague. Everybody smoked in those days and the smoke and the haze and the autumn light made it difficult for an outfielder to pick up the ball as it left the bat, even if the outfielder was not suffering from bouts of vertigo, which Reiser was. Dizzy and queasy, Pete had to face a dreadful chiaroscuro.

Game two went terribly for him. In the third inning George Stirnweiss hit a line drive just over Eddie Stanky's head into right center. Reiser broke late and never caught up with the baseball. He reached it on two bounces but it deflected off his glove and rolled behind him. Stirnweiss was credited with a triple. Reiser was puffing a little and looking grim when John Lindell, two batters later, hit a long fly to straightaway center. Essentially a routine out. But Reiser could not pick up the ball this time, either. He started in, turned awkwardly, ran and lunged, and the ball bounced a few feet beyond him. "DiMaggio puts that in his pocket," someone said.

"Two DiMaggios pocket it," someone else answered. "Joe and Dom both make that play."

Another triple. Another ball Pete Reiser played into a triple. The Yankees took a 2 to 1 lead.

Dixie Walker opened the fourth inning for the Dodgers by lining a rocket into the lower stands in right. Tie score.

Billy Johnson led off the Yankee fourth with another long high fly to center field. Reiser started late yet again, backed up awkwardly, and, as the ball was descending, he tripped and fell backwards. The ball struck his glove and glanced off it. Another triple. A third triple. Phil Rizzuto lifted a fly to left field and Gene Hermanski, not suffering from dizzy spells, just an uncertain outfielder, lost sight of the ball. It dropped in front of him, almost landing on a great toe. Johnson scored and Rizzuto had a gift double. Then, in the fifth inning with a runner on second base, Reiser let a ground single go through his legs, for a two-base error. After that when Reiser caught an easy fly, some in the crowd of 69,865 cheered sarcastically. "Hey, lookit that. Pete Reiser didn't drop the ball."

The Yankees won the game for Allie Reynolds, 10 to 3, and the press was less than kind. "The Dodgers," Rud Rennie wrote, "reverted to the style of play that has made Flatbush famous in song and story. And the Yankees slaughtered them." Red Smith called Reiser's performance "a re-birth of vaude-ville.

"Pete," Smith wrote, "had appalling difficulties with the sun on fly balls, and on ground balls too, for that matter. This at least will be spared when the carnival moves on to Ebbets Field for Game Three. The sun no longer shines in Brooklyn."

Reiser would play parts of five more seasons, but that sunny October day at the Stadium was really the end. He couldn't play much after that. The best prospect Leo Durocher ever saw was washed up at the age of twenty-eight.

Reiser, a trim five foot eleven in his youth, began to drink heavily. He put on a round belly and flapping jowls. In 1952 he played thirty-four games for Cleveland. He stole one base and batted .136.

Afterwards, coaching and managing in the minor leagues, Reiser was dominated by bitterness and drink. He lost his last bush league job, managing St. Petersburg, for drunkenness. When they told him he was through, ol' Pete called a final team meeting.

The young players rallied round, wondering what message the great Pete Reiser could offer to help them on with life.

"I jes got one thing to tell you guys," Reiser said. He paused and ran a finger along his teeth.

"None of you sonsabitches is ever gonna make the major leagues."

The greatest prospect of his time died a forgotten man when he was sixty-two years old. The record book lists the date of his death as October 25, 1981.

How little the record book tells us. The great Pete Reiser

died years and years before, in the hazy October sunlight at Yankee Stadium.

Surely it is worth remembering that once, before Willie, Mickey, and the Duke, there was a kid called Pistol Pete.

As Durocher liked to remind people, mister, this was a guy who could do it all . . .

Joe DiMaggio sat silently in the Yankee clubhouse, shirtless and puffing a cigarette. Younger players were making noise, triumphant noises, but DiMaggio was quiet.

"That was rough out there on Reiser, wasn't it?" Bob Cooke of the *Tribune* asked.

"It's always like that in the fall," DiMaggio said, matter-of-factly. He wasn't gloating. He was just saying how it was. "It gets a lot darker around home plate and the haze settles in from all those smokes. It's no cinch to see a fly ball coming out of those shadows."

"You didn't have any trouble yourself," Cooke said.

"Don't you worry about the old boy. I've been playing in this park for a long time."

The Reliable Jersey House quoted the Yankees to win the Series at 1 to 8. That is, you would have to put up eight dollars on the Yankees to get back one, when and if they sent the Dodgers home. The great confrontation, the Fall Classic, was turning into an October fizzle.

On Thursday, October 2, Mohandas K. Gandhi marked his seventy-eighth birthday and said, with what bystanders called "a terrible weariness," that the masses in India were violent despite his pleas for peace. "Friends had hoped I would live to be 125," Gandhi said, "but I have lost all desire to live long. I do not want to go on living at all while hatred and killing fill the atmosphere."

That same day Mueller Macaroni of Jersey City, New Jersey, one of America's largest pasta houses, was reorganized as a nonprofit corporation with all its net income earmarked for

New York University Law School. Under sharp questioning, an attorney named John Gerdes, of 1 Wall Street, conceded that "technically, yes. I can't deny it. This does put NYU law school in the spaghetti business."

At Ebbets Field, in a shabbily played and intensely exciting game, the Dodgers defeated the Yankees, 9 to 8. It was not purists' baseball but it was a festive Flatbush day. Barred from managing, Leo Durocher was attending all the games, officially as a fan, accompanied by his actress bride, Laraine Day. "The slightly musical organization known as the Dodger Symphony [actually a reasonably competent four-piece band] materialized in the lower stands and serenaded Mr. and Mrs. L. Durocher with 'For He's a Jolly Good Fellow,'" Red Smith reported. "Mr. Durocher arose and shook the leader's hand. Mrs. Durocher, a music lover, blushed."

The Dodgers tore into the Yankee starter, Bobo Newsom. "As soon as the attack began," Smith wrote, "the species of fauna described as typical of Brooklyn began coming out of the woodwork. With half the capacity of Yankee Stadium the joint shuddered with twice the noise. Colored balloons floated from the stands. A blimp rode overhead, almost obscuring Bobo Newsom in its shadow. The joint was jumping."*

Joe Hatten managed to subdue the Yankees in the first. George Stirnweiss whaled a line drive off the right field wall. Dixie Walker played the carom deftly and held Stirnweiss to a single. Then Tommy Henrich bounced into a double play and Lindell grounded out.

The Brooklyn crowd made throaty noises as the Dodgers

---

*Numbers of writers for the New York newspapers adopted a patronizing tone when writing about Brooklyn, the Dodgers, and Ebbets Field. Smith, for example, never referred to Yankee Stadium as "a joint." The Dodger ballpark was a forty-five-minute subway trip or a five-dollar cab ride from Manhattan, neither popular with sportswriters. As Duke Snider mentioned, a number of Dodger players, including Jackie Robinson, picked up on the patronizing and resented it. Smith went to his grave insisting that Brooklyn was a provincial outpost. He himself was born in Green Bay, Wisconsin.

came to bat. Stanky bounced out to Newsom. Jackie Robinson lined a single to center. As he took his daring, hopping lead off first, the crowd began to bellow. The rooting was palpable. Come on, Jackie. Come on, big guy. Steal these Bronx bums blind.

Yogi Berra was not catching for the Yankees. He had thrown a ball away the day before and he had failed to catch a pop fly near home plate. "Worst World Series catching I ever saw," grumbled the tall patriarch Connie Mack. Bucky Harris had heard of Connie Mack. He benched Berra for the rookie, Sherman Lollar.

Robinson's big lead rattled Newsom, who fell behind as he pitched to Pete Reiser. When the count reached 3 and 1, Robinson stole second. The ball got through Rizzuto, and Robinson took a few steps toward third. Stirnweiss backing up the play flipped to Rizzuto, who tagged out Robinson.

Reiser walked. With Dixie Walker batting, he raced for second, but Lollar's accurae throw to Rizzuto caught him. Then Reiser could not rise. He had jammed his ankle. He felt better after a while but the pain came back and he had to leave the game (and the Dodger starting lineup) a little later.

The Dodgers broke out in the second. With one out Gene Hermanski walked and scored when catcher Bruce Edwards doubled off the left field wall. Reese singled to left center, scoring Edwards. After a fly ball, Joe Hatten singled Reese to second. Both advanced when Lollar mishandled a low pitch. Eddie Stanky doubled them home.

Harris lifted Newsom for Vic Raschi, and Robinson lined a missile into right. Henrich scooped it on a bounce and held Stanky at third.

Reiser was the next hitter, but by now he could barely walk. Shotton sent Carl Furillo in to hit for Reiser, a move sportswriters questioned. The criticism of Furillo, then twenty-five years old, was that he couldn't do much with tough right-handed pitchers. Raschi was one tough right-handed pitcher.

The sporting press buzzed querulously and Furillo slammed an outside fastball off the scoreboard in right. Stanky and Robinson ran home and the Dodgers led, 6 to 0.

The Yankees came back with two runs in the third inning. The Dodgers scored one more. The teams clawed at one another through the day. DiMaggio hit a long two-run homer in the fifth. Berra, whose Series batting average up to this point was nothing, literally .000, went in to bat for Sherman Lollar in the seventh inning, at which point Lollar's Series average was .667.

Before the second-guessing of Bucky Harris could gain much footing, Berra cracked a fastball over the scoreboard in right field. The score was now Dodgers 9, Yankees 8. Shotton finally sent for his glowering, guzzling relief star, Hugh Thomas Casey, out of Buckhead, Georgia. The game came down to a fascinating eighth inning.

Tommy Henrich walked and Lindell singled him to second base. No one out, a one-run game, and Joe DiMaggio coming up to bat.

"What would you do now, if you were Hugh Casey?" Red Smith said to Rud Rennie.

"DiMaggio's swing is grooved," Rennie said. "He's got two hits already. I'd walk him. Third base is empty. Walk DiMaggio, load the bases, and pitch to George McQuinn."

That wasn't the way Hugh Casey played the game. He snapped a curve ball across the outside corner. Strike one. Another curve missed wide. One and one.

DiMaggio was looking for a third curve, but Casey fooled him with a fastball, up and in. DiMaggio started an awkward swing, then tried to hold up. The pitch hit his bat and rolled to Stanky, who tagged Lindell in the basepath and tossed to Jackie Robinson. DiMaggio was doubled up by thirty feet. Henrich, the tying run, moved to third, but there he stayed as Robinson made a nice play on George McQuinn's hard bounder. The Yankees did not threaten in the ninth. The Dodgers won,

9 to 8, after three hours and five minutes of play, up to then the longest game in World Series history.

DiMaggio neither shunned the press nor granted usable interviews. He sat smoking and cursing himself for taking a half swing into a double play.

"You hit a good homer, Joe," Harold Rosenthal said, trying to shake free a quote.

"Fuck that," said the Yankee Clipper. "We got beat."

On May 3, 1947, Branch Rickey had dealt the Pittsburgh Pirates five shopworn Dodger ballplayers for $300,000* and an obscure five-foot, six-inch left-hand-hitting outfielder named Albert Francis Gionfriddo, from the metropolis of Dysart, Pennsylvania. The Dodgers owned a rich supply of young left-hand-hitting outfielders: Duke Snider, George Shuba, Dick Whitman, Marv Rackley, all of whom seemed to be better ballplayers than Al Gionfriddo. No one could understand why Branch Rickey wanted him. Then someone was struck with a punch line. Rickey was bringing Gionfriddo in from Pittsburgh because he needed somebody to carry the money, the three hundred grand.[†]

By 1991, Al Gionfriddo had evolved into a delightful and spirited party of sixty-nine, residing in Goleta, California, just outside Santa Barbara, where he supported himself by selling golf clubs and fishing lures he crafted with sure hands. "I know you want to talk about the catch," he said, when I came calling. "Red Barber called it the impossible catch. Joe DiMaggio said it was better than the catch Willie Mays made in 1954. Joe D.

---

*Macmillan's *Baseball Encyclopedia* lists a figure of $100,000. Dick Young of the *Daily News* said the true number was $300,000. My suspicion is that Young was more accurate than Macmillan.

[†]Rickey's contract with the Brooklyn National League Baseball Club, Inc., provided that beyond salary he was paid ten percent of all player sales. He pocketed a snappy $30,000 on this one May deal. Some, notably Walter O'Malley, regarded the Rickey arrangement as a conflict of interest. It figured prominently in the O'Malley-Rickey shootout, down the lane.

said it was the best catch in Series history. I'm not arguing with that. Heck, I *made* the catch. But can I tell you something else, first?"

"Sure, Al."

"When I came over to Brooklyn from Pittsburgh, the locker next to Jackie Robinson was empty and that's the locker they gave me, next to Jackie.

"And that was fine. I come from Pennsylvania. I was not a southerner. A lot of southerners were against Jackie comin' up, the southern players, the southern managers. Some *owners* were against him. But Jackie held himself together real fine.

"I'll tell you this and I won't say any more about it. When I got to Brooklyn in May, Jackie would not take a shower with the other players. He always waited and he showered last.

"And I seen this and I said, 'Jackie, what the hell are you doing? You're part of this team. You're one of the main members.'

"Most of the old Dodgers ignored me, when I come over from Pittsburgh, like I didn't belong. I said to Jackie, 'You know, they're treating you a little like they're treating me and, hey, we're *both* members of this team.

"'Jackie, let's go in the shower together. If those southern guys don't want to be in a shower with you — with you and me, Jackie — let 'em get the hell out.'"

They walked into the shower together, Jackie Robinson and Al Gionfriddo, and nobody got out. Nobody said a word. Another barrier, that shouldn't have existed in the first place, came tumbling down.

Game 4 is Cookie Lavagetto's triumph. It belonged to Big Bill Bevens for eight and two-thirds innings and then, with one level swing, Cookie Lavagetto took it away. That's true. The game is Lavagetto's triumph. But Little Al Gionfriddo owns a piece. Without Small Al, Cookie could not have swung his famous swing.

Floyd Clifford "Bill" Bevens, out of Hubbard, Oregon, stood

almost six foot four, and he could throw. Firing was never a problem for Bill Bevens. Firing on target was something else. Still, Bevens won sixteen for the somnolent Yankees of 1946. During the regular season of 1947, he won seven games but lost thirteen. Successful pitchers give up fewer than one hit for every inning pitched. Bevens worked 165 innings and yielded 167 hits. Good pitchers strike out significantly more batters than they walk. Bevens struck out seventy-seven and walked seventy-seven. There was no indication on his 1947 record that Bill Bevens was about to pitch the ballgame of his life, the World Series ballgame of the half century.

On the afternoon of Friday, October 3, Bevens walked ten Dodgers. No pitcher had walked ten batters in a World Series game before. But until the end, the very end, he yielded not a hit. Rud Rennie wrote: "Bill Bevens, in the most strangely beautiful performance ever seen in a World Series, broke three records* only to have Lavagetto break his heart." Nobody who saw that game or played in that game can forget it. "I remember very well," says Pee Wee Reese. "The golden time. I was the fella who was gonna come up after Cookie. And was I glad Lavagetto came through. Whatever the ballplayers tell you, nobody *wants* to come to bat in a situation like that, with all the pressure in the world on every swing."

"Holy cow, that game was something," Rizzuto says.

"Not a classic," Henrich says. "You know, Bevens couldn't find the plate. But exciting. There just can't be a more exciting ballgame for the fans."

"Did Tommy mention," asks Rizzuto in a bland, impish way, "that he kinda bobbled the ball Lavagetto hit?"

Harry Taylor started for the Dodgers. Taylor was a black-haired handsome kid with a fine curve ball and a flawed attitude. "Nothing that went wrong," someone remembers, "was ever Harry Taylor's fault. If somebody got a hit, it was the catcher didn't give Taylor a good target. He was a real good-

---

*Fewest hits, most walks, longest stretch of no-hit pitching.

looking guy. Like a movie star. A real good-looking guy who was always complaining."

He had plenty to complain about in a hurry. George Stirnweiss lined Taylor's first pitch safely to left. Henrich singled up the middle. Berra, back catching, bounced to Robinson at first base who threw to Reese at second to retire Henrich. But Reese dropped the throw and the bases were loaded. Taylor walked DiMaggio on four pitches, forcing in a run, and now he could complain in privacy.

Hal Gregg, another Dodger pitcher who was pretty good but no more than that, replaced him. George McQuinn popped out and Billy Johnson hit into a double play, ending the inning. A war of attrition had begun.

Bevens walked two Dodgers in the first inning. Gene Hermanski fouled out, stranding them both. Bevens walked another in the second. No damage.

DiMaggio drew another base on balls in the third and McQuinn topped a ball, an infield single, that the Dodger catcher, Bruce Edwards, threw over Robinson's head, toward a sign in foul territory on the right field wall advertising *The Secret Life of Walter Mitty,* a movie starring Danny Kaye and Virginia Mayo, the Blonde Bombshell.

Maybe the Blonde Bombshell distracted DiMaggio. He had a weakness for such items. He rounded second base, rounded third, and Dixie Walker's throw caught him by a good margin at home plate. DiMaggio didn't slide, a rare bad play.

In the fourth, Billy Johnson hit a triple off the center field fence, well beyond the reach of Carl Furillo. Johnny Lindell doubled to right, scoring Johnson. The Yankees were ahead, 2 to 0.

The Dodgers came back after a fashion in the fifth inning. Bevens walked third baseman Spider Jorgensen and pitcher Gregg. Stanky bunted the runners to second and third. Reese grounded to Phil Rizzuto, who threw out Gregg, wrong-headedly trying to advance to third. But Jorgensen scored on the play. The Dodgers had a run. Reese stole second and went to third when Berra's throw sailed into center field. With the tying run at third, Bevens struck out Jackie Robinson.

Bevens walked one in the sixth. He walked another in the seventh. Journeyman Hank Behrman replaced Gregg in the eighth and managed to retire the Yankees. Then came a ninth inning to remember. Rud Rennie wrote of the Brooklyn crowd that "33,443 spectators were dying 33,443 deaths, hanging in suspense to know whether Bevens would have a no-hit game or whether the Dodgers would do something." But the first thing the Dodgers had to do was retire the Yankees in the ninth.

Lindell singled to left. Rizzuto bounced to the mound and Behrman turned and threw out Lindell at second. Bill Bevens bunted. Edwards charged out from behind the plate and threw the ball to second. Rizzuto beat the throw. Two on, one out.

George Stirnweiss popped a short single into center field. The Yankee scouting reports on the Dodgers were, as we shall see, imperfect. But you didn't have to be a superscout to note the throwing arm of Carl Anthony Furillo. It was a wonder of the age. Rizzuto, fast but also smart, stopped at third base.

At this point Burt Shotton woke up. He yanked Behrman for his great relief pitcher Hugh Casey. (Why on earth hadn't he had Casey pitching the entire ninth?) Mighty Casey threw one pitch to Tommy Henrich, a marvelous clutch hitter, and it was an even more marvelous down-breaking curve. Henrich rapped the ball to Casey, who threw to Edwards, forcing Rizzuto. Edwards threw on to first and the Dodgers had their third double play.

Everybody knew, you could see it on the big scoreboard in right, Bill Bevens was just three outs away from a no-hitter.

Bruce Edwards led off the bottom of the ninth inning with a fly ball that DiMaggio caught against the wall in center. Carl Furillo, often an impatient hitter, walked. Spider Jorgensen lifted a pop fly near first base. Dick Young of the *Daily News* reported that George McQuinn "was white as a sheet as he made the catch."

Two out. The Yankees led, 2 to 1. Furillo was at first, but Bevens was only one out away from pitching the first no-hit game in the forty-four-year history of the Series.

"Gimme the little guy," Burt Shotton said. Ol' Burt at last came fully awake. "Hey, Reiser, can you run from home to first?"

Al Gionfriddo, the little guy, went to run for solid Carl Furillo. Limping on a tightly taped ankle, Pete Reiser made his way to home plate to bat for Hugh Casey.

Bevens threw a ball, a strike, another ball. He wound up and Gionfriddo broke for second base, getting a fair jump, not a great one. Yogi Berra's throw sailed a shade high. Gionfriddo slid into second base head first.

"I think I got him," Phil Rizzuto says. "Not a good throw from Yogi, but I had it, and I was coming down from a jump and I'm sure I tagged him before he reached the base." One man who disagreed with Rizzuto was Ralph Arthur "Babe" Pinelli. A civil disagreement among Romans, but an important one. Pinelli was the second base umpire. He called Al Gionfriddo safe. A call of out would have secured Bevens's no-hitter and ended the game.

"Phil tells you he got me?" Gionfriddo says. "I'll tell you how it really was. Phil *almost* got me."

The pitch had been high. The count on Reiser was now 3 and 1. With no hesitation, Bucky Harris signaled Berra to step out from behind home plate. Throw the fourth one wide. Put Reiser on base.

One enduring rule of baseball strategy goes like this: Never willingly put the winning run on base. If Gionfriddo somehow scored, the game would be tied. Should Reiser score, however improbable that was, the Dodgers would win. Keep Reiser, the winning run, off base by all means short of gunfire. Bucky Harris knew the rule and he defied it. A small tragedy for Harris was under way.

Reiser limped to first. Ed Miksis, a reserve infielder, ran for him. Shotton called for Harry Arthur "Cookie" Lavagetto to bat for Eddie Stanky. Lavagetto was an old Brooklyn favorite but he had appeared in only forty-one games that season. His time was winding down.

Bill Bevens and Yogi Berra both knew what the Yankee scouts said about Lavagetto. This feller was almost thirty-five, a baseball ancient. Don't throw him slow stuff. The old guys love to take their swings at changeups. Don't throw them curves. If there is one thing old batters still can do, it's hit the curve. Throw hard. Throw the ball by them. At thirty-five the reflexes begin to slow.

Lavagetto liked to pull the ball. The Yankees knew that also. Tommy Henrich in right field shaded several steps toward center. Bevens fired a fastball, high and away. Lavagetto swung and missed.

Berra put down one finger again. Another fastball. He made a fast hand waggle, up and away. Same pitch.

"I didn't want to throw it there," Bill Bevens said, years later. "I don't know if I wanted to throw a fastball but I definitely didn't want to throw him a fastball up and away. I kinda felt he was zeroing in on that."

Then why did you throw it, Bill?

"Because that's what Berra called for. Yogi was a smart kid, whatever you hear."

Why did you call for the outside fastball, Yogi?

"Because that's what them scouting reports told me to do."

Lavagetto cracked a sharp line drive toward a sign in right field advertising Gem Single-Edged Razor Blades. Tommy Henrich lost the smallest fraction of a second, picking up the ball against the crowd. He ran toward the wall, an unfamiliar wall, and made a little leap. He couldn't reach the ball and now he was positioned too close to the wall, the carom point.

The drive crashed off concrete and glanced between Henrich's legs. It hit a part of his glove and spun to the grass. Henrich grabbed once or twice and threw the ball in to George McQuinn.

Al Gionfriddo was scoring. The game was tied. Ed Miksis,

the twenty-one-year-old pinch runner, never slowed. He slid across home plate on his bottom, wearing a broad and insolent grin.

Bill Bevens, a disciplined Yankee pitcher, was backing up home plate. Gionfriddo scored. Young Eddie Miksis scored. The Dodgers won the ballgame, 3 to 2.

Slowly Bill Bevens walked out from behind home plate and started toward the mound. He had thrown 136 pitches. Still, he was ready to face another hitter.

He who had pitched with such a strange and moving beauty did not understand that the game was over.

Dodger fans stood under the Gem sign, as the lame and the halt stand at the shrine in Lourdes. Dick Young of the *Daily News* wrote an extravagant lead:

> Out of the mockery and ridicule of "the worst World Series in history," the greatest ball game ever played was born yesterday.

Young knew better than that. But like everyone else, he was wildly excited (or suddenly depressed).

I admire Red Smith's final sentence on this stirring drama, played out at Ebbets Field.

"The unhappiest man," Smith wrote, "is sitting up here now in the far end of the press box. The 'V' in his typewriter is broken. He can't write 'Lavagetto' or 'Bevens.'"

"I'm benching McQuinn and Berra," Bucky Harris announced truculently. "We're no worse off than when we started. They're just about out of pitching.

"I wouldn't trade places with them . . ."

DiMaggio walked up to Bevens in the clubhouse. "Tough luck, stud," he said. "We'll get them tomorrow."

Bevens made a little shrug.

"My husband," Bevens's widow, Mildred, was remembering not long ago, "was very quiet when we got home that evening. Just very quiet. He was as disappointed as could be, but he knew you could win them and you could lose them. He never was a very talkative person.

"He was real quiet and we went to bed early. There wasn't anything that we could say about the ballgame, that we wanted to say about the ballgame. I gave him a little kiss and we went to sleep."

They played a lovely game at Ebbets Field next day, combining sturdy elements of drama. Rex Barney, the fastest, wildest pitcher in captivity, started for Brooklyn. He pitched bravely. Spec Shea, the Naugatuck Nugget, finally glowed for New York. DiMaggio homered. Jackie Robinson crashed a clutch hit. Gionfriddo found work as a pinch hitter. Cookie Lavagetto pinch hit once again.

What a ballgame.

Except, except . . . .

The day before, the players had staged *Hamlet*. Now *As You Like It* (if you were a Yankee fan) came across as anticlimax.

Rex Edward Barney, out of Omaha, Nebraska, could throw yet harder than Bill Bevens and he was yet wilder than Bill Bevens. He survives as a footnote to lighthearted sportswriting. Summing up his effort one day, Bob Cooke wrote in the *Herald Tribune*, "Barney pitched as though the plate was high and outside."*

Here was how he made his first World Series start while Branca, the best Dodger starting pitcher, sat on a bench.

Barney walked George Stirnweiss on five pitches. Right-handed Clyde King began warming up in the Dodger bullpen, down the right field line. Tommy Henrich cracked a double off the wall in right center. Knowing Furillo's arm, Stirnweiss stopped at third.

Barney walked Johnny Lindell on four pitches. He struck

---

*Trying to sharpen Barney's control, Rickey ordered the young man to throw with a patch on one eye, then a patch on the other. The experimenting did not cease. For mysterious reasons, at the age of twenty-five, Barney dropped out of the major leagues.

out Joe DiMaggio on five pitches. George McQuinn — Harris
had not benched him, after all — tapped to Barney, who tossed
home, forcing Stirnweiss. Barney struck out Bill Johnson. Two
walks; one hit; two strikeouts; no runs. Something was happening every minute.

Aaron Robinson was catching for the Yankees. Harris did
bench Berra, but only for one day. After that Yogi played two
games as an outfielder. Harris was too smart to bench the Berra
bat.

Shea handled the Dodgers easily. In the second inning, Aaron
Robinson slammed a long fly that Furillo caught at the wall in
right center field. Barney walked Rizzuto. He wild-pitched
Rizzuto to second base. Rizzuto tried to steal third but Bruce
Edwards's throw caught him. Spec Shea lined out.

With one out in the third inning and the game still scoreless,
Barney threw four straight balls to Henrich. Then he walked
Lindell. DiMaggio bounced into a double play, ending the
flurry.

Someone in the press box remarked that Barney was playing
with disaster, using DiMaggio to get his important outs. Someone else observed the Dodger Symphony tootling through the
stands. All the musicians wore threads and patches — part of
the act — except for the second cornetist. He sported clean
pressed slacks and a neat bright yellow sweater. "It could be,"
Harold Rosenthal remarked, "that the feller's tramp clothes are
at the cleaners."

The Dodgers weren't hitting Shea. Then with two out in the
fourth, Barney walked Aaron Robinson and Phil Rizzuto. Basic
Barney. Now the Yankee pitcher came up. Barney pressed.
Trying to throw a strike, he let up on a fastball. Shea lined it
to left field. The Yankees led, 1 to 0.

Then in the fifth with one out, DiMaggio stopped playing
Barney's fall guy. He slammed a high drive three rows deep
into the upper stands in left. One batter later, Rex Barney was
gone.

The Dodger rally came in the sixth. Gionfriddo pinch hit and drew a walk. With one out, Reese walked. Robinson cracked a low drive up the middle that glanced off Spec Shea's glove and carried into center field. Gionfriddo scored and when Di-Maggio threw to third, trying to get Reese, Robinson advanced to second. Home run or not, DiMaggio was having a rocky day. He turned things around a bit by running down Gene Hermanski's long fly for the third out.

It came down again to the ninth inning. The Yankees led, 2 to 1, as they had the day before. Bruce Edwards singled. The pitcher Vic Lombardi ran for Edwards. Furillo bunted the tying run to second. After a fly out, Cookie Lavagetto pinch hit for the second day in a row.

He took an inside fastball for a strike.

Ball one. Low.

Ball two. Outside.

Ball three. Outside.

The noise level at Ebbets Field rose mightily.

Spec Shea threw a fastball past Lavagetto. Three and two. The game was on the line.

Shea threw another fastball. Lavagetto swung and missed. Heroism in the batter's box is a sometime thing. At the request of photographers, DiMaggio kissed Spec Shea in the Yankee clubhouse.

The Series was moving back to the Bronx. The Yankees led, three games to two.

Some of these wonderful games came down to an inning. Others to a single at bat. Now, game six came down to what everyone called "the Catch."

"Dammit," said Al Gionfriddo forty-four years later, when he was sixty-nine. "I didn't even think to keep the ball. I made the catch and Carl Furillo says somethin' nice and I'm runnin' in with Carl, you know, all excited. I made the catch and saved three runs and like a fool I drop the ball at the pitcher's mound. I'm the first hitter next inning. They give me a big hand. I foul the first pitch into the seats. That's the ball!

"Some fan got it. Maybe he kept it. Maybe he never knew that was the ball I saved a home run with, and saved the Dodgers."

These teams pounded each other. The Dodgers scuffed Allie Reynolds for two runs in the first inning, two more in the third on successive doubles, cuffed by Reese, Robinson, and Dixie Walker.

The Yankees knocked out the journeyman left-hander Vic Lombardi with four in the third. They went ahead in the fourth when Berra, now a right fielder, singled home Aaron Robinson.

Branca, working relief, held off the Yankees fairly well into the sixth. Then the Dodgers broke through for four runs and an 8 to 5 lead. As a defensive measure, Shotton sent Gionfriddo to left field in the bottom of the sixth.

Joe Hatten replaced Branca and quickly pitched into trouble. Allie Clark hit a sharp line drive that Reese flagged down. Stirnweiss walked. Henrich poled a long drive to right that sailed into the stands a few feet foul. Then he popped out. Berra singled. Hatten was being pounded. Now this staggering left-hander was called upon to pitch to DiMaggio, among the best right-handed batters of all time.

If Shotton was not comatose, he was dozing. He had Hugh Casey in the Dodger bullpen. He let Hatten pitch to DiMaggio. A home run, and DiMaggio was swinging hard, would tie the game. In left field, Al Gionfriddo knew that. He knew DiMaggio would be trying to pull the ball against a left-handed pitcher. Gionfriddo moved toward the left field foul line.

In doing that, he also moved closer to home plate. The left field foul pole at the Stadium was 301 feet away from home. Dead left was a kind of box. If you shaded a man to pull, you played him shallow. A deep fly down the left field line was out of reach, except to customers in the stands who would have had to put down their beer cups to catch it.

Gionfriddo shaded DiMaggio left. Some have criticized him for playing shallow, but those were ignorant of Yankee Stadium geography. Nobody tells what happened next more vividly than the principal, Gionfriddo.

"DiMaggio comes to bat and we were leading 8 to 5, and they had two men on base and there were two outs and I'm playing him to pull, which was in close. It had to be.

"He hits the ball to left center. Very deep. I mean Joe really hit it. He took some swing.

"At Yankee Stadium, the left field bullpen, where the visiting relief pitchers warmed up, there were these gates that the relief pitchers walked through when they went in to pitch. The gates were metal, with an iron frame. Something between three and four feet high.

"I picked DiMaggio's ball up good. He hit it high and deep toward those iron gates. I didn't think I had a chance. I'm maybe three hundred forty, three hundred fifty feet out. Next to those gates, there's a sign, big capital letters. It says: 415 FT.

"I put my head down and I ran, my back was toward home plate and you know I had it right. I had the ball sighted just right." After all these years, Gionfriddo laughs in gorgeous triumph.

"The ball is going at the bullpen gate and I look over my left shoulder. My back is to the plate. Over my left shoulder. I am left-handed. I throw left. So the glove is on my right hand. I see the ball coming and as the ball is coming in, I make a jump.

"Since I am left-handed I have to reach my glove, which is on my right hand, over my left shoulder. I do that. I jump and make the reach.

"I'm turning in midair. I'm turning and reaching and I catch the ball. I crash the gate. I hit it hard, against my right hip. I hold the ball.

"I'm with DiMaggio years later. We're talking to kids. Joe D. is a lot more famous than me.

"He tells the kids, 'Al's kind of small. You know a small guy has to work extra hard to make it to the major leagues.

"'Some big guy' — this is still DiMaggio talking — 'he probably wouldn't have ever *made* the Catch. A big guy woulda backed off and left it to go over the fence.

"'But this little guy. He always had to work harder than anybody else. That's the way it is in baseball. The little guys always have to work harder. So he was used to working, Al, this little guy, and he never gave up and he made the greatest catch that anybody ever made in the whole history of baseball.'"

Bald now, with wisps of white hair, Al Gionfriddo, a little guy who doesn't want to brag, affects a shrug. "Anyway, that's what Joe DiMaggio says."*

The Dodgers won the sixth game, 8 to 6.

Shotton, dull, obdurate Burt Shotton, shuffled his lineup for the seventh game. And the first thing he did was bench Al Gionfriddo. He replaced him in left field with Gene Hermanski, in turn replaced by reserve infielder Eddie Miksis. And before long Miksis was playing a fly ball into a triple.

Bench Gionfriddo? After the greatest catch in history? If there is a God and God follows baseball, He noticed that Gionfriddo was benched. Surely Burt Shotton was foredoomed.

Al Laney, an elegant journalist, wrote a fine paragraph in the *Herald Tribune*. "This extraordinary World Series of 1947, which has provided perhaps more thrills and more hysteria than any other, finally came down to a pleasant, sunny afternoon on which people could sit back and enjoy an ordinary ball game without having their nerves worn raw or their emotions too heavily involved. This was a straight-forward game with reason and logic in it and never once did panic sit up and make a noise."

*

---

*DiMaggio saw Willie Mays's famous catch at the Polo Grounds. "That was a great one, too," he says, "but Mays had plenty of room. Running back, all he had to worry about was the ball. On my drive, Gionfriddo had to worry about the ball and those iron gates. He had to worry about running out of room, about getting hurt. With all that, I say he made the greater catch."

The Western world focused on the Series. But as the cold war gathered, Eastern Europe didn't seem to care. The Soviet army was throwing a party near Budapest, Walter Kerr reported in the *Tribune*, with vodka toasts and great bowls of rich food, to demonstrate its peaceful intentions. "Toward the end of the evening, the Russian commander escorted his guests through his quarters, including a secret map room that showed the disposition of Soviet forces.

"An American officer, suspecting the display was not genuine, deliberately forgot his gold-braided hat. Three hours later he returned to pick it up.

"The entire 'headquarters' had vanished."

The Bronx was mighty and would prevail. Shotton started Hal Gregg, who was, quite simply, not a winning major league pitcher. (His lifetime record: 40 won and 48 lost.) Even though Branca had pitched the day before, a better manager might have started him, saying simply, "Throw as hard as you can for as long as you can." A genius manager, a Casey Stengel, might have started Hughie Casey. The Yankees didn't care for Hugh's slants at all. He was a hostile man who liked to knock down hitters. DiMaggio. Henrich. The great ones. Hughie Casey put them on their butts.

There was no quit in this dogged Dodger team. Swinging against Spec Shea in the second inning, Hermanski tripled around Berra in right field. Bruce Edwards, the stolid catcher, singled Hermanski home. Furillo singled Edwards to second base.

Bucky Harris lifted Spec Shea for Bill Bevens. Spider Jorgensen bounced a double into the right field stands and the Dodgers led by two runs. But Rizzuto singled home a run in the bottom of the second and the Yankees went ahead with two runs in the fourth. Johnson walked. With two out, Rizzuto lined a single to left. Bobby Brown hit for Bevens and doubled to left. Behrman replaced Gregg.

Where was Branca?

Where was Casey?

Where was Shotton?

Behrman walked Stirnweiss on four pitches. Henrich singled Rizzuto home. The Yankees had a lead they would not relinquish.

In the top of that inning Bill Bevens had retired three Dodgers, with a man on first. The last of the three, Gregg, bounced to second. Following that pitch Bevens grabbed for his right shoulder. Few noticed.

Joe Page replaced Bevens in the fifth inning. Across the final five innings of this Series, Page allowed only one hit, Eddie Miksis's one-out single in the ninth.

Experienced people can tell about such things. The Yankees were going to win. A crowd of sportswriters swarmed about outside the Yankee dressing room in the Stadium catacombs, while the ninth inning still was being played.

Abruptly Larry MacPhail, the hard-drinking Yankee boss, cleared a path among the writers. "If we win this," he bellowed, and the Yankees were going to win this, "I'm outa baseball."

"What's that?" asked Harold Rosenthal of the *Tribune*.

"You heard me. If we win this fucking game, I quit."

"Why, Larry?"

"Cause I wanna. That's why. That good enough for you?"

Relaxed in comfort at what he calls "Varicose Villa," a retirement community in northern New Jersey, Rosenthal remembers that moment with electric memory.

The *New York Times* of 1947 employed pedestrian writers to cover baseball. The paper's passion for lively sports coverage had not yet been born. The best *Times* baseball writer, though far from the best in New York, was James P. Dawson. "Jimmy could write better than the other two dinosaurs," Rosenthal says, "but writing wasn't his forte. Eating was Dawson's forte. His particular forte was eating free food.

"The Series is handout time. Free eats for everybody.

"So we're standing under the Stadium stands, waiting to

cover the winning dressing room, and Jim Dawson is eating the biggest free hot dog in the world.

"And MacPhail announces he's quitting. For emphasis, he smacks Dawson in the back.

"I remember that. What I remember even more is James Dawson of the *New York Times* damn near choking on his seventeenth free hot dog. That is a Series record, I believe."

The Yankees won the seventh game, 5 to 2.

At some cost, MacPhail stole the next day's headlines from his team.

6

Larry's Leavin';
Leo's Weavin'

◆

I MET LARRY MACPHAIL for the first time five years after certain episodes that followed the 1947 World Series. "The wildest, rowdiest and most sensational affair ever staged," J. G. Taylor Spink, the publisher of *The Sporting News*, wrote of these events in a front-page story that mixed hyperbole, hyperventilation, and — surprise! — tough, honest reporting.

The postbellum MacPhail I encountered on a cold March afternoon in 1952 was subdued, hoarse, sober, and so determined to avoid controversy that the Once Roarin' Redhead struck some as being dull.

Not I. As a child in Brooklyn I had seen from a distance how MacPhail created the modern Dodgers and I brought to our meeting profound respect. MacPhail responded warmly. He spoke softly and kindly of his Brooklyn days. "The franchise was dying," he said. "Remember when I put lights into Ebbets Field?"

"Yes, sir."

"The lights were a pulmotor. They kept the Brooklyn franchise alive."

"Is it true you actually tried to kidnap the Kaiser, Mr. MacPhail?"

"Sure is. We wanted the bastard brought to justice as a war criminal. Right after the Armistice in '18, a few of us drove into Holland, which was neutral territory, in our army uniforms, and we got right up to Kaiser Wilhelm's citadel in a town called Doorn. But before we got the bastard, a neutral Dutch infantry company opened up with machine guns. Some neutrals! We had to back off."

MacPhail mentioned in an uncomplaining way the battle he was waging against throat cancer. He even forgave me for being, as I was at the time, a member of the New York press. But when I tried to lead him into a discussion of a controversy rocking baseball — a controversy that really was wild, rowdy, and sensational — he withdrew. "No comment." Then, "Can I trust you, if I go off the record?"

I was twenty-three years old. "You can trust me, Mr. MacPhail."

"Well, son, let me tell you this. Ty Cobb may have been the best player in the history of the game. That's a possibility.

"But here's a certainty. Ty Cobb is the craziest son of a bitch on earth."

"I can't write that?"

"You can't write that," MacPhail said.

"I'd like to write that, Mr. MacPhail."

"I'm sure you would, son. But you gave your word."

Across twenty-four major league seasons, almost a quarter century, Ty Cobb batted .367. That is a lifetime average beyond approach and just about beyond belief. Indeed, Cobb's lifetime average is *the* major league record that will endure from here to eternity.

Cobb was also the best base runner of his time, some say of

any time. He stole 892 bases, and ploughing the basepaths he intimidated infielders as no one before or since. Often, during pregame warm-up, Cobb sat in the dugout, ostentatiously sharpening his spikes. Although no such record is kept, Ty Cobb must have spiked more infielders than anyone in the annals. To tag out Cobb was also to yelp in pain.

His salary never exceeded $30,000, but beyond the ballfield Cobb invested his way to a fortune. For years, he played down his financial skills, but in 1947, when Cobb's wife, the former Charlie Marion Lombard of Augusta, Georgia, sued for divorce, court papers established Cobb's wealth as "in excess of $7,000,000." His two prime winners, selected generations ago, were a soda pop company down in his home country, known as Coca-Cola, and a vehicular growth stock in the town where he played ball, called General Motors. "In many ways," the late Vincent X. Flaherty wrote, "Ty Cobb, the greatest of the Tigers, became symbolic of Detroit itself. He came along at a time when a lot of struggling mechanics were founding an industrial empire — mechanics who in after years became fabulous millionaires and grand dukes of industry."

In the spring of 1952, Ty Cobb, perhaps the greatest player of all time, surely the richest ex-player anywhere, lent his name to two unusual articles published in *Life* magazine. "They don't play baseball anymore," Cobb said. "They've ruined the game." *Life* promoted the stories with strident full-page newspaper advertisements. The magazine published photographs of Bob Feller, Stan Musial, Ted Williams, Jackie Robinson, Joe Di-Maggio, Ralph Kiner, Phil Rizzuto, and Eddie Stanky. Then the advertising copy asked:

"According to Ty Cobb, which two are the only *great* ball players?"

It was a rousing two-part piece, written or rather typed by Marshall Smith, the sports editor of *Life*, but fueled, generated, and thought out by Mr. Cobb. Hype aside, much of what Cobb had to say was applicable then and may be even more applicable today.

Cobb came charging off the pages like a famished lion charging a well-fed lamb. Today's ballplayers (today being 1952)? Growl. Sniff. Roar. Why, the blokes don't bother to learn fundamentals.

What's that, Ty? Big league ballplayers don't know fundamentals? Roar. Growl. They don't even practice, or anyway not enough, or anyway not in the right manner. Most of them don't even train seriously.

But, Ty, the big leaguers want to make money, don't they, and training pays off. Maybe they did, Cobb admitted, but all they *really* cared about was cashing in on home runs. Cobb himself led the major leagues in homers across the season of 1909. He hit nine. Now, in 1952, Cobb argued, the home run had become so commonplace it had "lost its thrill."

What about the pantheon stars Ted Williams and Joe Di-Maggio? They "limp along on one cylinder," Cobb wrote. He amplified in interesting but debatable ways.

When Williams came to bat, most ballclubs shifted hard to the right, the better to collar the hard drives that Williams pulled. Usually only one man, the third baseman, covered the entire left side of the infield. Against a shift of this sort, Cobb claimed, Babe Ruth would have hit the ball to left or bunted, defeating both his opponents and the shift. Williams neither bunted nor hit to left. He was not a great hitter, according to Cobb, because he had not mastered the fundamental of slapping singles to the opposite field.

DiMaggio? A lazy layabout. Cobb wrote that DiMaggio was perhaps the greatest natural player who ever lived, possessed of speed and grace, agility, a good eye, and long, strong muscles. But, Cobb commented, DiMaggio "hated exertion" and never took "a lick of exercise" all winter. As a result, DiMaggio went to spring training with muscles "weakened and soft," which, Cobb said, led to his frequent injuries.

When Cobb was a ballplayer, he played with his mind as well as his body and he stayed in condition all year. In the winter he claimed to have walked twenty to thirty miles a day, every day, tramping the snows of Canada in heavy boots or marching over the red-clay fields of Georgia in shoes weighted down by lead.

The champion Yankees seemed particularly to enrage Cobb. After one World Series, he wrote, Yogi Berra took a job as a greeter in a restaurant; Phil Rizzuto sold men's clothing, and DiMaggio just sat around. "Ribbon clerk" jobs, Cobb stormed. The men should "go deliver ice."

In fairness, some refutation of Cobb's charges is in order. Williams could have hit to left field; he knew how to do that. His argument was — and is — that pulling the ball to right, even against the shift, was what he did best. As stubborn as Cobb, Williams was damned if he was going to change or let others dictate how he should swing.

DiMaggio was never Spartan, but his worst physical problems probably proceeded not from indolence but from arthritis. If exercise cured arthritis, the world would be full of bankrupt aspirin companies.

It is the theory of Jon Miller, as astute broadcaster who reports on the Baltimore Orioles, that each generation produces at least one harsh attack on contemporary baseball players and a concomitant glorifying of those who went before. As Cobb in the 1950s lionized players of the 1920s, so today we lionize the very 1950s players Cobb derided. In twenty-five years, according to Miller, people will exalt the players of today, who are currently regarded as overpaid and undercommitted. "It's the nature of things," Miller says.

While I'm inclined to agree, the Cobb articles in *Life* remain unique, not for his exalted reasoning but for the sulfurous heat that was Ty Cobb.

Despite Rizzuto's soft job as a suit salesman, Cobb named him as one of the two genuinely great ballplayers of the Era. Rizzuto and Musial were the men Cobb had in mind when he said "only two players" could stand comparison with those from earlier times.

Not Pee Wee Reese, not Enos Slaughter, not George Kell, not Jackie Robinson — *pointedly* not Jackie Robinson — just to mention a few players Cobb spurned who have since been chosen for the Hall of Fame.

What did Cobb have to say about these worthies?

Here is his copyrighted opinion:

"Throw them a bag of peanuts."

For several days, everyone talked Cobb. Columnists wrote Cobb. Editorial writers deplored Cobb. And, of course, *Life* magazine sold out throughout the country.

Eisenhower won the New Hampshire Republican primary, defeating Robert Taft by 12,000 votes. On the Democratic side, Senator Estes Kefauver defeated Harry Truman by 3,000. Backed by machine gunners and tanks, Fulgencio Batista took over Cuba in a bloody coup that lasted seventy-seven minutes.

Fine, fine. Eisenhower was probably better than Taft or Dewey.

Kefauver was preachy, but we were tired of Harry Truman and his self-righteous Korean war.

Batista? Dictators came and went in Havana, but the whorehouses never closed.

Such was the stuff of chatter. Getting serious, people said, "Wait a minute here, let's talk something important. Can you really *believe* Ty Cobb?"

That week Bob Cooke, the sports editor of the *Herald Tribune*, assigned me to interview Larry MacPhail, who had emerged from a sort of self-imposed obscurity as the new president of Bowie Racetrack. I'd covered horse racing a bit and enjoyed some horsemen, but to me in those years racing was a sport, or maybe a business. Baseball was something else. In Prospero's term, baseball was "rough magic."*

*It still is.

"Could be a nice little story," Cookie said, "MacPhail moving into another world. Don't try to get him mad. Don't try to drink with him. Don't press. Just write what you see."

I nodded and the boss and I talked about softball prospects for the *Herald Tribune* team. Cookie played shortstop. I played third. Cooke was a patrician gentleman. He couldn't hit.

As I mounted my honeydew Chevrolet convertible — the pale green car was $200 cheaper than the red one — I began working out numbers of questions to trap MacPhail away from racetrack talk.

Was the great DiMaggio really a lazy layabout? (Here comes the Jersey Turnpike.)

Was the great Williams just a free-swinging bum? (Look at these trucks. Every truck in New Jersey wants to crush my little green car and me.)

There's no arguing about Musial, but is Rizzuto really that good? What about Reese? It was MacPhail who brought Reese to Brooklyn in 1940. (Watch that damn trailer. Where the hell is Maryland? Why didn't I take the Pennsylvania Railroad?)

With all the Cobb furor, MacPhail anticipated what I planned to do. He blocked my moves by putting our interview on a personal basis and, manipulating with great skill, played the off-the-record game to a fare-thee-well. It is almost always a bad idea to let an interview subject take you off record; at twenty-three I was learning my trade.

On the record MacPhail said that he was a novice at running racetracks. Yes, he had brought night ball to the major leagues, but he didn't like the idea of night horse racing. He went on in a mildly interesting way and then helped out in the dedication of a statue to a horse called Billy Barton, a steeplechase jumper who lived thirty-five years. My story began:

> Larry MacPhail made his debut as a racing executive this after-noon at a party where he shared top billing with a horse.

I dealt with his subdued manner indirectly:

He guarantees no more racing improvements than increased park space. He refuses to rap anybody famous. As a new member of Maryland's gentry, Larry seems to feel that loud talk and bickering are not seemly.

The quiet of countrylife may have had its effects.

"Nice piece," Cooke told me.

"I blew Cobb," I said. "I couldn't get MacPhail to talk Cobb on the record."

"I'm tired of Cobb," Cooke said. "You wrote a nice piece and you didn't press."

"I let him take me off record and then I felt I had to honor that."

"You did right," Cooke said. "No one story, none, *ever*, is worth losing a source like Larry MacPhail."

Cooke liked my work considerably more than I did. Exactly three days after the MacPhail piece appeared, he pulled me out of a drab Manhattan March and sent me to Florida — or was it Eden? — to cover the Brooklyn Dodgers.

The MacPhail we are about to meet, back in October 1947, is not someone I knew personally. He does not seem well. Some of his conduct traces to whiskey but some clearly goes beyond that. I don't think it is reaching to assert this: After the 1947 World Series, when the Yankees of Larry MacPhail won the World Series from a Dodger team significantly shaped by Larry MacPhail, the creator, MacPhail himself, underwent a nervous breakdown.

By tradition, World Series winning teams threw victory parties. The players and the manager and coaches were invited, of course, along with wives and selected, which is to say non-confrontational, writers and sports announcers and hangers-on. By tradition the parties were off record. The mood was manic — the host team had just won the Series — and the abundance of good whiskey and attractive women on top of a manic mood, encouraged excessive behavior. "When I go to one of those things," said Rud Rennie of the *Tribune*, whom MacPhail twice tried to have fired, "my understanding is that I'm a guest, not a reporter. A guest who doesn't tattle, if he is a gentleman." Which Rud Rennie was.

A full complement of reporters attended the Yankee victory party in 1947, held in the Grand Ballroom of the Biltmore Hotel on the night of October 6. Neither MacPhail nor the old gentlemanly press code really survived the evening.

As the Yankees moved toward their final victory, MacPhail began serious drinking. He left his box during the seventh inning and began to mix Scotch and beer, with speed and gusto.

A minute after Dodger catcher Bruce Edwards bounced into the double play that ended the Series, MacPhail was standing in front of the Yankee dressing room, ignoring his players, making a speech to sportswriters.

"You fellows have been wonderful to me," he shouted, waving a bottle of beer. "Aw, hell. Just wonderful." He began to sob. "I'm out of the picture now. I got what I wanted. We won the World Series. I can't take anymore. My health. My health . . ."

Writers came running down the corridors far below the three-tiered stands at Yankee Stadium. MacPhail pushed his way through them, tears running down his face, and threw an arm around dour, chipmunk-cheeked George Weiss, his farm director.

"Here, you guys," MacPhail shouted at the reporters. "I want you to say this in your stories. I'm the guy that built up the losers, the Brooklyn club. Here's the man who really built the Yankees." He raised George Weiss's right arm.

"Now I gotta talk to my players . . ."

The Yankees were drinking champagne and peeling off uniforms. MacPhail climbed on a trunk.

"I want to congratulate you fellows. Nobody beat you three in a row all season. That's something. Isn't that something!

"The two Joes [DiMaggio and Page]. Just wonderful. You're all just wonderful.

"I wanted to leave at the top. You've made it possible. I'm through, fellows. I'm quitting right now."

He started crying again. Then he went looking for Branch Rickey and found him amid another swarm of reporters. "You've got a fine team," MacPhail said. "I want to congratulate you."

Rickey leaned in very close. His whisper was ice. "I'll shake your hand because I have to with these people watching. But I don't like you, sir. Don't care for you at all." MacPhail wheeled away. He needed another drink.

Toward eight P.M. he came staggering into the press room at the Biltmore Hotel.

"I got some things to tell you writers," he said. "Stay away from me or get punched.

"I'm not a Happy Chandler man. I'm charged by him with saying something detrimental to baseball. Never. I gave New York another championship, didn't I?

"And what do you writers say?

"I'm nothing but a pop-off. Maybe I am but I deliver the goods. Who won the Series?"

Sid Keener, the sports editor of the St. Louis *Star-Times*, had known MacPhail for thirty years. "Larry," he said mildly, "everyone gets criticized in your business even when they win. Branch Rickey won in St. Louis and . . ."

"Rickey?" MacPhail shouted. "Bible-quoting, hypocritical, tightwad son of a bitch. He's worse than Chandler, worse than that goddamn hayseed we have as commissioner."

MacPhail was shouting all this at reporters from every major newspaper in the country.

"Gotta have a victory celebration," he said. "Have one for myself. Don't want to have my private celebration in the Grand Ballroom where everybody's dancing and eating roast beef." He paused for breath. "I don't want to have my celebration party with the damned press." Then, doing what he said he would not do, he lurched toward the elevator to join the Yankee victory crowd, which included writers. There he came apart.

MacPhail stumbled into the party and dropped into a chair beside John McDonald, who had worked for him in Brooklyn. He began a fresh assault on Rickey.

"I got no complaints with him," McDonald said. "Rickey looks after people he likes."

"You're defending Rickey here?" MacPhail said. "Here where you're my guest, the Yankees' guest? You Judas. Stand up."

As McDonald rose, MacPhail swung a right hand into McDonald's left eye. The two were separated.

MacPhail lurched about and spotted George Weiss, the man he had praised generously a few hours before. "You gonna do what I tell you from now on," MacPhail said, "or are you gonna quit?"

Weiss blinked in confusion.

"Look, you son of a bitch. You got forty-eight hours to make up your mind. What are you going to do?"

"We've all been drinking, Larry," Weiss said. "Why can't we talk tomorrow?"

"You're going to talk with me now, or you're fired. Wait. I just changed my mind about that. You're fired now, Weiss. Tomorrow? I'll give you tomorrow. Stop by my office for your final check tomorrow, Weiss. You're through."

"Oh, dear," said Weiss's wife, Hazel. "Larry. Please. We need the job."

"Stay away from me," MacPhail said. Hazel Weiss began to weep. MacPhail continued to lurch around the room. He spotted Dan Topping, big, Anaconda Copper–rich Dan Topping, who owned one-third of the Yankees.

"Hey, Topping," MacPhail said. "You know what you are? A guy born with a silver spoon in his mouth who never made a dollar in his life."

Topping seized MacPhail's left arm. "Listen, you," Topping said. "We've taken everything from you we're going to take."

Topping wrestled MacPhail into the hotel kitchen. He was bigger than MacPhail, younger by twenty years, physically stronger, and considerably more sober. He shook MacPhail roughly in the kitchen, punched him with a few body blows, and ordered MacPhail to behave. "If you act up again, Larry," Topping said, "I'm gonna knock your head off. Now go into the washroom and clean yourself up and for Christ sakes, comb your hair."

About half an hour later — ten P.M. — a subdued MacPhail returned, properly groomed. But the whiskey and the mindless rage still burned within him.

He walked up to Joe Page, who was sitting with his wife. "What were you, Joe, before I picked you up? A bum. You and this broad here, you were nothing. I bought a home for you. You're wearing nice clothes now. You're drinking champagne. But without me, the two of you would be starving."

Topping was approaching with a murderous look. Mrs. Page burst into tears.

MacPhail weaved away from the couple. Then this wondrous, bizarre, driven character staggered out of the room and out of the victory party and out of baseball.

"My dad made a lot of money," Lee MacPhail said recently, "and he spent a lot of money, too. Don't take this in the wrong way. Nobody has more appreciation for my dad's brilliance than I. But in a sense he lived too long. He insisted on managing his own financial affairs, even when it was clear that age was taking its toll. By the time my father died in 1975, he'd gone through every cent he had.

"Dad died broke."

The gentleman's agreement on not reporting victory parties was dead by the morning of October 7, 1947. An extraordinary New York newspaper called *PM*, which accepted no advertising, had hired an acerbic Brooklyn Irishman named Tom Meany to write its baseball. Meany recounted some of MacPhail's behavior and concluded his column:

Larry retains his title as headline champ. MacPhail is more emotional, without needing a warm-up, than Sarah Bernhardt. Larry always said he wanted to quit while on top. It should be recorded that Joe Page, with his winning performance, drove Larry out of baseball. Through the first six games, it looked as though it might have been vice versa.

The World Series and MacPhail finished simultaneously. Larry was sobbing when he announced that he was through. He set a record for sobbing in a seven-game series.

It took hard digging to ascertain what had been happening fundamentally in the Yankee front office. Behind an episode of apparent alcohol-induced psychosis lay very rugged fiscal stuff.

Some weeks earlier MacPhail had begun private talks with several Wall Street firms — Bear, Stearns and John J. Bergen & Co. — with an eye toward selling Yankee stock to the public. He produced books indicating that the Yankees of 1946 earned a profit of $1.35 per share. Since shares had a par value of $10, the team was returning better than thirteen percent. And 1947, with the pennant and the World Series, was going to be even better.

MacPhail and the brokers proposed to sell to the public 300,000 shares of new stock at $10 or possibly $15 a share. In restructuring the franchise, this would represent half of all Yankee stock, minus 100 shares. MacPhail, Topping, and Webb would retain operational control, and the public, getting not quite fifty percent, would pump $3,000,000 or possibly $4,500,000 worth of new money into the Yankees. MacPhail could then put a third of that, at least a million dollars, into his pocket or into a horse farm he had purchased in Bel Air, Maryland. "What Larry wanted most," Tom Meany remembered, "was not just to be a winner. He wanted to be a squire, like Thomas Jefferson, only richer."

In 1947, as today, organized baseball discouraged public ownership. Almost every major league club is privately held. In essence, baseball's books are closed. Profit figures are kept secret — if anything, more so today than in the 1940s.

But even in 1947 various owners did not want to see baseball's flagship franchise go public. MacPhail's partners, Dan Topping and Del Webb, had personal fortunes. They didn't need to raise cash as MacPhail felt he did. After furious exchanges, Topping and Webb agreed to purchase MacPhail's third interest in the Yankees for an even $2,000,000. (Remember, MacPhail had come in with a million dollars two seasons before.) MacPhail would have pretax profit of a cool million. The Yankees would sell zero stock, none at all, to the public. Their books would remain closed.

Before the weeping and the punching, the assault on George Weiss, the humiliation of Mr. and Mrs. Joe Page, MacPhail had accepted the Topping-Webb offer. He had his million. But that was not all he wanted.

Larry MacPhail wanted to have his million and he wanted to keep running the Yankees. He wanted to live like Jefferson from Monday to Friday and weekend like Louis XIV. He wanted to breed horses and win pennants and bend people to his will. He wanted a coterie of vassals, a bowing press, and, oh yes, he wanted very much to be loved.

As I say, the MacPhail I met in 1952 seemed recovered and resigned to a life outside of baseball. By that time the Yankees had evolved into a different kind of organization: cold, efficient, impersonal, openly bigoted against blacks, perpetually triumphant.

In a weak moment at the Players Club during the summer of '52 Red Smith admitted that he did, as a matter of fact, root for those antiseptic Yankees.

An unemployed actor was Smith's bar companion.

"But Red," the actor said. "How can you root for the Yankees? That's like rooting for U.S. Steel."

What happened to the Yankees in 1948, immediately after MacPhail's departure? What became of them?

Nothing happened to the Yankees in 1948. They didn't become. DiMaggio had a fine year, with thirty-nine home runs, but Page drank his way to a mediocre season. Discipline faded under Bucky Harris, who could not control his team or get along with George Weiss. The Yankees finished third behind the Cleveland Indians and the Red Sox.

Joe McCarthy, the famous old Yankee manager, now was managing the Red Sox. Casey Stengel, fifty-eight years old, was managing the Oakland Oaks of the Pacific Coast League.

The Yankee future was in doubt.

◆

LEO ERNEST DUROCHER, of West Springfield, Massachusetts; Brooklyn, Manhattan, and Beverly Hills, seldom drank spiritous liquids. Durocher's vocabulary would make a longshoreman wince.* He gambled incessantly, unscrupulously fleecing innocents. His pursuit of women was relentless. Leo was one foul-mouthed pool hall hustler of a rake. But unlike Larry MacPhail, he seldom drank. Durocher never, ever, wanted to lose control.

My first extended exposure to Durocher came in February and March of 1954, when I was sent to Phoenix to cover a spring training. Durocher dominated the Giant press corps with a combination of charm and threats. He supplied bourbon to the alcoholic man from the *New York Post*. He lent money to the reporter from the *Daily News*. ("But if you ever knock me in the paper, Jim, I'm calling in my fucking note.") He promised me a variety of exclusive stories, if I wrote them from his point of view. Providing only that I compose the gospel according to St. Leo, I could scoop all of New York, at least once a week.

---

*Lester Rodney, the sports columnist for the Communist newspaper *The Daily Worker*, has retired to northern California. *The Daily Worker* has long since stopped publishing, but Rodney's memories of Durocher remain vibrantly alive. The two were talking in a dugout one afternoon, Rodney recalls, when Durocher suddenly exclaimed: "For a fucking Communist, you know your baseball."

He fascinated me. He was a fascinating character. He told baseball stories beautifully and Hollywood stories just about as well. He knew Sinatra, Hope, Crosby. He knew everybody. That spring, Paramount was shooting a comic circus movie near Phoenix, with a cast that included Dean Martin and Jerry Lewis, then still speaking, and a radiantly bleached blonde actress of wide repute.

One day I stared after the actress, who was passing through a hotel lobby, and Durocher said, "Like that?"

"Umm."

"I'm fucking her, you know," Durocher told me.

"Who?"

He said her name. "That's why you don't see me around the lobby in the nighttime."

I could not believe what I was hearing.

"You," I said, very slowly. "You and that movie star?"

"Sure, kid," Durocher said, "but I gotta stop fucking her Wednesday."

"Why?"

"Because my wife is flying in."

Leo Durocher had to stop sleeping with one gorgeous actress because his wife, gorgeous Laraine Day, was coming to town. My face showed amazement. "Stick with me, kid," Durocher said. "Write what I tell you, good positive stuff.

"Do that and I'll teach you how to get movie stars to go to bed with you."

Durocher's season in exile, 1947, was troubled. Branch Rickey told reporters as background — material to use, but without specific attribution — that Chandler's decree suspending Durocher was unfair. The Brooklyn franchise was putatively bound by the rulings of the commissioner, including his order of silence. But for his part, Rickey said, he intended to see that, suspended or not, Durocher received his full salary as manager — approximately $30,000.

To hold Durocher's interest, Rickey had an assistant send a

daily telegram to California reporting on the progress of the Dodgers. The telegrams arrived regularly at Durocher's home. The paychecks did not. Durocher did some card table hustling and made a little money, but not enough.

Rickey ducked urgent calls. "I got that message," Durocher said. He then telephoned George V. McLaughlin, a banker who was in essence the Dodgers' chief financial officer.

"Send me a wire right now," McLaughlin said. "Make it read 'Please send $10,000 advance on my salary.' Phrase it like that and I'll personally make sure your check goes right out."

To his dying day, Durocher maintained: "I sent the wire. I got the check. I never got another."

Rickey could forgive Durocher most of the sins of Satan. But he would not forgive Durocher for dunning him. The friendship between the two began rapidly to fade.

Durocher told the author Ed Linn, "You know, if you asked me to explain mixed feelings, I could give you the old joke. It's watching your mother-in-law go over a cliff in your new car. Actually I liked Laraine's mother. Mixed feelings for me was sitting in California in the summer of 1947 and watching *my* team — the team I had worked like a dog to put together — win the pennant without me."

In *Nice Guys Finish Last,* an entertaining book written with Linn, Durocher boasts that he pursued other Dodger trustees until finally his 1947 salary was paid in full. On page 269, he swears he was never paid in full. Then on page 270 he gets his money. I do not suggest that *Nice Guys Finish Last* is coherent or accurate, only that it is entertaining (and as accurate as Linn could make it, given his collaborator).

Durocher next describes Laraine sensing Rickey as a false friend. He quotes his wife: "'Rickey speaks with a forked tongue. I know the type. We have them in the Mormon Church, too.'"

He is setting up a story of betrayal. Leo, the wronged knight, forced out of Brooklyn by the evil parson, Wesley Branch Rickey. That version is rather less than the whole story.

Jackie Robinson was the future in Brooklyn. You didn't have

to be a superscout to realize that. The Dodgers set up a spring base in Santo Domingo in 1948, specifically to avoid racial explosions in the South. Robinson had finished the 1947 season at a lean, hard 185 pounds. He showed up in the Dominican Republic at 210, a full 25 pounds over good playing weight.

The Dodgers paid Robinson $5,000 for 1947. With success came invitations to speak, to put on batting exhibitions, to appear onstage. Robinson needed money; he accepted every offer. As the black journalist Carl Rowan observed, "Jackie's admirers fed him until he was fat and futile."

Robinson loved to eat; rich meals abrim with sugars, starches, cholesterol. His attack on a wedge of apple pie, topped with two scoops of vanilla ice cream, was an exercise in passion. His discipline had been saintly across the season of 1947. After the World Series, it collapsed.

Rickey was disappointed, a fact he registered by putting Robinson on the waiver list. Any National League team could purchase Robinson's contract for $10,000 in 1948 unless Rickey withdrew his name from the waiver list within twenty-four hours of the claim. Nobody, not one of the seven other ball-clubs in the league, bothered to claim the great Jackie Robinson.

For his part, Durocher raged. "That colored son of a bitch stayed in shape for Shotton, who meant nothing. I'm the guy who knocked down the petition. I'm the guy who fought for Robinson. And when he shows up to play for me, he looks like a black tub of lard."

Durocher ordered Robinson to put on a tan rubber shirt that covered the entire upper body and arms. He stationed Robinson between first and second base and hit ground balls to Robinson's right and left. The temperature on the Caribbean field approached 90 degrees. Durocher ran Robinson back and forth, barking constantly: "Move, Robinson. Move. There's plenty of fat left back in the States. Leave some of *your* fat in Santo Domingo."

Whoosh. A grass-cutting hopper to Robinson's left.

Whoosh. A grass cutter to the right.

Overall, Durocher's ringing voice kept bawling. "Move it, fat boy. Move it."

After hours of this daily routine, Durocher turned to the press. "That's enough for the fat boy today, fellers. Stick a fork in him. He's done."

By the time the Dodgers broke camp at Santo Domingo, Robinson had lost fifteen pounds. He remained ten pounds overweight. And he and Durocher were locked into a blood feud that lasted for six years.

"I was wrong to report overweight," Robinson said long afterwards, "but Durocher was wrong to humiliate me, every day, in front of the other ballplayers, in front of the rookies, in front of the sportswriters. To tell the truth, I hated the loud-mouthed bastard."

With manager and star not speaking, the Dodgers started miserably in 1948. In July, with the best talent in the league, the team was tied for fourth, eight and a half games behind the first-place Boston Braves. The Dodgers were tied with the New York Giants, by far the best home-run-hitting team in baseball and just about the slowest.

Manager Mel Ott had joined the Giants in 1926, as a teenager. At the age of twenty Ott, a solid right fielder, hit forty-two home runs and batted in 152 runs. Across his career, he hit 511 homers. The Giants appointed him manager in 1942 and he brought the team home third. After that Ott's Giants finished last on two occasions. They usually lost more ballgames than they won.

By 1948, with a powerful and expensive Giant ballclub going sideways, Horace Stoneham decided he had to make a change. He had known Ott since childhood. Ott was one of the most pleasant people on earth, but he wasn't what Stoneham needed: a winning manager.

Burt Shotton *was* a winning manager. Or so he appeared. He'd brought the Dodgers home first in '47. One day early in July of 1948, Stoneham telephoned Branch Rickey: "I want permission to negotiate with Shotton. I'd like to bring him to the Polo Grounds."

"Shotton is under contract to the Brooklyn club," Rickey said. "At the moment, he's working as my chief scout."

"I want him to manage," Stoneham said.

"He's not available."

"Damn," Stoneham said.

After a pause, Rickey said, "If you're interested in somebody else, we might come to an agreement."

"Who?" Stoneham said.

"Leo Durocher."

Rickey's idea was for Durocher to resign. On July 4, he sent that request to his manager through Harold Parrott, the Dodgers' traveling secretary. "I hate to tell you this," Parrott said in Durocher's office under the first base stands at Ebbets Field. "But I gotta. Mr. Rickey wants you to quit. He says don't worry. He's got something else for you that you'll like."

"Harold, tell the old bastard that if he wants me to resign, damn it, I will, but he's gotta have the guts to come down here and tell me himself."

"Mr. Rickey is away for a few days. He's on the farm he bought in Maryland."

"Wait a minute," Durocher shouted. "I won't resign. He's gonna have to fire me and he's gonna have to do it man to man."

Fencing went on for several days.

"What is Leo going to do?" Rickey said. "Give me both barrels? Tell him I need more time to work out a special deal. Tell him I say to win ballgames. Win and keep on winning."

"Keep winning?" Durocher bawled at Parrott. "Nobody knows better than that old bastard, that if I knew he was gonna fire me in the third inning — Poof! Out of work and on the street in the third! — I'd still be trying to score ten runs for him in the second!"

Durocher flew off to St. Louis on July 13 to manage the

National League team in the All-Star Game. Stan Musial hit a two-run homer for Durocher, but the American Leaguers under Bucky Harris won, 5 to 2. Writers second-guessed Durocher's lineup. They wondered why in the sixth inning, with the bases loaded and two out, he had not used Ralph Kiner or Sid Gordon to pinch hit for Richie Ashburn. Kiner and Gordon were long-ball hitters. Ashburn struck out.

Durocher's mood was foul. When he returned to Brooklyn, Rickey ordered him into the Dodger office at 215 Montague Street. He offered Durocher Horace Stoneham's unlisted number. "If you're interested in managing the Giants, you have only to call him," Rickey said.

"Gimme the number," Durocher said. He telephoned the president of the Giants from the office of the president of the Dodgers. "Sure, I'll manage for ya," Durocher said.

"We have to meet," Stoneham said. "Someplace quiet. We don't need press here yet."

"My place," Durocher said. "I live at 46 East 61st Street. See ya there in half an hour."

The Dodgers were playing in Cincinnati. (Rickey had told reporters that Durocher was "off on a special scouting trip to find the right young players to help the Dodgers get back into first place.")

Horace Stoneham beat Durocher to the East 61st Street apartment. He introduced himself to Laraine Day Durocher and asked for a drink. "I'm waiting for Leo to get here," Stoneham said. "I expect he'll be managing the Giants tomorrow."

The radio console was tuned to WHN, 1050, which carried Red Barber's broadcast of the Dodgers' game at Cincinnati. Laraine walked briskly to the set. "Then why am I listening to this?" She clicked off the radio and said easily, "Scotch, Mr. Stoneham, or bourbon?"

On Saturday, July 17, 1948, the front page of the *Daily News* cried out:

LIP REPLACES OTT!
BURT BACK WITH FLOCK!!

The *Herald Tribune* also played the story on the front page, but more sedately:

DUROCHER REPLACES OTT AS MANAGER OF GIANTS
RICKEY BRINGS SHOTTON BACK TO PILOT DODGERS

Horace Stoneham was so upset at dismissing Mel Ott that he announced, even as he introduced Durocher, that the Giants were retiring Ott's uniform number "in tribute," Stoneham said, "by golly, to a swonnerful guy."

Some Dodgers, notably Jackie Robinson, felt relieved. "I loved playing for Shotton," Robinson said. "It's gonna be a lot different. When Shotton bawls out a player, he takes him aside and does it in private. If Leo has something on his mind, you hear about it in front of everybody."

Gene Hermanski, the outfielder, said, "It makes no difference, none at all. All I want to know is who's pitching."

Ralph Branca said, a little glumly, "You have to play as hard for one as you do for the other."

Carl Furillo, who five years later would assault Durocher at the Polo Grounds, sounded philosophical. "Hell, may the best man win."

The Giant players truly were shaken. Everybody liked Mel Ott. The team was in Pittsburgh, staying at the Hotel Schenley, a block and a half from Forbes Field. Al Laney wrote: "It was as though a wake were being held in the lobby. Men sat around or wandered around, saying nothing. Ott was through. The players had an air of bereavement, as though a well-loved member of the family had died suddenly and unexpectedly. Most appeared stunned."

As soon as Durocher flew into Pittsburgh, he called a team meeting. "You're a good ballclub," he said, "but from now on I want more life out on the field. I want more spark."

"Cooper." This to Walker Cooper, the mighty catcher. "You're a good ballplayer, Coop, but from now on when a pitcher throws up a lazy pitch, I want you to fire that baseball back at him. Wake him up.

"Mize." To Johnny Mize, the huge first baseman. "You're no Hal Chase [a legendary great fielder] out there, but you're a good ballplayer and a wonderful hitter. I want you to show some *life* out there."

One by one Durocher went down the Giant lineup, mixing criticism with controlled praise.

"And tonight," he said, "we're really gonna show the people something. Winning baseball. Winning baseball, gentlemen." That night it rained and the game had to be postponed.

Later in a suite at the Schenley, Durocher sat soberly with Stoneham and a few friendly, hard-drinking writers. "Pally," Stoneham said. "Tell me the truth. What do you really think of this team?"

"The truth?"

"Sure, pally. The truth is what I want."

Durocher issued a withering critique. "Back up the truck."

"Whas that, pally?"

"He means a moving van, Horace," the columnist Bill Corum said. "He wants some changes. He wants to ship some people out."

"Back up the truck," Leo Durocher repeated.

Harry Truman said the state of the nation worried him. The Republicans and a number of southern democrats were trying "to fool the people with poppycock." Truman urged Congress to reconvene, in the heat of midsummer, and pass legislation "that deals with eight critical areas."

1. Control skyrocketing prices. Sirloin steak had reached $1.10 a pound.

2. Provide housing to ease the present shortage. Home construction had stopped during World War II. Now, three years after the war, couples were crammed in with parents and grandparents.

3. Increase federal aid to education.

4. Provide a national health insurance program. Doctors were charging more and more; surgical fees were getting ridiculous. The medical monopoly hooted at national health insurance as "creeping socialism."

5. Guarantee civil rights. The Jackie Robinson experience was echoing through America.

6. Increase minimum wages. How else could you afford $1.10 a pound for sirloin steak?

7. Broaden social security coverage. Large numbers of small businessmen and independent contractors were unprotected.

8. Fight the utility monopolies by providing more low-cost public power "through quasi-government agencies like the Tennessee Valley Authority."

"The Democrats clearly are desperate," began a statement from the Republican National Committee. "They know that this President is sure to be voted out of office in November" [when the Republicans would run mustached Tom Dewey].

The next day the *Daily News* skipped the political debate. But the *News* ran an editorial on the Durocher-Shotton switch. The headline announced: REALLY MOMENTOUS NEWS!

The Dodgers played better baseball for Shotton than they had for Durocher, but they could catch neither the Braves, who won the pennant, nor the St. Louis Cardinals. Incredibly, a superb Brooklyn team finished no better than third.

The Giants played better baseball for Durocher than they had for Mel Ott, but only slightly. The team finished one game above .500, in fifth place. With such mighty musclemen as Cooper and Mize, the Giants hit 164 home runs, better than 50 homers more than any other team in the league. (The winning Braves hit 95.) But the mighty musclemen couldn't run much. The wisecrack said that Mize and Cooper could score *only* when they homered. Their top speed was a walk around the bases.

Durocher didn't like slow-moving baseball. "What are your plans?" a reporter asked as the season waned.

"I got plans," Durocher said. "You can damn well bet on that. I'm gonna put a better ballclub in the Polo Grounds."

"What kind of ballclub, Leo?"

"I'll tell you what," Durocher roared. "My kind of team."

Some writers laughed at Leo the Loud. The laughter did not finally die down until three seasons later when Leo, helped by the young and the swift, Mays and Lockman and Thomson, passed the Little Miracle of Coogan's Bluff.

The year 1948 was a rare triumph for out-of-towners. In St. Louis, Stan Musial slugged and poked his way to just about the best season any hitter ever had. Musial led the National League in batting (.376); slugging percentage (.702), hits (230) doubles (46), triples (18), runs scored (135), and runs batted in (131). He hit 39 home runs, one fewer than Johnny Mize and Ralph Kiner, who shared the title at 40. "Actually," Musial says, "I hit forty-one homers in 1948, but I lost two when games got rained out. If it hadn't been for the rain, I would have led the league in every single batting category that there was."

Cleveland won the American League pennant and defeated the Boston Braves, four games to two, in the World Series.

No one imagined — it was beyond imagining — that nine years would pass before a ballclub not based in New York City won the Series again.

7

The Second Coming

◆

The old Yankee tradition ceased to exist
several years ago. There is, therefore, nothing
incongruous in the notion of a comedian
running the Yankees.
— *Red Smith on Casey Stengel,*
October 14, 1948

THE LATE JOHN LARDNER, whose sportswriting is an
overlooked American treasure, knew Casey Stengel better
than Casey Stengel wanted to be known. Like most, Lardner admired Stengel as a manager and, to a smaller degree, as
a humorist. Uniquely among the admirers thronged in Manhattan, Lardner had known Stengel since his own childhood
and even, in a sense, before.

John's father, Ring Lardner, was Stengel's contemporary —
the two were born four years apart — and Ring was already
established in sports journalism when Stengel crashed into
the major leagues, with lots of line drives, some neat running catches, and, Stengel being Stengel, rivers of verbiage.
"Dutch" Stengel intrigued the elder Lardner. Indeed, Ring
Lardner used Stengel as a character in his final baseball novel,
a touching seriocomic work called *Lose with a Smile*. (In today's
climate, such genial literary license would loose a legion of
lawyers on all our heads.)

John Lardner, who grew up amid his father's Stengel stories, was a bit put off by the sports page bouquets that at length commenced to fall at Stengel's feet.* As we shall see, Stengel was delightful, vindictive, cordial, alcoholic, calculating, and thoroughly mean. Press portraits were sometimes tin-eared, often downright misleading.

The young Stengel broke in with the Brooklyn Dodgers in 1912 and a season later became the original center fielder at Ebbets Field, a direct ancestor of the last center fielder there, Duke Snider. Stengel's salary as a Dodger never exceeded $5,400, good for the time but not suitable for Stengel's lifestyle. As a young player, Stengel loved dice, poker, hand-tailored suits, and whiskey. With his expenses exceeding income in 1914, Stengel cashed a number of bad checks at a bar on Flatbush Avenue, the Broadway, so to speak, of Brooklyn. As the bar owner protested, Stengel promised to cover the rubber with the proceeds of his next Dodger stipend. Meanwhile, here was another check for $100. Sure it was good. Whadaya think! Thanks a lot. Now gimme an Ol' Overholt.

After three months of this, the saloonkeeper grew desperate. One morning he taped the bad checks — there were more than twenty — to the window of his bar. Passersby on a broad and busy Brooklyn avenue saw two items of interest in the window, each repeated many times: a genuine autograph of Charles D. Stengel; a bank stamp reading INSUFFICIENT FUNDS.

By the time Lardner told me this story, in 1960, Stengel not only was being acclaimed as the greatest manager in modern baseball; he was also president of a bank in Glendale, California. "From bad check passer to bank president in fifty years," Lardner said. "I think if you could get that on paper, with a

---

*Lardner was particularly annoyed by Arthur Daley, the genial and inept sports columnist for the *New York Times*, who wrote enraptured accounts of a saintly Casey. Groping toward realism, Daley spelled one verb coming out of Stengel's mouth "w-u-z." "Now how else would you spell that word?" John Lardner asked me. "W-a-s?" That was Lardner's only comment on Daley's efforts to reproduce Stengelese.

little baseball, you'd have a book about Stengel and in a way about America."

A lot was going on around us. Literary editors of the time spoke frequently about someone composing "the great American baseball novel." Several even offered small advances. "We want," one editor said, "the baseball novel Thomas Wolfe would have written if Thomas Wolfe had written a baseball novel. We're willing to offer twelve hundred dollars up front."

John Lardner felt that in *You Know Me Al*, his father had already written the great American baseball novel. He was himself a meticulous and disciplined writer, and as such no great fan of Thomas Wolfe. Finally, as a gifted essayist, John resented America's worship of the novel, a rival form.

Why didn't I try and see if I could write the great American *nonfiction* book, framed about Stengel's picaresque life? Lardner's health was failing. The project was quite beyond his energies. I was younger, stronger, promising in certain ways, prolific.

The idea was John Lardner's final gift to me. A month later, he was dead at the age of forty-seven.

Stengel was a student of sportswriting, specifically sportswriting about himself. He could have given President Kennedy lessons in manipulating the media. He was kind to me, even when I wrote critically about the Yankees, but as far as Stengel was concerned, two things were loudly wrong with John Lardner's idea. Stengel's bad-check days had been forgotten by the 1950s. Stengel meant for those days to stay forgotten. He didn't want a serious, dimensional, variegated book written about him, or even by him. He preferred something adoring and drippy, along the lines of *A Boy's Life of Theodore Roosevelt*. So, he explained over breakfast in his suite at the Essex House one October morning, "I like ya fine, kid, but I ain't gonna help you do no book about me and I don't want you trying to get with my brother or my wife, neither, because they won't talk to you, I told them not to, and it's nothing against you personal, kid. Why ain't you eating your eggs?"

As I say, Stengel's first objection was directed against my bent toward adult reporting. His second was entirely impersonal. My projected book would not earn him any money.

In 1961, after Stengel collected a $150,000 advance from Random House and *The Saturday Evening Post*, there appeared a putative memoir called *Casey at the Bat: The Story of My Life in Baseball*, written with Harry T. Paxton, who was sports editor at the magazine.

Trying to change substance, look, and image in one majestic swoop, the directors of the *Post* announced that on September 16, 1961, the "new" *Saturday Evening Post* would be "like no magazine you ever read before." Indeed, they promised that with the September 16 issue, "Suddenly reading becomes an adventure!" The centerpiece of that issue was a long excerpt from the drab and drippy Stengel-Paxton book.

Above the blaring ballyhoo for the "new" magazine, someone remarked, "Harry Paxton has achieved the impossible. He's made Casey Stengel dull." Criticism of the old *Saturday Evening Post* maintained that the magazine was mostly trivial and usually flat. The new *Post* offered glitzy layouts, including a full-page color photograph of Stengel sniffing a red rose. But the story — and the *Post* was a storytelling magazine — was sheer old *Post*. The Madison Avenue crowd, whose advertising dollars were lifeblood to the magazine, laughed at — not with — the memoir. "How come the 'new' *Post* reads worse than the 'old' *Post*?" ran the gibe.

The new-old *Saturday Evening Post* went into a tailspin from which it never recovered. Stengel went on to manage the Mets with astonishing good humor.

The old man outlived *The Saturday Evening Post* by fully six years.

Casey Stengel, circa 1948, had not yet gone cosmic. He was famous in a minor way as a quintessential old Dodger, a good but less than great ballplayer, and assuredly a bit daft. (Writers called long-ago Brooklyn teams "the daffiness boys.") Once Stengel tipped his hat to a Brooklyn crowd and a sparrow flew out. To this day, I am not certain how he trapped the bird. When I asked, Stengel said, quite clearly, with none of his customary curlicues or detours, "I don't want to talk about that anymore. There were funnier things when I was in Brooklyn."

"Such as?"

"Well, one day I'm in a hurry to leave Ebbets Field and I forget my wallet. I'm on the street with a lot of stuff and there, on Bedford Avenue, is a nice-looking kid on a bicycle. I want to run back without carrying stuff so I say to the kid, 'Here. Hold my glove. I'll be right back.'

"I get my wallet and run back to the corner. The kid and the bike and my glove — they're all gone. And you know the lesson I learned from that, that I never forgot to this day?"

"What's the lesson, Case?"

"Never trust a boy on a bicycle."

As Jimmy Durante said of his own jokes, Casey had a million of 'em. But with all the fun and even some success in Brooklyn — the team won the pennant in 1916 — center fielder Stengel was forever running out of money. He was disinclined to change his lifestyle, cut back on the gambling and the rest. Instead he muttered and roared that Charley Ebbets, who ran the Dodgers, was a cheapskate. That was so, and all the more reason why Ebbets did not like to hear it. In 1918 Ebbets shipped Stengel to the Pittsburgh Pirates, who presently sent him to Philadelphia, a club that dealt Stengel to the New York Giants on July 1, 1921.

Stengel gave the Giants two good seasons. On October 10, 1923, in the first World Series game at Yankee Stadium, his playing career reached a climax. The Stadium was new and vast and the largest crowd in baseball history, 55,307, herded into the Bronx. The Yankees, with Babe Ruth, were brash, muscular, nouveau. The Giants, under John McGraw, were old New York.

With the game tied, 4 to 4, in the ninth inning, Stengel came to bat in an unpromising situation. Two men were out. The bases were empty. "Bullet Joe" Bush, the Yankee pitcher, threw a three and two fastball on the outside corner. "I threw it as hard as I could," Bush said later.

Stengel, a left-handed batter, crashed the ball on a long high line into left center field. No one has described what happened more grandly than Damon Runyon in the New York *American*. Runyon wrote:

> This is the way old "Casey" Stengel ran yesterday afternoon running his home run.
> This is the way old "Casey" Stengel ran running his home run home in a Giant victory by a score of 5 to 4 in the first game of the world's series of 1923.
> This is the way old "Casey" ran, running his home run home, when two were out in the ninth inning and the score was tied and the ball was still bounding inside the Yankee yard.
> This is the way —
> His mouth wide open.
> His warped old legs bending beneath him at every stride.
> His arms flying back and forth like those of a man swimming with a crawl stroke.
> His flanks heaving, his breath whistling, his head far back.

Such is the stuff of legend. Stengel won the third game for the Giants, 1 to 0, when he cracked a home run into the right field bleachers at Yankee Stadium. Two home runs in a single World Series was extraordinary, but in the end, magnificent though Casey was, the Yankees won, four games to two, and the Yankees' star slugger outdid Stengel. Babe Ruth hit *three* homers. Summing up, Heywood Broun wrote in the New York *World*, "The Ruth is mighty and shall prevail."

In 1924, when he was thirty-four years old, Stengel married Edna Lawson of Glendale, California. Edna was a tall, willowy sometime actress who came from a monied background. The family's wedding gift to the couple was a two-story house on Grandview Avenue in Glendale, surrounded by flower gardens and citrus trees. The property included a swimming pool and a tennis court. Ring Lardner's rascally check bouncer was poor no more. Soon Stengel was investing in oil wells, real estate, and the family bank. His brother Grant had to drive a taxi in Kansas City to survive, but by the time "Dutch" Stengel reached the age of forty, he could have settled back into the life of a California squire. Almost all the investments paid handsomely. He had become a wealthy man.

But by nature he was an anti-squire. He needed tumult. He managed at Worcester and Toledo, drinking hard, brawling, often winning. The Dodgers hired Stengel to manage in 1934 and he held the Brooklyn job for three seasons. He finished sixth, fifth, and seventh. He was fired.

The Boston Bees hired him to manage in 1938 and he held that position twice as long. Under Stengel, the Bees finished fifth once, sixth once, and seventh four times. What everyone remembered was the tough wit. The Boston right fielder, Max West, was no Carl Furillo. West could hit and that was all. In pursuit of a fly ball one afternoon, West ran head first into an outfield wall. Stretcher bearers toted West from the field. Stengel looked down at his right fielder, who was moaning in pain, and remarked, "You got a great pair of hands, Max."

Stengel went back to the minor leagues, first with the Milwaukee Brewers and the Kansas City Blues of the American Association and then with the Oakland Oaks of the Pacific Coast League. Inside baseball, the Coast League was called "the Brother-in-Laws League." Old ballplayers seemed to gravitate toward California, and their style of play was less than fierce. Pitchers didn't throw at batters. No one tried to knock down a second baseman on a double play.

In 1948, when Stengel was fifty-eight years old, he flowered. His Oakland team, mostly gentle veterans with the exception of the second baseman, won 114 games, the pennant and the playoffs. (The second baseman, a loudmouthed twenty-year-old named Alfred Manuel Pesano, became famous in later years as Billy Martin.)

"The thing which is very good managing in Oakland," Stengel said, "is there is this bridge from Oakland to San Francisco, that is a very long bridge. Now it maybe don't matter much just how long it is, but when you're a manager, if you get my drift, it's a good idea to be near a bridge, *any* bridge."

When the Yankees brought Stengel to New York and a press conference at the 21 Club on October 12, 1948, Arthur Patterson, the team publicist, tried to stress Stengel's hard baseball background. "It's twenty-five years to the day," Patterson said, "since Casey hit his second homer in the 1923 World Series."

"Yeah," Casey said. "Arthur was trying. But I know writers and I kept hearing a hum from writers in the room. And the writers were looking at me, damn near sixty years old, and they're saying, in this hum: 'That old bum managed nine years before in the major leagues and he never once got out of the second division.'"

"Stengel. You were asking me about Stengel. . . . When George Weiss signed him, we had a problem. Drinking? No, it wasn't Casey's drinking. He could handle the stuff. It was everybody else's drinking. Ballplayers' drinking. That was part of it." The speaker was Arthur E. Patterson, a bright, abrasive character from Long Island, once a sound baseball writer for the *Herald Tribune,* but by 1948 publicity director of the Yankees. Prior to the Era, ballclubs assigned a minor official, usually the traveling secretary, to shepherd and corrupt the press, as a sidebar to such other duties as booking hotel rooms and assigning Pullman berths. (Rookies had to sleep in uppers; rebels were sentenced to berths over the clattering wheels.)

Skilled traveling secretaries — Eddie Brannick of the Giants was the best — bought meals and drinks for sportswriters, the basic device employed in keeping a benign press nonmalignant. "Ya got everything you need? We'll have dinner next week. Bring yer wife. What? Ya short a couple bucks. Say, here's a fifty, and don't worry about it. If ya can't give it back, the New York Giants won't come looking for ya." Such was the state of the art.

After World War II, the Yankees hired Patterson as publicity director. "I invented the damn job," Patterson said when we talked in 1991. "I was the first full-time press agent in baseball history." Coincidental with Patterson's emergence, reporters, editors, and publishers were struggling toward the beginnings of self-discipline. It was then that the *Herald Tribune*, the *Times*, and later the *Daily News* started paying travel expenses for their writers. Subsequently, several reporters wrote hard-nosed stories about Larry MacPhail's drunken breakdown.*

"What I did," Patterson said, as we lunched at a restaurant near his home in Anaheim, California, "is what today people call managing news. I'm not apologizing. I was damn good at managing news.

"Look, I saw that the Yankees were not just competing against the Giants and the Dodgers. They were competing against every leisure-time activity that you have in summer. If you decided to go to Jones Beach, you didn't go to Yankee Stadium. You didn't buy our tickets, pay our parking charge, eat our hot dogs, or drink our beer. I was trying to make the Yankees more interesting than the Giants *and* Jones Beach as well.

"In '49, we had a lot of injuries. Some — DiMaggio's heel — were serious. Some weren't. But I got the idea of keeping count on any injury more serious than a shaving nick. Mel Parnell and Bob Lemon [premiere pitchers] can't stop Casey's Yankees. Neither can Ol' Man Injury Jinx. Come to think of it, I may have *counted* shaving nicks. The total came to seventy-

---

*Writing about drunkenness had been absolutely beyond the bounds of sports pages. The famous Yankee manager Joe McCarthy went on a bender during spring training in 1938 and failed to show up at the ballpark for five days. The few reporters who mentioned that manager McCarthy was missing from the Yankee bench attributed his absence to "Florida flu."

one, about one injury every other day. The writers ate it up. Come to Yankee Stadium and see the walking wounded hit home runs. You couldn't see that at the Polo Grounds or at Jones Beach State Park, either.

"When Mantle came up, we knew he could hit very long homers. I made a point of leaving the ballparks [after homers went out] and measuring them, down to the last inch. Or so I told the writers. Did that get ink! Duke Snider hit very long home runs for the Dodgers, but nobody in the Brooklyn organization realized the extra press mileage they could get with a two-dollar tape measure . . ."

The 1948 Yankees finished third behind Cleveland and the Boston Red Sox, and attendance reached a club record, 2,373,901.* But dour George Weiss thought that numbers of players — reliever Joe Page, left fielder Johnny Lindell — were drinking too much. He wasn't happy with Joe DiMaggio running after showgirls. "Bucky Harris," pronounced George Weiss, "is too damn easygoing. He's lost control of the team."

Harris had to go, Weiss decided, and his employers, Dan Topping and Del Webb, agreed. Casey Stengel and George Weiss had known each other for more than twenty years, at least since Stengel managed Worcester in the Eastern League (he finished fourth) and Weiss operated the New Haven franchise. Across decades they had stayed in touch, Comical Casey and Glum George, an early odd couple. Stengel's Oakland Acorns won 114 games in the Pacific Coast League in 1948, the year in which Stengel celebrated his fifty-eighth birthday. Wealthy now, successful in California, Stengel was finally considering retirement when Weiss offered him baseball's golden apple, the Yankee job. "I at once commenced not thinking of retirement," Stengel said.

This would make Stengel the fifth Yankee manager in four

---

*The record was not broken until 1979 when a well-remembered Yankee ballclub, starring Reggie Jackson and Lou Piniella and managed by Bob Lemon and Billy Martin, drew 2,537,765. Curiously that Yankee team finished no better than fourth.

seasons, troubling to many connected with a team once as stable as Gibraltar. In a series of private meetings, Webb, Topping, and Weiss on one side and Stengel on the other agreed on a two-year contract calling for about $35,000 a season. A two-year contract, Red Patterson argued, would show that stability was returning to the Bronx.

In truth, the situation remained uncertain and Stengel's previous record as a major league manager was not comforting. "What we did about them particular matters," Stengel told me years later, "is a kind of verbal agreement, the owners, Mr. Weiss, and me. If in one year, they didn't like my work, or if I didn't like their baseball methods, I could leave or be removed and so forth, without hard feelings, which you did not know before, because it is a bad custom to talk about private agreements, which you yourself know very well and cannot argue with."

At one point, Weiss showed Stengel dossiers that two private detectives had compiled for him on a number of players — "night crawlers" in the argot of the time. "I don't like what I read here," Weiss said. Although he himself had been a ranking night crawler. Stengel said he would address the problem. He didn't personally favor private detectives, although Weiss would continue to employ them. Stengel's device for getting players into their hotel rooms before dawn was more direct. He sat in a prominent place in hotel lobbies into the wee hours. Like everyone else, the players knew he was there. Anyone coming in late had to walk past the manager and endure withering Stengel sarcasm.

"When the hiring was settled, we decided to have a press conference," Red Patterson remembered. "We knew that Casey could be funny. Weiss said he was a great baseball man. Still, we were nervous. The writers might kill us for firing Harris, a sweet guy. We spread the word Harris wasn't coming back during the World Series, when the writers were preoccupied with Lou Boudreau and Warren Spahn.

"Then we scheduled Stengel's conference for lunchtime.

More free food and free drink for the writers. We hired the 21 Club. We were the Yankees. We went first class. The day we picked, October 12, was one day after the World Series ended. The writers would maybe be so preoccupied wrapping up the Series that they wouldn't get around to knocking us.

"I know that sounds crazy, but there it is."

The *Herald Tribune* put the story on page one:

YANKEES NAME
STENGEL PILOT
FOR TWO YEARS

*Former Manager of Braves
and Dodgers Is Chosen
as Harris's Successor*

The piece began halfway down the front page. The *Tribune* of October 13 was more interested in Soviet and American arms negotiators ranting at one another and in Thomas E. Dewey's drab campaign to bounce Harry Truman from the White House. Stengel wasn't even the biggest story in New York City. On the day the Yankees unleashed Stengel, Columbia University installed its thirteenth president, General of the Army Dwight David Eisenhower. With an audience of 20,000 gathered below the steps of Low Library, the general disappointed conservatives by saying in his inaugural address: "Academic freedom includes the right to teach straightforward courses on communism."

The same day, at "21," Stengel disappointed just about everyone. Dan Topping, the Yankee president, arrived to introduce him. Topping had a brother named Bob; both Toppings had been married to a sensual brunette movie actress named Arlene Judge. But where Dan became a working baseball man, Bob Topping's ambitions led him toward nothing but a lush life. The brothers were not close.

Dan Topping introduced Stengel as the man who's going "to lead our great Yankee ballclub to a pennant."

Lips pressed together in tension, Stengel moved to the mi-

Perhaps the greatest hitter of the Era,
Stan "the Man" Musial of the St. Louis
Cardinals. (*Courtesy of the National
Baseball Hall of Fame Library,
Cooperstown, New York*)

(*Top left*) Bobby Thomson's famous home run wins the 1951 pennant for the Giants at the Polo Grounds.

(*Bottom left*) Recovered from a knee that was injured during the second game of the 1951 Series, Mickey Mantle spent the winter working in a lead mine near Commerce, Oklahoma. Here he poses with his father, Elvin "Mutt" Mantle, left, and veteran Yankee outfielder Cliff Mapes.

(*Above*) In the racially charged South, Pee Wee Reese and Jackie Robinson stretch together during spring training at Vero Beach, Florida, 1952. (*Courtesy of Mark Reese*)

(*Above*) Two friends, two Hall of Famers: Jackie Robinson and Pee Wee Reese. (*Courtesy of Mark Reese*)

(*Top right*) The New York press corps meets with Leo Durocher at Phoenix in 1954. From left, Milton Gross, *New York Post*; Louis Effrat, *New York Times*; Jim McCulley, *Daily News*; Joe King, *New York World-Telegram*; Barney Kremenko, *New York Journal-American*; Durocher; Mel Woody, *Newark Star-Ledger*; Charles Feeney, *Long Island Press*; Arch Murray, *New York Post*; Ken Smith, *Daily Mirror*; and the author, in jacket and tie, representing the *New York Herald Tribune*. (*Courtesy of the author*)

(*Bottom right*) Despite a relatively undistinguished record of 81 wins and 91 losses in fifteen major-league seasons, Don Larsen achieved immortality when he pitched a perfect game against the Dodgers in the 1956 World Series.

Known as the "Reading Rifle" for his strong throwing arm, Carl Furillo, during a fourteen-year career with the Dodgers, was also a good hitter with some power and base-running speed—but he never quite fit in with the Boys of Summer.

Jackie Robinson and the author on the grounds of Robinson's home in Stamford, Connecticut. Photo was taken in 1970. Robinson died two years later.

crophone. He looked at his employer Dan Topping and said, "Thank you, Bob."

Nervous laughter.

"Uh, Dan. I am happy to be back in New York, which is where I played before. I had some other offers regarding managing, but I didn't want to leave Oakland, where the owner has been very good." After a while, he threw the room open for questions.

"What are your plans for the Yankees?"

"I, uh, last seen the Yankees play a couple years back. Now I must study the Yankee situation and then, uh, I will commence to draw conclusions."

To indicate old guard support for the new man, Topping asked DiMaggio to linger in Manhattan and attend the Stengel press conference. DiMaggio sat quietly on the dais.

"What do you think about managing a great player like Joe DiMaggio?" a reporter asked Stengel.

"I can't tell you much about that, being as since I have not been in the American League so I ain't seen the gentleman play, except once in a very great while."

DiMaggio, with an ego as mighty as his bat, grimaced. In their few years together, he and Stengel never got along.

Then it was done. In half an hour Stengel had gotten the boss's name wrong and offended the biggest star in town.

This is the way old Casey Stengel stumbled at "21" on the first day of the biggest job of his life.

This is the way —
His mouth wide open
His warped old tongue
    Saying
       the
          wrong
             bloody
thing.

"Most observers," commented John Drebinger, senior baseball writer at *The New York Times*, "were kindly disposed toward Stengel. But after that press conference they were view-ing his forthcoming performance with misgivings."

"I knew what I was getting," George Weiss insisted twen-ty years later. "I was not hiring a comedian. In the minors Casey was wonderful working with veterans and great with difficult youngsters like Billy Martin, too. Nobody pushed Casey around.

"He had an uncanny knack for getting the right hitter up at the right moment, handling pitching, running a game. He had been studying for years. He had learned a lot from John Mc-Graw. Everybody agreed that Casey did a wonderful managing job his first Yankee season. But what did they think, that he learned how to manage, all at once, in 1949?"

After the press conference, Stengel retreated. This tough, competitive roustabout was hired not to charm the press or, as some have suggested, ex post facto, to humanize "the lordly Yankees." Weiss hired Stengel to win the pennant. That was the sine qua non. If Stengel finished second — far higher than he ever had finished before in the major leagues — he would be fired.

"Late in that season," Stengel later said, "everyone was talk-ing about platooning the players, which I very much did, but we come to a point against Boston where it come down to this: I had to win two games to win the pennant. I was gonna platoon myself out of a job, or platoon myself in, which is what hap-pened as I am certain you recall."

As a rookie manager, Stengel was given limited authority. Weiss would listen to Stengel on trades and even a bit on whom the Yankees might hire as coaches. But the decisions were made by Weiss.

"I know the league better than you," Weiss said.

"Yes, sir, you do," Stengel said. "But there is one pitching coach, who has been working in Portland, Oregon, which is very good."

Stengel recommended Jim Turner, gruff, gray-haired Milk-man Jim, who had had one fine year with the Boston Bees and had closed out his career as a wartime reliever for the Yankees. Turner came from outside the Yankee establishment but Weiss respected his work and hired him. Weiss then told Stengel that Bill Dickey, the greatest catcher in Yankee history, would be another coach, along with bald, quiet Frank Crosetti, who had played shortstop across seventeen seasons. Between them, Dickey and "Crow" had spent thirty-four years as major league ballplayers. Neither had played an inning for any team except the New York Yankees. Weiss was blending his roustabout manager with pillars of Yankee tradition. But the world was less than awed.

"Well, sirs and ladies," wrote Dave Egan in the Boston *Record*, "the Yankees have now been mathematically eliminated from the 1949 pennant race. They eliminated themselves when they engaged Perfesser Casey Stengel to mismanage them for the next two years and you may be sure the perfesser will oblige to the best of his unique ability." As Frank Graham, Jr., commented in *Casey Stengel*, the most winning and insightful of the Stengel biographies, "Uneasy lay the crown upon this old gray head."

Stengel spent the winter quietly getting ready to become a manager in New York, meeting from time to time with baseball men, gathering information on Yankee ballplayers, players he had seldom seen at work. He joined the Yankee delegation at the baseball winter meetings in Chicago, where Weiss made a questionable trade. He gave the St. Louis Browns Sherman Lollar, a promising catcher, two other players, and $100,000 for a pitcher named Fred Sanford. The season before, Sanford attracted attention by starting thirty-three games for the Browns and losing twenty-one. In 1948, Fred Sanford led the major leagues in losses.

Red Patterson told the writers that Sanford was "a great acquisition. Last year, like somebody's ex-wife," Patterson said, "he shoulda sued the Browns for non-support. Whenever he pitched, all those Brownie fielders went to sleep." But remember that two measures of pitching are essentially independent of position players. A pitcher should allow fewer than one hit an inning and should strike out more batters than he walks. Sanford allowed 250 hits in 227 innings; he struck out 79 batters but walked 91. His greatest merits, on the record, seemed to be that he was inclined to go to bed early and he didn't drink much. If Stengel wondered about this curious acquisition, he kept his counsel. Writers who pressed him in the lobby of the Blackstone Hotel gained neither jokes nor specifics. "There is very many good ballplayers on the New York Yankees," he said. "More than I ever managed on one team before. I think we can win."

Few newspapermen agreed. When *The Sporting News* polled 206 baseball writers, the forecast for 1949 looked like this:

1. Boston Red Sox (119 votes)
2. Cleveland Indians (79)
3. Yankees (6)

Platooning — playing more than one man at a position — traces to John McGraw, who so mightily impressed Casey decades earlier. Generally, a right-handed batter has more trouble hitting the deliveries of a right-handed pitcher than he does hitting a left-hander's stuff. (These assertions apply in exact reverse for left-handed batters.)

When a left-handed pitcher throws, the right-handed batter "sees the ball better." Actually, he picks up the baseball in flight a fraction of a second sooner than he can when facing a right-hander. An unimpeded fastball goes from pitcher's hand to catcher's glove in two-fifths of a second. Every millisecond counts.

A right-handed pitcher's curve and slider break down and away from a right-handed batter. Put simply, if you are a right-handed batter, the right-handed pitcher's curve ball starts on a collision course with your head. The left-handed pitcher's curve starts wide and then veers in. Tricky but less unsettling.

"The curve that starts at your head," said Stengel's colleague Charlie Dressen, "is so bad I call that pitch, and not John Dillinger, Public Enemy Number One."

Essentially, a manager wants to play as many right-handers as he can against a left-handed pitcher. But platooning is not simply right against left.

Batters have favorite hitting zones; there are high-ball hitters and low-ball hitters. Every batter is stronger in one zone or the other. Now suppose you are managing a team with two good left fielders. The right-hand-hitting left fielder likes low stuff. The lefty hitter paddles high balls. The rival manager starts a left-hander with a zipping high hard one. Whom do you start? The right-handed batter who prefers low stuff? He won't see low stuff, but he has an edge facing the left-handed pitcher. Or the left-handed batter who loses something to the lefty pitcher but likes swinging against the sinkers that he will see?

The equation becomes more complicated, quadratic at the least.

Left versus right.

High versus low.

Who's batting next?

Who's hot?

Who's cool?

Who's hurt?

Who just broke curfew?

Who's in their bullpen?

Who likes to pinch hit?

Who plays tomorrow?

And what about the psychology of it all?

Other extraordinary baseball men, Leo Durocher among them, felt that Stengel's creations with and about the Yankee lineup transcended managing. "The guy," Durocher said in his ceaselessly elegant way, "was a fucking genius." The course of genius never did run smooth.

Stengel met with his squad for the first time at St. Petersburg on March 1. He spoke quietly and quite clearly in the clubhouse. He had been around for a long time, he said, but he was new to the league. All the men were professional players. They were Yankees. He expected them to win. He wanted them to expect that of themselves. He was not going to make a lot of changes, Stengel said, after which he began to announce a lot of changes.

Instead of the customary single workout, he was instituting two-a-day practice sessions. "Never before," wrote James Dawson in the *Times*, "was both morning and afternoon practice known in St. Petersburg. The last time double workouts were a Yankee spring training practice was in New Orleans, 27 years ago."

Stengel decreed a midnight curfew. "Yer professionals on yer honor to keep it. Don't make us go and do bed checks now. Just keep the curfew.

"There is, uh, some concern about going to the dog track too many times a week. So the rule is, now, one night a week. That's all. Thursday night is dog track night. Other nights think about baseball, as I'm sure you will.

"We have, uh, the best group of coaches I think is available as instructors and you can learn from them. You young fellers, I expect you to be willing to learn from the many stars we have here, too, which I wished I coulda done when I was breaking in.

"Good luck.

"All right. Let's run around the field."

Stengel split the squad break into individual groups. Jim Turner met with the pitchers; Crosetti spoke with the infielders; Johnny Neun, a functionary who had managed the Yankees for fourteen games in 1946, was placed in charge of first basemen. Simple enough. Delegation of authority. But just a moment, please. Who *were* the first basemen? Before the 1949 season ended, Stengel would use seven men to play first base.

As outfield coaches-without-portfolio, Stengel appointed DiMaggio and Henrich. That raised another question. Who were the outfielders? Yogi Berra had played fifty outfield games the year before. On the other hand, Bill Dickey wanted to teach Berra catching. Stengel liked that idea. John Lindell, six foot four and 220 pounds, had come up as a hard-throwing pitcher. After that he evolved into an outfielder. What was he now?

Both?

Neither?

"Uh, Mr. DiMaggio and Mr. Henrich, you are experienced men, and would you commence working with the outfielders?"

"Sure," Henrich said. "Who are the outfielders, Skipper?"

"We will get to that matter very presently, Mr. Handricks."

DiMaggio was appalled. A few days later he asked Arthur Daley of the *Times*, "What do you think of the new manager?"

"I never saw such a bewildered guy in my life," Daley said.

"That's what I think," DiMaggio said, "and damned if the other ballplayers don't feel the same way."

I traveled with Stengel for many months in later seasons. By then he had divided the American press into categories: "my writers and the goddamn other guys, like them gentlemen from the magazines who take what you say and sit with it for a month so when they use it, everything you said comes out all twisted."

Simply by being assigned to the Yankees, I became one of "my writers." Each day Stengel made a careful effort to see that I knew what was going on. When I wrote that the team was flat, he accepted my judgment as fair comment. When I moved on, I thanked him and offered my hand. His gnarled, aged mitt met mine. "Nah, kid," he said. "I wanna thank *you*. Ya wrote splendid."

I talked to Stengel and listened to Stengel on trains and buses, in dugouts and bars. By this time he was famous and revered. He was very proud of his work with the Yankees and here is what he told me about his beginnings with the team:

"I was gonna platoon right from the start. George Weiss

knew that and I gotta say he left me alone to do that. We had differences, which I will get to, but he left me to do whichever lineups I commenced to choose.

"We had some great ballplayers, which was getting old, and whatever they felt about it, could not play in a hundred fifty-four games with the old bodies which they had.

"Take Mr. Henrich" — Stengel pronounced that name in various ways. "Handricks" became the favorite — "Mr. Henrich [who was thirty-six years old in 1949] had a knee that would get loose in its socket, although we had a very excellent trainer, Gus Mauch. So I knew Mr. Henrich would not be able to play every day and I would have to platoon him. Henrich was a very sharp hitter, who generally got the pitch he wanted. When they got two strikes on him, he fouled off pitches time and again until he finally got them to throw him the fastball he wanted. He could hit fastballs very hard. He was a great player.

"Mr. Keller" — Charlie Keller — "looked so strong they named him after the big gorilla you remember [King Kong Keller]. He was another beautiful hitter, never afraid of the ball, but he had a bad spine and after he played hard he'd get a stiff back. He couldn't sleep at night.

"These were two aged players, not their years but their bodies, and I platooned them because of that, also bearing in mind who was pitching and how these two great players would go against that pitcher.

"When a man is aged and you rest him, he will get limber again with his muscles and he runs faster and he becomes quicker with the bat. You do this, rest him good, and then his legs are fresh for five or six days.

"My other outfielder, which I would say was the most famous player in baseball, was DiMaggio, and this excellent trainer, who was working for me now, said that DiMaggio had very bad arthritis. So he would be coming up hurt, which means he would be platooning himself, if you get my drift. And DiMaggio was a very great player.

"So here is what I have, and the writers tell me this should be my outfield, for 1949: DiMaggio, Henrich, Keller. Which is all great and not a one kin play every day. Three years later they're all retired. You could look that one up, but I'm telling ya, and now some commence to write, 'What is that crazy old Stengel doing there, platooning great players like DiMaggio, Henrich, Keller?'

"If I made 'em play every day, I coulda killed them.

"I coulda killed all three. Killed them three great players.

"And what would the writers commenced to have written then, kid?

"You tell me."

The old ballplayers were tremendously significant for success in 1949, as was the Yankee team's collective sense of itself. King Kong Keller batted .389 during the Yankees' great victory over the Dodgers in 1941. Although he stood no more than five feet, ten inches, Keller was broad and massive, with thick eyebrows and a swart, intimidating look. Henrich, full-faced, a wide-framed six-footer, was such a staunch clutch hitter that he became famous, in Mel Allen's nickname, as Ol' Reliable. DiMaggio was a faultless hero to the reigning columnists, Red Smith and Jimmy Cannon, who called him Joltin' Joe, the Yankee Clipper. (DiMaggio's nickname among teammates was Daig, short for Dago.) The new Yankee manager was well advised to treat King Kong, Ol' Reliable, and the Jolter like diamonds. To Yankee fans they were jewels beyond price. But age and Stengel's good sense moved them in and out of the lineup. None played more than 115 games that season. A second platoon — younger replacement players — had to be ready.

Stengel: "Platooning is also good for the young players, which they is the last to agree, because they get to come along at a slow pace. Now it is possible to see a young player who thinks he can hit any pitcher, which he did in the minor leagues. And he goes to the plate [in the majors] and gives it a great fight but those balls coming in have too much stuff for him to handle, too much curve, because the pitchers are more expert, which is not even talking about the change of speeds.

"After a while the young player don't think he can hit any pitcher anymore. When a young player loses confidence in hisself, that is a terrible thing. I have seen them, good ones, blow up in a single season. They never make it back. They have been humiliated in professional baseball and will go somewhere else for their livelihood. You platoon the young players depending on the pitcher and so forth but you also platoon them when they are getting distressed. You platoon them for their mental condition.

"Which they do not like. When these strong, young men are being platooned for their mental condition, they get angry."

As Stengel knew, I had heard platooned players complaining about him, with hot fury. The players believed that days spent on the bench worked against them during salary negotiations. More than today, there existed a stigma in "not being good enough to play every day."

One night at the old North Station in Philadelphia, I chatted briefly with Stengel as we waited for a train, then moved on. Gene Woodling, a splendid left-hand-hitting outfielder, muttered in my general direction. "The son of a bitch. I wouldn't want him in my house. I wouldn't want him near my wife and kids."

"Who are you talking about, Gene?" I asked.

"Stengel, that son of a bitch."

Beneath a controlled manner, stocky, round-faced Gene Woodling thundered with intensity. The outburst against Stengel meant mostly that Woodling resented being platooned.*

---

*I never reported this episode in the *Herald Tribune*, and readers may well ask why I did not. I felt that if a quote was pretty much nonsense, then I wasn't going to report it, even though a nonsensical quote might make headlines. And the Woodling quote was nonsense, as Woodling himself agreed, once his rage passed. I was employed by the *Tribune*, not the Yankees, but we were never encouraged at the paper to lob grenades just to see how loud a bang they would make.

"Ya don't listen to what the players say," Stengel maintained, "because the ones which is mad at you can win the most games." He jabbed a finger into my forearm. "Now that's something which I would say you never knew, kid, even though you been to college and have read numerous very learned books."

Stengel had no fewer than seven major league outfielders looking for work in St. Petersburg: DiMaggio, Henrich, and Keller, Big John Lindell and strong-armed Cliff Mapes, plus two wonderful rookies, Hank Bauer, a right-hand-hitting strong boy with the visage of a gargoyle, and Woodling, up from the San Francisco Seals, where he batted .385.

Stengel encouraged DiMaggio, as coach-without-portfolio, to teach the others the mysteries of his own outfield play. Stengel noticed at once the quick grace with which DiMaggio ran down fly balls, the early break, the smooth striding run.

That style was a matter of concentration, vision, hearing, and knowing intricate pitcher-batter patterns, not matters that are easily taught, if at all, even if one loves teaching, which DiMaggio did not. He did not rebel, but his enthusiasm was limited.

Stengel had two good third basemen. Billy Johnson, who had "an amazing arm to first base, never threw bad," batted right-handed with decent power. Bobby Brown's classwork at Tulane Medical School forced him to report late, but when Brown did arrive he would tote a major league bat, along with *Gray's Anatomy. Platoon.*

George "Snuffy" Stirnweiss, the veteran second baseman, had good speed, fair bat, not much power. Stengel respected Stirnweiss, but he *liked* a tall, diffident rookie named Jerry Coleman. "He throws beautiful overhanded. On the double play, he jumps up in the air and whilst in there throws overhanded to first base, very accurate. He's like a great basketball player that jumps and makes a perfect shot."

Stengel also liked the way Coleman wore his uniform. "Instead of putting the pants way down, which some do, he rolls his pants tight over the knees, which shows all them nice baseball stockings. The umpires are less likely to call low strikes on a player which wears his pants like that, which made him harder to pitch to. And this kid is a fighter. Soft-spoken and so forth, but he can be vicious to a pitcher." *Platoon.*

At first base Stengel had Jack Phillips and Dick Kryhoski, and Joe Collins. He sent Collins to the minors, which he said later was a mistake. (Collins, born Joseph Kollonige in Pennsylvania coal country, spent most of '49 tearing up the American Association.) *Platoon.*

There was not much question that Yogi Berra could hit. He swung at bad pitches. He belted bad pitches. A joke held that Berra's weakness was a fastball down the middle. (He also hit those hard, to be sure.)

Berra's problems as a catcher were technical and physical. Blocking low pitches. Moving into position to throw out runners trying to steal. Dickey wanted to work with Berra. "He wants to steady him," Stengel said. A few weeks later Berra reported that things were "going very good. Dickey is learning me all of his experiences."

Ever flexible, Stengel moved away from platooning catchers. Berra would be the Yankees' regular catcher for the next eight years, paralleling the career of Roy Campanella in Brooklyn. "My other catchers were fine men," Stengel said, "but they could not hit the ball for distance like Mr. Berra." *No platoon.*

Curiously, the smallest, lightest Yankee was the bulwark. Shortstop Philip Francis Rizzuto would start 153 of the Yankees' 155 games. Rizzuto stood about five foot five. Fourteen years earlier Rizzuto had presented himself at Ebbets Field for a tryout before Dodger manager Casey Stengel. After the workout Stengel said irritably, "Yer too small. Ga wan. Go home. Get a shoebox."

Unlike DiMaggio, Rizzuto is not inclined to brood. "I liked him right away when he came to the Yankees," Rizzuto says. "I was established. I'd been the shortstop since 1941. He came on low-keyed. What did I care in 1949 with the Yankees what had happened in 1935 over in Brooklyn? Casey wasn't the only guy who didn't think I could make it. That was just so much water over the dam. By 49, I didn't need a shoebox, anyway. The clubhouse boy at the Stadium shined my Yankee spikes every day."

Stengel would not discuss his early wrong call on Rizzuto. He was hypersensitive to any criticism of his baseball judgments and, when pressed, exploded into profanity. Harold Rosenthal of the *Herald Tribune* questioned him on a minor judgment once, more intensely than Stengel wanted to be questioned. In front of a mixed assemblage of sportswriters and ballplayers in the Yankee dugout, Stengel shouted at Rosenthal, "Yer fulla shit and I'll tell ya why."*

Stengel said Rizzuto "had somewhat hurt his arm previously [to 1949]. I was asking around and some players told me it was hard for him to throw out a man, once he went deep for a ball toward third base.

"I said in the spring, why don't he loft the ball to first base, which he commenced doing, getting rid of the ball with an amazing quick throw. It would fly in the air but he'd get the throw off so fast he would beat the runner, which is better than a bullet throw, which takes the shortstop so long to get rid of that the runner to first base beats the bullet to the bag."

Stengel's views of Yankee pitching were complex. Reynolds, as he said, could start and relieve better than Cy Young. Glowering Vic Raschi was "the greatest I ever had to be sure to win one game." Ed Lopat was "a first-class starting pitcher, and Joe Page, they called the fireman because he put out fires, could do an amazing job in relief. I believed in platooning with relief pitching. It was different when the ball was dead. Now I didn't

---

*Rosenthal was outraged. He telephoned me at home and announced, "I'm not speaking to Stengel. I thought you'd want to know." Since Rosenthal was the reporter, the note taker, the important question seemed to me whether Stengel was still speaking to Rosenthal, which, of course, he was. Rosenthal's indignation softened quickly but recurred for decades afterwards, whenever someone suggested that "Casey must have been a sweet old guy."

want to put extra strain on my starting pitchers who you need over a long pennant race."

During Stengel's great years, no Yankee pitcher was permitted to work 300 innings in a season, not even the bellwethers, Reynolds and Raschi, both broad-shouldered and imposing specimens.* "In the dead-ball days [Christy] Mathewson and Cy Young, they could just throw it in there on some hitters when they were ahead because there wasn't gonna be a home run. But I ain't managing this club in the dead-ball days, which my pitching coach, Mr. Turner, and I remember every day."

Stengel had an extraordinary, mystical (to me) sense of when to lift a pitcher. When I asked him to explain how he perceived pitchers at work, the answer was no more than partly satisfactory. "If I see a man getting hit hard, which is even if the balls are caught, very long flies, line drives hit at somebody, and so forth, I take him out after an inning where he has given no runs, no hits, and some say how could you take him out so soon?

"But he is throwing as hard as he can and they are hitting the ball hard and he'll just get worse from here on in. So I bring in another pitcher and when I do that I have a third one warming up, in case my second pitcher is not right on that particular day, which gives me another shot at stopping them, and does that answer your question for you, sir?"

When Stengel took over the Yankees, American League managers warmed up relief pitchers one at a time. Sometimes you'd see a starter hit hard. Then the relief pitcher was hit hard. By the time a backup reliever warmed up, the game was lost. Stengel's thinking was a full generation ahead of that of his

---

*As Reynolds and Raschi anchored Stengel's Yankees, the Dodgers of the 1960s were anchored by Don Drysdale and Sandy Koufax. Drysdale pitched more than 300 innings for four consecutive seasons. Koufax pitched more than 300 innings three years out of four, reaching a peak of 336 innings in 1965. A year later arthritis in his pitching elbow forced Koufax to retire when he was thirty years old. In essence Koufax at his peak was pitching seven or eight more complete games a season than Stengel permitted Reynolds or Raschi or Whitey Ford to work.

colleagues. I think it is fair to say that the modern pitching staff, with short relievers and long relievers, with carefully chosen left-handed and right-handed spot pitchers, this whirling, complex, twenty-armed beast, the pitching staff of today, was invented by Casey Stengel of Kansas City, Missouri, St. Petersburg, Florida, Glendale, California, and the Bronx.

How did the Yankee ballplayers respond to their first exposure to managerial genius? DiMaggio was profoundly negative. He didn't care for Stengel's long-winded style and thought platoon baseball was chaotic. DiMaggio was a laconic and introverted man. Before retiring at night, he habitually stacked his coins on the bedroom dresser, one pile for pennies, others for nickels, dimes, and quarters. Stengel's platooning offended DiMaggio's sense of order.

"I don't get this guy," he complained to Phil Rizzuto. "Nobody knows when he's playing or where. With this guy managing, we can't possibly win." Unhappy, DiMaggio came down with heel spurs and missed the first sixty-five games of the season.

Others were more tolerant. "You see, whatever he was doing with the club, Casey came on in a very low-keyed way to us veterans," Rizzuto says. "He didn't tell us all his ideas all at once. He was really pretty humble. To me and the other veterans, he said, in one way or another: 'I know you're big leaguers. You know what you're doing. Just whatever little input I can give you I will.'

"If he had come in with a big speech, telling us a whole lot of stuff up front, there would have been trouble. Casey did a lot of smart things with the Yankees but the smartest thing he ever did was come on slow."

Charlie Silvera, a backup catcher for nine years, is renowned among teammates for his vivid memory.* "Remember," Silvera

---

*During our talk, Silvera described himself as "a spear carrier among a bunch of emperors and lords. You gotta have spear carriers and I was a damned good one."

says, "I was a rookie Yankee catcher the same year Stengel was
rookie Yankee manager. I was only twenty-four, but I knew the
tradition, that Joe McCarthy had been a stern taskmaster and
that Bucky Harris was looser.

"I caught for Portland in the Coast League, playing against
Casey's teams for two years. He could get noisy. He put on a
pretty good show just in the dugout."

"But there was none of that in St. Petersburg, none of that
the whole first year. Starting out, I think the first thing was to
put that clown background behind him. He wanted to get the
players on his side and the writers on his side, as a sound
baseball man."

I mentioned Stengel's gruffness and sarcasm.

"Face it, he was one gruff old man," Silvera said. "With the
platooning, some players said he wasn't fair and then he'd say,
quietly, 'Well, you don't like me very much now, but when
you get your check for playing in the World Series, you'll like
me a little better.'

"And, of course, he kept on platooning, which caused the
guys being platooned to play even harder when they got into
the lineup. They'd say, 'I'll show that crooked-legged old bastard.'

"That was fine with Casey. He wanted to win. And win
today. None of that wait-till-next-year stuff. That was Brooklyn.
None of that we'll-get-'em-tomorrow.

"You were a Yankee. You got 'em today.

"Anybody who didn't understand that did not play for Casey
very long."

Jerry Coleman, he of the rolled-up knickers, was a bright,
sensitive California kid, tough enough to fly fighter planes during the Korean War.

"First of all, about the pants," Coleman says. "I didn't wear
'em the way I did to shrink the strike zone, whatever Casey
said. The truth is when I wore 'em longer I could feel fabric
against my knee and that was inhibiting. Rolled up they felt

comfortable and I believed I could run better. But if Casey thought I was being shrewd, I won't argue.

"When he came to the Yankees, he was up against an old-school-tie type of thing. Rizzuto, Henrich, DiMaggio, Keller all became stars under Joe McCarthy. They loved McCarthy, and why not? They looked at Stengel as an outsider.

"Everybody was wary that first spring. Stengel treated Joe DiMaggio the way everybody else treated Joe DiMaggio. Like an icon. Whatever may have been *muttered,* there never was a *confrontation* between them. Even when Casey thought Di-Maggio was past his peak in center, he never said anything like that directly.

"But Casey was not exactly a wimp. That first spring, the squad split one day in Texas. One squad went to Austin. One went to San Antonio. We lost both games to Texas League clubs.

"Casey went crazy. Nuts. You're professionals. You're Yankees. Minor leagues beat you! *Damn you! GO OUT AND WIN!!*

"Nobody knew about DiMaggio's bad heel, but one day Joe just disappeared. We read about it in the papers. Joe was just gone. You look around. There's rookie Gene Woodling, rookie Hank Bauer, almost rookie Bobby Brown, Yogi Berra who never caught regularly before, three pitchers nobody knew that much about, and rookie Jerry Coleman. They were picking us anywhere from third to sixth.

"There are four basic parts of managing," Coleman said. "Keep the fans interested and happy. Get along with your front office. Handle the team. Contend with the media.

"Great as Stengel was with our team, he was just as great with the media.

"Somebody says, 'Hey, Case, who's a greater player, Di-Maggio or Ruth?' and he doesn't want to answer that question. For obvious reasons.

"So he says, 'Well, Mr. DiMaggio can do this, and Mr. Ruth

could do that, and don't forget Mr. Cobb,' and now he's back to 1912 with John McGraw and then he's telling the reporter what was going on in Kansas City when he was a child.

"By this time the reporter has forgotten the question.

"I've never seen a manager to match him.

"Casey Stengel was a brilliant man, but you knew that, didn't you?"

Well, I suspected.

8

The Red and the Black

◆

THE THREE NEW YORK CITY ballclubs drew more than five million fans in 1949, despite a disappointing finish by Leo Durocher's evolving Giants. Durocher had uttered one classic comment on his well-liked predecessor at the Polo Grounds, stumpy, congenial, uncomplicated Mel Ott. "Nice guys finish last," Durocher said.

"Right," pronounced the *Daily News*'s tart-tongued Dick Young when the 1949 baseball season ended. "And not-so-nice guys finish fifth."

Both the Yankees and the Dodgers battled through pennant races that turned and twisted and blossomed until Sunday, October 2, the very last day of the season. The Giants, who finished twenty-four games behind the Dodgers, made news somewhat more subtly. On the eighth of July, the team was integrated.

Earlier the Giants had signed two distinctly different black athletes and assigned them to the Jersey City farm team in the International League. During a barroom brawl somewhere in

Texas, Henry Curtis "Hank" Thompson, an infielder who stood a broad-beamed five feet, nine inches, had beaten a man to death. "The way things worked in the South then," reported Garry Schumacher of the Giant front office, "when one colored guy killed another colored guy, it didn't count. The white cops wouldn't even make arrests." Thompson proved pleasant enough, except when an occasional rage gripped him, and not notably bright. Baseball integration was proceeding at a most lethargic pace. But history often moves unevenly. Just two years after Robinson's first Brooklyn season, the stern character barrier to blacks — no drinkers, no rowdies — was coming down. Henry Curtis Thompson was a bibulous man.

Along with Thompson, the Giants signed a black of faultless character and keen intelligence, Monford Merrill Irvin, an outfielder who had graduated from Lincoln University, a small Negro college in Pennsylvania, affiliated with the Presbyterian Church. Irvin was thirty years old. Racism kept big Monte Irvin out of the major leagues during most of his prime playing seasons. Irvin was courteous, thoughtful, soft-voiced. To Robert Creamer of *Sports Illustrated*, perhaps unconsciously mouthing some prejudice of the time, "Monte Irvin sounds like a Latin professor."

Into July, Thompson hit .303 for Jersey City. Irvin hit .373, with fourteen steals and fifty-two runs batted in across sixty-three games. They were then promoted to the Polo Grounds. "Of course we knew segregation was wrong," says Charles "Chub" Feeney, vice president of the Giants at the time. "My uncle [Giant president Horace Stoneham] knew it and I knew it, but pure idealists we were not. Competing in New York, against the Yankees and the Dodgers, the resource we needed most was talent. Whatever Durocher told you, Leo's brain alone was not enough. In 1949, the Negro leagues were the most logical place in the world to look for ballplayers."

Still, the best young player in Negro baseball, indeed the best young player in the world, was not allowed into white baseball for another season. Quite simply, Willie Howard Mays, the eighteen-year-old center fielder for the Birmingham Black Barons, was a wonder. But opportunities for blacks, even wonderblacks, remained restricted.

With the addition of catcher Roy Campanella and the very large, very fast right-hander Don Newcombe, the Dodgers of 1949 were solidly integrated. Some days a third of the starting Brooklyn lineup was black. For the time being, that was enough, Branch Rickey decided. The Giants wanted to see how things went with Thompson and Irvin before they undertook further black hiring.

Three major league teams were integrated — Cleveland, the Dodgers, and the Giants. Three teams were integrated and two of them were based in enlightened New York. The Yankees felt a certain pressure.

Between them, Dan Topping and Del Webb had no discernible social conscience. Topping was comfortable in an all-white, all-wealthy Southampton social world. Webb's construction company had built one of the concentration camps used to imprison Japanese Americans during World War II. With some drinks in him, Webb boasted that he had completed the concentration camp "ahead of schedule." Citing his responsibility toward his employers' investment, George Weiss was determined to keep the Yankees white. Besides, personally Weiss didn't care for blacks and didn't trust them. (In later years Weiss unloaded an outstanding black Puerto Rican prospect, Victor Pellot Power, informing people at the *Times* and the *Herald Tribune*, "Maybe he can play, but not for us. He's impudent and he goes for white women.")

But social pressure remained and, besides, it was illegal for an employer in New York State to discriminate. Seeming to bow to the law, but actually sidestepping, Weiss sent Bill "Wheels" McCorry, sometime scout and full-time road secretary, to look at Mays in a few Negro League games in Alabama. Although McCorry was born in upstate New York, he had the attitudes of a southern Klansman, which he made little effort to conceal. He reported back to Weiss that Willie Mays could run some and could throw a little but wasn't worth signing because "the boy can't hit a good curve ball."

"That's just about the worstest scouting report I ever heard of," Roy Campanella says. "Willie couldn't hit the curve! He was eighteen years old. No way an eighteen-year-old kid is *ever* gonna be a good curve ball hitter. That takes time. Mickey and Duke, great as they were, they didn't hit good curve balls when they were eighteen.

"The onliest thing McCorry had negative on Willie was something else: the color of Willie's skin."

The Yankees could have signed Willie Mays in 1949 for a bonus of $5,000. They made no offer. If they had signed Mays, the Yankee outfield through the 1951 pennant race would have been remembered through the corridors of time: DiMaggio, Mantle, and Mays.

One has to conclude that bigotry is not simply wicked. It is also pretty damn dumb.

Two absolutely extraordinary episodes in 1949 removed the base-ball focus from the field. One was a deed of psychopathic violence that wrecked at least two lives. The other, less obviously violent, haunted and troubled Jackie Robinson until his death.

Both the Dodgers and Yankees broke training camp in fine style. Robinson was back to a good playing weight of 190 pounds. With the arrival of Campanella, he was no longer the only black regular in the National League. His teammates increasingly felt more comfortable with him and he felt increasingly comfortable with himself.* Robinson flowered through-

---

*Robinson traced a certain amount of this comfort back to August 24, 1948, in Forbes Field in Pittsburgh. During the fourth inning of a Dodger-Pirate game, umpire Walter J. "Butch" Henline called a questionable strike on outfielder Gene Hermanski. The Brooklyn bench yapped at Henline and continued jeering after a warning to stop. Suddenly Henline whirled, ripped off his mask, and shouted: "You! Robinson! You're out of this game!" Robinson recalled, "That made me feel great. Henline didn't throw me out because I was black. He threw me out because I was getting on his nerves. It was wonderful to be treated like any other ballplayer."

out the summer of 1949. With a batting average of .342, he led the league, outhitting Musial by four points. Robinson batted in 124 runs and hit 38 doubles and 12 triples. In a period of cautious base running, he stole 37 bases. That is almost routine for a good base runner today, but it was 11 more than anyone else in the majors stole in 1949. And he stole in punishing ways.

Somebody wrote a song:

Did you see Jackie Robinson hit that ball?
Did he hit it, man, and that ain't all.
He stole home!

There was no musical background for Stengel's platoons in the Bronx, but without Joltin' Joe DiMaggio — who had been sanctified in song ("Joltin' Joe DiMaggio") eight years before — they performed wonderfully well. Vic Raschi won nine of his first ten decisions. Tommy Henrich hit sixteen home runs across three months. In June the Yankees had a four-game lead.

The integrated Dodgers against the dominantly southern Cardinals. The Yankees and Casey Stengel against the world. A gripping time for baseball, with excitement aplenty, when suddenly, on June 15, gunfire exploded into the major leagues.

A tall, rather drab, black-haired Chicago woman named Ruth Ann Steinhagen, daughter of a hard-working die maker, had become infatuated with a graceful but quite ordinary-looking first baseman named Eddie Waitkus, a native of Cambridge, Massachusetts. Waitkus had fought in the South Pacific during World War II and been awarded the Bronze Star for courage under fire. He was quiet, in no way a hell raiser, and he sometimes mentioned that he had turned down a Harvard scholarship to play pro ball. He was a bachelor, a fact not lost on Ruth Ann Steinhagen.

Ruth Ann noticed Waitkus when he was playing for the Cubs at Wrigley Field in 1946. He was a smooth fielder who hit for a .304 average, without much power, but he moved well around first base, a slick fielder; in the argot, a fancy Dan. Ruth Ann Steinhagen began spending whatever spare money she could find to buy tickets to Wrigley Field. She always sat as close as possible to first base. She was sixteen and gawky; after a time she felt she was in love. She saved newspaper photos of Eddie Waitkus and Cubs ticket stubs. She wrote to the ballclub and obtained more photographs of Waitkus. She graduated from high school and found work as a typist. There is no record of a serious boyfriend in her life.

Ruth Ann was a gay and happy child who changed markedly on reaching adolescence. She became quite prim, fastidious about her hair and fingernails. She worshiped regularly in a Lutheran church. But suddenly, her parents said, as an adolescent, she announced that she did not want people to look at her.

She grew interested in music, in a pop singer named Andy Russell, who sang love songs in English and Spanish. Then she turned to Franz Liszt, the great romantic pianist and composer; she confessed to a girlfriend that she had a "crush on Liszt." Franz Liszt died in 1886.

Her lonely passion for Waitkus took hold across the seasons of 1947 and 48. Waitkus wore number 36. Ruth Ann bought every phonograph record she could find that was produced in 1936. Since Waitkus was born near Boston, Ruth Ann began eating baked beans. Her parents said she "wanted Boston baked beans all the time."

At length her parents convinced her to see a psychiatrist, Dr. Abraham A. Low, who reported later that Ruth Ann appeared "very disturbed and confused." Her mother disputed that version saying, "The doctor told us there was nothing wrong with Ruth, except she should forget about Eddie Waitkus."

Ruth Ann could not forget Waitkus, whose background was Lithuanian. She began giving herself lessons in the Lithuanian language. In December 1948, the Cubs traded Waitkus to the Phillies for Walter "Monk" Dubiel, a right-handed pitcher who lost as often as he won. It was a roundly bad deal for Chicago, a poorly run ballclub playing in handsome Wrigley Field, where ivy vines climbed the outfield walls. Ruth Ann took to bed and cried for several days and nights.

She moved into a rooming house, near her parents' home, and worked as a typist. Her obsession with Waitkus sometimes elated her but sometimes depressed her so severely that she thought of suicide. Early in the 1949 baseball season, Ruth Ann Steinhagen conceived a bizarre plan.

The first week in May she went to a pawnshop and ordered a .22-caliber rifle that was on sale for twenty-one dollars.

"What do you want the gun for, miss?" the pawnbroker asked.

"Father's Day is coming," Ruth Ann said. "I want it as a present for my father."

The pawnbroker showed her how to disassemble the rifle and gave her two boxes of shells. The Phillies, with Eddie Waitkus at first base, were coming to Chicago for a three-game series starting on Tuesday, June 14. The Phillies and Eddie Waitkus would stay at the Edgewater Beach Hotel, close by Lake Michigan on the North Side of Chicago.

On about June 10, Ruth Ann Steinhagen made a three-day reservation for "a nice room" at the Edgewater Beach. Then she went to her bank and withdrew eighty dollars, all she had in her savings account.

On Monday, June 13, Ruth Ann packed a suitcase with three days' clothing, the bullets, the rifle, and a knife with a blade that was five inches long. She checked into the Edgewater Beach at four P.M. and was given a room on the twelfth floor. She was feeling agitated and ordered a daiquiri from room service. Then she ordered another. She wanted to be able to think clearly, but she felt very strange. At one minute, she wanted to use the rifle to kill herself. In the next minute, she wanted to use it to kill Eddie Waitkus, whom she had never met but who tomorrow night would be sleeping under the same roof as she.

The Phillies traveled to Chicago by overnight Pullman car. The team stopped at the Edgewater Beach Hotel just long enough for check-ins. Then the ballplayers rode a bus for the fifteen-minute trip to Wrigley Field.

Ruth Ann had a light breakfast in the hotel coffee shop. Then she went to Wrigley Field and bought a general admission ticket. She arrived at noon when the gates opened and moved to a seat close to first base.

The baseball calendar was full for Tuesday, June 14. Back in New York, the Yankees maintained a three-game lead in first place by defeating the Chicago White Sox, 15 to 3. That was Vic Raschi's tenth victory.

At Cincinnati, Larry Jansen pitched a four-hitter and the Giants defeated the Reds, 2 to 0. Trying to create a team that could run, Durocher had gotten the Giants to trade massive, muscular, immobile Walker Cooper, his slugging catcher, to Cincinnati and call up young Wes Westrum. "He's thirty pounds smaller but twice as quick," Durocher said.

"I ain't gonna answer Durocher with no words," Cooper told Ed Sinclair of the *Herald Tribune*. "But tonight, he better watch it. I'm fixing to bust some fences."

That night Westrum contributed a clutch single for New York. "Cooper wound up with no hits at all," Sinclair wrote. "He looked the same as ever, or somewhat worse, when he grounded into a game-ending double play."

"Yeah," Durocher said, merrily. "I told ya he couldn't run. My wife coulda beat the fucking relay to first base. Cooper couldn't, and yeah, yeah, I know. Laraine's legs are better looking, too."

In St. Louis the Dodgers moved three games ahead of the Cardinals on the pitching of their skinny left-handed ace, Elwin "Preacher" Roe of Ashflat, Arkansas. The Dodgers won, 7 to 2, and would have won by more if the Cardinals had not executed a triple play.

The biggest baseball story of the day unfolded in Chicago. The Cubs had won the pennant in 1945 under manager Charlie Grimm, a genial, storytelling midwesterner nicknamed Jolly

Cholly who liked to sing, accompanying himself on the banjo, which he played left-handed. After 1945, the Cubs began a drift (which some suggest continues to this day). Jim Gallagher, the general manager who had made the mindless Waitkus trade, now fired Grimm and replaced him with Frankie Frisch, the old Fordham Flash, who was every bit as easygoing as a drill sergeant.

Frisch met with his new team, players named Verban, Ramazzotti, Jeffcoat, Reich. "We're going to hustle just like my ballclub in St. Louis," Frankie Frisch said, "that great club they called the Gashouse Gang."

A morning drizzle wet Wrigley Field. It was hard to hustle, even in spikes, without slipping. The Phillies scored five runs in the third inning and defeated the Cubs and Frisch, 9 to 2. Eddie Waitkus made eleven putouts at first base, in his graceful way, and got a hit.

Waitkus went back to the Edgewater Beach on a cheerful team bus. The Phillies were coming along. They would win some games.

Ruth Ann Steinhagen returned to the hotel in a taxi. She felt a little breathless. She ordered a few more drinks. She still felt breathless. She had been properly brought up. She was a proper person. She was conscious of a sense of sexual arousal, without understanding much about it, and she felt acutely uncomfortable. She loved Eddie Waitkus, but he had done this to her. In a careful hand, she wrote a note:

Dear Eddie:
It's extremely important that I see you as soon as possible. Please come soon. I won't take up much of your time. I promise.
Ruth Ann Steinhagen

She called for a bellhop and told him to deliver the note to Waitkus. She tipped the bellboy fully five dollars. (One dollar was a healthy tip in 1949.)

Now Ruth Ann waited in her room. When she heard nothing by 9:30, she became angry and depressed. When and if Eddie

Waitkus did call, she would stab him to death and then turn
the gun on herself. Then she felt calmer. If Waitkus called, she
would simply *show* him the knife and the gun, tell him of the
murder-suicide plan and let him call the police. After a while,
Ruth Ann undressed, put on a nightgown, and went to sleep.

The phone woke her at 12:40 A.M. "This is Eddie Waitkus.
What's so darned important?"

Ruth was startled. ("He was so, you know, informal.") She
said she could not discuss anything on the phone. "Can you
come up tonight for a few minutes?"

Waitkus said he could.

"Give me a half hour to get dressed."

When Waitkus knocked at 1:10, Ruth Ann hid the knife in
the folds of her skirt and let him in. Waitkus moved past her
quickly. He said something, but Ruth Ann later told a psychol-
ogist that she was so excited she did not hear the words.

Waitkus dropped into a chair near the window. "What did
you want to see me about?" he asked, staring at her.

"Wait a minute," Ruth Ann said. "I have a surprise for you."

She went to the closet where she had hidden the rifle. Then
she turned and pointed it at Waitkus. He said, "Baby, what's
this all about?" He rose from the chair. "What's this all about?
What have I done?"

"You've been bothering me for two years," Ruth Ann Steinhagen said. "Now you are going to die." She pulled the trigger.

Waitkus slammed backward against a wall, a bullet in the
right side of his chest. He rolled to the floor. "Oh, baby, what
did you do that for?" he said.

Ruth Ann knelt beside the broken ballplayer. She took his
hand. "You like doing that, don't you?" Waitkus said.

Ruth Ann withdrew her hand. She thought, Now is the time
to shoot myself. But she suddenly felt frantic and couldn't find
the box of bullets. Waitkus began to moan.

Ruth Ann called the hotel operator and said someone had
been shot. "Please send a doctor."

Waitkus continued to moan. Ruth Ann couldn't stand his cries of pain.

She was standing in the hall with her hands over her ears when a doctor and a house detective arrived.

An ambulance took Waitkus to Illinois Masonic Hospital. He had lost a great deal of blood and was "deeply critical." Two days later, he began slowly to rally. Surgeons performed a series of operations, cutting away part of Waitkus's right lung and chest musculature. After excruciating rehabilitation, he was able to resume his baseball career with good success in 1950.

The hospital bill, $4,000, was sent on to the Philadelphia ballclub. The Phils declined to pay and eventually took Waitkus to court, forcing him to settle the bill.

Ruth Ann Steinhagen was arrested on the charge of "assault with intent to kill." Psychiatrists and psychologists diagnosed her condition as "acute schizophrenia in an immature individual." At an Illinois state mental hospital, clinicians called her neat, cooperative, and generally cheerful. Only twice did they record intense emotional outbursts, once when she described the trade that sent Waitkus to Philadelphia and once when she was required to undergo a complete physical examination, disrobing in front of a male physician.

In 1952, Ruth Ann was found to have recovered her sanity. The charge against her was dropped because when she shot Waitkus, doctors said, she had not known right from wrong. In 1955, she was released into society, a free woman. Her present whereabouts are not known.

Waitkus suffered recurrent episodes of pain. "So bad," he once remarked, "that I wished that the girl had finished the job."

After his major league career ended in 1955, he worked in several department stores as a public relations man. "By then," says his teammate Russ Meyer, "he was in pain all the time and drinking too much. He'd go out for a three-hour lunch, get stewed, and come back and be rude to the customers."

Waitkus entered a Boston hospital in 1972, suffering from cancer in the lung that had been torn up by Ruth Ann's bullet. He died on September 15, at the age of fifty-three.

The shooting fired the imagination of Bernard Malamud, who fictionalized the episode in his famous novel *The Natural*. Ballplayers were troubled by the incident, but only briefly. Their patterns of behavior did not change. Ballplayers on the road were a heedless, wanton lot; they still are, risks be damned.

Besides, I doubt that one major leaguer in a hundred has heard the story of Ruth Ann Steinhagen and poor, dead, reckless Eddie Waitkus.

◆

OUT FRONT, pages ahead of the sports sections, headlines bannered the Great American Red Scare. "The scare had been unsettling the country for some time," Gordon J. Kahn, a historian and the author's father, summarized in an early edition of the *Information Please Almanac:* "Back in 1939, Representative Martin Dies, a Texas Democrat, threw suspicion on little Shirley Temple, who was eleven. Maybe she was a Red! Now ten years later it became a favorite sport for eager-eyed legislators to hunt for communists in government, schools, movies, even the clergy.

"Bigger Red Scares were developing abroad. In September of 1949, a fourteen-word White House announcement broke the news that Russia had exploded an atomic bomb.

"The 'secret' was no longer ours."

Some who confused baseball with Shangri-La assert that the game transcends politics. It did not in the tortured summer of 1949.

Across an epic life, Paul Robeson was a Phi Beta Kappa scholar, an All-American end, a lawyer, an actor, a singer, and an orator of unforgettable power. During the 1930s he came to admire the socialist ideal, and later the Soviet Union. There is no evidence that he ever joined the Communist party in the United States or anywhere else. He was an American radical, strong, sensitive, outspoken, headstrong, and described to this day in Harlem as "the tallest tree in the forest."

In 1943 Robeson's basso rang across Broadway in a performance of *Othello* that was dark thunder. He was forty-five years old and at his very peak. "I marvel," he said, "about the patience and the patriotism of my own Negro people. They cannot vote in some places, but they buy bonds. They cannot get jobs in a *lot* of places — but they salvage paper, metal, and fats. They are confronted in far too many places with the raucous, Hitleresque howl of 'white supremacy' — but they give their blood and sweat for red, white, and blue supremacy."

A few weeks before Christmas 1943, Robeson and several black newspaper publishers presented themselves at the winter meetings of the sixteen men who owned major league ballclubs. Robeson's prestige and presence were such that he was permitted to address the owners and Commissioner Kenesaw Mountain Landis.

"I come here," he began in the matchless basso, "as an American and as a former athlete. I come because I feel deeply." He spoke first to the theme of disturbance — riots in the stands — which some argued would inevitably follow baseball integration. He had played football at Rutgers, three varsity seasons of integrated games. There were no disturbances at all. Now on Broadway, he was Othello, a Negro protagonist who seven times a week strangled a white heroine, played by the beautiful, young Uta Hagen. There had not been a single disturbance at the Royale Theater, either. Robeson's voice rose in passion. Negroes were fighting for America on distant seas and far-off continents. They were fighting for their country. Some were dying for their country. It would be a fine thing, would it not, to give these self-same Negro soldiers, and every other Negro who was good enough, a chance to play baseball in the major leagues?

When Robeson finished, the owners erupted in applause. Cold-eyed, thin-faced Kenesaw Mountain Landis spoke to reporters later. "No law," he said, "written or unwritten, exists to prevent blacks from participating in organized baseball." This was not true. Apartheid was the greatest unwritten law in baseball history; it was baseball's First Commandment.

When Jackie Robinson was permitted to join the Dodgers four years after this speech, Robeson attended a small reception and promised Robinson whatever support he could provide. Robinson thanked Robeson and moved on.

By 1949, with feral Red baiting abroad, Robeson took certain extreme positions. On a tour of Europe, he spoke against the cold war. Should hot war break out between the Soviet Union and the United States, Robeson added, blacks would not or should not fight for America. They had nothing to fight for.

Robeson amplified in Harlem on June 19. "I love the Negro people from whom I spring. . . . Yes, suffering people the world over — in the way that I intensely love the Soviet Union.

"We do not want to die in vain anymore on foreign battlefields for Wall Street and the greedy supporters of domestic fascism. If we must die, let it be in Mississippi or Georgia.

"Let it be wherever we are lynched."

The *New York Times* headline the next morning read: LOVES SOVIET BEST, ROBESON DECLARES.

Each of thirty-seven newspapers owned by William Randolph Hearst, from the New York *Journal-American* to the *Los Angeles Examiner*, published an editorial labeled AN UNDESIRABLE CITIZEN. "It was an accident unfortunate for America that Paul Robeson was born here."

Representative John S. Wood, a conservative southern Democrat from Georgia, who was chairman of the notorious House Un-American Activities Committee, decided to convene a special hearing. The issue: loyalty of American Negroes. The NAACP wired Wood in protest: "There never has been any question of the loyalty of the Negro."

Wood responded that he had not meant to imply that there was. His committee was merely answering requests from Americans of "the colored race" for a forum to "express views contrary to the views of Paul Robeson." Wood sent a telegram to Jackie Robinson inviting him to testify.

This was a request, not a subpoena, but it was weighty. If Robinson declined to testify he could, in the perfervid climate, stand accused of agreement with Robeson's politics and indeed with the politics of Joseph Stalin. Robinson went at once to Branch Rickey.

In a highly emotional meeting, Rickey told Robinson that it was an honor to testify in the Congress of the United States. This was indeed a wonderful opportunity to speak out beyond the world of baseball. Some might oppose his testifying. Such men might well be secret Communists themselves.

"I'm not sure, Mr. Rickey. I'm not a politician. I'm not a speech maker. You know. I'm a ballplayer."

"And an uncommonly fine one," Rickey cried. "Don't worry about the speech. The congressmen expect a prepared statement, of course. Don't worry about that. I know you pretty well, Jackie. I'll write the statement."

Rickey enlisted the help of two former newspapermen who worked for him: Arthur Mann and Harold Parrott. Neither had any idea how to write what Rickey envisioned: the credo of an American Negro.

Rickey tried himself. The result was flowery, wordy, preachy. It was not in Rickey's nature to concede that he had failed, but he admitted to me long afterward, "I was a bit presumptuous to believe that I, as a white, could speak for a Negro."

More meetings followed, and Robinson expressed serious doubts about testifying. Some congressmen leaked the plan to invite Robinson to the Capitol, and scores of letters arrived at Ebbets Field urging Robinson "not to be a tool of witch-hunters." Phone calls to the Robinsons' tidy brick home in St. Albans, Queens, warned him that to speak out against Robeson was to be "a traitor to the Negro." Robeson himself sent a letter to Robinson saying, "The press badly distorted my remarks in Europe."

But Rickey persisted in trying to sweep away Robinson's doubts.

"To tell you the truth," Robinson told his employer, "I don't like having to defend the patriotism of Negroes. It's like having to defend my own patriotism, when you think about it."

"Not at all, Jackie," Rickey argued. "The issue here is not patriotism. It's your sense of social responsibility.

"The issue is how best can an enlightened Negro right the glaring wrongs in America?

"To say, as Mr. Robeson has said, that Negroes everywhere are waiting to betray Americans in mortal combat against the Reds?

"To suggest, as Mr. Robeson suggests, that the only hope for freedom American Negroes possess is a bloody Red revolution?

"Your triumphs on the ballfield give the lie to that.

"Speaking responsibly to the Congress of the United States can be your greatest triumph of all. It will forever establish the Negro's place in baseball and all America."

Years later Robinson said, rather glumly, "With Mr. Rickey putting it that way, what the hell could I do? I didn't know everything I should have known about the cold war. I had a sense that anti-Communist stuff, the witch-hunts, were dangerous. They came out of a lynching mentality. I didn't think this white congressman from Georgia, Wood, was any hero. My mother, who grew up in Georgia, got out as quickly as she could.

"I wasn't politically smart but I sensed — and my wife, Rachel, sensed — some of what was going on.

"Hell, we weren't idiots. But Mr. Rickey *demanded* that I go. At that point in my life, if Mr. Rickey had told me to jump off the Brooklyn Bridge, I would have said 'Head first or feet first?'"

Rickey enlisted Lester Granger of the Urban League, the most conservative of the national Negro organizations, to help Robinson in his dilemma. Granger and Robinson finally put together a twenty-three-paragraph statement.* Granger did the actual writing, but Robinson was no voder, simply sounding programmed words.

His voice was high-pitched. He was not a dramatic public speaker. The force of his delivery in Congress — and it was forceful — came from the pain and the sincerity with which he spoke.

Robinson flew to Washington and testified on Monday, July 18. "It isn't very pleasant," he began in a crowded hearing room,

> to find myself in the middle of a public argument that has nothing to do with the standing of the Dodgers in the pennant race — or even the pay raise I am going to ask Mr. Branch Rickey for next year. [Laughter.]
>
> So you'll naturally ask, why did I stick my neck out by agreeing to be present and why did I stand by my agreement in spite of advice to the contrary? It isn't easy to find the answer but I guess it boils down to a sense of responsibility.
>
> I don't pretend to be any expert on communism or any other political "ism." . . . But put me down as an expert on being a colored American, with thirty years' experience at it.
>
> Like any other colored person with sense enough to look around, I know that life in these United States can be tough

---

*I collaborated with Robinson on a series of articles that ran under his byline in the black magazine *Our Sports* during 1953. Robinson came to our meetings with a vivid sense of what he wanted said. I typed, organized, punctuated, and spelled and occasionally questioned. Robinson provided the ideas. That was about how he had worked with Granger, Robinson said, "except Granger's questions and suggestions were more than occasional, since we were dealing with a tremendous topic."

for people who are a little different from the majority in their
skin color or the way they worship. . . .

I'm not fooled because I've had a chance. . . . I'm proud that
I've made good on my assignment to the point where other
colored players will find it easier to enter the game. But I'm
well aware that even this limited job isn't finished yet. There
are only three major league clubs with only seven colored players signed up,* out of close to four hundred major league players
on sixteen clubs. . . .

A start has been made. Southern fans as well as northern
fans like the way things are working. We're going to make progress in other American fields, if we can get rid of some mis-
understanding.

The white public should start appreciating that every single
Negro worth his salt resents slurs and discrimination. That has
absolutely nothing to do with what Communists may or may
not be trying to do. . . .

White people must realize that the more a Negro hates communism because it opposes democracy, the more he is going
to hate any other influence that kills off democracy in this country — racial discrimination in the army, segregation on trains
and buses, job discrimination because of religious beliefs.

If a Communist denounces injustice in the American courts,
or police brutality, or lynching, that doesn't change the truth. . . .
A lot of people try to pretend that the issue [of discrimination]
is a creation of Communist imaginations. . . . But Negroes were
stirred up long before there was a Communist party and they'll
stay stirred up long after the party has disappeared. . . .

I've been asked to express my views on Paul Robeson's statement to the effect that American Negroes would refuse to fight
in any war against Russia. The statement, if Mr. Robeson actually made it, sounds silly to me. But he has a right to his
personal views and if he wants to sound silly when he expresses
them in public, that's his business, not mine.

There are some colored pacifists and they'd act like pacifists
of any color. Most Negroes and Irish and Jews and Swedes and
Slavs and other Americans would do their best to keep their

---

*Robinson, Newcombe, and Campanella with the Dodgers; Thompson and
Irvin with the Giants; and Larry Doby and Satchel Paige with Cleveland.

country out of war; if unsuccessful, they'd do their best to help their country win, against Russia or any other enemy.

The public is off on the wrong foot when it begins to think of radicalism in terms of any special minority group. Thinking of this sort gets people scared because one Negro threatens an organized boycott by 15 million members of his race.

I can't speak for 15 million, but I've got too much invested for my wife, my child, and myself in the future of this country to throw it away because of a siren song sung in bass. . . .

That doesn't mean we're going to stop fighting race discrimination. It means we're going to fight it all the harder.

We can win our fight without Communists and we don't want their help.

Robinson put down his papers in the hearing room. Someone shouted "Amen!"

There followed tumultuous applause.

Robinson flew back to New York in time for batting practice before a night game against the Chicago Cubs at Ebbets Field. He took over the Brooklyn ballpark in the sixth inning. Bob Rush, a hard-throwing right-hander, walked him with one out. Robinson stole second and went to third when catcher Mickey Owen threw the ball into center field. Robinson led far off third base, bluffing a break for home. With one out, the percentage demanded that he stay at third. A fly ball or a grounder would score the run.

But Robinson was all adventure, all surprise. As Rush went into a high-kicking windup, Robinson broke for the plate. Hurrying, Rush threw a fastball over Owen's head. Robinson had stolen two bases in the inning; he'd stolen home.

Finally, in the eighth inning, he tripled to drive in Brooklyn's third run. The Dodgers defeated the Cubs, 3 to 0, moving three and a half games ahead of the second-place Cardinals. Robinson had manufactured two of the three runs. That night he was batting .363 and leading the league in hits, runs, runs batted in, and stolen bases.

In an arch sidebar story, Louis Effrat of the *Times* focused on Robinson's remark to Congress that he was going to ask Rickey for more money the next season.

"No comment" is all Rickey would tell Effrat.

Actually, Rickey's cold frugality did not extend to Robinson, who had already moved up to a salary of $19,000, fine for the time. And, of course, Rickey knew in advance everything that Robinson would tell Congress and approved in advance everything that Robinson would tell Congress.

Teasing Effrat in the Ebbets Field press box, Dick Young of the *Daily News* said, "What would you do with a guy playing as great as Robbie? Give him a pay cut?"

"It's a fresh angle," Effrat protested. "They love the way I do that at the *Times*. They call me the Kid with the Twist."

"Aaff," Young said. "For God's sake, Jackie's *got* to get a raise." He thought for a moment. The Dodgers were still having trouble finding accommodations for Robinson in Cincinnati and St. Louis. "He leads the league," Young said, "in everything but hotel reservations."

Viewed objectively, or with as much objectivity as I can muster, Robinson's statement seems an outstanding articulation of an informed 1949 centrist position, black or otherwise. Segregation and implicitly segregationist congressmen were rebuked in an extraordinary way. Newspapers applauded with headlines:

JACKIE HITS ROBESON'S RED PITCH

JACKIE ROBINSON HITS A DOUBLE —
AGAINST COMMUNISTS AND JIM CROW

The only immediate criticism appeared in a cartoon published by the *Baltimore Afro-American*. A little boy labeled Jackie Robinson was pictured carrying a huge gun and tracking the gigantic footprints of Paul Robeson.

Robinson's wife Rachel conceded years later "we didn't fully understand what was going on with the House Un-American Activities Committee." In essence, she says, right speech, wrong forum.

Robinson went further to me in 1972. Blinded by virulent diabetes, but more insightful than ever, Robinson said across morning coffee at his sunlit home in Stamford, Connecticut, "I would never criticize Paul Robeson today."

"You disagreed with him," I said.

"That was between us," Robinson said. "We both had and have a larger disagreement with white society.

"Whites took away Paul's career. They took away his wealth. Then white men called this a blacklist. . . .

"The salient fact of my life and the salient fact of Paul Robeson's life is the same. We are black men in a prejudiced white country."

Robinson died that October. Paul Robeson died in 1976. Two brave men had borne frightful pain.

9

Field Marshal
Casey von Stengel

◆

I got this fella who sucks up all the glory and
plays only when he feels like playing.
I never had one like that before.

— *Casey Stengel on Joe DiMaggio*

THE EMPEROR HAD TAKEN to his bed.

His marriage to Dorothy Arnold, the blonde actress, was shot. She'd thrown him out and lured him back and thrown him out again. She was still shooting her mouth off to the gossip columnists. Bad husband. Out all night. Indifferent father.

The Emperor was coming off a rousing season. In 1948, he hit thirty-nine home runs, fourteen more than the Boston Blowhard. Plus *he* could catch a fly and make a throw. But now it was another season and the emperor couldn't play at all. Play ball? He couldn't walk without wincing. He was thirty-four years old and shrewd beyond his years. Joe DiMaggio always knew the score. It could be over. He could be all washed up.

And after that? Icon, deity, emperor, DiMaggio faced questions that tore at every ballplayer approaching the middle of the journey.

Alimony and child support ran to almost $10,000 a year. How could he make those payments if he didn't play ball?

There was the family restaurant back in San Francisco, but the family was large. The money got cut up a lot of ways. If he didn't play ball, how would he make a living?

The Yankees were paying DiMaggio $100,000 for the season of 1949. But if he didn't get better, DiMaggio knew, that cold-eyed bastard George Weiss would stop paying him anything at all.

And after that? What was he going to do with the rest of his life?

The Emperor was feeling poorly. He listened to the radio and read the papers and watched television and took pain-killers. Without him, and with a clown for a manager, the Yankees were running up a big lead. Tommy Henrich. Bobby Brown. Allie Reynolds. Stengel. Stengel. Stengel.

The Emperor sulked in his suite at the Hotel Edison and told the operator that he didn't want any calls today, or any visitors except for Toots Shor and Georgie Solotaire.

DiMaggio had been suffering from heel spurs, tiny spikes of calcium growing like needles out of the bone. The spikes cut into soft tissue with each step. Walking hurt. It was impossible to run.

In April, Yankee medical people dispatched DiMaggio to Johns Hopkins Hospital in Baltimore, where an orthopedist named John Bennett was renowned for successful surgery on athletes. Bennett told DiMaggio that he could remove the calcium spikes but that pain would persist for some time. "Eventually, Joe, the pain should go away. It's a mysterious kind of thing. But there have been cases where a month or so after this operation, a patient went to sleep one night in pain and woke up feeling fine."

As orderlies wheeled DiMaggio toward the surgical theater, a photographer appeared in the white hospital corridor and flashbulbs popped. DiMaggio sat up and began to curse. Then he said to the photographer, "I've always cooperated with you guys. Why are you doing this to me?"

The photographer stopped shooting. "It's my assignment," he said.

"I've cooperated with every photographer who ever wanted a picture," DiMaggio said, white-draped on the hospital gurney. "All I'm asking for now is personal privacy."

"Sure, Joe," the photographer said. "I'll tear up the negatives. I'll tell my boss I couldn't get a shot."

A few days later, DiMaggio returned to New York on crutches and boarded up in the Edison, near Times Square, his home for half a year. DiMaggio was a hotel fella, not subject to domestication.*

George Solotaire was a short, stocky ticket broker who spoke glib, Damon Runyon English. Divorce was "splitsville." Bankruptcy was "brokesville." Want two tickets in row F? "I'll see if I can get ya a coupla Freddies."

Solotaire idolized DiMaggio, hung his clothing, sent out his laundry, and ran huge Broadway-Jewish sandwiches from the Stage Delicatessen to the convalescent. With ties to theater, Solotaire seemed always able to find showgirls aquiver to meet DiMaggio. Solotaire became DiMaggio's closest New York friend during the Era.

Toots Shor worshiped at Shrine DiMaggio in a different fashion. "Daig is the greatest ballplayer ever," Shor lectured favored patrons, columnists Bob Considine, Red Smith, and Bill Corum, and the repetition had the effect of magnifying DiMaggio's formidable skills. You got nowhere, or at least I got nowhere, in later years submitting to Shor that Willie Mays ran faster, threw better, was more durable, and caught fly balls DiMaggio couldn't have reached. Shor's response: "Don't advertise yer ignorance."

Solotaire handled food, laundry, and show girls. Shor was supervising press secretary, minister of propaganda. The most

---

*Years afterwards he traveled to Vietnam with Pete Rose on a trip to cheer up servicemen. The publicity man for the trip, Robert O. Fishel, said, "I had to pack and unpack for DiMaggio every day. He said he didn't know how to pack a suitcase. All his life he'd gotten somebody to pack and unpack for him."

favored chronicler was Jimmy Cannon of the *New York Post.* Cannon was passionate, egocentric, talkative, unmarried, and gifted in remarkable ways. Describing many years later one boorish sportscaster, Cannon wrote, "If Howard Cosell were a sport, it would be Roller Derby."

"Jimmy had certain excesses," says Ed Fitzgerald, who edited *Sport,* the dominant sports magazine during the Era, "but I believe, even including Hemingway, Cannon was the greatest writer in the world on two topics: Joe Louis and Joe DiMaggio."

In his bestselling *Summer of '49,* David Halberstam suggests that Cannon "created not just the legend of Joe DiMaggio as the great athlete, but, even more significant, DiMaggio as the Hemingway hero, as elegant off the field as on it." Actually, Cannon did not create the image of a silent, towering hero. DiMaggio himself created that. Joe DiMaggio and nobody else invented Joe DiMaggio. Cannon was merely the scribe, albeit a good one.

To this day, debate continues to hum about the point: How good was Joe DiMaggio, really? How much of his reputation is image and hype? One interesting, although negative, perception comes to us through an unusual statistical gauge of offensive performance called relative performance measurement, or RPM. This was created by an Illinois statistician with a name that might belong to one of those old Chicago Bear linebackers: Ron Skrabacz. "The concept of dominance," Skrabacz writes in *The Baseball Research Journal,* "can easily be quantified and can be useful in comparing players with their peers or with players from other eras. Relative performance measurement shows which players were most dominant over their careers. . . . Can you compare Babe Ruth against Hank Aaron based on seasonal numbers or even career statistics? They hit against different pitchers and fielders and played with different advantages."

Ruth, of course, played only against whites, which made his working day easier. Aaron played against whites, blacks, and

Latins. Ruth played by day and made his trips by train. Aaron traveled by jet and mostly played at night. Aaron hit against fielders armed and armored with big gloves. Ruth had to swing at spitballs. Aaron was cared for by skilled trainers and modern doctors. In Ruth's time, sports medicine was primitive.

To pick up Mr. Skrabacz, "What you *can* compare definitively is how Ruth measured up against his peers and how Aaron stacked up against his. By neutralizing era-specific factors [jet travel vs. train travel], you can judge the players on how well they dominated their peers."

Skrabacz considers fifteen familiar categories, including runs, hits, singles, doubles, triples, homers, walks, steals, runs batted in, and batting average. Then he measures each player's performance in each category against the performances of contemporaries. Since Skrabacz is seeking excellence, he flags only the top five players in each category, examining every season from 1900 to the present. "I calculate the numbers with simple arithmetic," he says. "A point system awards the top player five points. That is, if you're the leading hitter you get five. Second leading hitter gets four, down to the fifth leading hitter who gets one."

With a little more arithmetic, Skrabacz has calculated the twenty-five most dominant offensive players in major league history. Here is his list:

Rank	Player	Combined RPM	Total Top 5 Finishes
1	Ty Cobb	724.33	151
2	Stan Musial	618.66	135
3	Babe Ruth	569.83	112
4	Hank Aaron	543.91	130
5	Honus Wagner	542.64	118
6	Lou Gehrig	537.27	120
7	Rogers Hornsby	518.25	107
8	Ted Williams	507.25	104
9	Sam Crawford	489.39	120

10	Willie Mays	470.83	111
11	Tris Speaker	429.16	111
12	Pete Rose	415.96	97
13	Mike Schmidt	365.83	81
14	Mickey Mantle	360.33	78
15	Mel Ott	350.53	84
16	Joe Medwick	334.75	81
17	Jimmie Foxx	325.50	75
18	Frank Robinson	314.19	82
19	Johnny Mize	313.67	71
20	Napoleon Lajoie	312.43	67
21	Paul Waner	301.75	74
22	Joe DiMaggio	299.16	75
23	George Sisler	294.64	70
24	Sherry Magee	284.93	71
25	Eddie Collins	284.86	75

From this list, Musial, Williams, Mays, Mantle, Mize, and DiMaggio played significant portions of their career during the Era. DiMaggio's finish, twenty-second, places him in the second echelon of the top offensive players of all time. Commendable, but less than godlike.

Arthur Patterson suggested a rebuttal shortly before his death in 1991. "DiMaggio played for us at Yankee Stadium for thirteen years," Patterson said. "During that time we won ten pennants. I'm sure I'm not as good with numbers as Mr. Skrabacz, but ten for thirteen isn't bad, and we don't win ten, or anywhere close, without DiMaggio."

"Red," I said, "after DiMaggio quit, the Yankees still won the pennant in six of the next seven seasons."

"That tells us nothing about DiMaggio," Patterson said. "It just says that Mantle was great and Stengel was a genius."

As he lay about his hotel suite in sharp, persistent pain, DiMaggio did not want to see any sportswriters, not even Cannon. Any one of them, Cannon included, might start asking

questions. Would he ever play again? DiMaggio did not want
to see teammates, either. He missed playing ball. He missed
the cheers. Seeing his teammates could just make that longing
sharper. It hurt not playing and, to tell the truth, it hurt that
the Yankees were winning all those games without him.

DiMaggio later said, "I guess I was . . . a mental case. . . .
The team kept sending me checks. Whenever one came, I told
myself, 'You've certainly done a swell job of earning this money.'
. . . I had trouble getting to sleep. . . . If my playing career
was over, what was I going to do? Lying awake, sometimes
until five in the morning, I figured out at least a half dozen
careers. I must have been really upset, because right now I
can't remember any of them."*

He was close to emotional collapse one morning in June
when the pain in his left heel eased, as mysteriously as doctors
at Johns Hopkins had foretold. DiMaggio had looked over the
abyss and hadn't liked what he saw. He threw himself back into
the world. He took batting practice and swung until his hands
bled. He had special high shoes crafted, with heavy padding
at the heel and toe spikes only. Eliminating heel spikes cut
down on impact where the spurs had grown.

On June 27, DiMaggio went out to play his first game of
the year. He had missed three months. His intensity glowed
like Vesuvius, circa A.D. 79. Then he popped out four straight
times.

The game was on a Monday night, an exhibition between
the Yankees and the Giants to raise money for sandlot baseball
and determine what the *Herald Tribune* called "the Trans-
Harlem championship of Manhattan and the Bronx." The Yankees defeated the Giants, 5 to 3.

DiMaggio did not hide from reporters. "I thought I was
ready," he said. "Now I'm not sure."

---

*DiMaggio told these things to Marshall Smith, the sports editor of *Life*
magazine, later in the 1949 season. Still worried about money, he sold his byline
to *Life* for $5,000.

The Yankees caught the Owl, an overnight train for Boston, where on Tuesday they would open a three-game series against the Red Sox. DiMaggio declined to accompany the team. Next morning he took two more hours of batting practice in empty Yankee Stadium.

He caught a three o'clock plane for Boston but declined to check in with Casey Stengel.

A dozen writers pressed Stengel at Fenway Park. Was he going to put DiMaggio in the lineup?

"I don't know," Stengel said loudly. "I'm waiting for him to tell me whether he can play."

DiMaggio was sitting twenty-five feet down the bench, adjusting the laces in his high-topped semi-spikes. "What about it, Joe?"

"Yeah," DiMaggio said, clearly, distinctly. "I'm going to play."

He was not asking. He was announcing. Stengel silently prepared the Yankee lineup:

Rizzuto, ss
Coleman, 2b
Henrich, 1b
J. DiMaggio, cf
Berra, c
Johnson, 3b
Lindell, lf
Bauer, rf
Reynolds, p

DiMaggio led off the second inning with a line single to left field off Maurice "Mickey" McDermott, a twenty-year-old left-hander from Poughkeepsie, New York. McDermott walked Long John Lindell, and Hank Bauer slugged a fastball over the left field wall. The Yankees had a 3 to 0 lead.

Rizzuto led off the third with a single. McDermott struck out Jerry Coleman and Tommy Henrich. Then DiMaggio cracked a fastball high over the left field wall. The Yankees won the ballgame, 5 to 4.

Next afternoon, the Red Sox went with a tall, bourbon-gulping right-hander named Ellis Kinder and seemed to be making off with the game. Kinder was cruising in the fifth, two out, nobody on, and the Red Sox leading, 7 to 1. But he walked Rizzuto and Henrich, and DiMaggio hit another home run high over the left field wall, scoring three runs.

By the eighth inning the Yankees had tied the score. Earl Johnson, a tall left-handed pitcher who had been having arm trouble, was the Boston reliever. Johnson threw a breaking ball low and inside and DiMaggio hit his second home run of the game. As he loped across home plate, Stengel scrambled out of the dugout and began a series of ostentatious salaams. Di-Maggio looked embarrassed. The Yankees won the ballgame, 9 to 7.

From Rud Rennie's story in the New York *Herald Tribune* two days later:

Boston, June 30 — The DiMaggio did it again. For the third day in succession since returning to active duty, Jolting Joe walloped a home run over the wall. This one in the seventh inning was good for three runs, the margin as the Yankees defeated the Red Sox, 6 to 3, sweeping the series.

Joe is stealing the show and headlines from coast to coast with a devastating performance in which he has hit four home runs in three games for a total of nine runs driven in. He has the writers searching their brains for superb super superlatives and his teammates beaming in the reflected splendor of his stardom.

The Red Sox did not fold. They regrouped and played tough baseball and going into the final weekend of the season led the Yankees by one game. Williams was having a wonderful summer; he would bat in 159 runs. DiMaggio gave the Yankees a wonderful half summer, but late in September he retreated into his hotel suite again. This time it was flu or mild pneumonia or a ferocious cold or — none dared say this in the sporting world — just overwhelming pressure. DiMaggio looked pale. He felt weak. The pennant was unsettled. The last two games pitted the Yankees against the Red Sox at the Stadium.

DiMaggio's status was uncertain, but the Yankees placed advertisements in each of New York's nine daily papers:

Saturday Is Joe D. Day
at the Stadium
A Great Day for a Great Player
1:15 P.M.

"But will you play him?" Leonard Koppett of the *Herald Tribune* asked Stengel.

"If he feels better," Stengel said tightly.

"Joe told me there was no sense in his playing," Koppett said, "if he was going to be a detriment to the team."

Stengel's answer sailed over Koppett's head. "It would be hard for him to be a detriment in any condition, wouldn't it?" Stengel said. A very young reporter and a passionate Yankee fan, Koppett was too wide-eyed to recognize the bitterness between the tough old manager and the temperamental star. "Play or not," Koppett wrote blithely, "Joe will be on hand today as the central figure in the greatest one-day baseball show ever put on in New York."

"I got this fella," Stengel remarked to his wife, Edna, "who sucks up all the glory and plays only when he feels like playing. I never had one like that before. What am I gonna do?"

Edna Lawton Stengel was a practical person. "Let him play whenever he wants to play, dear."

The American League pennant race closed with a positively Aristotelian unity of place. The Yankees and the Red Sox, DiMaggio and Williams, Old Casey Stengel and Older Joe McCarthy eyeball to eyeball, nostril to flaring nostril at Yankee Stadium. By contrast, the National League race, though equally close, was diffuse. The Dodgers and the Cardinals would settle their great rivalry playing third parties. Here is the way the races stood on the morning of Saturday, October 1.

NATIONAL LEAGUE

	W.	L.	Pct.	Games Behind	To Play
Brooklyn	96	56	.632	—	2
St. Louis	95	57	.625	1	2

Remaining games: Brooklyn at Philadelphia (2); St. Louis at Chicago (2)

AMERICAN LEAGUE

	W.	L.	Pct.	Games Behind	To Play
Boston	96	56	.632	—	2
New York	95	57	.625	1	2

Remaining games: Boston at New York (2)

Often during the Era, Dodger managers assigned important ballgames to Ralph Branca, the large, hawk-nosed, right-handed pitcher out of Mount Vernon, New York, by way of New York University, where he starred on both the baseball and the basketball teams. Ralph was sensitive, open, and likable, with a fine fastball and a big snapping curve. He was just the kind of major leaguer you'd want to take the kids to meet. As a big-game pitcher, he evolved into a disaster.

He would go on to marry a wealthy woman and enjoy great business success in later years, but to this day anger and sadness play on Branca's face when he discusses his pitching career. A twenty-one-game winner at the age of twenty-one, he was out of baseball, selling insurance, by the time he was thirty. He blames injuries. Others are not so sure.

"The tree that grows in Brooklyn is an apple tree," Dick Young wrote in the *Daily News,* "and the apples are in the throats of the Dodgers." Young meant that the Dodgers could not swallow, that they were choking. "Not all the Dodgers, of course," Young told me. "No one in his right mind would call Reese or Robinson a choker. I meant the pitchers. Specifically

I meant Ralph Branca. The other players agreed with what I wrote. Quietly they agreed with me. Sometimes it looked like everybody on the Brooklyn club knew who the chokers were, everybody except the ballclub manager."

Branca started strong in Philadelphia on Saturday, but abruptly lost command in the sixth inning when Dick Sisler tripled and Del Ennis, a free-swinging right-handed slugger, cracked a home run into the upper deck in left field at Shibe Park. Branca went no further. The Phillies won, 6 to 4. But the Cardinals lost in Chicago. The Dodgers stayed one game out front.

On Sunday the Cards played a powerful ballgame at Wrigley Field. Musial hit two home runs and St. Louis won, 13 to 5. The Dodgers pulled ahead in Philadelphia but the Phillies overcame a five-run deficit and tied the score. Two in the tenth inning at last won the ballgame, 9 to 7, and the fiercely contested pennant for Brooklyn.

"C'mere," Burt Shotton bellowed at Harold Rosenthal in the Dodger clubhouse. Shotton hugged the reporter and bellowed, "How about that win, Rosenbloom?"*

St. Louis had now finished second three straight times. Despite Musial, the Cardinals, the closest thing extant to a Confederacy team, were in decline. By the time the Cardinals won another pennant, long afterwards in 1964, their best pitcher and most of their best hitters were black men.

Joe DiMaggio's haul, on October 1, was without precedent, either in baseball history or in the annals of excess in the Bronx. Gifts from "fans and organizations" included two automobiles, one motorboat, three watches, two television sets, one foam mattress with box spring, three sets of luggage, a deer rifle, a

---

*Rosenthal says that Shotton, like numbers of old baseball men, disliked Jews. "When I finally stood up to him and told him to stop mocking my name, he shouted at me, 'Okay, *Rosenberg.*' After that, I never again mentioned Shotton's name in the *Herald Tribune.* I'd write 'the Dodger manager' but not his name. A disservice to readers, perhaps, but that was how I felt."

case of oranges, a pack of walnuts, a cocker spaniel, three sets of cufflinks, three hundred quarts of ice cream, a golf bag, a case of shoestring potatoes, a set of fishing tackle, an electric blanket, three money clips, and a set of rosary beads.

"How do you feel?" Red Smith asked DiMaggio.

"You know something, Red?" DiMaggio said. "I'm kind of worried."

"You've been through tough ballgames before," Smith said.

"I'm not talking about the ballgame. I've got to say thank you. It's my speech that has me worried."

DiMaggio withdrew into silence, mentally rehearsing what he would tell the crowd — 69,551 people assembled in triple-tiered, autumn-shadowed Yankee Stadium. After a while Mel Allen walked up to a microphone set up close to home plate and said, "It's always best to be brief when introducing a great guy. Ladies and gentlemen, Joe DiMaggio."

"The cheers that followed," Smith wrote, "ricocheted off the eardrum, made conversation impossible and gave Joe an opportunity to rehearse his speech once more." People screamed in adulation. DiMaggio stood silent and solemn.

Facing the seats behind home plate, DiMaggio began very gracefully: "First of all, I'd like to apologize to the people in the bleachers for having my back to them." That started the ovation again.

"This is one of the few times in my career," DiMaggio said, "that I've choked up. Believe me, ladies and gentlemen, right now there's a big lump in my throat.

"Many years ago a friend of mine named Lefty O'Doul told me, when I was coming to New York, not to let the big town scare me. This day proves that New York City is the friendliest town in the world.

"I thank the good Lord for making me a Yankee."

A fine, tough ballgame followed. Stocky, bespectacled Dom DiMaggio opened the game for Boston with a single to right field. After Johnny Pesky forced little Dom, Ted Williams hand-cuffed Tommy Henrich with a bounder. Williams hit ground balls with so much overspin that infielders likened them to grenades. Allie Reynolds bounced a curve ball past Yogi Berra and both runners advanced. Vern Stephens lined out to Johnny Lindell in left field and Pesky scored.

In the third, with the Red Sox still leading by one run, Reynolds walked Pesky, Williams, and Stephens. Early though this was, Stengel sent for lefty Joe Page, his great closer. Before Page got his head into the game, he walked two more. The Red Sox now led, 4 to 0. At this point Mr. Page went fully awake. Across the final six innings, he allowed the Red Sox only one hit.

Joe DiMaggio got the Yankee offense going in the fourth inning with a line drive to right that bounced over the low railing for a ground-rule double. Before the inning was done, the Yankees scored twice. In the fifth, Rizzuto, Henrich, and Berra singled on successive pitches for another run. With two out in the eighth, Johnny Lindell crushed a fastball deep into the lower left field stands. Noise ricocheted off the eardrums once again.

The Yankees won the ballgame, 5 to 4. With one day left and one game left in the season, the teams were tied.

Sunday, October 2, was an unsettling day. The Soviet Union announced that it was severing relations with the Nationalist China, now based on Taiwan, and would recognize the People's Republic, ruled by Mao Tse-tung. The *Times* reported that the Russians would demand that the Chinese Communists replace the Chinese Nationalists at the United Nations. The world was moving slowly toward a withering war on the redolent peninsula of Korea.

Justice William O. Douglas, the preeminent liberal on the Supreme Court, was bucked off a horse near Yakima, Washington, and broke thirteen ribs. But next day, the big news was baseball. Even the grim, gray *New York Times* published a breathless baseball story as its lead.

The Stadium was overflowing with fans — 68,055 paid — under a bright early autumn sky. The weather was gentle — high 60s. "Hey," Casey Stengel said to Joe Cashman of the Boston *Record*, "how is your team today, Cashbox? Confident?"

"I think they are," Cashman said.

"Well, so is my club," Stengel said. He grinned without mirth. "But one team is gonna lose all its confidence before dark."

Boston manager Joe McCarthy was tense and clipped. Managing the Yankees, McCarthy had won eight pennants from 1932 through 1943. A month into the 1946 season, Larry Mac-Phail fired him. The Red Sox hired McCarthy in 1948 on the supposition that a man who had won with the Yankees might know how to defeat the Yankees, as if, say, George III commissioned Benedict Arnold to lead an army attacking Washington's Continentals.

McCarthy did outpace the Yankees in 1948, but still finished second to Cleveland. Now, at sixty-two, older even than Stengel, Joe McCarthy wanted to wrest the pennant from the Yankees, the team that he'd helped build and shape, the team that had fired him. McCarthy wanted to beat the Yankees as a climax to his life.

"Yeah, we're ready," he said tightly. "We been ready all year." Plump Johnny Schulte, the Red Sox bullpen coach, was merrier. "I've got myself a couple of train reservations," he said to Arthur Daley of the *Times*. "If we win, I'm on the six o'clock for Boston, and the World Series. But just in case, I'm also booked on the seven-thirty for St. Louis. That's home."

Joe DiMaggio allowed himself one light moment. "Joe," he said archly to Page, the team's preeminent pub crawler, "how did you sleep last night?"

"Good," Page said. "I always sleep good. That is, I always sleep good when I get to sleep."

Then it was time to play ball: Vic Raschi, 20 and 10, against Ellis Kinder, 23 and 5, for three months the most effective pitcher in baseball. Raschi handled the Sox easily in the first inning. Rizzuto led off for the Yankees with a line drive over third base. It was only 301 feet down the line. The drive looked good for two bases at most. Williams rushed over but did not get his glove down, and the ball skittered past him for a triple. "Ted played that," Red Smith said, "as though the baseball were a viper."

Ellis Kinder was a country boy, a drinking man. He had been up much of the night, but he was rugged. He felt okay. Hell, Kinder wondered, what was going on with Williams? He *knew* what was going on with Williams. Pressure was going on. Then Old Joe McCarthy played the Boston infield back. McCarthy was conceding a run for an out. That's what baseball textbooks said to do, go for the out early; you'll get the run back.

Except . . .

except . . .

The Sox were swinging against Vic Raschi in a big game. The textbooks, such as they were, told you also that in big games, runs against Raschi came very, very hard.

McCarthy, managing the biggest game of his career, was playing it safe. Henrich grounded out to second and Rizzuto scored.

Joe DiMaggio lifted a fly down the right field line. Al Zarilla ran hard but fell down. DiMaggio slid safely, painfully, into third base. Another triple. One inning. Two bad Boston outfield plays. A questionable call by the Boston manager. Still, DiMaggio was stranded at third.

Raschi gave nothing away, no runs at all. Bulky, big-shouldered, glowering, black-browed, superb. The Yankees led, 1 to 0, in the eighth inning and Kinder was scheduled to hit first. McCarthy called him back and sent up a left-hand-hitting rookie outfielder, Thomas Everette Wright, who had behind him a total of six major league turns at bat.

Kinder began to curse. He could hit better than that kid. The way he was pitching, Kinder thought, how the hell could you take him out?

Wright walked. Dom DiMaggio grounded into a double play. The Yankees retained their one-run lead, and Kinder was out of the game. The Yankees broke through with four more runs against the Boston bullpen.

Boston came back in the ninth inning. With one out, Williams walked. Vern Stephens singled. Bobby Doerr hit a long fly to center. DiMaggio broke slowly and the ball sailed over his head, good for three bases and Boston's first two runs.

With Birdie Tebbetts batting, DiMaggio suddenly shouted, "Time. Time out!" to Charlie Berry, the second base umpire. DiMaggio shook his head. He felt dizzy, he said. He began a slow jog from center field toward the Yankee dugout. He was taking himself out of the game. With that, he drew an ovation, sucking up, as Stengel said, more glory.

Raschi threw a high fastball and Birdie Tebbetts hit a pop foul that Tommy Henrich caught. The game was over. The Yankees had won, 5 to 3. The Yankees had won the pennant. Coach Bill Dickey leaped with jubilation. His head hit the dugout ceiling and Dickey went bubble-eyed.

"That is the seventy-second injury our courageous ballclub has suffered this season," Arthur Patterson announced in the press box.

Afterwards, Casey Stengel sought out McCarthy. "Well, you won a lot of pennants for this here New York nine. You been splendid," Stengel said. "I guess this year it was just my turn."

After Stengel and the photographers and the reporters left, Ellis Kinder sought out McCarthy with harsher words. "You gutless old clown," Kinder said. "You choking old bastard. You couldn't manage my dick."

McCarthy had managed a pantheon of stars: Rogers Hornsby, Gabby Hartnett, Babe Ruth, Lou Gehrig, Joe DiMaggio. Twenty-three years managing in Chicago, New York, Boston, the greatest players in the greatest towns. No ballplayer had cursed him out before.

Overall, McCarthy teams won nine pennants. His World Series winning percentage, .698, was and is the loftiest in history. He hadn't managed badly against the Yankees, just routinely, which was not good enough when opposing Stengel.

After the Kinder confrontation, McCarthy lost both authority and respect. The Red Sox fired him the next season. He retired to Buffalo, New York, where he pursued obscurity and declined to grant interviews, much less compose his memoirs. He was approaching his ninety-first birthday when he died in 1978 on a cold January day. The local ballfields were buried under two feet of snow.

◆

ON WEDNESDAY, OCTOBER 5, Sherman Minton of Indiana, a new appointee to the Supreme Court, paid an afternoon call on the White House and found Harry Truman staring at a television set.

"Sit down, sit down," Truman said. "We'll talk business later. This big colored guy for Brooklyn is throwing hard. I wonder if DiMaggio will get to him."

"He better watch Henrich," Sherman Minton said. "Henrich is the Yankees' best clutch hitter now."

"Down home in Missouri," Truman said, still watching intently, "we called a good clutch hitter Mr. Pork Chops. He was the guy who'd bring the pork chops home."

"Henrich has a German background, Mr. President," Minton said, "but believe me, he sure is Mr. Sauerbraten."

The great pennant races had focused almost everybody's attention on baseball. Still, John Foster Dulles, a dour and doctrinaire Republican functionary, maintained weaponry trained on the Red Menace. Running for the Senate in New York, Dulles charged that Herbert H. Lehman, the Democrat, was the darling of the radical left. Lehman, a devout capitalist, had inherited a Wall Street banking fortune and resided in opulence at 820 Park Avenue. Meant nothing, said Dulles. Lehman was soft on communism; he was just one more Park Avenue pinko. How nice, many thought, to flee such lewdness for the ballpark, where with minimum peril you could admire real left wingers, Joe Page and Preacher Roe.

This would be Casey Stengel's first World Series since 1923, the season of his ninth-inning home run, and he made a grand return to the sold-out ballparks with three-colored bunting, the raucous folk festival with hustlers, which is what every World Series used to be. Casey would employ only five pitchers in five games. Burt Shotton by contrast used nine. One, Rex Barney, posted an earned run average of 16.88; two others, Carl Erskine and Joe Hatten, recorded ERAs of 16.20. Embarrassing.

Pee Wee Reese is the only man who played in every game in every one of the great Brooklyn-Yankee World Series, from 1941 through 1956, seven confrontations, forty-four games. Not Rizzuto, not DiMaggio, not Berra, but Reese, a thin, well-muscled, graceful athlete.

Reese had a gentle, compassionate nature, formed about a core of pure competitive flame. His seamless youthful face led writers to describe him as "puckish." He stood five feet, ten inches and played at 160 pounds, hardly a pee wee. Indeed, the nickname came not from his size but from the game of marbles. Reese won the national boys' marble championship when he was fifteen years old. The large marble was called a shooter. The small marble, the one you aimed for with the shooter, was a pee wee. "What I got in this young feller," Durocher remarked, when Reese reached Brooklyn in 1940, "is the Babe Ruth of marbles. On our ballclub, he's a rookie. In the world of marbles, he's an old man."

Durocher was phasing himself out of the Dodger infield; he wanted to concentrate on managing. He loved to strut in silk shirts, gold cufflinks, wingtip shoes; he intended to put his playing days behind him and Reese was a perfect instrument toward that end.

"Kid," Durocher said, "anything you want to know about playing shortstop in the majors, come to me."

Reese nodded. He was a quiet rookie. Durocher talked about shading hitters, cheating toward second, moving with the pitch, going into the hole, turning the double play. He talked and talked, begging Reese to ask questions. But no questions came.

Finally, in late June Reese said, "There is something I do want to ask you, Skipper."

Durocher beamed. Several thousand ganglia snapped to attention.

"Anything, kid. Anything."

"Leo," Reese said, "where do you buy your clothes?"

Reese became a dominant Dodger through quiet leadership rather than flash. You had to see him every day to realize what a wonderful ballplayer he was. He became captain of the Dodger team in 1947 and he championed Jackie Robinson's cause, without ever deifying his double play partner. Robinson was often loud, often cutting. Sometimes Robinson's needling became downright nasty.

"You know, Jack," Reese remarked one day, "some of those pitchers knocking you down are throwing at you because you're colored. But for some others color has nothing to do with it. They just plain don't like you."

Robinson winced and nodded. No other ballplayer, white or black, spoke to Robinson as Reese did. There was touching love between them and touching candor.

With all this, it was possible to forget how splendidly Reese played under pressure, how tough he was when a game was on the line. "You throw him a good curve," Stengel said, in admiration and annoyance, "and he goes down with that bat of his and gets it like a fisherman getting his hook down for a fish. The little son of a bitch hits my good pitchers' very good pitches, which shows that hitting is more than batting average,

as my very good pitchers will confirm if they feel like talking
to you."

Reese had a good Series in 1949, batting .316, with a home
run. But Duke Snider and Jackie Robinson, both Hall of Famers, batted under .200 and Carl Furillo, plagued by a torn
muscle, could start only two games. "Where did you tear it,
Skoonj?" Harold Rosenthal asked. "Where does it hurt?"

"It's in my groining," Skoonj Furillo said.

Furillo's unusual nickname came from his fondness for scun-
gilli, chopped conch served in a spicy Neapolitan sauce. Sturdy
Carl had come into his own at the age of twenty-seven. Earlier,
he'd had a nasty time playing for Durocher. "That bastard said
I couldn't hit right-handed pitchers," Furillo told me in anger
and disgust. He was a guileless man never schooled beyond
the eighth grade. "Durocher was making it seem like I was
afraid of curve balls. That I was backing off. That I was gutless.
Hey, Meat, the year I like to squeeze his fucking head off,
Durocher found out how gutless I was, right?"*

Healthy, Furillo was a good Series hitter. Now he was hurt.
Reese and Gene Hermanski, an irregular outfielder, were the
only Dodgers who batted over .300 in the Series. Dodger fans
said, as the Series seemed to slip away, "It's a damn shame our
good hitters slumped. Otherwise we woulda kilt them Yankee
crumbs."

This is the Flatbush version of the Grand Illusion. The Dodgers never had a true fence buster of a Series against the Yankees. Twice Duke Snider hit four home runs in one Series, but
overall the Yankees consistently outhit and outslugged the Dodgers. In their thirty-nine Series games from 1947 through 1956,
the Yankees hit forty-five homers. The Dodgers hit fourteen

---

*At twenty-two, I weighed 138 pounds. With great geniality, Furillo nick-
named me "Meat." I thought the nickname Skoonj had a distressing racial tinge,
rather like addressing a Jew as "Matzo-ball." Furillo called me Meat. I called
him Carl. The astounding head-squeezing episode with Leo Durocher occurred,
as we shall see, in 1953.

fewer, a significant difference, some thirty-one percent. Life-time, Jackie Robinson was not much of a World Series hit-ter, batting only .234. By contrast, Billy Martin hit five Series home runs against the Dodgers and batted .333. Gil Hodges, Brooklyn's strongest right-handed slugger, got no hits at all in the seven-game Series of 1952. He went 0 for 21 and 0 for Oc-tober.

This was not coincidence, or what was damned in Brooklyn as Yankee luck. It is a tested axiom that good pitching stops good hitting and this is what worked mightily against Robinson, Hodges, and the others. The Yankees had very good pitching and a manager who knew how to use good pitching better than anyone else on earth. Didn't the Dodgers have splendid pitch-ers as well? Indeed they did. "A lot of their fellers really threw hard," as Bobby Brown points out. "Newcombe, Branca, Bar-ney were very fast. But it happened we were a great fastball-hitting team." Brown speaks without smugness, although when he retired to work in medicine full-time, his World Series bat-ting average, pounded mostly against Brooklyn fastballs, stood at .439.

Allie Reynolds started the first game against Don Newcombe, power pitcher against power pitcher. The Dodgers brought back stars from a 1916 Brooklyn team that won a pennant, and Stengel chattered cheerfully with old teammates Zach Wheat, "Chief" Meyers, "Rube" Marquard. "Damn," Stengel said, clearly and sadly, "where did all those years go?"

"For eight and a half innings," Red Smith wrote, "nothing happened yesterday at Yankee Stadium. Reynolds and New-combe wouldn't allow anything to happen. There were no fielding plays of great distinction, no hits of special note. Hum-phrey Bogart and Lauren Bacall sat looking on, as silent as the 66,224 other witnesses. They've put on more spectacular bat-tles themselves in El Morocco."

Across nine innings, Reynolds struck out nine Dodgers, including Snider three times. Across eight and a half innings, Newcombe struck out eleven, every Yankee but Rizzuto and Henrich. He walked nobody.

Henrich led off the ninth inning. Newcombe missed with an inside fastball. He missed with another. His curve was a fast, sharp-breaking pitch. He threw the curve to Henrich, low, where he wanted it. Henrich cracked a long drive to right. Newcombe gave the ball a quick look and started off the mound. Henrich's homer won the ballgame, 1 to 0. At the White House, Harry Truman clapped Sherman Minton on the back.

"Taking nothing away from the Brooklyn team," Stengel told the sportswriters, "you would have to agree after what you just saw, that they are pretty nice, the ballplayers I got."

"The plate umpire [Cal Hubbard] is an American League guy," Jackie Robinson said, "and he called an American League game. I've never seen so many bad strikes called against us. Reynolds was missing the corners all day."

When A. B. "Happy" Chandler, the commissioner, read Robinson's remarks, he ordered Robinson to wire an apology to Hubbard or face suspension. Then Chandler issued a press release stating that he personally had ordered Robinson to "stop popping off."

"Is this because of my color?" Robinson said, echoing a question someone asked. "Ask yourself this. There are fifty ballplayers on the field and most of them yap at the umpire. One ballplayer is singled out by the baseball commissioner. The one ballplayer is colored. Aside from that, I have no comment."

Brooklyn's best pitcher — as distinct from hardest thrower — was a left-handed stringbean, all bones and angles and Adam's apple, out of northeast Arkansas hill country. Elwin Charles Roe had been nicknamed "Preacher" during a gabby childhood, and Preacher Roe was a droll and remarkable character.

His father, a failed pitcher, practiced medicine out of a tin-roofed house in Viola, the only doctor in a wide area, patching and treating farm families, collecting his fees in grain and dairy products, and dreaming about the major leagues. "Arkansas," Preacher recalled, "was Cardinal country, and when I finished college down at Searcy, muh Dad came up to St. Louis with me to meet Mr. Rickey and read the contract afore I signed." Roe pitched a single three-inning stint for the 1938 Cardinals and gave up four runs. He was then dispatched into the farm system — baseball people called it Rickey's Chain Gang — and languished there, a fast, wild hillbilly of uncertain promise.

At length Roe made the major leagues with a good wartime Pittsburgh team in 1944 and a year later led the National League in strikeouts. Winters in Hardy, Arkansas, Roe taught high school math and coached basketball. "One night," he said, "I didn't care for a referee's call and I shouted something.

"The ref shouted back at me, 'Shut up.'

"I thought he shouted, 'Stand up.'

"He decked me. My head hit the gym floor. I got a skull fracture and a lacerated brain. The fracture ran eight inches long."

Recovering slowly, Roe stayed with the Pirates through two more seasons. Both went badly. He could throw an occasional hard one but would not be a consistent strikeout pitcher ever again. "I commenced thinking," Roe said, "about pitching to spots, changing speeds, fooling them hitters instead of overpowering them, and, of course, I commenced to develop my wet one."

On December 8, 1947, Branch Rickey dispatched three ballplayers to the Pirates: Vic Lombardi and Hal Gregg, journeyman pitchers, and Fred "Dixie" Walker, who wanted to be traded rather then play on the same club with a Negro. In exchange, the Dodgers got Billy Cox, who became the finest fielding third baseman of his time; Gene Mauch, who was to become better known as a manager; and the remarkable, evolving spitball-throwing Preacher Roe.*

Twice in Brooklyn Roe would lead the league in winning percentage. With success he went to considerable lengths disparaging his fastball. "I got three speeds," he said. "I got my change of pace [slow ball]. I got my change off my change [slower yet]. And I got my change, off 'n my change, off 'n my change." Slow, slower, slowest. Actually he could throw a good fastball now and again, but he tended to keep that pitch high and wide. He wanted batters to see it, to upset their timing. He wanted them actually to swing at slower and deceptive breaking balls.

The spitball is thrown with a straight fastball motion. At the instant of release, you squeeze, as when squirting a watermelon seed. Properly squeezed, a spitter breaks down sharply, a most difficult pitch to hit. Roe jiggled through interesting tableaus on the mound. He moistened his fingers and then carefully dried the fingers on the bill of his cap. Or he pretended to moisten his fingers. He wanted his spitter to surprise, when it broke down, but Roe was aware that a fake spitball, yet another pitch, helped keep hitters off balance.

The fingers were not his repository of moisture. What Roe wet purposefully was the meaty part of the hand below the thumb. Then, in an intricate gangling windup, he transferred the moisture to his left index finger before the delivery and squeezed. Once in a while a Dodger infielder walked a moistened ball in to Roe with a quick remark, "It's there if you want it."

How come Roe was never caught? He was not only droll but

---

*After retiring following the 1954 season, Roe sold an article to *Sports Illustrated* which editors titled "The Outlawed Spitball Was My Money Pitch." Roe reported that Beech-Nut chewing gum provided ideal saliva and demonstrated in a series of posed photographs how he "loaded" the ball. He later regretted collaborating on the article and made certain sounds of recantation. His real regret may be that he gave the magazine a sensational (and factual) article for a fee of only $2,000.

tricky. Once, when Roe was holding a premoistened ball, umpire Larry Goetz came charging in from second base yelling, "The ball, Preacher. I want to see the ball."

Roe tossed the ball obediently to Goetz. By this time Roe was the best control pitcher in baseball. Somehow the soft toss went over Goetz's head. Pee Wee Reese scooped the ball and flipped it to Jackie Robinson, who rubbed the ball and tossed it to Gil Hodges. After another rub, Hodges tossed the ball to Billy Cox who flipped it to Roe. Ten hands had now rubbed the baseball dry.

"Here, Larry," Roe said mildly. "Here's the fucking ball."

Red Smith called Roe "an angular, drawling splinter of gristle." The Preacher stood six foot two and weighted 163 pounds. Stengel started broad-shouldered Vic Raschi, and Jackie Robinson led off the second inning by cracking a double to left field. Gene Hermanski hit a foul pop fly into short right and Jerry Coleman made a good running catch with his back to the infield. Robinson sprinted to third. When Gil Hodges singled to left, the Dodgers had a run.

That was all Roe needed this mild October afternoon. Roe showed his fastball but kept it out of reach. He broke curve after curve around the black borders of home plate. From time to time, Preacher broke a spitter down below the knees.

In the fourth inning, Johnny Lindell cracked a line drive that caught Roe on the fourth finger of his right hand. He made the play but soon had to have a hole drilled in the nail to relieve pressure. "The pain made me sick to my stomach," Roe said later, "but good thing it wasn't my pitching hand."

His slow stuff and his remarkable control stopped the Yankees on six hits. Roe did not walk a man. The Dodgers won, 1 to 0.

"You must have had great stuff," Harold Rosenthal told Roe after the shutout.

"My breaking stuff was better than usual," Roe said. "My fastball wasn't hardly no use. I was lucky I had my forkball working good."

"Forkball?" Rosenthal said. He had covered the team for two years. "I never knew you threw a forkball."

"Sure do," Roe said. "I struck out DiMaggio with my forkball."

Like the spitter, a forkball drops. "He was telling me in his country-slick way that his spitball was working well," Rosenthal said afterwards. "But he was too slick for all us city guys, including me, including Joe DiMaggio."

After back to back 1 to 0 games, the Series was tied.

New York Telephone Company operators reported the precise time to any caller dialing Meridian 7-1212. During the Series, the company also provided the World Series score throughout the afternoon to callers dialing the time number. The volume of calls for scores, the company reported, reached 224,526 on the afternoon of October 6. The shutout Series, Reynolds and Raschi, Newcombe and Roe, held New York, and the nation, in thrall.

Ralph Branca was twenty-three. He had started twenty-seven times that season and won thirteen, including every decision at Ebbets Field. Shotton chose him to start game three, on Friday afternoon in Brooklyn.

Stengel went with Tommy Byrne, a strong left-handed pitcher who walked more batters than anyone else in the American League. The Dodgers, a solid right-hand-hitting lineup, seemed good bets to win on the dyed green grass of home. But Branca was on the way to constructing that strange and troubling career. Too nice and too softly sensitive, some say until this day, to win big games in the caldron that was the major leagues around New York during the Era.

Branca pitched two perfect innings. Then in the third he walked Cliff Mapes, a journeyman outfielder who didn't hit much. (Mapes's lifetime Series record: one hit in fourteen turns at bat.) You don't want to walk the first man to come to bat in an inning; you particularly don't want to walk him if he doesn't hit much. Branca struck out Jerry Coleman, but Tommy Byrne

bounced a single to center and Mapes went to third. Phil Rizzuto scored him with a fly to right. "Damn," Pee Wee Reese
remembers thinking. "They haven't hit a ball solid and we're
losing."

Reese straightened that out soon enough. He slammed a
home run into the lower stands in left, tying the score. Byrne
gave up a single and, with one out, walked Robinson and
Hodges, loading the bases. Joe Page had pitched the ninth
inning for Stengel the day before. Page chiefly worked at short
relief, two or three innings at a time. But here Stengel saw —
he was phenomenal at this perception — the ballgame at an
absolutely critical point. What might happen in the seventh or
eight inning wouldn't matter if the Yankees lost the ballgame
in the fourth.

The Dodger hitter was Luis Olmo, a right-hand-hitting backup outfielder who had batted .305. Stengel sent for Page, bringing in a left-handed relief pitcher to face the right-handed
batter. Olmo fouled out. "Stengel," someone said, "knows
things that nobody else does." Duke Snider bounced out. The
game remained tied.

Gene Woodling had doubled for the Yankees in the top of
the fourth, but after that Branca retired fourteen consecutive
hitters. Lefty Joe Page all but matched him. Going into the
ninth the game was still tied at one run. Then Branca's mastery
fled.

Robinson's great stab robbed Henrich of a hit, but Branca
walked Yogi Berra. After DiMaggio fouled out, Bobby Brown
singled and Branca walked Gene Woodling, loading the bases.

The batter was Cliff Mapes. Clyde Sukeforth, the Brooklyn
pitching coach, walked to the mound. "Get ahead of him,"
Sukeforth said. "You've got great stuff. Just throw it in there."
Branca nodded. Sukeforth returned to the dugout. Suddenly
as Branca was about to pitch, Stengel called time. As Red Smith
wrote, "Field Marshal Casey von Stengel called for Johnny
Mize, who has devoted a long and blameless life to the abuse
of National League pitchers." Long John Mize, of Demorest,

Georgia, was a powerful left-hand-hitting slugger who had led the National League in home runs four times, twice with the Cardinals and twice with the Giants, and played in the All-Star Game nine times. High cheekbones gave him a feline look; Long John was the Big Cat.

"Cat was a helluva hitter," Leo Durocher recalled, "but was he my kinda player? Not by 1949. Not anymore. They said Mize was strong as a tank, but by '49 he couldn't move. On the bases he was a tank, all right, a stalled tank. At first base, he covered a dime on a good day. So when Horace Stoneham said he could get rid of him, I said, go right ahead. We got some young guys who move better than him."

Under baseball rules, before selling Mize to the Yankees in an interleague transaction, the Giants had to offer him to every team in the National League. No one bid for the slugger, then thirty-six years old. George Weiss brought Mize from Manhattan to the Bronx for $40,000 on August 22.

Now in October the Dodger brain trust had primed Branca to pitch to Cliff Mapes. But here came Mize, six foot two, 220 pounds, all slugger. "I knew the bases were loaded," Mize said. "I knew the score. Even if the kid walked me, it would force in a run."

Clyde Sukeforth did not make a second trip to the mound. Branca fell behind Mize, two balls and one strike, and then threw a fastball that Mize said "looked big and fat.

"When I hit it, I didn't know right off whether it was going to hit the right field screen or carry over it into the street there. I didn't care. I just knew that nobody was going to catch the ball."

The baseball struck the screen and scored two runs. Carl Furillo played the carom perfectly, holding Mize to a single, a rocketing 330-foot line-drive single. Still, two runs scored.

Jack Banta replaced Branca. Jerry Coleman singled in another run. The Yankees led by three.

The Dodgers didn't quit; they were a gritty team. Luis Olmo

and Roy Campanella hit home runs off Joe Page in the bottom of the ninth. Stengel tramped out to talk to Page. "Don't hurry," he said. "You'll get him." With two out, Joe Page had just enough left to overpower pinch hitter Bruce Edwards with a fastball that was called strike three. The Yankees won by a single run, 4 to 3. This tense and exciting game, on a gray day in Brooklyn, effectively settled the 1949 World Series.

"Damn. It had to be a Giant [Mize] to do it," Burt Shotton said loudly in the Dodger dressing room afterwards, where one reporter said "the silence was so heavy it seemed to make even breathing difficult."

Long-faced Ralph Branca sat in front of his locker. "One out away. One out away," he mumbled. He had thrown Mize a good high inside fastball, he said. "I had good stuff. I got it in there. It just got hit."

Cheerful and naked in the visiting clubhouse, Stengel said, "They got to win three out of four to beat us now. I don't think they can do that." The nude manager twisted his face into an enormous wink.

"Mize," Rud Rennie said, trying to grasp Stengel's thinking. "What made you decide to pinch hit Mize?"

"They tell me he always hit Branca hard," Stengel said, "which I didn't actually see because I wasn't in the other league, but what I do know is that he is one of the great hitters in baseball and in that spot, tie in the ninth in the World Series, I want to have one of the great hitters in baseball at the plate for my team."

Upstairs in the press box, Red Smith observed to Grantland Rice that Branca had walked four batters and three scored.

"Jack London ought to be covering this ballgame," Rice replied. "Title it *The Call of the Wild*."

"Steinbeck, Granny," Smith said. "I'd go with Steinbeck."

"Why is that, Red?"

Smith said, *"Of Mize and Men."*

Smith's great rival Jimmy Cannon curled over a Remington

typewriter, trying to describe Casey Stengel's craggy face. "Stengel had the look," Cannon wrote, "of an eagle that had just flown through a sleet storm."

To some of us, the press box during the Era was as exciting as the ballfield.*

Desperate, Shotton called on Don Newcombe to start with two days' rest. Stengel tapped Edmund Walter Lopatynski, a stocky, genial, left-handed New Yorker who worked under the name of Ed Lopat and specialized in changing speeds. Newcombe threw three good innings. Then the Yankees knocked him out and continued pounding old Joe Hatten until they had moved ahead, 6 to 0, after five innings. The Dodgers chipped away at Lopat for single after single, seven sixth-inning singles in all, until Stengel called on Allie Reynolds to relieve. Like Newcombe, Reynolds was working on two days' rest. Unlike Newcombe, he was not asked to go nine tough innings.

"Throw as hard as you can for as long as you can," Stengel told him. Reynolds ended the long inning by striking out pinch hitter Spider Jorgensen. Then he blazed past the Dodgers, retiring nine in a row across the last three innings. The Yankees won the ballgame, 6 to 4.

Branch Rickey, integrator of baseball, empire builder in St. Louis and Brooklyn, elected to take over managing a team, that was losing the World Series three games to one. "I want Roe to pitch the fifth game," he told Shotton.

"He's a skinny guy to start with two days' rest," Shotton said. "Besides, he tells me his finger hurts real bad."

"That's on his *right* hand. Send him to my office immediately."

---

*Alistair Cooke covered game one of this Series for the Manchester *Guardian*. "Baseball," Cooke wrote, "is an industrial development of rounders [an English game enjoying great popularity with schoolgirls]. The object is to hit the ball and run all around the bases and back to the wicket. Altogether, 54 batsmen came to the wicket yesterday [in Allie Reynolds's 1 to 0 game]. Fifty three of them made a duck [failed to score]."

Gangly Preacher Roe, in a suit and tie, walked into an ante-room at Ebbets Field and showed a swollen, misshaped finger to Branch Rickey. "Ah cain't get my glove over that finger," Roe announced.

"You could if you wanted to," Rickey said. "This is the World Series. The team needs you."

"I want to help," Roe said, "but Ah cain't pitch without a glove and with all this pain."

"It wouldn't be that Ebbets Field is a small ballpark and you don't want to face those Yankee hitters here?"

Roe simply stared.

"It wouldn't be that you're afraid? I don't want to think it is that," Rickey said.

"Ah cain't pitch with this finger, Mr. Rickey, in Brooklyn or anywhere else."

Rickey glared at Roe in fury. He said a single word. "Coward."

The Dodgers started Rex Barney in the fifth game. Barney was wild, fast, erratic. Concluding that Barney's wildness was a problem of attitude more than coordination, Rickey had ordered him to visit a psychiatrist in Brooklyn.

A highly nervous but possibly well adjusted Barney lasted two innings. Stengel started Raschi and relieved with Page. The Yankees won the game, 10 to 6, and the World Series four games to one. Johnny Mize had a sore right shoulder. Di-Maggio was still recovering from his respiratory infection. Yogi Berra had a badly swollen thumb. Tommy Henrich's back was raging.

In defeat Dodger fans cited Roe's finger and Carl Furillo's groin. "Not everybody on either side was healthy," Rud Rennie wrote, "but the fair conclusion is that the Yankees outplayed the Dodgers and *outgamed* them, as well."

Rickey said, "We didn't go into the Series at our peak. I'm concerned now with building a pitching staff to beat the Yankees." He never would. For the rest of his time in Brooklyn, Rickey pitted himself against Walter Francis O'Malley in a battle beyond the ballfields for control of the Dodger franchise.

Stengel had given the world a lesson in modern managing. He'd won the Series with three pitchers, Reynolds, Raschi, and Page, plus a pinch hitter who was supposed to be washed up and platoon players who starred — Gene Woodling and Bobby Brown. In Stengel's first triumphant Yankee series, Joe Dimaggio batted .111.

Not everyone immediately recognized the range of Stengel's gifts, but baseball writers polled by the Associated Press did vote him manager of the year, with 101 votes out of a possible 116.

"I am, uh, pleased to accept this award from you gentlemen," Stengel told the press, "and am fortunate to have it as I have been fortunate to be able to make a career in baseball, which is important, because as you know, not many people would actually have put their trust in a left-handed dentist."

He was still funny, but after 1949 no one again called Stengel a clown.

10

Scouts, Center Fielders, and Schemers

◆

THE OLD BASEBALL SCOUT comes down to us as a wise codger. His manner is gruff, his face is grizzled, and his car, in the old baseball movies, is a 1924 Model A, the one Henry Ford said you could get in any color you wanted, so long as the color you wanted was black.

The old scout doesn't have much money. Never has. Although he'll take a drink, he's blind to women. The old scout's life is a celibate journey, never brightened or distracted by a pretty smile, in search of the Rookie from Olympus.

In legend, the climax always is the same. Above the steaming radiator of his faltering car, the old scout suddenly perceives a ball in flight. It seems to be leaving village, county, state. Then he sees the kid who hit it.

Music pipes in here, a horn call commanding our attention.

The old scout has found his Rookie from Olympus. And, because he is an old scout, and wondrous wise, he knows at once what he has discovered.

The horn music fades. The rookie trots into the picture.

"Say, son," the old scout says, in his gruff and kindly way,
"have you ever heard of the. . .

major. . .

leagues?"

Three Olympian prospects who strode to glorious maturity
during the Era were Willie, Mickey, and the Duke. Mays,
Mantle, Snider; Giant, Yankee, Dodger; speed, power, grace,
and youth, as well.

The Dodgers signed Snider out of Compton High School, in
Greater Los Angeles, and brought him east to Bear Mountain,
New York, where the team gathered for spring training in 1944.
Ballclubs had to abandon spring training in the South during
World War II, when the military commandeered the country's
rolling stock.) "Was I green?" Snider says. "It was late February
and I didn't bring a topcoat. Being a California kid, I didn't
own a topcoat."

"Did you buy one in New York?"

"The Dodgers only gave me a bonus of $750," Snider said,
"and my family needed the money. No, I didn't buy a topcoat.
I was just cold a lot."

After watching Snider exercise within the army fieldhouse
at West Point, the Dodgers sent him to Newport News, in the
Piedmont League, the bottom of the minors. There, at the age
of seventeen, Snider batted .294.

The old scout in charge was one Jake Pitler, out of Olean,
New York, later coach and caddy to the gabby Brooklyn manager Charlie Dressen. Old Scout Pitler filed his Snider report
on September 2, 1944. His enthusiam was restrained.

"Well-built and moves good," Pitler wrote. "Has lots of ability, but must improve on hitting curve ball."

Pitler rated Snider's outfield throwing as "very good," an
A minus. But in other categories — hitting, power, running,
speed, and fielding — Pitler rated Snider only as "good," no
more than a straight B. Snider had a magnificent throwing
arm. He was certainly among the ten best center fielders of

modern times. He had astounding power. Pitler saw none of these things. Indeed, he reported that Snider "throws right, bats *right*." Snider hit 418 major league home runs batting left-handed. He had batted left-handed from boyhood days.

Wise Old Scout Jake Pitler did not seem to have known what he had come upon in Snider. Later, after a hitch in service, Snider moved up quickly. By 1950, he led the National League in hits.

"He's a great kid," Old Scout Pitler said, reemerging as a Dodger coach the following spring.

By then *everybody* knew Duke was a great kid. Pitler's on-scene 1944 scouting report draws an F.*

Tom Greenwade, an old Yankee scout, is credited with having discovered Mickey Mantle, one early summer night in 1948, when he stopped off to watch a team of teenagers play a ball-game at Baxter Springs, Kansas. Greenwade dined out for years on Mantle stories. But there was little shock of recognition when Greenwade first saw Mantle, and precious little hurry to sign the young man.

Mickey's father, Elvin "Mutt" Mantle, worked in lead and zinc mines in the northeastern corner of Oklahoma, literally scratching a living out of unyielding earth. He taught his son switch hitting, drilled the boy at shortstop, and once, about the time Snider was moving up through the minor leagues, drove all the way to St. Louis to ask the Browns to give Mickey a tryout. Sturdy Mutt Mantle had press clippings in his hand and his son in tow. The Browns, baseball's weakest franchise, were not interested.

Later a St. Louis Cardinal scout named Runt Marr called on the Mantle home in the town of Commerce, Oklahoma. "I got to do a little more work, folks," Runt Marr said, "but promise me this: Mickey won't sign with another club until

---

*"Don't be *too* harsh on old Jake," urges Leo Laboissiere, a crack scout with the Baltimore Orioles. "Most of us are wrong more often than we're right."

you give me a chance to make an offer." That was in 1948. "I'm still waiting to hear from Runt," Mantle said in 1992.

The Browns refused to discover Mickey Mantle. The Cardinals discovered him, then never made an offer. Tom Greenwade, who finally did sign Mantle, moved, as the southern saying is, slow as molasses in winter.

On the night in 1948 that Greenwade saw the Baxter Springs Whiz Kids, Mantle hit two home runs right-handed and another home run left-handed.

The exact date is lost. The precise postgame conversation is not. "Son," Old Scout Greenwade said, "do you think you'd like to play for the Yankees?"

Mantle was not much at eloquence. His clear blue eyes looked right at Greenwade. "Shit, yeah," he said.

Mantle was still a junior at Commerce High. The rules of organized baseball decreed that scouts could not sign boys until they had graduated or, since some players fell before algebra and history, the class with which they had entered high school graduated. Greenwade moved on, without further romancing Mantle. It was ten months before Mantle saw Greenwade again.

"That was my high school graduation day," Mantle says. "Tom Greenwade talked to the principal. He wanted to see me play some more. He said could I skip the graduation ceremonies that night so I could play another game for the Baxter Whiz Kids. When Greenwade told the principal he was a Yankee scout, the principal said sure, whatever he wanted. The principal got real excited meeting a big league scout. I don't remember being that excited myself. We didn't have a television but we had a radio and I used to listen to the broadcasts from St. Louis. The best games were National League, the Dodgers and the Cardinals. My two idols were Stan Musial and Pee Wee Reese.* I wasn't that much turned on by the

---

*During game one of the 1952 World Series, at Ebbets Field, Mantle slid hard into second base, breaking up a double play. He crashed into shortstop Reese, who came tumbling down on top of him. "All I could think," Mantle says, "was, 'Oh, my God, I've killed my idol.'"

Yankees. But they were the only big league team that wanted me."

Greenwade's first offer was a $500 bonus.

"My boy can do better than that staying here playing semi-pro," Mutt Mantle said.

After considerable haggling, Greenwade agreed to make the bonus $1,500. Since that was the only offer, Mantle took it.

How, then, to rate Old Scout Tom Greenwade's pursuit and evaluation of Mantle? Probably a B minus. In semipro ball, Mantle was playing shortstop, the wrong position, but speed and strength and power, the matchless switch-hitting power, must have been visible. Greenwade was less excited than he should have been. Indeed, if the forgotten Cardinal scout, Runt Marr, had been more alert, Greenwade would not have gotten to sign Mantle at all.*

Mantle went to play in Independence, Kansas, where he batted .313. The next year, 1950, he batted .383 at Joplin, Missouri. The following spring, Stengel saw him.

Casey, a better old scout than Hollywood scriptwriters could imagine, knew just what he was looking at right away. "You gonna send that flashy kid to Kansas City, Case?" a reporter asked in 1951, when Mantle was nineteen.

"I think," Stengel answered, "it might be safer for the boy if he spent the summer up in New York City with me."

The first pro baseball man to observe Willie Mays was Willie's father, who played with Negro teams around Birmingham, Alabama, in the 1920s and '30s. The father, named William Howard after Taft, who was president when he was born, was fast and lithe. His baseball nickname was "Kitty-Kat" Mays.

I met Kitty-Kat late in the 1960s, after he had left the South

---

*We would then have seen a pretty fair St. Louis Cardinal outfield, come 1951 or 1952: Stan Musial in left field, Enos Slaughter in right field, and Mickey Mantle in center. I suspect that outfield would have wrenched pennants away from the Dodgers and the Giants. The Era would have been a very different time, indeed.

and gone to work in Harlem as a supermarket checkout clerk. He was chubby by then, with a significant belly. "Sure," Kitty-Kat Mays told me in a dugout at Shea Stadium, "I'll be glad to tell you 'bout my boy, Willie. Ask anything you want."

"When, sir, did you first begin to think your son was going to become a great ballplayer?"

Kitty-Kat offered a quick smile. "The neighborhood where we all lived" — Willie's parents had been divorced — "had this ballfield, and when Willie was eight years old, he was so good he had to play with older kids."

"I mean even before that, if possible."

"Well, I'll tell you a truth I ain't never told no one," Kitty-Kat said, slowly and seriously. "I knew he was gawna be special soon as he started walking, right around the time he got to be one year old. He's one year old and I bought him a big round ball. Willie would hold that big round ball and bounce and chase it. If it ever got away from him, he'd start to cry.

"You couldn't believe how good Willie was, one year old, chasing down that big round ball. Little bit of a thing, but even then his hands were sure and strong.

"I'm telling you the truth. Right then, when he was one year one, I knew he'd be a great one."

It was sixteen or seventeen years before Mr. Mays's magnificently prescient scouting report drew outside confirmation. Young Willie had started playing for the Birmingham Black Barons, which is where the Yankees spurned him out of bigotry. The Boston Red Sox also knew about Mays and, like the Yankees, went through the motions of scouting him. They declined to make an offer. (No black played for the Red Sox until 1959.) Finally, the Dodgers knew about Mays as well. There is no written evidence (this is not the sort of thing people put on memo pads), but by 1949 the Dodgers were backing away from further good black prospects. With Robinson, Campanella, and Newcombe already signed, Rickey elected to slow down integration, even if it meant losing good ballplayers. He thought three blacks in a starting lineup of nine was a good balance. "It would not have been prudent," he remarked privately years later, "to have had too many Negroes on any one club."

The road was open for the Giants. "We decided we were going to integrate in 1948 or '49," Chub Feeney says, "so we were looking at the black leagues pretty carefully. We sent one of our scouts, Ed Montague, who was white by the way, down to Birmingham to look at a first baseman named Alonzo Perry. He wasn't impressed by Perry, but he burned up the telephone lines about a kid named Willie Mays. Quick bat. Great hands. Terrific speed.

"You know, Willie's parents split when Willie was young and the main person in Willie's life was his Aunt Sarah. As I understand it, after the divorce he went and lived with her.

"Aunt Sarah was a pretty good agent. She said we could have Willie, all right, but we'd have to pay a bonus. Five thousand dollars. That's what, fifty thousand dollars today? And mind you this is in an Alabama town that's so poor they haven't been able to pave the streets.

"Eddie Montague argued a little with Aunt Sarah, but his heart wasn't in it. All Eddie wanted to do was sign the kid.

"So we came up with the $5,000 bonus and no, don't ask me, I have no idea whether Aunt Sarah charged Willie a commission."

The Giants dispatched Mays to their farm team at Trenton, class B in the old minor league classifications. These ran from Triple A down to D. Trenton was four rungs from the top, a lower level of baseball, Mays says, than he had been playing for the Birmingham Black Barons. "I had to hit against Satchel Paige for Birmingham. There wasn't nobody, no way, near Satchel Paige playing baseball down in class B." (Mays batted against Paige in only one game in Negro ball. He remembers it. He went one for two.)

Mays hit .353 at Trenton, but the assessment of manager Frank "Chick" Genovese remained conservative. Genovese evaluated Mays's throwing arm at 4, the highest number in the Giant rating system. But Genovese gave Mays only a 3 in power, a 3 in hitting, a 3 in running, and a 3 in fielding. (He actually gave the greatest outfielder in history a B in fielding!)

It was not until a year later, 1951, that a stocky, weary old catcher out of Savannah, Tennessee, named John Herman "Hank" DeBerry filed a scouting report that is more than a report. Old Hank DeBerry wrote a scouting poem.

In thirty-five games that season at Triple A Minneapolis, Willie Mays would bat .477. Hank DeBerry watched Mays play minor league ball from May 6 through May 10. This is what he sent to the Giant offices, overlooking Bryant Park on 42nd Street in New York City:

"Sensational.

"The outstanding player on the club.

"He's now on the best hitting streak imaginable.

"He hits all pitches. He hits to all fields.

"Everything he does is sensational.

"He runs and throws with the best.

"He makes the most spectacular catches.

"He slides hard. He plays hard.

"The Louisville pitchers knocked him down plenty. It had no effect on him at all.

"He's as popular with local fans as can be — a real favorite.

"This player is the best prospect in America.

"It was a banner day for the Giants when this boy was signed."

On September 10, 1951, the Giants were closing in on the Dodgers. After a torporific start, the team had fallen thirteen games behind. But with Mays in center field, the team awakened. By September 10, the Dodger lead was less than six games. That day in Savannah, Tennessee, a heart attack killed the old scout Hank DeBerry.

I like to think that before he died, when he gazed at Willie Mays, Hank DeBerry saw his promised land.

In 1950, when Mays was dominating in Trenton, Mantle was tiring outfielders in Joplin, and Snider was becoming a major league star, the Yankees called up a slim, sandy-haired left-handed pitcher out of the borough of Queens, a bartender's son who by his own account "was all bright and street smart. I knew my way around." Rookie Whitey Ford would win nine games and lose only one that season and the Yankees needed just about every victory. Quite suddenly old 100-proof Joe Page was finished at the age of thirty-two. Page lost seven games in relief and his earned run average jumped to a sorry 5.04. The booze turned his arm to rust all at once.

Around the American League fans groused about the Yankees' damnable good luck. "Just when that lefty Joe Page is drinking himself out of the league, they come up with this slick kid left-hander." And, of course, luck had nothing to do with the Yankees' getting Ford, who, sportswriters later wrote, was really a Cadillac pitcher.

"I always loved to play ball," Ford remembers. "I just *loved* it. When I was five years old, I used to play with a broom handle and a red rubber Spalding ball. I played in high school, Manhattan School of Aviation Trades, mostly first base. Then I went to a tryout at Yankee Stadium. I'm five foot, eight inches tall and they figure I'm too small for a first baseman. But Paul Krichell, the scout, sees me throwing in infield practice and says I ought to think of switching and becoming a pitcher. I had a good arm. Krichell gave me tips on throwing the curve. The good curve ball just came to me real easy."

Ford became a New York City sandlot pitching star. The Red Sox and the Giants grew interested but hesitated. The kid still looked awfully small. The Yankees signed Ford in September 1947 for a $7,000 bonus, which they split into two equal payments. Ford cashed the first check, taking seventy $50 bills, and walked to Times Square. There he bought his parents a radio-phonograph combination priced at $175.

"I was wearing dungarees and a T-shirt and when I whipped out my roll, thirty-five hundred dollars in fifties, the salesclerk called the police.

"A cop grabs me and says, 'Where did you steal this money, kid?' After a while, I got them to call my mother, and she explained that the cash was really mine. I didn't get arrested buying a present for my parents, but the cops sure spoiled my plans. I meant the radio-phonograph to be a surprise."

Three seasons later, in 1950, Ford became a Yankee star. The team pumped his dimensions on its roster sheet, claiming he stood five feet ten and weighed 180, exaggerating by two inches and fifteen pounds. Hype, to be sure, but there was no luck in the Yankees' landing Ford, no luck at all. The Yankees had him switch from first base to the mound, taught him the curve ball, tracked his progress with great care, and then out-bid two other wealthy teams to sign him. (Scout Krichell gets an A.)

The 1950 Yankees finished three games ahead of the De-troit Tigers, who were bunched with Boston and an improving Cleveland team. Since Ford saved one game, in addition to the nine victories, he had a major hand in ten games the Yankees won. Older chaps named DiMaggio and Mize helped with good home run years, but without ten big victories from twenty-four-year-old Edward Charles Ford, Field Marshal von Stengel could not have won his second straight pennant.

In 1950 the Giants, with two blacks in the line-up, had their best season in eight years, finishing third. Most regarded the Dodgers — Robinson, Reese, Campanella, Snider, just to men-tion future Hall of Fame players in the Brooklyn lineup — as the strongest team in the National League. But Burt Shot-ton could not fire up the club, which dawdled about in third place as late as September 19, nine games behind a fast, young Philadelphia squad, nicknamed the Whiz Kids and managed by a gentle, fatherly character called Eddie Sawyer. The Phillies were still all white, but their days of spewing apartheid garbage were done.

Through late September, the Dodgers closed like thunder, winning thirteen out of sixteen games. The Whiz Kids lost Curt Simmons, a wonderfully fast left-handed pitcher, to the military. Injuries and pressure took tolls. While the Dodgers were, in Red Barber's recurrent phrase, "tearin' up the ol' pea patch," the Phillies were losing nine out of twelve. In another recurrent phrase, sportswriters took to saying "The Whiz Kids are looking like the Fizz Kids."

On Sunday, October 1, 1950, the last day of the regular season, the Phillies led the Dodgers by a single game. The drama of things working with a vivid flair, the Phils would have to play their final regular season game at Ebbets Field, and on a curiously superheated autumn afternoon. The temperature climbed to 88 degrees and Red Smith announced that pulses ran rapidly "in the old Flatbush ballyard. A Dodger victory would force a play-off between a spurting Brooklyn ballclub and the Phading Phils. Few doubted who would then speed away with the pennant."

A magnificent game developed with intensity, comic relief, and unrelenting excitement. Indeed, this would be yet another of what magazine editors like to call the Greatest Ballgame Ever Played. Some in Philadelphia still believe it really was.

Shotton started Mighty Don Newcombe, out of Madison, New Jersey, six foot four and 220 pounds, the first successful black pitcher in the major leagues.* Big Newk, the players said, could throw through a damn brick wall. Sawyer countered with sturdy six-foot Robin Roberts, just two years out of college but already in full stride toward a career that won him election to the Hall of Fame. Not only could these right-handers throw

---

*Bill Veeck brought Satchel Paige to Cleveland in 1948, when Paige was forty-two, or possibly forty-eight, and past his prime. Across six major league seasons, Paige won twenty-eight games but lost thirty-one. As Langston Hughes might have remarked, that is what happens to a dream deferred.

very hard; each had control. Fast balls high and tight, hopping and buzzing up toward the letters. Sharp, low curve balls cutting the black outer marker of home plate. In Brooklyn, this day was particularly warm for hitters.

The seating capacity of Ebbets Field varied over its forty-seven-year life. In 1950 the park seated 32,111. Somehow on this October day a crowd of 35,073, almost 3,000 above capacity, paid its way into the old arched ballpark. People stood behind seats and sat in the aisles and climbed girders and settled into uncomfortable iron nests. Crowds milled outside on Sullivan Place and Bedford Avenue. A swarm stormed the roof of a six-story apartment building at 250 Montgomery Avenue. From that roof, you could see the infield and the mound, much of right and center field, none of left. Wasn't this ballgame televised? Indeed it was, on channel 9. But in 1950, people preferred to see baseball live, live and visceral and bloody and real, no matter how distant or perilous the perch.

"General admission fans," Harold Rosenthal reported in the *Herald Tribune*, "began collecting outside the Ebbets Field gates at midnight. "Police and fire officials estimate that by game time, as many people had been turned away as gained admission."

"I remember very clearly," Rosenthal said forty-two years later, "that I took the BMT subway to the ballpark and I got out at the Prospect Park station. There was a terrific crowd in the streets and I had to push a little. But it was a genial crowd, all upbeat. 'We can do it,' people were saying. 'We've come from way back and we can do it.' Remember, an upbeat 1950 Brooklyn crowd was nothing alarming, nothing like an angry urban crowd today."

The two right-handers dominated through five innings, with Roberts a shade more imposing. Nobody scored. Eddie Waitkus, now in a remission from tragedy, led off the sixth for Philadelphia with a sharp grounder to the right of first baseman Gil Hodges, who made a lunging snare. Then Hodges tossed to Newcombe covering first base for the out. Richie Ashburn, a fine center fielder who lived to become a New York Met a generation later, hit a replica of Waitkus's smash. Another out, Hodges to Newcombe. Dick Sisler, on the biggest day of his life, smoked a single to right. Del Ennis, a strong right-handed slugger, followed with a short fly ball into right center. Duke Snider, playing Ennis to pull the ball into left center, couldn't race in fast enough. Nor could Carl Furillo, playing a deep right. Jackie Robinson at second base had a chance to make the play but broke slowly. The short fly dropped beyond Robinson for a base hit. Then Willie "Puddin' Head" Jones, a strong country boy from South Carolina, lined a Newcombe fastball cleanly into left field and Sisler ran home with a Philadelphia run.

Pee Wee Reese, the Dodger captain, batted .260 in 1950, but Reese was the best .260 clutch hitter on the planet. With two out in the sixth inning, Reese cracked an outside fastball high and deep to right.

The right field wall in Brooklyn angled back for about eight feet, then rose vertically to a point fifteen feet high, where it was topped by a stiff screen that went forty feet into the air. Right field in Brooklyn wasn't deep — 297 feet down the line and 344 to right center — but it was high. Reese's drive struck just at a point where the screen rose from the fence. And there, for the only time in Ebbets Field history, the baseball stuck. It neither bounced off the screen nor dribbled down the fence. The baseball stuck, wedged between fence and screen.

Reese sped around the bases.

"Slow down," Frank Dascoli, the second base umpire, shouted. "Slow down, Pee Wee. The ball is stuck."

Reese did not slow down. ("I knew the ground rules," he says. "If that ball started rolling down the right field wall, it was in play.") He rimmed the bases at top speed, turning his head two or three times to see the baseball but never slowing, sprinting all out until he crossed home plate with the tying run.

No one had ever seen a ball stuck on the wall before. No

one would ever see a ball stuck there again. "The Dodgers," growled Red Smith, who always rooted against them, "have adopted germ warfare."

A boy of twelve or fourteen crawled out along the top of the right field wall between innings and retrieved the baseball. Scrambling back, he tossed it to a cohort in the crowd. Before ballpark police could react, boy, ball, and cohort escaped into a keyhole of history.

The game itself remained tied into the last of the ninth inning. The Dodgers had gotten only four hits; Reese had two of them. Cal Abrams — Calvin Ross Abrams, born in Philadelphia and raised in Brooklyn — was a left-handed, opposite-field hitter. He led off the Dodger ninth by drawing a walk on a three and two pitch. Reese tried to sacrifice Abrams to second but fouled off two bunt attempts. Then he lined a single to left center, his third hit. The Dodgers had men on first and second with nobody out.

The hitter was Duke Snider, a poor bunter. But Richie Ashburn in center field suspected the bunt anyway, at least on the first pitch. He moved in, playing more shallow than he normally played Snider, to back up the infield in the event of a bunt and a subsequent throw to second base.

Snider cracked Roberts's first pitch on a hard low line into center. The ball bounced. The Brooklyn crowd made a great triumphant sound. Surely Abrams would score the winning run. But quick Richie Ashburn raced in from his shallow post, scooped the ball, and fired it toward catcher Stan Lopata. Milton Stock, the Dodger third base coach, waved Abrams home. The throw was perfect and beat Abrams by fifteen feet. Lopata, a six-foot, two-inch 210-pounder, set his body and blocked the plate. Abrams ran into the tag gently, like a pacifist.

The Dodgers were a good base-running team. Reese reached third and Snider took second on the play at home. Two men on for Brooklyn, only one out, and Jackie Robinson, the best batter in the league that year (after Stan Musial) stepping in to hit.

Roberts walked Robinson deliberately, a move that both took the bat out of Robinson's powerful hands and set up a potential double play.

Bases loaded now. Still one out. Tie game. Roberts jammed Carl Furillo with a fastball and Furillo swung weakly and lifted a low pop foul to Eddie Waitkus. Two out. Then Gil Hodges hit a long fly ball to right center that Ennis caught. The Brooklyn flurry was over. The game went into the tenth inning.

Roberts bounced a ground single up the middle. Waitkus lifted a pop fly single to center. Ashburn bunted, but Newcombe threw to Billy Cox at third base, forcing Roberts. Newcombe got two strikes on Dick Sisler, wasted a pitch high, and then tried to throw an outside fastball past the hitter. Sisler batted left. He slapped the fastball into left field where it carried 350 feet, into the first row of box seats in the lower deck.

Home run. 4 to 1, Phillies.

The Dodgers went out in order in the bottom of the tenth. The Phillies had won their first pennant since 1915. Roberts's victory was his twentieth, the first Philadelphia pitcher to win twenty since Grover Cleveland Alexander had a great year in 1917.

October 2, 1950, was an unsettling day in Brooklyn and beyond. The Korean War, which had quieted, flared into fresh violence on that day when South Korean troops rolled north across the 38th parallel and General Douglas MacArthur called upon the North Korean army to surrender "and avoid useless shedding of blood and destruction of property." MacArthur's arrogance would wane in November when the Chinese Communists intervened with a million foot soldiers and put his armies to rout. President Truman removed MacArthur from command the following April and the general made his famous farewell speech to Congress. ("Old soldiers never die; they just fade away.")

MacArthur settled in Manhattan after that and became a

frequent visitor to Ebbets Field. The American Caesar, as William Manchester called him, turned out to be an enthusiastic Dodger fan.

Walter O'Malley was flattered to have the general as a guest, but in time MacArthur annoyed the sportswriters. The general insisted on riding the press elevator to O'Malley's private box but would not enter an elevator occupied by reporters. An aide-de-camp imperiously cleared out all journalists before the general would step aboard.

"What are we, cholera?" Dick Young wanted to know.

Having exhausted their ace in the great Sunday victory, the Phillies did not start Robin Roberts against the Yankees on Wednesday, October 4, when the World Series began in Philadelphia. Instead, Eddie Sawyer worked a rugged right-hander from upstate New York, Casimir James Konstanty, who answered to Jim. Konstanty threw with reasonable speed; his "out" pitch was a palm ball, which dipped sharply as it approached home plate, much like the popular split-fingered delivery of recent years. He had appeared in seventy-four games that year, winning sixteen and saving twenty-two, but he had not started any at all. Konstanty was a relief pitcher. Before the 1950 Series, he had not started a ballgame since 1946.

He pitched with surprising endurance, giving up only a single run. But Vic Raschi pitched a two-hitter and the Yankees won, 1 to 0, the second straight October in which they opened the Series with a 1 to 0 victory.

Roberts returned to work on Thursday and pitched another fine game. Allie Reynolds was just a little finer. Joe DiMaggio hit a homer in the tenth inning and the Yankees won this one, 2 to 1. "Yes, sir," Stengel told the swarming reporters at Shibe Park, "them Philadelphias is a very fine team, make no mistake. It is difficult to beat them, which is why it took us an extra inning today."

Back at the Stadium next afternoon the Yankees won the

third game 3 to 2, scoring the winning run with two out in the ninth on successive singles by Gene Woodling, Phil Rizzuto, and Jerry Coleman. Never had there been three such close games at the start of a World Series. "The Phils," Jimmy Cannon said, "are playing just well enough to lose."

"After this tense and exciting contest," Rud Rennie wrote, "manager Eddie Sawyer left the field in a daze. Following three one-run losses, he felt like a man on an operating table, trying to fight the anesthetic."

"Yes, sir," manager Stengel said, "the Philadelphias are very difficult to beat, as I have told you. Why today, as you gentlemen saw, my fine team was unable to beat them again until the very last inning we were permitted to play."

Factors at work this October included toughness, pressure, and the remarkable tenacity of Stengel and his field hands. Those who despised the Yankees — there was no shortage of Yankee haters in the country — railed once more against Yankee luck. But winning close World Series games is not primarily a matter of fortune.

With their third victory, Stengel's Yankees now had a World Series winning streak of six, three against the Dodgers in '49 and three more against the Phillies in '50. Across those six games, the Yankees had made only one error. They didn't give anything away. By contrast, the Phillies actually invited the Yankees back into game three, after taking a 2 to 1 lead.

In the eighth inning, Ken Heintzelman, a thirty-four-year-old left-hander, got two quick outs and walked three Yankees in a row, loading the bases. Sawyer brought in Konstanty to pitch to Bobby Brown, a devastating World Series hitter. Konstanty bothered Brown with the sinking palm ball; Brown stroked a routine grounder to shortstop. Then Granny Hamner having a great Series — he would bat .429 and steal a base — dropped the ball. It was his only error of the Series; the tying run scored.

Is it luck when you score the tying run on three walks and an error? Possibly, although one is reminded of Branch Rickey's metaphysical pronouncement: "Luck is the residue of design." The Phillies handed the Yankees a run, but that happens all the time in baseball. *The Yankees handed Philadelphia nothing back!*

Consider the principal players:

Heintzelman pitching the only World Series game of his life, trying to remain composed at vast, intimidating Yankee Stadium, where he had never pitched before, while a crowd of 64,505 looked on. Heintzelman had never pitched in front of that many people either. He kept his poise for seven and two-thirds innings. Then he cracked.

Young Hamner, a shortstop with great fielding range, had never played in the Stadium either. With bases loaded and two out in a one-run game, he suddenly became unable to pick up a ground ball. Errors under pressure happen often, but the Yankee shortstop, Phil Rizzuto, did not make an error all World Series. Like Reynolds and Raschi and DiMaggio and the rest, Rizzuto had played under World Series pressure before. "It never gets easy," Rizzuto says. "But you learn how to live with it, block out the crowd and the noise, and you make yourself play not the situation but the grounder."

Little Phil, white-haired and trim at the age of seventy-six, offers a twinkly smile. "Now you know, huckleberry, what I just told you is easier to talk about than to do."

Bobby Brown: "As a cardiologist, I've had to apply heart massage in an emergency room. Could I keep my patient alive or would I lose him? The stakes are completely different in the World Series, of course, but just in terms of personal pressure, will I succeed or will I fail? . . . On that level the pressure of a life and death emergency, for a conscientious doctor, which I was, and a tight spot in a World Series, for a dedicated ball-player, which I also was, can be said to be comparable."

For game four, Stengel could have come back with Raschi, "my finest pitcher to win one game," but with a lead of three games to none, he could take a bit of a chance. He chose the Astoria rookie. Before Whitey Ford was finished in baseball, he started twenty-two World Series games, more than any other pitcher. (Christy Mathewson and Waite Hoyt, in second place, each started eleven.) Ford leads in Series victories, strikeouts, and also losses, with eight. (Mathewson lost five.)

"I remember when Casey told me I was going to start," Ford says. "We were way ahead in the Series so I wasn't *too* nervous, but I had to run around buying a bunch of tickets for all my relatives and a lot of friends."

The Yankees scored twice in the first inning and three more times in the sixth. Ford carried a 5 to 0 lead into the ninth inning. The Phillies scuffed him a bit, getting runners on first and third with two out. Then Andy Seminick, the Phillies' starting catcher, hit a high fly to left field. "It was just a fly ball with two out in the ninth," Rud Rennie wrote. "It was the end. But it wasn't the end."

Gene Woodling had trouble picking up the fly through haze and cigarette smoke and slanting late afternoon sunlight. He finally spotted the baseball, lunged, and dropped it. The Phillies scored two runs. Then Mike Goliat singled, bringing the tying run to the plate.

Stengel tramped to the mound and lifted Ford for Allie Reynolds. "Casey got a lot of booing for taking me out," Ford says. "'Let the kid finish. Give him a chance.' Stuff like that. Hell, half the people booing were my relatives. But I admire Casey for what he did, making the move he thought he should, and the hell with the booing.

"The way Allie Reynolds looked when he come in, with those high Indian cheekbones of his. . . . He was the meanest-looking pitcher I ever saw. Walking off the mound, I was happy about one thing. I wasn't going to have to hit against Allie Reynolds."

Reynolds threw three fastballs past Stan Lopata and the 1950 World Series was done. The Yankees and Stengel were establishing baseball dominance without precedent.

"I'm sorry I had to take the young man out," Stengel said

later, "but as I have been telling you, the Philadelphias is hard to defeat, and I am paid by my employers to defeat them, which is why I went for the feller with the big fastball. Have a nice winter."

◆

THE BROOKLYN FAMILY O'MALLEY, destined to change the face of baseball, crossed paths with my own family long, long ago, in 1937. Viewed from the declining years of this century, the setting was unlikely: an Episcopally oriented grade school, called Froebel Academy, located at the corner of Brooklyn Avenue and Prospect Place, such a conservative institution that in 1936 a straw poll of upper school students showed Alfred M. Landon defeating Franklin Delano Roosevelt by a margin of 10 to 1. (In the November election, Roosevelt won forty-six of the forty-eight states.)

Froebel education was rooted in Anglican traditions: chapel every morning with psalms and hymns and sermonlike talks by the headmaster. Very early, Froebel students were required to memorize the Gettysburg Address and "An Old Athenian Oath" and to sing the Doxology. Most of the student body was staunchly Protestant, but the entry of two Roman Catholic children named O'Malley was accepted easily enough. Shanty Irish would have been unwelcome, but Terry O'Malley and her younger brother Peter were well dressed and generally well behaved. Terry was a spirited tomboy; Peter, tall for his age, bespectacled, serious and skinny, wasn't much good at sports. In the gossip that buzzed through recess or preceded football practice, I learned that the father was a lawyer, not particularly wealthy, but one who could pay his bills.

At the request of Carlton M. Saunders, M.A., the headmaster, my father took over the Froebel athletic program in 1937, actually coaching football and baseball across many afternoons on the gravelly field that stretched behind the schoolhouse. At the same time, Walter O'Malley moved on to the board of trustees of Froebel, eventually becoming chairman. Neither my father nor O'Malley accepted a fee. My father loved sports and seemed to enjoy coaching us, which, helped by several paid assistants, he did with verve and towering authority. When he said jump, we jumped without comment, except perhaps to say, "How high, sir?" (The noun *Coach* had not yet become a title, like Professor or Doctor.)

O'Malley enjoyed making policy and manipulating, and it was under his aegis that Froebel, in a startling break with tradition, replaced Mr. Saunders with someone named Florence McCormack. She would work more cheaply than Mr. Saunders, which pleased O'Malley mightily, and she, like Walter, was Roman Catholic. O'Malley was burningly aware of ethnicity and in time created in Dodger management an entirely Roman Catholic hierarchy.

I have known the O'Malley background intimately since my own childhood. No version I have read is close to accurate, hardly the fault of the writers. Walter O'Malley, the Great Manipulator, was something of a novelist. He enjoyed making up stories, inventing familial wealth and creating for himself a distinguished career, say as an admiralty lawyer, which had not in fact existed. There was a touch of megalomania to O'Malley, but aside from that he loved games, golf, poker, even baseball. Getting *The New York Times* to print his fabrications as truth amused him. He sure had put one over on that old Scotch-Irish Protestant sportswriter Roscoe McGowen and on that silk-stockinged Park Avenue publisher Arthur Hays Sulzberger, who by the way just happened to be Jewish.*

---

*When caught in a misstatement, O'Malley never missed a swaggering step. "Surely, you realize," he told me once when I nailed him, "that only half the lies the Irish tell are true."

One favorite O'Malley whopper: That Joseph Kennedy tried to buy the Dodgers in 1946 so his wounded son Jack could become club president. "If I'd let that deal go through," O'Malley boasted some years after Oswald, "John Kennedy would be alive today."

Another: "As president of the Dodgers I'm like everybody else at Ebbets Field. I'm just a fan."

O'Malley's father, Edwin, was a Democratic party ward heeler, who became commissioner of markets for New York City and was dismissed after a contentious — but now obscure — scandal in 1922. O'Malley's mother's family was southern German and as staunchly Catholic as the Irish-American father. Even after his dismissal, Edwin O'Malley retained some money. He sent his son to the University of Pennsylvania to study engineering, and later to Fordham, where Walter got his law degree.

O'Malley graduated from Fordham Law while the Depression raged and set about wheeling and dealing. He claimed to have made the definitive feasibility study for construction of the Triborough Bridge and after that — "with my engineering background" — rewritten the New York City building code. Perhaps. But when I was at Froebel Academy late in the 1930s my father knew O'Malley simply as "a lawyer for a bank." O'Malley handled collections out of an office in Manhattan but also was a familiar figure in the courthouses and Democratic clubs of downtown Brooklyn. He was a glad-handing sort, offering cigars and buying drinks for what he called "the higher-ups." Although O'Malley's legal acuity left the famous lawyer Bill Shea unimpressed, his swarming, energetic style attracted the attention of George V. McLaughlin, president of the Brooklyn Trust Company, the bank that held the mortgage on Ebbets Field. O'Malley was an ingratiating, hustling young feller. McLaughlin came to trust him with problem collections.

The problem at Ebbets Field was clear. The Dodgers were not paying down the mortgage, said to exceed three hundred thousand Depression dollars. As Larry MacPhail began generating revenue by bringing in Pee Wee Reese, Dolph Camilli, and Billy Herman, he insisted that he needed more time before taking on the mortgage. "I need every cent I've got, George, to keep operating this club. We're taking on the Cardinals and the Yankees. The mortgage comes next."

McLaughlin accepted that, but bank examiners for New York State found the situation intolerable. They delivered an ultimatum: Either the Brooklyn Dodgers commenced making timely interest payments on the mortgaged ballpark or they would order the Brooklyn Trust Company to foreclose on Ebbets Field.

McLaughlin summoned O'Malley. "I want you to get over to Montague Street and tell me exactly what's going on."

"I'll need to attend board meetings to get a good picture," O'Malley said.

"I've arranged for that," McLaughlin said. "I'm having you appointed lawyer for the Brooklyn Dodgers.* Understand, we simply *cannot* foreclose on Ebbets Field. The public reaction would be disastrous for the bank. We'd lose half our depositors. Aside from that, Walter, I'm a Dodger fan."

O'Malley presently described the financial profligacy he found in the Dodger offices with wincing horror. Large sums of money came in at Ebbets Field, from ticket sales and hot dogs and beer. Concession receipts ran to about ten percent of the gate. A sold-out Ebbets Field meant receipts of about $75,000. That money, in dimes and quarters and dollar bills, was loaded into duffel bags and transported to the bank in downtown Brooklyn, where the duffel bags were dumped into a vault. "The bags weren't sealed," O'Malley recounted years afterward, "and some of our employees were supplementing their income by dipping into the unsealed duffel bags."

"That's called skimming," I said.

"I know what that's called," O'Malley said irritably. Matters were so bad, he told McLaughlin, that he could not do much to correct the situation even as club lawyer.

"Terrible mess, George," O'Malley insisted in his Tammany basso. "The only way I can get something meaningful done is if I myself become a director of the team."

---

*The previous Dodger lawyer was Wendell Willkie, the Republican presidential candidate in 1940. A remarkable and independent character, Willkie was too involved in such questions as U.S.-Soviet relations to give the Dodgers the time that Brooklyn chaos required.

McLaughlin accepted O'Malley's approach. The Brooklyn Trust Company lent O'Malley $250,000, with which he purchased twenty-five percent of the stock in the Brooklyn National League Baseball Club, Inc.* Timely interest payments on the Ebbets Field mortgage began soon after.

O'Malley sized up major league baseball with that consuming nonromantic intelligence of his and saw something both akin to and remote from grass and gloves and basepaths. He detected the road to El Dorado.

O'Malley set out immediately to invent a baseball background for himself. "I played a little ball and pretty damn well," he began one of the whoppers, "until at Penn a ground ball intersected with my nose and I thought better of participation on the field." O'Malley has been described as looking like a cartoon of a capitalist drawn for a socialist magazine: jowls, glasses, paunch, cigar. But reporters accepted his story of athleticism partly because he had the sense to tell it with self-deprecating charm.

He'd always loved sitting in the box seats at Ebbets Field, O'Malley maintained. Even though his law office was "high up in the Lincoln Building in Manhattan," he had taken favored clients to Dodger games "for many years." Was this true? Probably not. But again O'Malley offered soothing self-deprecation. "I wasn't fancy enough to get good seats at Yankee Stadium. That's why I had to take my clients to Brooklyn. And when I got to Ebbets Field, darned if I didn't like what I saw." There was no stuffed shirt about O'Malley. Most people quickly liked him; his charm could have warmed an igloo in January.

After inventing the baseball background, O'Malley moved to form alliances with other stockholders, each of whom controlled a quarter of the Brooklyn ballclub shares. (Rickey held the other quarter.) John Smith owned a booming pharmaceuti-

---

*For all his bluster of early affluence, O'Malley entered baseball on borrowed money. After the Dodgers moved to Los Angeles, Bill Shea told me, "George McLaughlin never again spoke to O'Malley. George loved the Brooklyn Dodgers. He hadn't lent O'Malley money to kill his favorite team."

cal company, Pfizer Chemical, which was brewing and selling penicillin. A woman called Dearie Mulvey had inherited stock; her husband Jim, the eastern boss of Metro-Goldwyn-Mayer, often represented her. O'Malley made fast friends of Smith and the Mulveys.

Rickey was the man who signed Jackie Robinson. ("But he couldn't have done it without my approval," O'Malley later said.) Rickey was the man who made the trades, hired and fired managers. In essence, Rickey ran the ballclub. But increasingly in the late 1940s, O'Malley ran the ballclub bank accounts. They moved onto a collision course.

O'Malley's march toward power was subtle, leading Rickey to tell Red Barber, "He is *the* most devious man I've ever met."

For his part, O'Malley conceded Rickey his flare and baseball brilliance. "But," he told his fellow shareholders Smith and Mulvey, "we are never going to have a profitable franchise as long as that man is in charge."

He cited Rickey's own contract, which paid him a straight ten percent commission on all player sales. That, O'Malley said, caused Rickey to sign players who would not be right for Brooklyn but who could later be sold to lesser franchises such as Pittsburgh and the Chicago Cubs. Clearly a conflict of interest. "Besides," O'Malley said, "he keeps bamboozling the writers by telling them Bob Ramazzotti and Joe Tepsic are great players. He uses the press clippings to make sales. But when the writers find out how bad Ramazzotti and Tepsic really are, they get mad at Rickey and everybody else at our ballclub for bamboozling them."

Indeed, Dick Young at the *Daily News* and his boss, sports editor and columnist Jimmy Powers, ran frequent attacks on Rickey and the Dodgers. Young said he found Rickey duplicitous and pompous and also — perhaps the worst sin of all — not terribly interested in Dick Young. Like many driven newspapermen, Young had an ego as big as the Ritz. His distaste for Rickey carried over to Rickey's manager, whom Young dubbed, with heavy tabloid sarcasm, KOBS, for Kindly Old

Burt Shotton. The nickname was meant to suggest that Shotton was a mean old man, doddering and vicious. He was neither, by general testimony, although he was only a mediocre manager.

Jimmy Powers, a militant Roman Catholic, despised Rickey for championing Leo Durocher against the Brooklyn Catholic hierarchy. Powers couldn't attack on the specific point, but he moved on and nicknamed Rickey "El Cheapo." Rickey was indeed tightfisted but once, in 1946, when he wanted to give his entire team Studebaker cars as a bonus for good effort, the Dodger directors were talked out of authorizing the plan, an expenditure of about $20,000, by, of all people, the newest director, Walter O'Malley.

Powers ignored that episode. Unlike Young, he wasn't much of a reporter. But Powers was shrill and his column was prominent in the *News*. El Cheapo was ruining the Dodgers. El Cheapo was breaking everybody's spirit! El Cheapo was a windy fraud! El Cheapo was, well, very cheap!!

In the season of 1950, when these assaults peaked, the *Daily News* sold two million copies a day. It was by far the most popular paper in New York. Coincidentally, Dodger attendance dropped sharply; crowds fell off by more than one-third from the 1.8 million figure reached in 1947.

Was the *Daily News* driving away fans? Were Dick Young and Jimmy Powers, the tabloid twins, that powerful? After all, the Dodgers were televising their complete schedule, 154 games, and more and more fans owned television sets. Surely that was taking a toll on attendance. Regardless, O'Malley told Smith and the Mulveys, it was very bad business for a ballclub to go to war with the biggest newspaper in town.

Rickey regarded Young, whose philandering was well known, as a guttersnipe, and Powers, who hired ghosts to write his columns, as an ignoramus. He refused to salve Young's ego or to buy Powers dinner. The assaults continued. Finally, after the grinding 1950 season, O'Malley had his way. Led by O'Malley, the directors decided to dismiss Rickey as Dodger president.

As Charlie Dressen, later a Dodger manager, told me, "They wasn't just gettin' rid of no Ned-in-the-third-reader [innocent youth]. That Rickey had been around." Indeed, Rickey's contract stipulated that if he were not rehired to run the team, others — in this case O'Malley — would have to buy his stock — twenty-five percent of the Brooklyn National League Baseball Club, Inc. In the interests of fairness, the others and O'Malley would have to match the highest outside offer, "I knew that the value had gone up," O'Malley told me, "since I had bought my own twenty-five percent for two hundred fifty thousand. I guessed the value might have doubled."

To O'Malley's horror, Rickey produced an offer, from William Zeckendorf, a Manhattan real estate speculator, of one million dollars for twenty-five percent of the Brooklyn club. Although O'Malley believed until he died in 1979 that the offer was "fraudulent as a four-dollar bill," he couldn't prove fraud. O'Malley paid Rickey $1.25 million for a second twenty-five percent of the Dodgers. Rickey had to go to work in Pittsburgh. O'Malley had won control in Brooklyn for what turned out to be a bargain price. But O'Malley, the manipulator, raged at having been manipulated.

Walter O'Malley acceded to the Brooklyn Dodger presidency on October 26, 1950. "From this day forward," he said, making his point but masking his anger, "anyone in the Brooklyn Dodger offices who mentions the name of Branch Rickey will be fined one dollar on the spot."

O'Malley quickly fired Burt Shotton and also Milton Stock, the coach who sent Cal Abrams home, and engaged Charlie Dressen to manage. He named Buzzie Bavasi as vice president and de facto general manager. "Buzzie," he said, "I want you to get these fellows Young and Jimmy Powers off our backs right away. Buy them dinner. Buy them suits. A full wardrobe if you have to. Spend what it takes. Just get them off our backs."

Suddenly, Dick Young and Jimmy Powers appeared better dressed than they had ever been before. Young and the *Daily*

News consistently came up with inside Dodger stories that somehow eluded the *Tribune,* the *Post,* and the *Times.*

Blessed with news leaks and clothing, Young and Powers underwent an epiphany. They and, with them, the powerful, popular *Daily News* became born-again Brooklyn Dodger fans.

◆

THE NATIONAL LEAGUE PENNANT RACE OF 1951 belongs to the ages. There has been nothing like it before or since. Nor will it come again. Summarizing the 1951 race is akin to summarizing *King Lear.* Before anything else, your effort will diminish majesty.

Here is an episode. The Giants are lollygagging, going nowhere with Bobby Thomson playing center field. Thomson is swift and skilled but the team wants fire. Durocher has seen Willie Mays once and has a passion. All right. All right. The front office agrees to bring him up. "I'll call him myself," Durocher says.

The twenty-year-old Mays is playing for the Minneapolis Millers and he doesn't want to leave Minneapolis, for two reasons. He's afraid to play in the major leagues. He has fallen in love with a Minneapolis girl.

Durocher reaches Mays in a hotel room.

"You don't want me, Mr. Durocher," Willie says.

"Now just why is it I don't want you, son?"

Willie is flustered. What is there to say? Aha. He's got it. "You don't want me, Mr. Durocher, cuz I ain't good enough to play baseball for you."

"What are you hitting, Willie?"

"Uh, .477."

"Get your ass on an airplane, Willie, right now."

The Giants are in fifth place when Mays joins the team on May 25. He makes out twelve straight times, hits a huge home run off Warren Spahn, then slumps again. His batting average slips to .039. He sits in front of his locker in the green blockhouse at the Polo Grounds and begins to cry.

Durocher approaches and puts a hand on Willie's shoulder. "What the fuck is the matter with you, kid?"

Mays speaks amid sobs. "Send me back down. I knew I couldn't hit big league pitching. Send me back down, Mr. Leo. I'm begging you."

"Now look, Willie," Leo says. "You are my center fielder. Today. Tomorrow. For as long as I'm managing this club. I'm not sending you back down. You are my center fielder. Now stop your fucking crying."

Willie goes on a tear. "I got nine hits," he says, "the next twenty-four at bats." A small tear.

Willie proceeds, of course, to go on a larger tear than that. He becomes the greatest ballplayer in the world.

The Dodgers never really led the Giants by thirteen and a half games at sundown in 1951. On August 11, the Dodgers won the first game of a double-header against the Braves, moving thirteen and a half ahead; but the Dodgers lost the second game. At the end of the day, they led the Giants by an even thirteen games.

From that day forward, the Dodgers played .500 ball. The Giants won thirty-seven and lost seven. When the Giants defeated the Braves, 3 to 2, on September 30, they led the Dodgers by half a game. The Brooklyn club made an extraordinary comeback in Philadelphia and beat the Phils, 9 to 8, when Jackie Robinson hit a home run off Robin Roberts in the fourteenth inning.

"Just goes ta show ya," announced Irving Rudd, a peppery little publicity man O'Malley had hired for twenty-five dollars a week. "If a ballgame lasts long enough, Jackie Robinson will win it for ya."

A playoff, best two out of three, began at Ebbets Field October 1. Jim Hearn, a rangy and deliberate right-hander from

Atlanta, won the first game for the Giants, 3 to 1. Monte Irvin and Bobby Thomson hit home runs. Once again Ralph Branca lost an important contest.

The Dodgers won the next day at the Polo Grounds, 10 to 0, behind crewcut Clem Labine, a poised twenty-five-year-old rookie right-hander out of Lincoln, Rhode Island. The game turned in the third inning, when the Dodgers led by two runs and the Giants loaded the bases with two out. The count went to three balls and two strikes. Labine threw his curve, a courageous choice for a rookie pitcher in that spot, and Bobby Thomson, guessing fastball, missed it by a wide margin. The pitch was outside. Thomson struck out, swinging at what would have been ball four. After that the Giants rolled over.

On October 3, the Dodgers and Giants played the last game of the playoff. Some years ago, when all the principals were still alive, I reconstructed that encounter. Although I have learned some things since then about this famous baseball game, I want to set down here an account that is as close as I can offer to contemporaneous. The nearer we remain to a primary source the better.

The night before, nearly everyone slept well. Bobby Thomson was troubled because he had struck out with the bases full, but after a steak dinner and a few beers, he relaxed. Ralph Branca fell asleep quickly. He had pitched on Sunday, the last day of the regular season, and on Monday in the first game of the playoff. Tomorrow, October 3, 1951, would be Wednesday, and Branca did not expect that he would have to pitch again so soon.

Sal Maglie, who knew he was to start for the New York Giants, spent a comfortable night in his room at the Concourse Plaza Hotel. For all his intensity, Maglie had learned to control his nerves. So, to a degree, had Don Newcombe, who would start for the Brooklyn Dodgers. "I can always sleep," Newcombe said, a little proudly. "I don't need to take pills like some guys do the night before they pitch."

Charlie Dressen, who managed the Dodgers, went to an Italian restaurant called Rocco's and ate a dinner of clams, mussels, lobster, and spaghetti with hot sauce. A few people asked how he felt about tomorrow's game, and Dressen told them he wasn't worried. "Our ballclub is ready," he said.

One man who did feel restless was Andy Pafko, the new left fielder. The Dodgers had traded for Pafko at midseason, in a move the newspapers called "pennant insurance," and Pafko, reading the papers, was impressed. Now he felt that the pennant was his personal responsibility. Lying in his room at the Hotel St. George in Brooklyn, he thought of his wife, Ellen, in Chicago. He had sent her a Pullman ticket to New York so she could watch him play with the Dodgers in the World Series. Next year there would be time to find an apartment together in Brooklyn, but for the moment Andy Pafko was alone. Perhaps it was loneliness as much as pressure that depressed him.

Although New York City was bright with the quickening pace of autumn, none of the ballplayers went out on the town. Everywhere, harboring their energies, they went to bed at about eleven o'clock, and soon, everywhere, they slept.

These were two tough and gifted baseball teams. The Dodgers had been built around such sluggers as Duke Snider and Gil Hodges, and in Jackie Robinson they had the finest competitor in baseball.

Under Leo Durocher the Giants were combative, strong in pitching and opportunism. Bobby Thomson, like the other Giants, knew none of the Dodgers socially; the teams did not fraternize. He thought that Gil Hodges was a pleasant man but that the rest of the Dodgers were unpleasant. This was a sermon Durocher preached ceaselessly throughout the last months of the season until finally the ballplayers came unquestioningly to believe their manager.

No one expected the deciding game of the playoff to be easy, but no one, not Thomson or Branca or Durocher or Dressen, felt any dramatic foreshadowing of what was ahead. The game

would be tense, but they'd all been tense lately. It was against
this background of tension, which the players accepted as a
part of life, that everyone slept the night before.

Robert Brown Thomson, tall, swift, and brown-haired, said
good-bye to his mother at 9:50 A.M. and drove his blue Mer-
cury to the Staten Island Ferry. The Thomsons lived on Flagg
Place in New Dorp, once an independent village, now a community within the borough of Richmond. As he drove, Thomson thought about the game. "If I can just get three for four,"
he mused, "then the old Jints will be all right." The thought
comforted him. He'd been hitting well, and three for four
seemed a reasonable goal.

Ralph Theodore Branca, tall, heavy-limbed, and black-haired,
said good-bye to his mother at ten in suburban Mount Vernon,
New York, and drove off in his new Oldsmobile. He felt a little
stiff from all his recent pitching. It would take him a long time
to warm up, should Dressen need him in relief.

It was a gray day, darkened with the threat of rain. The
temperature was warm enough — in the high 60s — but the
crowd, waiting for the gates of the Polo Grounds bleachers to
open, was smaller than the one that had waited in bright sun-
shine the day before.

Most of the players arrived by car. Andy Pafko came by
subway, an hour's ride from downtown Brooklyn. "I'll beat the
crowd," he decided, "so there's no sense wasting money on a
cab." The crowd, it was to develop, was scarcely worth beating:
34,320, some 15,000 under standing room capacity.

Back of center field stood the squat green building, the
outsized pillbox that contained the clubhouses. Since both Durocher and Dressen believed in intensive managing, each team
was gathered for a meeting in the green building shortly before
noon. The announced purpose was to review hitters, although
the two teams had played each other twenty-four times previously that season and there was nothing fresh or new to say
about anyone.

"Jam Mueller on the fists," Dressen told Don Newcombe.

"Keep the ball low and away to Thomson. Don't let him pull it." Dressen concluded, with more warmth than he customarily displayed: "Look, I know it's tough to have to play this game, but remember we did our best all year. So today, let's just go out and do the best we can."

"Don't give Hodges anything inside," Durocher told Maglie. Then, later: "We haven't quit all year. We won't quit now. Let's go get 'em."

During batting practice Branca was standing near the cage with Pee Wee Reese and Jackie Robinson. "You guys got butterflies?" a reporter asked.

"No matter how long you been playing, you still get butterflies before the big ones," Reese said. Robinson grinned, and Branca nodded solemnly. Ralph's long face, in repose, was sad, or perhaps deadpan. One never knew whether he felt troubled by what was around him or whether he was about to laugh.

The game began badly for the Giants. Sal Maglie, who had won twenty-three games and beaten the Dodgers five times that season, walked Reese and Duke Snider in the first inning. Jackie Robinson came up and lined Maglie's first pitch safely into left field for a single. Reese scored, and the Dodgers were ahead, 1 to 0.

Newcombe was fast but not untouchable, and in the second inning Lockman reached him for a single. Thomson followed with a sharp drive to left, his first hit, and briefly the Giants seemed to be rallying. But very briefly. Running with his head down, Thomson charged past first base and had almost reached second before he noticed that Lockman had stopped there. Thomson was tagged out in a rundown, an embarrassing end to the threat.

When the day grew darker and the lights were turned on as the third inning began, the ballpark buzzed with countless versions of a joke: "Well, now maybe Thomson will be able to see what he's doing."

During the fifth Thomson doubled, his second hit, and Branca began to throw. Newcombe pitched out of the inning easily, but Branca threw a little longer. He wasn't snapping curves or firing fastballs. He was just working to loosen his arm, shoulder, and back.

Branca threw again during the sixth inning, and when Monte Irvin doubled to left in the seventh, Branca began to throw hard. He felt loose by then. His fastball was alive. Carl Erskine, warming up next to him, was bouncing his curve, but Branca had good control and good stuff.

With Irvin at second, Lockman dropped a bunt in front of the plate, and Rube Walker, the Dodger catcher, grabbed the ball and threw to Billy Cox at third. Irvin beat the throw, and now Thomson came to bat with the tying run at third base late in a 1 to 0 ballgame.

Bearing down, Newcombe threw only strikes. After two, Thomson fouled off a fastball. Then he hit another fastball deep into center field, and Irvin scored easily after the catch. As the eighth inning began, the score was 1 to 1.

"I got nothing left, nothing," Newcombe announced as he walked into the Dodger dugout. Jackie Robinson and Roy Campanella, who was not playing that day because he had pulled a thigh muscle, took Newcombe aside.

"My arm's tight," Newcombe said.

"Bullshit," Robinson said. "You go out there and pitch until your goddamn arm falls off."

"Roomie," Campanella said, "you ain't gonna quit on us now. You gonna hum that pea for us, roomie."

While the two built a fire under Newcombe, other Dodgers were making the inning miserable for Maglie and Thomson. Reese and Snider punched one-out singles to right, and when Maglie threw a curve in the dirt and past Wes "Nappy" Westrum, Reese scored and Snider sped to third. Then Maglie walked Robinson, and the Dodgers, ahead 2 to 1, once again had runners at first and third.

Pafko pulled a bounding ball up the third base line and Thomson, breaking nicely, reached backhand for it. The play required a delicate touch; the ball glanced off the heel of Thomson's glove and skidded away from him. Snider scored, making it 3 to 1, Brooklyn. Pafko was credited with a single. Then Billy Cox drove a fierce one-hopper, again to Thomson's sector.

One thought — "Get in front of it" — crossed Thomson's mind. He did, lunging recklessly. There were other times at third when Thomson had thought of hard smashes coming up and hitting him in the face. This time he didn't. He thought only of blocking the ball with his glove, his arm, his chest. But the ball bounced high and carried over his shoulder into left field. The Dodgers had their third run of the inning and a 4 to 1 lead.

Newcombe blazed through the last half of the eighth inning, his arm no longer tight, and Larry Jansen retired the Dodgers in the ninth. "Come on," Durocher shouted as the last of the ninth began. "We can still get 'em. Come on."

Newcombe threw two quick strikes to Alvin Dark. "Got to get my bat on the ball," Dark thought. "Just get my bat on it."

Newcombe threw again. Dark rapped a bounder into the hole in the right side of the infield. Both Hodges and Robinson broke for the ball and Newcombe ran to cover first base. Hodges, straining, touched the ball with the tip of his mitt and deflected it away from Robinson. Perhaps if Hodges had not touched it, Robinson could have made the play. As it was, Dark reached first. A single, ruled the scorer.

Then Dressen made a curious decision. He let Hodges hold the bag on Dark, as though Dark as a base runner were important. Actually, of course, Dark could have stolen second, third, and home without affecting the game. The Giants needed three runs to tie, not one, and the Dodgers needed only outs.

A fine point, except that Don Mueller, up next, bounced a single through the right side — close to Hodges's normal fielding depth. Now the Giants had runners at first and third. All around the Polo Grounds people stood up in excitement.

With Monte Irvin coming to bat, Dressen walked to the mound. Branca and Erskine were throwing in the bullpen, and Clyde Sukeforth, the bullpen coach, told Dressen that Branca was fast and loose. But on the way to the mound the Dodger manager thought about catching, not pitching.

Campanella had a way with Newcombe. He knew how to needle the big pitcher to fury, and this fury added speed to Newcombe's fastball. Walking to the mound, Dresen wondered about replacing Rube Walker with Campanella. There was only one drawback. Foul territory at the Polo Grounds was extensive. A rodeo, billed as colossal, was once staged entirely in the foul area there. Campanella could catch, but with his bad leg, he could not run after foul pops. Dressen thought of Hodges and Cox, both sure-handed, both agile. They could cover for Campanella to some extent. But there was all that area directly behind home plate where no one would be able to help Campy. Dressen thought of a foul pop landing safely on the sod directly below the press box. He thought of the newspapers the next day. Dick Young. Jimmy Powers. The second-guessing would be fierce. He didn't want that. No, Dressen decided, making the move he wanted to make wouldn't be worth the peril of second-guessing. He chatted with Newcombe for a moment and went back to the dugout. When Irvin fouled out to Hodges, Dressen decided that he had done the right thing.

Then Newcombe threw an outside fastball to Whitey Lockman, and Lockman doubled to left. Dark scored, making it 4 to 2, but Mueller slid into third badly and twisted his ankle. He could neither rise nor walk. Clint Hartung ran for him, and action suspended while Mueller was carried to the distant clubhouse.

"Branca's ready," Clyde Sukeforth told Charlie Dressen on the intercom that ran from bullpen to dugout.

"Okay," Dressen said. "I want him."

Branca felt strong and loose as he started his long walk from the bullpen. At that moment he had only one thought. Thomson was the next batter, and he wanted to get ahead of Thomson. Branca says he never pitched in rigid patterns. He adjusted himself to changing situations, and his thought now was simply to get his first pitch over the plate with something on it.

Coming into the infield, he remembered the pregame conversation with the newspaperman. "Any butterflies?" he said to Robinson and Reese. They grinned, but not widely.

At the mound, Dressen handed Branca the ball and said: "Get him out." Without another word the manager turned and walked back to the dugout.

Watching Branca take his eight warm-up pitches, Thomson thought of his own goal. He had two hits. Another now would give him his three for four. It would also tie the score.

"Boy," Durocher said to Thomson, "if you ever hit one, hit one now." Thomson nodded but said nothing. Then he stepped up to the plate.

Branca's first pitch was a fastball, hip-high over the inside corner. "Should have swung at that," Thomson told himself, backing out of the box.

"I got my strike," thought Branca. Now, he decided, it was time to come up and in with a fastball. Now it was time for a bad pitch that might tempt Thomson to waste a swing. If he went for the ball, chances were he'd miss. If he took it, Branca would be ready to come back with a curve, low and away.

The pitch came in high and tight. Thomson swung hard and the ball sailed out toward left.

"Get down, get down," screamed Billy Cox as the line drive sped high over his head.

"I got a chance at it," thought Andy Pafko, bolting back toward the fence.

Then the ball was gone, under the overhanging scoreboard, over the high wall, gone deep into the seats in lower left, 320 feet from home plate. For seconds, which seemed like minutes, the crowd sat dumb. Then came the roar. It was a roar matched all across the country, wherever people sat at radio or television sets, a roar of delight, a roar of horror, but mostly a roar of utter shock. It was a moment when all the country roared and when an office worker in a tall building on Wall Street, hearing a cry rise all about her, wondered if World War III had been declared.

As the ball sailed into the stands, Thomson danced around the bases, skipping and leaping. The Giants crowded from their dugout to home plate. Ed Stanky, the second baseman, ran to Durocher, jumped on the manager's back, wrestled him to the ground, and embraced him.

In left, Pafko stood stunned. Then he started to walk slowly toward the clubhouse, telling himself over and over: "It can't be." Most of the Dodgers were walking before Thomson reached second base. Jackie Robinson held his ground. He wanted to make sure that Thomson touched all bases before conceding that the pennant race was over.

Clyde Sukeforth gathered gear in the bullpen, and nearby Carl Erskine turned to Clem Labine. "That's the first time I've seen a big fat wallet go flying into the seats," Erskine said.

As Thomson touched home plate, the Giants lifted him to their shoulders. Then, inexplicably, they lowered him, and everyone ran for the clubhouse. Champagne was waiting. "Gee whiz," Thomson said. "Gee whiz."

Wes Westrum and Clint Hartung grabbed Ed Stanky, who liked to boast that he had never been drunk, and pinned him to a rubbing table. Westrum poured champagne into Stanky's mouth. "You're gonna get drunk now," he shouted. Westrum turned to the rubbing table, where Mueller lay, ice packs at his ankle. "Hey, Don," he shouted and emptied a magnum over the injured leg.

"Isn't this the damnedest thing you ever saw?" Durocher said.

"Gee whiz," Thomson said. "Gee whiz."

"How the hell did you go into second with Lockman there?" coach Fred Fitzsimmons said to Thomson. "But the hell with that," he added, and kissed Thomson damply.

"Congratulations," Charlie Dressen said to Durocher. "I told you we'd finish one-two. Well, we did, and I'm number two."

"Gee whiz," Thomson said.

In the Dodger dressing room Branca wept, showered slowly, and, after submitting to some questioning, asked reporters to leave him alone. Then he went to the Oldsmobile, where his fiancée, blonde Ann Mulvey, was waiting with Father Frank Rowley of Fordham.

"Why me?" Branca said inside the car. "I don't smoke. I don't drink. I don't run around. Baseball is my whole life. Why me?"

"God chose you," the priest said, "because He knew you had faith and strength enough to bear the cross."

Branca nodded and felt a little better.

Thomson went from the ballpark to a CBS studio where he appeared on Perry Como's regular Wednesday night television show. Everywhere he went he was cheered, and always three thoughts ran through his mind. The old Jints had won. He had pushed his runs batted in total up over one hundred. He had got his three for four.

When Thomson reached the house in New Dorp, his older brother, Jim, was waiting for him. "Do you know what you've done?" Jim said, all intensity and earnestness.

Only then, six hours after the event, did Bobby Thomson realize that his home run was something that other people would remember for all the rest of his days.

Several players have since been kind enough to offer further comment. "I don't agree that if Hodges had played me deep rather than holding Dark at the bag the outcome would have been different," Don Mueller says. "I always checked the fielders before I swung. [Mueller was such a deft place hitter that he was nicknamed Mandrake, after a popular comic strip magician.] I saw where Hodges was playing, that there was a hole on the right side, and I hit the ball through the hole on purpose. If Hodges had played deep, I would have swung differently and just as likely gotten a base hit."

Jackie Robinson said he did not remember Branca's first pitch to Thomson as being hip-high on the inside. "I thought it was right down the middle. I remember, Pee Wee and I exchanged looks. Like, if Branca throws another like that, we're cooked."

Branca's grandiosity about a role for God in a baseball game persists, and he accepts criticism poorly. But some years ago Sal Maglie demanded of him: "How were you pitching to Thomson?"

"I wanted to get ahead of him," Branca said, "throw a strike."

"You did get ahead of him," Maglie said. "Then what?"

"I wanted to get him with a curve. I threw the second fastball to set up a curve."

"If you wanted to get him with a curve in a spot like that," Maglie said, "you should have thrown the curve. What were you waiting for?"

Branca did not argue. Perhaps poor pitch selection, not the Divinity, was his undoing. God may not have been a Giant fan after all.

This ballgame had been televised from coast to coast on the brand-new coaxial cable. Thomson's home run instantly became a moment in the consciousness of a nation, without equal in American sport.

There has never been a better rendering of that instant than the one in the *Herald Tribune*. Against a deadline in the Polo Grounds, Red Smith wrote:

> Now it is done. Now the story ends. And there is no way to tell it. The art of fiction is dead. Reality has strangled invention. Only the utterly impossible, the inexpressibly fantastic, can ever be plausible again.

A talented feller with whom to share a press box.

11

Monte, Mickey, Clay, and Joe and Marilyn

♦

"She's a plain kid . . . She'd give up
show business if I asked her."
— *Joe DiMaggio,*
describing his second wife

THE BEST, THE MOST gloriously competitive, the most
wonderfully hostile, fastball-in-your-ear, spikes-in-your-
shin baseball ever played illuminated New York during
that decade half forgotten but also half remembered as the
drifty, shifty, not entirely nifty fifties. As Joe DiMaggio remarked when a *New York Times* reporter asked him to sum-
marize the experience of taking a shower with Marilyn Monroe, "Louie, you shoulda been there."

We moved into the time warbling "How High the Moon"
along with Les Paul and Mary Ford; proceeded mistily to "Secret Love" with that dewy, sexy sunflower Doris Day; and stumbled out as music became a wind of change, hammering, loud,
rock-rock-around-the-clock:

Scramble my brains,
And fry me, honey.
I'm more than just a good little egg.
(Shaboom.
       Doo-wop.

Yeah,

Yeah,

Yeah,

YEAH.

!

Some argue that baseball today, circa 1993, is better than ever. George Will, in the popular 1990 book *Men at Work,* declares that "things are better than ever . . . in baseball" and that talk about a "Golden Age" is "piffle." Even if one resists the temptation to dismiss Will as an arriviste, it is difficult to agree with his conclusion.

It is true, to be sure, that many things today *are* better than ever: color television sets, ball gloves, thermonuclear bombs, Olympic long jumpers, high blood pressure pills, tennis rackets, jet fighter planes, and sneakers. But many things are not better than ever: epic poems, violins, presidents, concert halls, blondes, plays about royalty, and — to put a point on this — managers and ballplayers.

Indeed, many things are demonstrably worse. AstroTurf is a poorer playing surface than grass. AstroTurf has given baseball the trampoline bounce and the ground ball triple. Multisport stadia, those vast concrete coffee cups in Cincinnati, Pittsburgh, and elsewhere, are worse than the old ballparks; they are not even designed specifically for baseball.

Generally the rich players of today are less driven to win than the forever hungry players who grew out of the Depression. Although one finds exceptions, today's ballplayer is more the pampered house cat and less the tiger focused on the hunt.

Aren't today's athletes faster, bigger, and stronger than their counterparts of the 1950s? Certainly that applies to football players, runners, and Olympic basketball stars. But baseball is not a faster-bigger-stronger game.* Given a certain minimum

---

*Leonard Koppett and John Thorn, two generally sound observers, also argue that ballplayers are better than ever. In *Clearing the Bases,* a wonderfully reasoned study, the late Bill Starr, former major leaguer, longtime minor league

standard, major league baseball is timing, coordination, and hand-to-eye response. Jim Thorpe, the strongest, fastest athlete of his time, was a bust as a big leaguer. For all his strength and speed, Big Jim could not hit major league curve balls.

The best recent big league shortstop has been Osborne Earl Smith, called Ozzie, who stands five foot ten and weighs 150 pounds. That is 10 pounds less than the playing weight of Harold Henry Reese, called Pee Wee, the Hall of Fame shortstop from the Era. (Are great fielding shortstops actually getting smaller?)

The strongest contemporary power hitter probably is Jose Canseco, who stands a formidable six foot four. But neither Canseco nor other large present sluggers, such as Mark McGwire (six foot five) and Cecil Fielder (250 pounds), hit for distance to match Mickey Mantle, who stands five foot eleven and played at 190 pounds. (Are great sluggers growing bigger . . . and weaker?)

An electronic timing device clocked balls fired by the Dodgers' Joe Black at 96 miles an hour one night in 1952. "Allie Reynolds," Black says, "was faster than me. When he was pushing it, he got up over one hundred." Reynolds was big, but no giant, at six feet, 195 pounds. Many pitchers today are bigger. None throws faster.

The skills of managers are harder to quantify. Durocher was matchless across pennant races, keeping his players furious, focused, and sullen yet not mutinous.

As Yankee manager, Stengel practiced necromancy. I don't believe you can say that about any baseball manager today.

During the Era, baseball had first and undisputed claim on the best athletes in America. Pro basketball was a minor sport, just

---

guru, rebuts the arguments of Koppett and Thorn, with icy logic and great good humor. Ralph Kiner calls *Clearing the Bases* "the most penetrating book ever on technical baseball."

bouncing out of armories and dance halls; pro football still struggled to convince fans and sports editors that not *all* of its heroes were potbellied, bald beer barrels. Baseball was totally dominant and baseball salaries were by far the highest offered in any team sport. An outstanding lineman during the Era, Don Colo of the Cleveland Browns, earned $6,000 a year. Before Allie Reynolds retired in 1954, the Yankees were paying him $65,000. With that sort of income differential, baseball was every athlete's first choice.

Then as now, great athletes were gifted in many sports. Stan Musial and Jackie Robinson were fine basketball players. As a youngster Joe DiMaggio loved tennis. Duke Snider was a wonderful football quarterback. Willie Mays could have become the greatest pass catcher in the annals. All these athletes chose baseball; under today's conditions they might make a different choice.

John Elway, quarterback at Denver, was a promising shortstop. Baseball lost him to the National Football League. Jim Courier abandoned baseball for tennis. Bo Jackson, a developing power hitter, has had his baseball career hampered by a football injury. Baseball stars during the Era were forbidden by fiat or contract to play another team sport.

"Football?" the Dodgers farm director Fresco Thompson roared in the face of a young prospect who wanted to supplement his baseball income on the gridiron. "Football? What is it you're looking for, young man? A major league contract or a limp?"

Today baseball has a harder time first in attracting the best athletes. Then, the best talent it does sign is diluted by endless mushrooming of new franchises. During the Era there were sixteen major league teams. With the newest expansion, we have twenty-eight. Once there were four hundred major league jobs for ballplayers. Today there are seven hundred. Some of the best baseball players in America are not playing ball; they're working in other sports. Many of today's major leaguers could not have made *any* big league team in the 1950s.

*

Approaching the years of the Era ruled by Walter O'Malley, we run into another persistent misconception. This one suggests that people, particularly New Yorkers and Brooklynites, lost interest in baseball. In his one-volume history *Our Game,* Charles C. Alexander, Distinguished Professor of History at Ohio University, describes the Era as a time of "shrinking crowds and shifting franchises." From 1947 to 1957, attendance at the three New York ballparks dropped from 5.6 million to 3.2 million. But these attendance figures mean less than they appear to mean. During the Era, televised baseball took hold.

The television set was exotic in 1947; televised baseball had novelty appeal. Earlier, during most of the 1930s, the three New York teams collectively (and probably illegally) blocked radio broadcasts of their games. They believed that fans offered baseball on the radio would not come out and buy tickets. When Larry MacPhail brought Red Barber to Brooklyn in 1937, it was established very quickly that broadcasts did not keep people away. Broadcasts *sold* tickets. Barber and later Mel Allen were the greatest ticket salesmen in town.

Considering television, the three teams determined not to repeat the radio blackout mistake. From 1947 on, the Dodgers, the Giants, and the Yankees televised every one of their home games and most road games as well. By 1955, the Dodgers earned $787,155 for local television and radio rights, roughly $250,000 more than the combined salaries of all their players. "We were in the black before Opening Day," Buzzie Bavasi remembers, "but we never told that to anybody. I mean, you don't exactly advertise a gold strike, do you?"

Unlike radio, television carried troubling side effects. More and more people bought sets from DuMont and Admiral and Philco, and old habits began changing. People grew accustomed to baseball on a 13-inch black-and-white screen, where a blizzard broke out every time an airplane flew over the antenna. When a sellout crowd jammed Yankee Stadium one summer afternoon in 1953, Rud Rennie wrote: "Many were surprised to learn that the grass was green and that there were nine men on the field at all times."

As people embraced televised baseball, fans grew querulous. The parking was crowded at the ballpark. The seats were harder than a sofa. Besides, it was just a little cloudy. A summer shower? You never could tell.

Let's sit at home tonight, people said, and watch the ballgame on the one-eyed box. It's cheaper that way and more comfortable and if the game gets lopsided we can switch to Milton Berle. *Fanus televiendis americanus.* The group proliferates.

Professor Alexander's observation on "shrinking crowds" is true in a narrow sense. The crowds at the ballparks shrank. The crowds watching televised baseball multiplied and grew.

Interest, as opposed to attendance, never flagged. The ballplayers were godlike. The managers were giants in the earth.

The Era was the greatest age in baseball history.

The captains and the kings depart (even as new legionnaires arrive) and in 1951, when Mays and Mantle reached New York, it had come time for Joe DiMaggio to go.

There was small glory in DiMaggio's final year. He batted .263 — 66 points below his lifetime standard — and threw out fewer base runners than any other center fielder in the league. He told Gus Mauch, the Yankee trainer, "I got arthritis in every joint. The pain is terrible." A wretched combination — slowed reflexes, physical pain, and resulting poor performance — produced a condition that seems akin to clinical depression.

Milton Gross of the *New York Post* reported in late summer: "DiMaggio no longer wants anything to do with his teammates. He won't ride the team bus from hotels to ball parks. He takes a taxi by himself. He has pulled himself totally into a shell as though he no longer even sees the many men with whom he has performed and traveled for so many years. He will no longer even speak to his manager, Casey Stengel."

DiMaggio's wonderful last bow, the World Series of 1951, is generally treated as an anticlimax. Even before that Series began, the Liggett and Myers Tobacco Company purchased a full-page advertisement in the *Herald Tribune* for a victory ode:

Our hats are off to the Giant crew
When the chips are down they sure come through.
Though things looked black at the start of the race,
They didn't quit 'til they had first place —

Sound Off!

To the leader of this fightin' team,
To the guy who kept them on the beam,
To *Leo* give a solid cheer
Our choice for manager of the year —

Sound Off!

Thomson with a mighty blast
Nailed the pennant to the mast
And Sal and Larry, Stanky and Dark
In triumph carried him from the park.

Sound Off!

Like the Giants, Chesterfield's number one
Around New York with most every one
The reason Chesterfield sets such a pace
Is *mildness* plus *no unpleasant after-taste*
Sound Off for Chesterfield!!!

"They still gotta play us for the championship of the world," Casey Stengel insisted, "which my men and I are much looking forward to, competing against them all, Mr. Durocher and his very excellent players, who will give us a fine contest, I am sure, when we play the Series games, which no matter what Mister Thomson has done remains as yet, if you catch the drift. My men are ready."

The 1951 World Series, sponsored by Gillette, was televised coast to coast — a first — with Mel Allen and Jim Britt calling play-by-play, and broadcast nationally with microphones manned by Russ Hodges, the Giant broadcaster, and a former sidekick of Red Barber's known as "Brother Al" Helfer.

"Al was not much of a broadcaster," remembers Frank Graham, Jr., publicity director of the Dodgers for five seasons, "but if you were having a huge party and you needed a greeter, Brother Al would be your absolute first choice."

As a World Series special, General Electric reduced the price on its 17-inch Black-Daylite television from $379.95 to $299.95. "Not a clearance!" GE announced. "Not a small screen model! Not plastic or metal! Television in genuine mahogany-veneered cabinet. Up to 78 WEEKS to pay. Weekly terms as low as $2.72!"

Out in Las Vegas, Clark Gable filed suit for divorce from the former Lady Ashley, and the Associated Press reported that Mrs. Gable was willing to leave the star for $200,000 down and $100,000 a year for life. Closer to civilization, Uta Hagen, the beautiful German-American actress who had been Paul Robeson's lover, was appearing in the Cort Theater as St. Joan. At the St. James, Gertrude Lawrence starred in *The King and I*. Betty Grable's latest movie was *Meet Me After the Show*.

All this supplied backdrop. On October 4, the stumpy left-hander George Bernard Koslowski, who pitched as Dave Koslo, subdued the Yankees with breaking balls and control. Mantle, DiMaggio, Berra, and Hank Bauer collectively went one for fifteen.

Monte Irvin, so long barred from the major leagues by bigotry, at last could show the entire country — "coast to coast" — what a great ballplayer he was. Irvin pounded out four hits and in the first inning, as Allie Reynolds went into a full windup, Irvin stole home. "Never before," Red Smith wrote, "in the history of postseason amusements, had a Giant been so impudent; never had such humiliation been worked on a team of Yankee champions." The Giants won in commanding fashion, 5 to 1.

But champions the Yankees were, and a day later Ed Lopat

outlasted Larry Jansen at the Stadium and the Yankees won, 3 to 1. Irvin hit three more singles, but the Giants made only two other hits. It was a hard-bought Yankee victory; Mickey Mantle tore ligaments in his right knee.

The injury came in the fifth inning when Mantle and Di-Maggio broke for a short fly hit into right center field. On hearing DiMaggio's commanding voice — "I got it" — Mantle stopped short. He lost his footing, crumpled, and lay motion-less. He felt no pain, but suddenly his knee and most of his right leg went numb.

"You okay, kid?" DiMaggio said.

Mantle was unable to speak. He was crying in terror.

Sid Gaynor, the Yankee orthopedist, said Mantle's knee had taken "a terrific jolt. Why, with an older man, the cartilage would have torn right out of there. He's out for the Series, of course. It's a bad sprain. I'll x-ray it tomorrow morning and he'll be all right."

Dr. Gaynor was a good orthopedist, but Mantle's knee would not be all right ever again. For the rest of his career he had to wear a cumbersome metal brace. Some of his magic speed fled forever.

This memorable short fly ball, rising above DiMaggio and Mantle, produced a remarkable confluence of center fielders. The man who hit the fly was Willie Mays.

Years later, in a Dallas drinking club, Mantle remembered the play with anger. "DiMaggio always wanted to look good out there. That was very important to him. So he waited to call Willie's fly until he was damn sure he could reach it in stride. That's why I had to stop so short. If DiMaggio called for it earlier — or if DiMaggio had backed off and let me take it — I don't believe I woulda hurt my knee."

Mantle looked into a glass of Jack Daniel's and said, "Damn."

The Giants took a 1 to 0 lead in the third game, as the Series moved a few thousand yards west from Yankee Stadium, at

161st Street, to the Polo Grounds, across the Harlem River on 155th.* On several occasions the Series has been played in a single ballpark, but 1951 presented the last World Series played at ballparks within walking distance of each other.

The Yankee Stadium crowds had been subdued and civil. "Corporate crowds," some called them, as opposed to the "lunch pail guys," who screamed themselves hoarse during the regular season as the Dodgers and Giants went at one another.

Then in the third game came a remarkable play. Writing in the *Herald Tribune* Al Laney observed:

"The somnolence and lassitude which had enveloped crowds at the first two World Series games passed suddenly and with something of a shock in the fifth inning yesterday. Up to that time everything had been about as it was at the Stadium. . . . People got up and wandered, seeking the refreshment stands rather than waiting to have things brought to them. Some sought out friends for visits. They seemed to feel they'd have plenty of time. . . . The weather helped the mood, midsummer in autumn. Laziness was easy to achieve. And then Eddie Stanky kicked the ball out of Phil Rizzuto's glove. . . . The first truly spontaneous shout of the Series went up. People behind the stands, who had been eating and drinking calmly, came scurrying back to their seats, getting in each other's way and obstructing the view. The voice of the crowd had a new note. . . . This was the real thing at last."

With one out in the fifth, Eddie Stanky, the combative five-foot, eight-inch second baseman, drew a full-count walk from Vic Raschi. Al Dark batted next and Durocher called for a hit and run. The Yankees picked off the sign and Berra signaled for a pitchout. His throw to Rizzuto had Stanky by ten feet. Rizzuto waited, ball in glove, directly in front of second base. Stanky slid hard and with his right foot kicked the ball into center field. Then he got up and ran to third.

---

*The playing field at the Polo Grounds was a few feet below the level of the Harlem. Drainage was terrible. A brisk shower at ten in the morning meant no Giant game that afternoon.

That is a legitimate play, just as it is legitimate for a fielder to tag a base runner on the nose. Rizzuto was charged with an error and the Yankees went into shock. Dark singled. Hank Thompson singled and, after another error, Whitey Lockman knocked out Raschi with a three-run home run. The Giants won, 6 to 2. Their best pitcher, Sal Maglie, was ready for game four.

"Tell me how you kicked that ball," Rud Rennie asked Stanky, who was sitting naked on a trainer's table.

"I consider that an incident of minor importance," Stanky said, managing to be nude and formal simultaneously. "Let us discuss Lockman's home run."

"Listen, gentlemen," Leo Durocher shouted. "You cannot tag Mr. Stanky with the ball held nice and easy in your glove. You got to hold it in your bare hand and go for him like that and maybe you get spiked but maybe you get him out. It ain't a fucking tea party out there. Not against my guys."

"It was a bad game by both teams, I would say," Stengel began, "but it was particularly bad for us, because we lost. You all saw what happened at second base." Stengel kicked, to remind the swarming press. "They come up with a field goal good for five points. That beat us. I may have my men work overnight on blocking field goals."

The next day, a Sunday, brought rain, a steady October rain soaking the Polo Grounds and washing away the ballgame everyone was awaiting. "That rain killed us," Monte Irvin says. "It took away our momentum. It gave them a chance to regroup. The Yankees always had the luck. I'm not denying that they were a fine team, but they always got a break when they needed a break most. And that gave them confidence. Those Yankee teams beat you with confidence and with Casey; the talent just flowed easily under those conditions."

Salvatore Anthony Maglie won twenty-three games in 1951. Scowling, heavy-featured, with hooded eyes and a jet-black beard that always showed a shadow, Maglie was Mephistopheles on the Mound. He was nicknamed Sal the Barber, to a small extent because so many Italian Americans cut hair and to a larger, much larger, extent because he threw fastballs at batters' chins. Sal the Barber offered terrifying shaves.

He was genial enough off the mound, and frank in discussing tactics. "You have to make the hitter afraid of the ball," he said. "A lot of pitchers think they do that by throwing at a hitter when the count is two strikes and no balls. The trouble there is with that count, a knockdown is routine. It's expected. You don't scare a guy by knocking him down when he knows he's gonna be knocked down."

"Then when, Sal?" I asked.

"A good time is when the count is two and two. You knock him down two and two, he gets up shaking. Then curve him and you have your out. Of course, you have to be able to get your curve over the plate on a three and two count. Not every pitcher can do that." Maglie could break two or three different curves over the plate with the count full. He worked his intimidating style so well under pressure that he beat Brooklyn, the National League's best hitting team, twenty-three times over the years, against only eleven defeats.

Maglie was thirty-four in the autumn of '51, and he had pitched 298 innings. He was tired. His back hurt. Durocher, compassionate and loving to Mays, respectful of Monte Irvin, believed in motivating Maglie with a lash. As it happened, on Monday, October 8, Sal Maglie felt considerable pain in the lower right area of his back. It was not his nature to complain; the steady needling to which Durocher subjected him had the effect of making it just about impossible for Maglie to complain, even when he should have.

On the Yankee side, Stengel called a meeting. "Now, uh, men," he began, "we have not done well, and I am including everybody when I say we, including you very excellent ballplayers and including the manager. You have not done well and the manager has not done well but we are going to be all right if you just go out and play the way you can and I commence managing as I should be managing. We have all been lousy together. Now, let's all be goddamn good."

The Yankees awoke. In the first inning, DiMaggio, who had not hit a ball well for three games, scorched a curve ball against the facade of the left field roof, just foul. Another pitch, another foul, this one a fierce low liner that crashed against a fence. Then Maglie fooled him with a fastball and DiMaggio was called out. He had come to bat twelve times without a hit. "Even though I struck out," he said later, "I felt good. I dropped my bat weight down from thirty-five ounces to thirty-four ounces. I was swinging better."

The Giants scratched a run off Allie Reynolds in the bottom of the first and the Yankees tied the score in the second. As Maglie came into the dugout, after having given up one run, Durocher said, "C'mon, you son of a bitch. Pitch like you can."

DiMaggio lined a single in the third inning. His first hit was a signal. The Clipper was back. In the fifth, with Berra on base, DiMaggio cracked the eighth and final World Series home run of his career, a line drive that rose into the left field stands.

Durocher called Maglie several names. The Yankees won, 6 to 2, and the Series was tied at two games.

Actually, the Series was over. Next day at the Polo Grounds, Gil McDougald, the young Yankee infielder, walloped the third grand slam homer in Series history, scoring Berra, DiMaggio, and Johnny Mize ahead of him. McDougald was an odd-looking hitter. As Smith described him, "he plants his right foot barely within the rear inside corner of the batter's box and spreads his legs like an adagio dancer . . . his left foot points toward third base, his right toward the box seats behind first. His body is twisted awkwardly as he peers slantwise at the pitcher. He holds the bat slackly as though it is too heavy . . . it droops behind him like a bent banana."

Still, the man hit a grand slam home run. "Red," Stengel said, "the kid won the most valuable player prize in the Texas

League last year and how do you think he did that? By goin'
around buyin' votes? However you think he looks, the kid can
hit." The Yankees won the game, 13 to 1.

Hank Bauer's three-run triple in the sixth inning of game six
gave the Yankees a 4 to 1 lead, which they carried into the
ninth.

Stanky singled. Dark bunted safely. Whitey Lockman singled, loading the bases. Monte Irvin hit a long fly that scored
Stanky and advanced the other runners.

The hitter was Bobby Thomson. Everyone remembered.
Thomson flied out. Another run. The teams now were a single
run apart.

Durocher ordered Sal Yvars, his backup catcher, to pinch
hit. "I hit .317 that year," Yvars says, "and Durocher didn't use
me up to then for the whole Series. We had an incident during
the season. I ended up taking a swing at him. I got a hot Italian
temper, but you better know, too, that Durocher was a vulgar,
filthy guy who treated me and Maglie like dirt. When I ask
why he ain't using me in the Series, Durocher says, 'I'm teaching you a lesson. Now get the fuck away from me.' He hated
me. I got so mad I went and broke all my bats, six Louisville
Sluggers. Now, finally, Durocher's *got* to use me. He's got
nobody else. And I gotta borrow a bat.

"I was a good contact hitter under pressure. I hit a helluva
line drive . . ."

The ball carried into right center where Bauer made a lunging, skidding catch. The Series was over. The Yankees had won
in six games.

"For me," Irvin says, "hitting in that Series was almost too
easy. Allie Reynolds threw me serious heat; it was brutal hitting
against him and Raschi. Except sometimes you're on a roll and
the pitcher, whoever he is, throws it and you see it and you hit
it and it drops. In that '51 Series for me, it was see the ball, hit
the ball, and the ball fell in.

"It wasn't *just* the rain that beat us. I think of games that got away, especially the second and the sixth, and then I remember Don Mueller getting hurt in the playoff.

"Don was a wonderful hitter. When he went down in the playoff, it took away an absolutely key element.

"There's no doubt in my mind, none at all, that if we had Mueller, we'd have beaten the Yankees."

Rud Rennie called the Giants "wide-eyed." In achieving their third consecutive World Series victory, the Yankees were "lordly."

On the same day, October 10, the FBI announced a victory of its own. Gus Hall, national secretary of the Communist party, was slapped into the federal prison in Texarkana to serve five years. His crime: "teaching the overthrow of the government."

Hall had done nothing violent. He was arrested because he *might* do something violent. The times were disappointing for Sal Yvars, the New York Giants, Gus Hall, and free speech.

Life magazine struck a week later and before that fallout settled, Joe DiMaggio broke down and cried. During the last month of the pennant race, the Dodgers assigned Andy High to scout the Yankees. High reviewed the Yankees clinically; most of his judgments were sound. When the Giants won the pennant, the Dodgers delivered High's scouting report to the Giants, in a gesture of National League solidarity.

The statistician for the Giant broadcast team was a young man called Clay Felker, quite frantic to further his career. Felker wangled an appointment with Sidney L. James, assistant managing editor of *Life*. He wanted to work for *Life*, Felker said. He could help because he had great baseball contacts.

"If your contacts are so great," James said, "get us a copy of the Dodger scouting report on the Yankees. If you bring that in, I'll hire you."

Felker approached Buzzie Bavasi, whom he knew slightly, and said that his career was on the line. According to Bavasi,

"Felker begged me to *lend* him a copy of the report. He promised he wouldn't show it to anybody else. He'd just make some
notes for a story. Then he could get this great job at *Life* magazine. I took a chance. I decided to help the kid."

Life published the entire Andy High scouting report in its
issue dated October 22, 1951. "I got three different scouting
reports," Larry Jansen remembers, "two from our people and
one from the Dodgers. Not one mentioned that Mickey Mantle
was a helluva bunter. He led off against me in the second game
and surprised all of us. He beat out a bunt. That led to a run.
I end up wondering why none of the scouts noticed Mantle's
bunting."

Life magazine was not interested in publicizing deficiencies
in Andy High's scouting. Instead the magazine quoted Leo
Durocher: "High's report was great. Never saw one like it. It
has everything, all the little details."

Life ran High's comments on Berra, Mantle, Woodling, Reynolds, and the rest, but had a little trouble with DiMaggio.
Here the report read:

JOE DIMAGGIO, CF

Fielding — He can't stop quickly and throw hard. You can take
the extra base on him if he is in motion away from the line of
throw. He won't throw on questionable plays and I would chal-
lenge him even though he threw a man or so out.

Speed — He can't run and won't bunt. [Actually High is talking
about two things here, speed and attitude. Reluctance to lay
down a sacrifice bunt is attitude, not speed.]

Hitting vs. Right-hand Pitcher — His reflexes are very slow
and he can't pull a good fastball at all. The fastball is better
thrown high but that is not too important as long as it is fast.
Throw him nothing but good fastballs and fast curve balls. *Don't
slow up on him.*

Hitting vs. Left-hand Pitcher — Will pull left-hand pitcher a
little more than right-hand pitcher. Pitch him the same. *Don't
slow up on him.* He will swing at a bad pitch once in a while
with two strikes.

*

After going hitless in twelve times at bat, DiMaggio hit his homer. Over the last three games he cracked out six hits in twelve turns, .500 hitting. Even *Life* conceded: "DiMaggio was a better player than the scouting report made him out to be."

Life hired Clay Felker, who next made a splash by reporting on Stengel's drinking. James subsequently was appointed the first managing editor of *Sports Illustrated*. "I am still waiting," Bavasi said in 1992, "for one of those guys to return the scouting report I lent them in 1951."

DiMaggio flew to Japan to barnstorm but quit after a few days. He knew, better than the people at *Life*, that High's scouting report was broadly accurate. He felt humiliated that his shortcomings had been pointed out in public. The Yankees wanted him to keep playing; DiMaggio still drew fans. Dan Topping offered him $100,000 for 1952.

This ballplayer turned that down. On December 11, 1951, two weeks after his thirty-seventh birthday, DiMaggio announced his retirement at a crowded press conference in the Yankee offices. Reading from a prepared statement, he said, "I can no longer produce for my ballclub, my manager, my teammates, and my fans the sort of baseball their loyalty to me deserves." Jolting Joe was history. He began weeping.

Stengel, relieved to be rid of a brooding, fallen star, announced with cynical charm: "He's the greatest player I ever managed. I just give away the Big Guy's glove and it's going straight to the Hall of Fame."

DiMaggio did not make major news again until January 14, 1954, at the San Francisco City Hall when in a civil ceremony he married Marilyn Monroe.

"She's a plain kid," he told his friend Jimmy Cannon. "She'd give up show business if I asked her. She'd quit the movies in a minute. Her career means nothing to her.

"Jimmy, this is one marriage that can't miss."

12

Recessional

◆

On dune and headland sinks the fire . . .
— *Kipling*

FRANK GRAHAM, JR., feels that the Era was foredoomed to its wrenching end. Graham worked as Dodger publicity director from 1949 until 1954 and saw Walter O'Malley almost daily. "His sense of rivalry with Rickey was ferocious," Graham says. "He knew, although he didn't like admitting, that when Rickey signed Jackie Robinson, the old man became baseball's pioneer.

"O'Malley wanted to match that, to become a pioneer himself. That drove him against the wishes of family and friends to break ground for the Dodgers in California. He *had* to go."

This being reality, rather than plotted drama, *Exodus O'Malley* did not proceed in a particularly ordered way. First O'Malley decided simply he would build the most wonderful baseball park in human history. Dos Passos reminds us that "man is a creature that builds." O'Malley, venal and mendacious though he may have been, was a master builder.

Under Rickey, the Dodger field at Vero Beach, Florida, was a basic country ballpark: an outfield fenced in with slatted green. Fans sat on open bleacher planks. Along with an engineer named Emil Prager, O'Malley conceived an innovative, organic Florida field. First, he had earthmovers dig a yawning hole. The excavated dirt was bulldozed and shaped into an outfield barrier. The new Vero Beach outfield "fence" was earthen. He replaced the bleachers with comfortable grandstands. The slope of the new outfield barrier was planted with Bermuda grass and topped with long-trunked royal palms. The little field was a beauty.

In his high-style, frugal way, O'Malley had underground streams tapped into the nearby yawning hole, creating a pond. He stocked that with trout. "Everything indigenous," he said with pride, "except the trout. But I can justify that expense. A lot of my players like to fish. The trout keep 'em on the base and out of paternity suits."

O'Malley claimed warm memories of Ebbets Field, a claim many found suspect. He was no more sentimental than a hippopotamus, which his enemies claim he resembled. He saw Ebbets Field not as a shrine but as a relic, with rotten parking and smelly urinals, both of which kept customers away. If a ballpark was a relic, businessman O'Malley reasoned, let it go. "The secret," he said, "is to eliminate the reasons people have for *not* going to your ballpark. Stated positively, you want your ballpark to be a place where a feller loves to take his girl on Friday night."

Although he has been dead since 1979, O'Malley still is hated in many quarters. Jack Newfield, a New York newspaperman, told the writer Peter Golenbock, "Once Pete Hamill and I were having dinner and we began to joke about collaborating on an article called 'The Ten Worst Human Beings.' " They agreed to each write on a napkin the names of the three worst. "Each of us," Newfield said, "wrote down the same three names in the same order: Hitler, Stalin, Walter O'Malley."

"Listen," says Harold Rosenthal. "Walter was straight with me on serious things and I was straight with him. Back in the 1950s, I'm trying to do magazine work, the *Herald Tribune* doesn't pay much, and O'Malley is going off on a safari to shoot polar bears. The first safari to the North Pole. *Sports Illustrated* wants to cover it and O'Malley says your photographer can come with us on one condition. Harold Rosenthal writes the story. They said *they'd* pick the writer, so Walter trying to help a friend, me, told this powerful media company to go to hell.

"I have no idea what Newfield is talking about. He wasn't there. I never saw Newfield at the ballpark or on a field or in a press box. Hamill, either. Haven't they got better things to do than knock the dead?"

After Thomson's home run, O'Malley was riding an elevator at the Biltmore Hotel, where the sporting press was gathered. Someone in the elevator, neither baseball man nor journalist, cursed Ralph Branca and O'Malley asked the man why he was angry.

"I lost a bet. Branca's home run ball cost me a hunnert bucks."

"I sympathize with you," O'Malley said. "I lost money, too." He did not identify himself nor mention his calculation that missing the World Series had cost the Dodgers at least a million dollars.

O'Malley told that story with brio to Red Smith and me during a time of triumph, 1955. When O'Malley moved on, I remarked that it was a pleasure to cover someone that available. "Blarney or no, he's always offering yarns."

"I understand why you like him," Smith said and sipped the Scotch O'Malley had bought us, "but I'm uncomfortable in his presence. He makes me feel as if I were a page sitting before a feudal lord. It may be personal taste, but O'Malley is too much the grand seigneur for me."

With the Dodgers defeated on the last day in 1951, O'Malley entertained thoughts of firing Charlie Dressen, brought in to replace Rickey's man, Burt Shotton, after the Dodgers had lost the 1950 pennant on the last day. The new man, Dressen, had now done the same damn thing.

But Dressen was getting along with the writers, including Dick Young of the *Daily News*. O'Malley had flat-out ordered him to get along with all the writers. At least once a week, when the Dodgers were traveling, Dressen threw a party in his hotel suite just for the press. The Dodgers bought food and drink and even paid to have a particular delicacy, crab fingers, flown north from Florida.

"All right," O'Malley said to his new general manager, Buzzie Bavasi, "Dressen gets along with Jackie Robinson and Dick Young. I give him that. But the son of a bitch lost me the pennant. For this team to make money, we have to win. I've studied history. In Brooklyn, your baseball team is either in first place or bankrupt."

Bavasi, earning $17,000 as general manager, had hoped to bring the conversation around to a pay raise for himself. Now that was impossible.

"Who the hell picked Branca?" O'Malley said.

"The bullpen coach, Clyde Sukeforth."

"Then that's the son of a bitch we fire. We'd better stay with Dressen. It doesn't look good to change your manager every year."

"I'll fire Sukey," Bavasi said. (This removed another Rickey loyalist from the Dodger organization.)

O'Malley puffed a cigar from a cache sent to him by Roberto Maduro, president of the great Cuban ballclub the Havana Sugar Kings. "One more thing, Buzzie," he growled. "Tell that son of a bitch Dressen that if he doesn't win the 1952 pennant — win, not second place — he's unemployed."

Charles Walter "Chuck" Dressen was the least of three remarkable New York managers during the Era. That is not a denigration any more than it is a denigration of Mantle to point out that he was not as good a center fielder as Duke Snider or Willie Mays. The basal line runs high as a mountaintop.

Dressen, a stocky fellow out of Decatur, Illinois, started as quarterback for the Chicago Staleys, ancestor of the Bears, at a height of five foot five and a weight of 145 pounds. He played eight major league baseball seasons, mostly at third base, and managed for four seasons in Cincinnati without finishing in the first division. By all accounts he was quick and observant. He was a good sign stealer. When Leo Durocher ascended in Brooklyn, he appointed Dressen a coach.

When the *Herald Tribune* assigned me to cover the Dodgers in 1952, manager Dressen, thirty years my senior, said, "Stick with me, kid, I'll learn ya the ropes." I had been playing baseball all my days and Dressen was extremely kind in helping me discover that the baseball I'd played and major league baseball were different games. He showed me how to throw a spitball and a wonder of details on everything from tag plays to a particularly favorite sign: clutching his throat. In general baseball lore, a throat clutch suggests your opponent is "choking up." Dressen used the clutch as his sign for the squeeze play. He might yell at an opposing pitcher, "Choke, ya bastard," and grab his throat. What appeared to be one more bit of nasty needling was an order for the squeeze. "Believe me, kid," Dressen told me, over and over and over, "there's tricks to this game. Believe me. I know 'em all. I ain't no Ned-in-the-third-reader."

Dressen talked — preached may be more accurate — on a variety of topics. Arm trouble was interfering with the career of Clem Labine, a young pitcher of courage and sensitivity. At least, judging by the visible muscle knot on his right forearm, it looked as if Labine had arm trouble. "Kid," Dressen told me, "it ain't his arm. I happen to know after Labine got borned in Rhode Island, he was put in a incubator. That's the problem. Them incubator babies can never last nine innings."

Dressen not only sounded absurd at times, he tended to extemporize extensively on his own wisdom. Some Dodgers liked to play a parlor game on the Pullman — guess a name from a set of visual clues. Branca once challenged a group by pointing toward his eye.

"Dressen," shouted relief pitcher Clyde King. The pun on "eye" and "I" was excellent by the standards of ballplayer wit.

Reese remembers a game at St. Louis in 1952 when the Dodgers, losing by three runs, went out to take the field in the eighth inning. "Hold 'em, fellas," Dressen said. "I'll think of something."

But Jackie Robinson regarded Dressen as the best manager for whom he played. In turn Dressen described Robinson as the best ballplayer he had managed. I was intrigued by the ease with which Dressen accepted black ballplayers and asked if he knew anything about prejudice.

"I know *everything* about prejudice," Dressen said. "My parents was Catholics, I don't go to church myself, and where we grew up in Illinois when you wasn't even born, there was a lot of Klan. One night to let my parents know how they felt about Catholics, the Klan set fire to a cross on our front lawn. Kid, there's nothing else you have to know about prejudice. See a cross burn on your lawn. I was nine years old."

Primitive, intuitive, Dressen also was capable of cruelty. He didn't care for Cal Abrams and Duke Snider remembers that on June 6, 1952, at Cincinnati he issued a hard order. "Abrams, you ain't hitting. The only thing that can keep you with this club is your mouth."

The Dodgers broke nicely in 1952. By June 9, the team was in first place.

"The guy managing the Reds is Rogers Hornsby," Dressen said.

"I know that," Abrams said. "I know who Rogers Hornsby is."

"If you want to stay with my club, get on him," Dressen said. "Call him every goddamn name you can think of. I want you to get him so mad he can't think straight."

Abrams spent the first game of a double-header bellowing and screaming taunts at Hornsby.

The Dodgers won the first game, 6 to 1. Hornsby was raging. In the clubhouse, Dressen said to Abrams, "Don't bother to dress here. You've been traded. You're playing for the Cincinnati Reds. Abrams, your new manager is Rogers Hornsby."

*

Dressen spotted the Dodgers' key deficiency. There was no big, rough, volcanic pitcher, no Allie Reynolds, no Vic Raschi, no Sal Maglie. In his second spring as Dodger manager, Dressen noticed Joe Black, a six-foot, two-inch right-hander out of Plainfield, New Jersey, who had graduated from Morgan State, majoring in psychology, and then gone to work in the Negro leagues. The Dodgers signed Black in 1950, but his minor league record during 1951 was undistinguished. Watching him in the spring of '52, Dressen liked the way this big and poly-syllabic right-hander carried himself.

"You throw great, Joe. Just throw where I tell ya. When we want it high, throw it high — and tight. When we want that hard curve low, throw it down — and away. When I want you to brush a hitter, I want you to go right at his head. I want to see his bat go one way, his cap go another and his ass go somewhere else. Do what I tell ya, Joe, and you're gonna be a big leaguer, and the hitter will be whoops, Good-bye Dolly Gray!"

"Okay, Number Seven," Joe Black said. By June of his rookie season, Black was the best relief pitcher in baseball.

Race hatred lingered like a plague. To rattle Black in Cincinnati, some bench player began singing "Ol' Black Joe."

The hitter was a rangy outfielder, Wally Post. Black threw a fastball toward Post's skull. The rangy outfielder hit the dirt. The singing stopped.

Increasingly, people wondered why the Yankees had no blacks. Increasingly people thought and feared that they knew. On one popular television show, *Youth Wants to Know*, a panel of young people guided by bright, blonde Faye Emerson, directed questions at a celebrity guest.

Jackie Robinson appeared on *Youth Wants to Know* and a young person asked if the Yankees were prejudiced.

"I'm not volunteering anything," Robinson said, "but you asked me a question and my job here is to answer questions." Robinson drew a breath. "Yes, in my opinion. The Yankees are prejudiced." Among Robinson's viewers that day was Casey Stengel.

The Dodgers rolled to the 1952 pennant and, with great help from Black, fought off another late Giant onrush. The Yankees also rolled. For the third time in six years, the Dodgers and Yankees met in the World Series.

Politics continued its ominous way. Stalin said war between capitalist nations was inevitable once "governments rise up against the imperialist slavery imposed on them by the United States." Speaking for the Democratic candidate, Adlai Stevenson, Harry Truman told a Montana audience that Dwight Eisenhower had misread Soviet intentions in 1945. "Liberal" Democrat Truman maintained that the Republican Eisenhower had been "soft and misguided" when he asserted the Russians wanted to be our friends.

Six New York City teachers were dismissed for declining to answer questions "about Communist party membership." On September 30, the day before the 1952 World Series began, the Office of Civilian Defense staged a "mock nuclear attack" on Manhattan. Flights of "hostile" bombers flew north over Times Square, where soldiers with searchlights tried to pick them out. The city's 572 air raid sirens sounded a red alert at 7:45 P.M. Ten minutes later a "simulated atom bomb" was dropped on the Upper West Side. More than fifty thousand civilian defense volunteers responded and Arthur Wallander, the civil defense director for New York City, announced that the imitation atomic holocaust was "a great success."

That was Tuesday night. On Wednesday afternoon, Joe Black outpitched Allie Reynolds, and the Dodgers won the first Series game at Ebbets Field, 4 to 2. Raschi won a game for New York. Roe won a game for Brooklyn. Reynolds started again in game four and, defeating Black, 2 to 0, struck out Jackie Robinson three times.

Stengel was grim in victory. He pointedly reminded the writers of Allie Reynolds's Creek tribal background and Jackie Robinson's remarks to Faye Emerson.

"Before he tells us we gotta hire a jig," Stengel said, "he oughta learn how to hit an Indian."

Sunday, October 5, was memorable; a crowd of 70,536 at Yankee Stadium was treated to a magnificent game. "Eleven tremendous innings," Red Smith pronounced. The passionately Republican *Herald Tribune* was reporting that Dwight Eisenhower's campaign to recapture the White House from the Democrats was more than a campaign; it was a crusade! Working to inform his readers rather than to delight his employers, Smith reported in the *Herald Tribune:* "Crowds at the Stadium yesterday expressed their emotions by wild animal cries, by boos and cheers for a California politician named Richard Nixon — first Republican to be jeered by a World Series crowd since Herbert Hoover got it in 1931."

Helen Rogers Reid, the Iron Maiden who owned the *Tribune,* was not amused, but neither did she want the column killed. The *Tribune* of the Era was a collegial place. Helen Rogers Reid and her son Whitelaw considered criticism of Nixon unfortunate. Censorship was unconscionable.

Carl Erskine pitched for Brooklyn and took a one-hit shutout and a 4 to 0 lead into the fifth inning. Erskine remembers: "I had first-class stuff. My curve was sharp. It was October 5. That was my fifth wedding anniversary.

"In the fifth inning my control slips. A walk. Some hits. Mize rips one. I'm behind five to four. And here comes Dressen.

"I'm thinking, 'Oh, no. I got good stuff.' I look at Dressen coming closer and I think, the numbers are against me. October *fifth.* My *fifth* wedding anniversay. The *fifth* inning. I've given the Yankees *five* runs. Five must be my unlucky number. . . . The fives have done me in. Suddenly Dressen says, 'Isn't this your anniversary? Are you gonna take Betty out and celebrate tonight?'

"I can't believe it. There's seventy thousand people watching, more than lived in my hometown, Anderson, Indiana, and he's asking what I'm doing that night. I tell him yes, I was planning to take Betty someplace quiet.

"'Well,' Dressen says, 'then see if you can get this game over before it gets dark.' I get the next nineteen in a row. We win in eleven. I took Betty out to dinner and we celebrated the first World Series game I ever won."

Without anointing anything as the greatest ballgame ever played, I can say that this was the most *enjoyable* ballgame I've seen. Jackie Robinson showed up the Yankees with brilliant base running, a delayed steal in the second inning. Snider homered and made a magnificent leaping catch in deep right center. ("Not quite as magnificent as you think," Snider said recently. "I could have gone closer to the wall, but I sorta shied. Hard catch, but if I'd played it better, I wouldn't have had to jump that high.") Andy Pafko and Carl Furillo each made leaping catches and they *did* have to leap as high as they did. They jumped well above box seat railings and snagged what appeared to be home runs. Billy Cox, the great third baseman, made a backhanded stab on Phil Rizzuto in the tenth inning that moved Stengel to a fuming rave: "He ain't a third baseman. He's a fucking acrobat." Finally, John Sain, a good-hitting pitcher who worked six strong relief innings, was called out on a ground ball in the tenth inning when he beat the throw. Red Patterson displayed a photograph in a press room at the Biltmore which showed Sain's foot creasing the bag while the baseball was still several feet from the glove of Gil Hodges. Art Passarella, an American League umpire, is calling Sain "Out!"

"That's how it goes in baseball," Fresco Thompson told Patterson. "You don't make decisions hours later, Red. Leave the photos to Belmont and Hialeah."

Erskine and Robinson; Rizzuto and Mize; Snider and Cox; Nixon and Stengel. And luck — the bad call — actually going against the Yankees. One's cup ran over, provided of course the cup itself had been forged in Brooklyn.

For the first time ever, the Reliable Jersey House installed the Dodgers as favorites to win a Series from the Yankees. To bet Brooklyn, you had to put up eight dollars to win five. For what seemed to have been eons, Brooklyn fans bleated in October, "Wait till next year." Now in 1952 it seemed that Next Year had arrived.

But on Monday at Ebbets Field, Stengel managed with triumphant desperation, and the Yankees won because Billy Loes, Brooklyn's starting pitcher, lost a ground ball in the sun. Stengel started Raschi and relieved with Reynolds. That meant he had no suitable pitcher for a seventh game. Tomorrow's problem. Today Stengel focused on making sure the Series actually went to seven games.

Duke Snider's home run in the sixth inning gave Loes a 1 to 0 lead. Berra tied the game with a home run in the seventh. Woodling singled. As Loes wound up to pitch to Irv Noren, the ball dropped out of his glove. Balk. Woodling took second.

Loes struck out Noren. Billy Martin popped to Cox. Two out, Woodling on second, Raschi up. The Yankee pitcher hit a bounding ball toward Loes. Late afternoon sunlight flooded into Ebbets Field through arches behind seats on the third base side. The grounder bounced up in front of the low October sun and Loes was blinded. The ball struck Loes's knee and skittered past Gil Hodges into right field. Running with two out, Woodling scored.

Eighth inning homers by Mantle and Snider canceled one another. The Yankees won, 3 to 2.

"There were only 30,037 persons at Ebbets Field for this game," Rud Rennie wrote, "which would have had the effect of an A-bomb with noodles if the Dodgers had won. It was the smallest crowd of the Series, probably because many did not think they would be able to get tickets; or maybe because many people did not want to stand in line and preferred to stay at home and look at it on television."

Stengel next started Ed Lopat, whose left-handed slow stuff

would not long stop a Brooklyn lineup consisting of seven right-handed batters in Ebbets Field. Stengel knew that. Lopat pitched three scoreless innings and, as soon as the Dodgers started to cuff him, Stengel summoned Allie Reynolds. Another three innings. Then Raschi again.

The Dodgers started Joe Black and relieved with Roe and Erskine. In the seventh, with the Yankees leading, 4 to 2, the Dodgers loaded the bases with one out. The batter was Snider, who had hit four home runs so far in the Series.

Stengel brought in a journeyman left-hander, Bob Kuzava, whose name reminded Red Smith of "some kind of melon."

"I knew Snider a little bit from the International League," Kuzava says, "and good as he was, I never had trouble with him." The count went full. Kuzava threw a rising inside fastball. Snider popped to second base.

"I thought," Kuzava says, "that Casey would lift me then for Johnny Sain, bring in a right-hander to face Jackie Robinson. Sain had pitched in the National League; he knew how to work Jackie. I turned and looked for Sain, but Casey kept me in."

Kuzava threw Robinson a snapping outside curve and Robinson hit a pop fly to the right side. "I saw the ball," Kuzava says. "I coulda caught it. But this is the major leagues. The World Series. Pitchers don't chase down pop flies.

"I hollered, 'Joe! Joe!' "

That was the call for first baseman Joe Collins. But Collins lost the pop fly, as Loes had lost the grounder, or he froze. Billy Martin, running at top speed, made a wonderful catch when the ball was barely shoelace high. That was the ballgame and the Series.

"Them Brooklyns is tough in this little park," Stengel said, "but I knew we would win today. My men play good ball on the road. Now, you are gonna ask me why I left in the left-hand fella [Kuzava] to face the right-hand fella [Robinson], who makes speeches, with bases full. Don't I know percentages and etcetera? The reason I left him in is the other man [Robinson] has not seen hard-throwing left-hand pitchers much and could have trouble with the break of a left-hander's hard curve, which is what happened."

Stengel now had managed four consecutive World Series winners. The benchmark managers, John McGraw and Connie Mack, won successive World Series on three occasions. No other manager matched Stengel and his lineal predecessor Joe McCarthy with four straight.

"Nice Series, young man," Rud Rennie said to Mantle, who batted .345. "What are you up to now?"

"Headin' back to Oklahoma. I got me a job working down in the mines."

"Work in the mines?" Rennie said. "You don't have to do that now."

"Yes I do," Mantle said. "You know my dad died and I got seven dependents who're counting on me." Mantle named three brothers, a sister, his mother, and his wife.

"That's six," Rennie said.

"A baby is due in March," Mantle said.

High above Ebbets Field, I looked at my Royal portable and quested for a lead. I was twenty-three, about Mantle's age, and seated between two elegant veterans, Red Smith and Rud Rennie. My assignment was the lead story that would run on the front page of the *Herald Tribune*.

I thought of Brooklyn's bent dreams, but I thought, too, of how the Yankees had responded with power and endurance and great courage. I began with a short sentence:

"Every year is next year for the Yankees."

◆

ON A SLOW PLANE TO FLORIDA one bright spring morning in 1953, Allan Roth was having difficulty reviewing charts. Roth was the Dodger statistician and kept extraordinary records, breaking down the performance of players in ways widely used today but novel then. He worked with pencil and graph paper but on this flight, as he tried to review "Hodges, G. vs. right-hand pitchers' curve balls," he was jabbed repeatedly by a T-square.

Hodges set a record in the 1952 Series by getting no hits at all in the seven games. He had small luck with hard outside curves and sliders and Dressen wanted to teach Hodges to hit to the opposite field. Roth was compiling a record of futility that Dressen hoped would convince the big first baseman to change his batting stance.

"But I couldn't get much done," Roth remembered. "The T-square hit me. Then a drawing board. Then the T-square again." In the cramped and crowded DC-3, Roth was sitting next to the eminent industrial designer Raymond Loewy. For the entire flight, six hours, Loewy scrawled and sketched. His assignment: design a new baseball park for Brooklyn.

O'Malley took me into his confidence that March. "Did you ever ask yourself," he began in the modest Florida office where he worked, "why in an electronic age we play our games in a horse-and-buggy park?"

I had never asked myself anything like that. Ebbets Field was a Brooklyn fixture, like the Soldiers and Sailors Monument at Grand Army Plaza and the Cyclone roller coaster at Coney Island.

"The aisles are too narrow," O'Malley said. "The stairs are too steep. Poles obstruct the views. We can't park enough cars. We need twice as many seats. The bathrooms smell. The girders holding up the whole thing are rusting away."

He puffed his cigar, looking unhappy, then brightened. "Imagine a new park. Seventy thousand seats just like the Yankees have. No poles. You can cantilever construction now. Escalators take the fans to their seats. Plenty of parking. Restaurants and train stations right in the park. Then, to end worries about rain, we put a dome over everything."

After a while I said, "Walter, as far as I know, grass won't grow under a dome."

"We can get agronomy people to work on that, or maybe we can find a substitute for grass." His face was beaming; he was serious.

"Where on earth did you get this idea for a dome?"

"History," O'Malley said. "I wondered about the Coliseum; did the Romans call off battles between gladiators when it rained? I did some research and found out they did not. The Romans developed a retractable canvas dome. It was tied in with winches. When rain started, slaves cranked those winches and the Roman citizens did not get rained on. Or overheated, either. There was a hole in the center of the Coliseum dome that let the warm air out. The warm air rushed up so quickly no raindrops fell through. A dome worked in Rome. It will work in Brooklyn."

O'Malley became intimate and deferential. "Just thought this might make a story for you sometime."

I thought it did, but when I wrote a brief piece, Bob Cooke, the sports editor, would not run it. "You're supposed to be writing baseball," he said, "not Walter's fantasies."

The author's son, Gordon J. Kahn II, an architect, recently ran down O'Malley's Roman tale in a professional library. The "Coliseum or Flavian Amphitheater" inaugurated by Titus in A.D. 80, was designed to take fifty thousand spectators. Those of "equestrian rank or higher" had cushioned marble seats. The seating higher up was wooden. "At the top," reports Fletcher's *History of Architecture*, "there are brackets and sockets to carry the masts from which a canopy, known as a velarium, was hung to give shade."

Not a retractable top, really, but enough to give O'Malley his inspiration for the dome. (How many other baseball men have ever had any clue to the architecture of ancient stadia?)

After Loewy built a model, people made dismissive jokes about O'Malley's Pleasure Dome. Walter was the wrong man to dismiss.

*

As the Dodgers worked their way North, I had a beer with Carl Furillo. "It's gotta stop," he said.

"What's gotta stop."

"Maglie throwing at my head. I know why he's doing it. Durocher orders him to do it. Next time Maglie throws at me, I go for him."

"Who?"

"Durocher. I'm gonna get him."

The Dodgers reached their mountaintop in 1953. As a team, Brooklyn batted .285. No club has matched that for more than a quarter century. The '53 Dodgers led all baseball with 208 home runs. They scored 955 runs, about 200 more than any other club in the league, and they were the best defensive team as well. The Dodgers made eleven fewer errors than any other team in the league. The Brooklyn weakness — and this was relative — was the pitching staff. The Dodgers had a good strikeout staff, but the team earned run average was unimposing: 4.10. By contrast, the Yankee pitching staff, with Reynolds, Raschi, and Ford, posted an ERA of 3.20. The difference, a run a game, would be significant.

The Dodgers ran off from everyone else and on September 6, eleven games out front, they played their last game of the season against the Giants. The Dodgers had beaten the Giants nine times in a row.

The Giants went ahead in the first inning when Al Dark hit a home run, but the Dodgers took the lead in the second on Roy Campanella's two-run homer.

Gil Hodges bounced out. Ruben Gomez threw an inside fastball that hit Furillo on the left wrist. Furillo walked toward the mound. He pushed aside two umpires who tried to stop him. He pushed into Charlie Dressen, who threw both arms around him. Gomez, a willowly six-footer, stood his ground. To reach him, Furillo would have to trample his own manager. Gomez now circled back toward second base. Dressen talked urgently, "Come on. Come on. Get hold of yourself." At length Dressen led Furillo to first base.

Order returned. Gomez threw two strikes and two balls to Billy Cox. Furillo stared into the Giant dugout. He saw Durocher glaring at him, lips moving. He could not hear what Durocher was saying. Durocher made a beckoning gesture with one finger. Furillo bolted from first base toward the Giant dugout.

Durocher, flanked by ten players, rose to meet Furillo. They grappled and fell to the ground. Furillo clamped a headlock on Durocher, who lost his cap. Durocher's bald pate went pink, then red, then purple. Two powerful Giants, Monte Irvin and Jim Hearn, moved to rescue their manager. Clawing and stomping they worked Durocher's bald head free. Someone stamped on Furillo's left hand. The umpires threw both Furillo and Durocher out of the game. (The Dodgers defeated the Giants, 6 to 3.)

Furillo's hand puffed. In the clubhouse, he seemed oblivious to pain but his breath came in snorts. "I told you I'd get him," he said. "He made them throw at me one time too many."

I said that taking on Durocher at the Giant dugout stacked the odds.

"I wasn't worried about the other players ganging up on me," Furillo said. "A lot of the Giants hate him too."

Furillo played no more that season. He suffered broken bones in his left hand. He was batting .344 and his average froze. While on the bench, Furillo won the batting championship, beating out Red Schoendienst of the Cardinals (.342) and Stan Musial, who hit his customary .337.

More than one baseball writer fell to temptation and wrote that Furillo's fractures were a lucky break.

Primed, rested, the Dodgers played a dreadful World Series. The Yankees, performing brilliantly and methodically, defeated them in six games. The highlight was a moment in game five when Mickey Mantle took one mighty, dramatic, and defining swing.

The teams had split the first four games. Stengel then started a forgotten right-hander, Jim "Hot Rod" McDonald, who would win only twenty-four games in nine big league seasons. Charlie Dressen started his sleek young left-hander Johnny Podres, who turned twenty-one on September 30. Dressen wasn't quite sure about using the youngster, so he also warmed up Russ Meyer, a thirty-year-old right-hander whose furious temper earned him the nickname "Mad Monk."

For an hour and five minutes, while Podres warmed up and worked his way into the third inning, Monk Meyer threw baseballs to Rube Walker in the Dodger bullpen. The Yankees scored a run in the first inning. The Dodgers scored a run in the second. Meyer continued throwing — this was not exactly a show of confidence in young Podres.

Starting the third, Podres walked Rizzuto. McDonald sacrificed. Podres seized Woodling's hard drive up the middle and threw him out, as Rizzuto went to third. Joe Collins grounded to Hodges and the ball kicked off the heel of the first baseman's glove. Rizzuto scored on the error. Pressure again asserted itself. In 145 earlier games that season, Hodges had made only nine errors, none critical.

Trailing now, Podres got ahead of rugged Hank Bauer with two strikes then hit him on the forearm. He walked Berra, and Dressen had seen enough of his boy starter. Russ Meyer came in to pitch to Mickey Mantle.

Mantle would be batting left-handed against the right-handed Meyer, whose best pitch was a screwball. "I want ya to set him up for the scroogie," Dressen said. "Give him good breaking stuff. Don't give him a fastball he can hit. Keep the breaking stuff at his knees."

Meyer had thrown perhaps a hundred pitches to Rube Walker in the bullpen. Now, as the game resumed, he threw one to Roy Campanella behind home plate. It never got there.

Mantle swung — at a hip-high curve — and crashed a monstrous fly ball to left center field. The ball sailed and sailed, carried and carried high into the upper deck, landing with such force that some said they heard the sound of furniture splintering.

That sort of thing just didn't happen, a left-handed batter reaching the upper deck in left center at Ebbets Field. Not many right-handed batters could clout a ball that far. I remember sitting in the press box in disbelief. Mickey Mantle's batting power was a thing apart.

Red Smith wrote: "Collins, Bauer and Berra trotted around to the plate and waited there for Mantle, the fourth man in Series history to hit a home run with bases loaded. Berra straddling home plate flapped his fins like a circus seal applauding his own cornet solo. They leaped upon Mantle as he arrived and struck him repeated blows. Jubilantly they convoyed him to the dugout where the whole Yankee squad had come boiling out onto the lawn to pummel the young man."

Mickey had arrived. In the press box I glanced toward the forlorn figure on the mound. "Meyer didn't warm up long enough," Rud Rennie said.

The Yankees won the game, 11 to 7, and won the sixth game, 4 to 3, on Billy Martin's twelfth hit. This was Stengel's fifth consecutive World Series victory, an unmatched accomplishment. On this occasion the Yankees defeated the very best of all the wonderful Brooklyn teams.

In the dressing room several Dodger players broke down and cried. "Not me," Pee Wee Reese says. "I didn't cry till I got home."

O'Malley was tiring of Dressen. The manager got along with the reporters, as ordered; better than ordered, in fact. The papers brimmed with stories of the guile and wisdom of Charlie Dressen. Walter O'Malley had difficulty with egos other than his own.

Dressen had finished second, then won two pennants and lost two World Series. He was working on annual contracts, which troubled Dressen's wife, Ruth, a slight woman and a great fancier of toy poodles. "Durocher has a long-term contract," Ruth reminded her husband. "So does Stengel. You deserve a long-term contract, too."

She prodded and nagged, and Dressen, one week after losing the World Series, presented himself at O'Malley's office. "I need a three-year contract."

"Chuck, as we are both aware, the policy of the Brooklyn ballclub is one-year contracts and only one-year contracts. It's clear to me you'd be happier managing somewhere else."

"Course, I would settle for just two years, not three, Mr. O'Malley."

"Somewhere else, as I was saying, and we'll call a press conference quickly to make clear that I won't stand in the way of your getting a multiyear contract somewhere else."

"The thing is, my wife says . . ."

"Buzzie!" O'Malley shouted. "Get in here and get Frankie Graham."

The next morning, October 16, O'Malley and Dressen jointly announced that Brooklyn would have a new manager next year. Reese was the popular choice, the logical choice. He was intelligent, respected, gentle, and a wonderful competitor. But Reese, as manager, could overshadow Walter O'Malley.

"With Dressen gone," Reese says, "I knew that people were saying I should manage. I wasn't sure if I wanted to.

"Bavasi came to me. I don't remember his exact words. The sense was, 'Pee Wee. You don't want to manage this club, do you?' I knew I didn't want to manage after a proposal like that.

"So you can't say they didn't offer me the job, but you can't say they did offer it to me, either."

Reese sighs slightly and says one word with affection and perplexity.

"Brooklyn!"

The Dodgers hired a drab organization man, Walter Emmons Alston, to manage in 1954. (Eventually Alston managed for twenty-three seasons, always on a one-year contract.) In his first year as Dodger manager Alston took the team out of the race. He quarreled with Jackie Robinson. He bickered with the press. His racial attitude was suspect. He provided no leadership. Few experienced players warmed to him. "He was used to managing in the minors," Dick Young remembered, "where you had a roster of seventeen players. He didn't know how to function with a twenty-five-man squad. In head-to-head contests, Durocher, who used everybody, ate Alston alive." The Giants won the pennant by five games.

While Alston was losing the pennant in Brooklyn, Willie Mays was winning it in New York. After two years in the army, Willie was discharged in March and flew to join the Giants in spring training at Phoenix. In his first appearance, Mays made two outstanding catches and hit a home run, bubbling and giggling and laughing exuberantly, passionately in love with playing ball.

Willie says that Jackie Robinson was the smartest ballplayer he ever saw and that Stan Musial was the best hitter. In the spring of 1954, Willie was the most *joyous* ballplayer ever.

We struck up an acquaintanceship. "You got to love the game," Willie said, "else how you gonna play good? How you gonna be good at something you don't love?"

"Some seem to be good, even when they complain all the time."

"Complainin' don't mean you don't love the game. You don't know how they feel. You goin' on your own."

"Couple a guys tell me you love baseball so much, you'd play for the Giants for free."

"Hey," Willie said. "They're going on *their* own."

That springtime forty years ago comes back in a whispering rush and I see Arizona again, the wide pellucid sky, and the baked hills wanting grass, and the desert winds blowing whorls of sand. Strange country to one used to Berkshire hills, strange and lonely. But not when Willie was playing ball on scruffy, alkaline soil.

He played pepper games with Durocher and Monte Irvin, the men standing close. Leo hit smashes at Willie's toes and knees, wherever. Mays's reflexes were such that he could field a hard line drive at ten feet. Once in a while Willie bobbled a ball. Then he owed Durocher a Coke. Durocher made great shows of cheating Willie. One morning Leo hit a hard smash on one hop, well to Willie's right. Willie knocked down the ball with a prodigious lunge but failed to glove it.

"Coke," Durocher roared. "That's six you owe."

"Ain' no Coke for that," Willie said. His voice piped high. "That's a base hit."

"Six Cokes you owe," Durocher said.

"Monte," Willie pleaded at Irvin. "What say, roomie?"

"Six Cokes," Irvin said solemnly. Willie's seamless face slumped into a pout. "I'm getting the short end," his expression said, "but I'll fix you guys anyway."

People started coming to the Phoenix ballpark early just to watch Willie and Leo and Monte play pepper. The skills were awesome. The clowning would have done honor to Chaplin.

We had conversations most days and Willie always became very solemn and gave me serious answers. "Who suggested," I asked, "that you catch fly balls that way?" The technique became famous: glove up, near the belt buckle.

"Nobody," Willie said. "I just start it one day. I get my throw away quicker."

"Nobody taught you?"

Willie's eyes, which sometimes danced, grew grave. "Nobody can teach you nothing," he said. "You got to learn for yourself."

Day by day the Giants grew more cheerful and more confident. Willie so illumined the spring that even long-faced Sal Maglie began to smile. "It's different pitching with the kid in center field," he said. "All I gotta do with Willie there is keep the baseball in the park."

A few hours' distant from the Giants base a wonderful Cleveland team was training, with great pitchers like Early Wynn and great competitors like Al Rosen. The teams met frequently.

My enthusiasm for Mays irritated a Cleveland coach named Ralph "Red" Kress, who said that Willie was flat-out overrated.

"I don't think so," I said.

"What the hell do you know about baseball?" Kress said.

Franklin "Whitey" Lewis, a Cleveland columnist, said, "Willie won't bat .300."

"Twenty dollars, Whitey," I said. "I'll let your friend Kress, here, hold the money."

"Nobody has to hold anything," Lewis said. "We'll see each other down the road."

Willie wouldn't hit .300? We made it, Willie and I, by 45 percentage points. Willie led the National League at .345 (with 41 home runs), and Whitey Lewis, an honorable man, mailed me a twenty-dollar check on September 1.

A lovely concession speech.

After a while the Giants and the Indians traveled East playing game after game in Wichita Falls and Beaumont and Shreveport and New Orleans. The teams had separate Pullman cars but a common diner, and I noticed that the Indian squad drank seriously before and after dinner. As Early Wynn remembers, "Martinis before dinner, stingers afterwards."

When I returned to New York, Red Smith asked if I thought the Indians might finally beat the Yankees.

"No chance," I said, "the way these fellers drink. Athletes can't drink that much and win."

Months later, when the season ended, the hard-drinking Indians had won 111 games and beaten the Yankees out of the 1954 pennant by eight games. Then the Giants, with Willie, swept the World Series from the Indians in four straight.

New York got good hitting from Al Dark (.412) and Don Mueller (.389) and Dusty Rhodes, who helped decide two games with home runs and a third with a pinch-hit single. This Series turned in the eighth inning of the first game, when the score was tied at two.

Bob Lemon was pitching against Maglie, who walked Larry Doby in the eighth. Al Rosen singled to deep short. The Indians had two runners on with no one out, and a tough left-handed batter named Vic Wertz came to the plate. Wertz had

hit Maglie hard, two singles and a triple. Durocher replaced
Maglie with left-hander Don Liddle, who threw a shoulder-
high fastball. Wertz walloped a high line drive to center field.
The green blockhouse in dead center at the Polo Grounds was
505 feet distant from home plate.

Mays turned his back and ran toward a point to the right of
the blockhouse. He sprinted toward the bleacher wall some
485 feet away, and toward the Harlem River beyond. Time
slowed. The ball was frozen in the air. Willie showed his back.
Number 24. Then time began again.

The ball was hit too far and too hard to be caught. Willie ran
and ran. He ran past the farthest edge of the outfield grass. As
his spikes touched the narrow cinder strip near the base of the
bleachers, he took the ball over his left shoulder and he whirled
and threw and went tumbling. His throw held Rosen on first
base. "This," Arnold Hano wrote, "was the throw of a giant."
The crowd at the Polo Grounds numbered 52,751; the roar of
that crowd was thunder.

The Giants won the ballgame in the tenth inning, 5 to 2,
when Dusty Rhodes pinch-hit a three-run home run. Rhodes's
homer traveled 251 feet. The ball Vic Wertz hit, the uncatch-
able wallop that Willie Mays caught, carried 455 feet.

"Leo," Harold Rosenthal said in the dressing room, "was
that the greatest catch Willie has made?"

Durocher was a nasty winner. "Fuck," he said. "What kinda
question is that? Willie makes great catches alla time. He's
made catches like that all year. Where you been!"

In the Cleveland clubhouse, manager Al Lopez said, "I don't
know what in the world Leo is talking about. I've been in the
major leagues since 1928 and that was the greatest catch I ever
saw. I believe that was the greatest catch ever made. I'm not
even factoring in pressure." Although the New York Giants had
only three years of life left, they were triumphant in the autumn of 1954 as no Giant team before.

After the sweep, Mays liked to amble out of his apartment
in Harlem. On mild days the greatest player in baseball wan-

dered into the streets and played stickball until dark with young people from the neighborhood.

Dwight David Eisenhower, president during most of the Era, was regarded with some ambivalence by the old Roosevelt Democrats, so numerous around New York. After Eisenhower spent several years as president of Columbia University, someone remarked, "In a community of scholars, his best friend was the football coach." Nor were austere Republicans that pleased with him. In 1952 as Eisenhower was wresting the nomination from the thin-lipped Cincinnati conservative Robert Taft, midwestern Republicans claimed that Eisenhower was as dangerously liberal as Thomas E. Dewey. "Pick Taft," their placards demanded. "Beat Eisen-hewey!"

History informs us that Eisenhower was a centrist, somewhat wiser than he was given credit for during his presidency. He never had the nerve or spirit directly to reprimand the demagogue Joe McCarthy, even when McCarthy called General George C. Marshall a dangerous leftist. Marshall had been military godfather to Eisenhower. But Eisenhower resisted increasing demands from the French that the United States send troops to Indochina, in the war that evolved into the Vietnam War.

Eisenhower did send France $60 million in 1953 to prosecute the conflict and even agreed to train South Vietnamese soldiers. But unlike his successors John Kennedy and Lyndon Johnson, Eisenhower refused to commit American combat troops. "It makes no sense for the country to become involved in a land war in Asia," he said.

By and large, despite jokes about Eisenhower's intelligence and syntax, the country trusted the old general. When Eisenhower suffered a heart attack in Denver on Sunday, September 25, 1955, shock was intense. "Few men," began James Reston's passionate outburst in *The New York Times*, "in the public life of the Republic have wielded such power yet retained such affection. Accordingly, his intimates were in despair tonight and political leaders of his party were dismayed." What Reston could not see was that the dismay was not simply a matter of fondness for Eisenhower. National distaste for Eisenhower's vice president was palpable. The vice president, of course, was Richard Nixon. "Can you imagine if Ike died and Nixon became President?" people asked one another. Many shuddered.

To enormous relief, Eisenhower held on to life at Fitzsimmons Army Hospital and a Nixon presidency was thus delayed for almost two decades.

On September 30, James Dean, smoldering and intense, was ticketed for driving a Porsche Spyder 65 miles an hour on Grapevine Road, south of Bakersfield, California. Two hours later Dean plowed into a larger vehicle driven by Donald Turnupseed of Tulare and lost his life at the age of twenty-four.

Back East, the champion Giants had been sagging, except for Mays, who hit 51 home runs. The Dodgers and Alston began to get along. Brooklyn finished in first place, thirteen and a half games ahead of the Milwaukee Braves. The Giants slipped to third. Durocher seemed to lose interest in his job, arriving at the Polo Grounds just a few minutes before game time. "You can't believe what I put up with," he told Spencer Tracy. "The boss [Horace Stoneham] is a full-time drunk."

"I used to be a drunk myself," Tracy said. "That was in the old heimerdeimer days."

"Not like Horace," Durocher said. "We got to make some moves. He says, 'We'll be okay, pally.' I'm sick of this."

The Yankees outlasted the Indians, and for the third time in four seasons the World Series matched the Yankees against the Dodgers. Each ballclub was somewhat past its peak. Allie Reynolds, who owned oil wells, retired to Oklahoma. George Weiss sold Vic Raschi to the Cardinals. At long last the Yankees brought up a black, the catcher-outfielder Elston Howard. But this was a lesser team. The shortstop, Billy Hunter, batted only .227. No one on the pitching staff won twenty games. Mantle had a strong year with 37 homers, but going into the World

Series his left knee hobbled him. He could not play every day.

The Dodgers, of course, were older too. Reese had reached thirty-seven. Robinson, at thirty-six, was having trouble with his legs and incipient diabetes. These teams were heavyweights, but flabbier than they had been. They were also crabby.

The Yankees won the first game, 6 to 5, on Joe Collins's two homers; Jackie Robinson stole home in the eighth inning. "What a lousy, showboat play," Berra announced in the Yankee clubhouse. "They're two runs behind. Anyway, I had him out. The damn umpire blew the call."

"Lousy?" Robinson said to a reporter. "Whitey Ford was winding up. With me on third? Anytime they give me a run that way, I take it. And Berra *didn't* have me. He made a lazy tag. He stayed *behind* the plate. By the time he put the ball on me, my foot was across the plate."

The Yankees won the next day, 4 to 2, knocking out Billy Loes in the fourth inning. They were up by two games. Mantle had not played an inning.

Al Laney interviewed fans at the Stadium. "The Dodgers got a better team," someone told him. "There ain't a doubt. But when they go up against the Yankees, they can't win. It's the hawks get em. The hawks. They can't get away from the hawks."

Johnny Podres held off the Yankees at Ebbets Field on his twenty-third birthday and the Dodgers won, 8 to 3. Mantle limped into action and hit a home run, but after that he was in too much pain to be a factor. ("If Mickey says he hurts, believe me he hurts," the orthopedist, Sid Gaynor, said. "His pain threshold is remarkable, ten times higher than DiMaggio's.")

The Dodgers won two more in Brooklyn. Snider hit two home runs in the fifth game and a small Cuban outfielder named Edmundo Isasi Amoros, nicknamed Sandy, knocked in two more runs with another homer. "Wait till you see this kid hit," Al Campanis of the Dodgers had told reporters. "His wrists are so quick, he hits the ball right out of the catcher's glove.

"I'll do some work for you guys. Give him a nickname Edmundo 'Miracle Wrists' Amoros! How's that?"

The nickname didn't work in 1955. "Miracle Wrists" batted .247. He was a cheerful sort, but he had a hard time learning English. Some said the only three words he knew were "shrimp cocktail" and "steak."

The Series returned to the Bronx, and the Yankees won the sixth game, 5 to 1. The Reliable Jersey House favored the Yankees, 7 to 5.

Duke Snider sprained his left knee in center field. He could play the seventh game, but he was hobbled. Jackie Robinson bruised his left heel so severely he could not play at all. Mantle could not start. The famous ballgame of October 4, 1955, matched a pair of tired, wounded clubs.

The deposed manager, Charlie Dressen, had spent months teaching Johnny Podres a change of pace. "Think fastball," Dressen said. "Throw a fastball. Just when you release — zip! Pull down the window shade." The downward motion takes speed off the pitch at the same time as it increases rotation. The batter sees a rapidly spinning baseball. Fastball, he thinks. But the rapidly spinning pitch is moving slowly. Rotation is the fooler. Podres frustrated the Yankees with good fastballs and spinning changeups. The Dodgers chipped away — "beating at the Yankees with butterfly wings" — and scored single runs in the fourth and in the sixth.

Alston started infielder Jim Gilliam in left field. In the last half of the sixth, he moved Gilliam to second base and sent Amoros to left. Billy Martin walked. McDougald beat out a bunt. Yankees on first and second. Nobody out.

Podres threw Berra an outside fastball and Berra stroked a drive far down the left field line. Amoros, left-handed, wore his glove on his right hand. He ran full tilt and speared the ball in the glove and threw to Reese, who spun and loosed a perfect throw to Gil Hodges at first base. McDougald, running on what might have been a hit, was doubled. It was a fine catch and an absolutely spectacular relay throw. Pee Wee Reese at his very best.

The game ended at 4:44 P.M. The Dodgers won, 2 to 0. Brooklyn had won its first World Series.

Francis Sugrue of the *Herald Tribune* described victory night in Brooklyn. "The Fourth of July, New Year's Eve, St. Patrick's Day, V-E Day, and Bastille Day, all in one. Add to that a touch of Mardi Gras. The minute Pee Wee Reese threw out Elston Howard for the last out at first base, Brooklyn police headquarters sent out an alert for all to be on the lookout for Dodger fans. As this edition went to press, there were no fatalities."

Somehow, Reese and I ended up toasting the universe on West 57th Street. His face was shining, a child's face when school is out, or when Christmas morning finally has come.

"Can I ask you something, Pee Wee?"

"Sure."

"Two out in the ninth. You've played on five losing World Series teams. You're one out away from winning a Series. Elston Howard's up. What are you thinking?"

"I'm thinking," said Pee Wee Reese, the greatest, bravest shortstop of the Era, "I hope he doesn't hit the ball to me."

Walter O'Malley summoned the press a few days later. He had commissioned "Buckminster Fuller of Princeton" to design the new Dodger Stadium as a geodesic dome.

A sportswriter asked how to spell the word.

"Dome," Buzzie Bavasi said. "D-o-m-e."

"Are you gonna give Podres a raise?" someone else asked.

"We're here to talk about the geodesic dome," O'Malley said. *Nobody took him or Bucky Fuller seriously.*

Durocher continued telling Hollywood friends that his employer was a drunk. A group of actors and agents threw a stag for Durocher at the Friars Club, and a special feature was Danny Kaye's imitation of a drunken Horace Stoneham. Kaye had the words right — "pally," "by golly." Kaye's mimic drunken diction was brutal.

"The greatest thing," Durocher said later, "was when Danny opened his fly and pulled out his pecker and put it on a saucer. He's doing Horace. I mean, the sloppy talk and the stupid speeches and the rest. He's doin' Horace with his pecker hanging out. I never laughed so hard in my life."

William Joseph Rigney of Burlingame, California, was hired to manage the Giants for 1956.

◆

DICK YOUNG INSISTED O'Malley told him he wanted to leave Ebbets Field "because the area is getting full of blacks and spics." O'Malley denied having said any such thing.

"Oh, yeah," Young parried when I pressed him. "O'Malley also said the trouble with Brooklyn was that the place had too many blacks and spics *and Jews.*"

Certainly O'Malley was most comfortable with his Roman Catholic cadre, Bavasi and Fresco Thompson. Jackie Robinson disquieted O'Malley, not just because Robinson was Rickey's man but also because he was a challenging, defiant black. Walter liked blacks docile. He preferred Pullman porters to Jackie Robinson.

The Dodgers brought Sandy Koufax to spring training in 1955. Al Campanis, who scouted Koufax, said, "Only twice in my life has my spine actually tingled. Once was when I saw the Sistine Chapel. The other time was when I saw Sandy Koufax throw a fastball."

Koufax was wild. Today he is remembered as a Hall of Fame player, but it was not until 1963, in Hollywood, that Koufax became a twenty-game winner. Alston and others in the Dodger organization handled him poorly. It may not, however, have taken Koufax eight years to throw a strike under pressure. He is a closemouthed man but he has remarked that Alston would have made him a starter earlier, except that he was Jewish.

O'Malley was aware of everyone's ethnicity. It is excessive to accuse him of bigotry, but he did harbor stereotypes. Brooklyn blacks were moving southward out of Bedford-Stuyvesant toward Eastern Parkway and Crown Heights. Ebbets Field stood in the path of the black advance. This became another reason he wanted to move.

O'Malley did not relish the Dodgers' great 1955 World Series victory as a sportsman would have relished it — triumph after half a century of failure. It was good; it was fine; but it cost him extra damn dollars for a victory party. Most of all O'Malley saw the triumph as a wedge. The mayor and the governor had better start working with him on his new Brooklyn ballpark forthwith, now that he was presiding over the greatest baseball team on earth.

Dodger attendance in 1955 ran slightly over a million, a disappointing total. The Yankees drew five hundred thousand more. The upstart Braves, who had moved from Boston to Milwaukee, drew two million.

"This is a very serious problem," O'Malley told me. "With the Braves making more money than we are, they'll hire the best scouts away from us and before you know it, they'll have a better team. That would be ruinous. You know what I say. In Brooklyn, you're first or bankrupt."

I had enough sense to ask for numbers and he had enough fondness for me to provide them. "Not for last year, those numbers aren't in yet, but for two years ago, 1953, typical Brooklyn numbers." This was the Dodger balance sheet Walter O'Malley gave me.

RECEIPTS

Tickets sales, including World Series, and minor league clubs	$4,500,000
Concessions and parking	450,000

Player sales	200,000
Total Dodger income	$5,150,000

EXPENSES

Federal, state, and city taxes	$ 926,000
Team salaries; players' pension contributions and all traveling expenses for major and all minor league squads	1,119,000
Team replacement costs: scouts, payments to free agents, spring training costs, minor league team deficits	428,000
Maintaining Ebbets Field	589,000
Games expenses; ticket printing and selling, ushers and staff	184,000
Advertising and publicity, office personnel and staff salaries, and insurance	80,000
Administrative expenses, including executive salaries, telephone, and office supplies	417,000
Total Dodger expenses	$3,743,000

The single-season profit O'Malley admitted was $1,407,000. He would not admit $750,000 from radio and television, but that ran his annual profit to more than $2,000,000. Gaining control of the Dodgers cost O'Malley $1,250,000. Now the team was making more than that each season. O'Malley was earning about two hundred percent on his investment. His team had won the World Series.

He was not satisfied.

In November, O'Malley told Irving Rudd, of his publicity office, that he was booking the Dodgers into an old minor league park, Roosevelt Stadium in Jersey City, for seven games in 1956. On December 12, he told Rudd to move into a one-room office at the Hotel Plaza on Journal Square (in Jersey City). "Thus, I became the only general manager of a major league baseball team in New Jersey history," Rudd recalled in a memoir called *The Sporting Life.* "Of course, if you take into account that the Dodgers were playing only seven of their regularly scheduled 77 home games in Jersey City, this made me the one-eleventh general manager of the Dodgers.

"More seriously," Rudd says, "it was clear what O'Malley was threatening.

"Today Jersey City.

"Tomorrow California."

Firing Durocher did not revive the Giants. The team had finished third in 1955. Under Rigney, the Giants did no better than sixth in 1956 and 1957. They traded Bobby Thomson to Milwaukee in February of 1954, a move defiant of decent sentiment, but one that brought them the good left-handed pitcher Johnny Antonelli. In the middle of the 1955 season, they sold Sal Maglie to the Cleveland Indians. The following year the Dodgers bought Maglie's contract from Cleveland.

The Brooklyn clubhouse was electric as Maglie entered it on the afternoon of May 16, 1956. He had knocked down Dodger hitters for six years. Carl Furillo continued to swear vengeance.

As Maglie entered, Erskine and Reese and Campanella looked curiously toward Furillo.

"Hello, Dago," Furillo said.

"'Lo, Skoonj," said Maglie.

Maglie won thirteen games for Brooklyn. The Dodgers won the pennant from Milwaukee by a single game; quite simply, Sal Maglie, Mephistopheles on the Mound, had won it for Brooklyn.

"That may be," Carl Erskine says, "but when I saw Maglie standing in *our* clubhouse, wearing *our* uniform, I knew nothing in this world would ever surprise me again."

Mickey Mantle came into his own in 1956, which he now calls "my favorite year." He batted .353, hit 52 home runs, and drove in 130 runs. Unlike Mays, Mantle had not been anointed rookie of the year. (Gil McDougald beat him out.) But in '56, Mantle was indisputably the American League's most valuable player.

The Dodgers jumped to a lead in the World Series. Maglie won the opening game, 6 to 3. Next day the Yankees knocked out Don Newcombe and handed Don Larsen a 6 to 0 lead in the second inning. But the Dodgers knocked out Larsen and won going away, 13 to 8.

Larsen broke in with the St. Louis Browns in 1953, the year the Browns went bankrupt. The team underwent a kind of breech rebirth as the Baltimore Orioles, and the Yankees acquired Larsen in an eighteen-player trade with Baltimore in the winter of 1954. Larsen quickly established himself as a pretty good pitcher and a free spirit.

He demolished a car at four A.M. one predawn during spring training at St. Petersburg, driving into a pole.

"The pole was speeding," Larsen told reporters. "I hope Stengel don't fine me."

"Fine him?" Stengel said. "He oughta get an award, finding something to do in this town after midnight."

The Yankees won the next two games at the Stadium. On October 8, with the Series tied at two games each, Larsen went out to pitch against the remarkable Mr. Maglie. Larsen felt stressed. He had failed in this World Series. He had failed in the Series of 1955. He was having trouble making ends meet. His estranged wife, Vivian, twenty-nine, had obtained a court order requiring the Yankees, Larsen, and Commissioner Ford Frick to show cause why his World Series share should not be seized by the Bronx Supreme Court.

"While this baseball hero is enjoying the luxuries of life and the plaudits of the public," argued lawyer Harry Lipsig, "he is subjecting his fourteen-month-old baby girl and his wife to the pleasures of starvation existence."

The night before the game, Larsen went out for drinks with a group that included the Yankee backup outfielder Bob Cerv. "I am not going to say much," Cerv told me, "I left him at four A.M."

"I got no comment at all on that night," Larsen says.

"I called his hotel in the morning," Cerv says, "to make sure he got out of bed. He said, 'Noooooo.' At the ballpark, he took a whirlpool bath, a cold shower, and had a rub. You know what happened next."

Maglie was marvelous, limiting the Yankees to five hits. Larsen was better. He pitched the only perfect game in the history of the World Series. Fastballs and sliders. A few slow curves. Superb control. A novel no-windup delivery.

With two out in the ninth inning and twenty-six men retired, Dale Mitchell pinch hit for Maglie. He took a ball, high and outside. A slow curve broke over for a strike. Mitchell missed a curve. Strike two. He fouled a fastball. He took a quarter swing at a fastball that seemed to be eye-high. Babe Pinelli, the umpire, called Mitchell out.

"Damn," Dick Young said in the press box. "The imperfect man just pitched a perfect game."

"Casey," Louis Effrat of the *Times* shouted in the winning clubhouse, "was that the best game you ever saw Larsen pitch?"

"So far," Stengel said.

Shirley Povich of the *Washington Post* wrote a lead people remember:

> The million-to-one shot came in. Hell froze over. A month of Sundays hit the calendar. Don Larsen today pitched a no-hit, no-run, no-man-reach-first game in a World Series.

By nightfall, Larsen dispatched four hundred twenty dollars to the lawyer for his wife and daughter.

"This man is still no hero," Harry Lipsig, the lawyer, said. "In these proceedings, he has brazenly suggested when his daughter was born she immediately was to be given out for adoption."

In California Larsen's mother, Charlotte, a housekeeper at a retirement home in La Jolla, said she had been weeping tears of joy.

*

Labine shut down the Yankees, and the Dodgers won the sixth game, 1 to 0, in ten innings. The next day the Yankees won, 9 to 0, putting Don Newcombe to rout in three innings. It was the seventeenth time the Yankees had won the Series.

"They beat the hell out of us," Walter Alston said.

In December of 1956, O'Malley sold Jackie Robinson's contract to the New York Giants for $35,000 and the rights to a journey-man left-hander named Dick Littlefield. O'Malley wrote the Robinsons a letter of farewell.

> Dear Jackie and Rachel:
> I do know how you and your youngsters must have felt. It was a sad day for us as well.
> The roads of life have a habit of recrossing. There could well be a future intersection. Until then, my best to you both.
> With a decade of memories.
>
> > Au revoir,
> > Walter O'Malley

"If it makes him so sad," Jackie said to Rachel, "why did he go and trade me to the Giants?"

Robinson quit and sold the announcement of his retirement to *Look* magazine for $50,000. Then he went to work for Chock Full o' Nuts, the coffee company, as director of personnel. In the summer of 1957, I traveled to Greenwood Lake, New York, to watch Sugar Ray Robinson train for a fight with Carmen Basilio. After a while, Jackie Robinson appeared carrying a carton and looking embarrassed. The carton contained cans of coffee. William Black, the president of Chock Full o' Nuts, had ordered Robinson to pass out coffee cans free "to get some publicity from the boxing writers."

Sugar Ray greeted Jackie with a hug; but a hero had been reduced to a handout man.

"By 1957 we had a terrible situation at the Polo Grounds," Chub Feeney remembers. "The park was deteriorating. People were afraid of the neighborhood. At the very least, we needed three million dollars as a minimum to break even and we weren't getting it. We offered Jackie fifty thousand dollars to play for us, although we knew he wasn't in great shape. We were hoping desperately to boost attendance with Robinson. We were drawing only six hundred fifty thousand a year in a metropolitan area of twelve million.

"We could have sold the club, but my Uncle Horace didn't *want* to sell the club.

"You knew him.

"He lived for baseball . . ."

Hulan Jack, borough president of Manhattan, proposed a new stadium for the Giants. It would be built on enormous stilts, Jack said, over railroad tracks on the West Side of Manhattan. This is where, thirty years later, Donald Trump proposed a development so enormous that its highest skyscraper would cast a shadow on Central Park. Hulan Jack was an eccentric; he talked of a 110,000-seat ballpark. He had no plan to raise construction money.

"We owned the Minneapolis Millers in the American Association," Feeney says. "By June of 1957, Horace and I were finishing arrangements to move the team there. Then Horace's phone rang. Walter O'Malley said, 'Why not move to California with me?'

No one paid appropriate attention in 1955 when O'Malley sold Ebbets Field for three million dollars to a real estate developer named Marvin Kratter. He also sold ballparks the Dodgers owned in Fort Worth and Montreal for one million dollars each. "That five million dollars," he said, "is the money that will, one way or another, go into our new Brooklyn ballpark." But he also invested some of the money by acquiring the Los Angeles franchise in the Pacific Coast League from the Chicago Cubs. He now owned territorial rights to Los Angeles. He was ready to play his special game: stroke and tomahawk.

"My roots are New York," O'Malley told Mayor Robert Wagner at City Hall on June 2, 1957. "People in Los Angeles want the Dodgers to move. They've made flattering offers. I am in no way committed."

"What do you want?" Wagner asked.

"Air rights over the Long Island Railroad station at Atlantic Avenue and Flatbush Avenue in downtown Brooklyn. The Dodgers don't want anything else. We'll pay for a new ballpark by ourselves."

Wagner was a pleasant person, part Tammany hack, part liberal reformer, and totally overmatched in negotiating with O'Malley. Robert Moses, New York's commissioner of parks, was the principal city player. Through a series of appointments, Moses controlled not only parks, but highways and urban projects as well. Urbanologists regard Moses as "the single most powerful figure in twentieth-century New York City government." Moses put hard questions to O'Malley.

"You aren't suggesting, sir, that four or five million dollars is enough to build the domed stadium you propose?"

O'Malley conceded that the cost would be higher. "The Brooklyn Dodgers are prepared to sell a bond issue to citizens of Brooklyn, backed by the full faith and credit of our franchise. I have no doubt, Mr. Moses, none whatsoever, about our ability to finance ourselves."

Further, O'Malley said, he was negotiating with Mathew Fox of Skiatron, Inc., "to put our games on subscription TV." The technology involved a coin box on television sets. Fans would have to put two quarters into the box to unscramble pictures of Dodger games. "These receipts will help pay for the new ballpark."

Moses looked incredulous. "Engineers and electronic experts," O'Malley said, "tell me coin box television is no problem at all."

"As a matter of fact," Moses said, "I just don't want to see a baseball field in downtown Brooklyn at all. The streets will never handle all the cars."

O'Malley said that his plans for the domed stadium, over

the Long Island Railroad station, included such good access that most people would come to the park by train.

"You are in error, Mr. O'Malley. If I let you build your domed stadium, your ballgames will create a China Wall of traffic in Brooklyn. No one will be able to pass."

"Where would you prefer that we relocate?" O'Malley said.

"I have a lovely parcel of land in Flushing Meadow, at the old World's Fair site in Queens."

O'Malley looked steadily at Robert Moses. "If my team is forced to play in the borough of Queens, they will no longer be the Brooklyn Dodgers."

Next day the front page of the *Herald Tribune* announced that a new aquarium was being dedicated in Coney Island and that Margaret Truman, wife of Clifton Daniel, Jr., assistant managing editor of the *New York Times,* had given birth to a son. A headline in columns four and five, more prescient than the copyeditor knew, described the meeting among O'Malley, Wagner, and Moses as "a scoreless tie."

In September the Los Angeles City Council voted to offer the Dodgers 307 acres in Chavez Ravine in exchange for a small parcel of land at the Los Angeles minor league park called Wrigley Field.

The last ballgame at Ebbets Field occurred on September 24, 1957. The Dodgers defeated Branch Rickey's Pittsburgh Pirates, 2 to 0.

Gladys Goodding, the organist, played sad songs for the crowd, 6,702 fans in — as O'Malley said — "a borough of fully two million." Goodding played in order:

"Am I Blue?"

"What Can I Say, Dear, After I've Said I'm Sorry?"

"Thanks for the Memory!"

"When I Grow Too Old to Dream"

"When the Blue of the Night Meets the Gold of the Day"

"Auld Lang Syne"

That night Casey Stengel's Yankees clinched their eighth American League pennant.

The Milwaukee Braves won the World Series, four games to three, with three complete-game victories from Lew Burdette, a right-hander out of Nitro, West Virginia.

I flew back on a United Airlines plane chartered by the Yankees. Stengel was angry and drank steadily for three hours. After we landed, he moved down the wheeled stairway to the tarmac at Idlewild Airport and a reporter from channel 11 rushed at him with microphone and cameraman.

"Did your team choke up out there?" the reporter asked.

"Do you choke up on your fucking microphone?" Stengel said. He turned around and clawed his buttocks.

"You see," he told me later, "you got to stop them terrible questions. When I said 'fuck' I ruined his audio. When I scratched my ass, I ruined his video, if you get my drift."

The Era was done. On October 9, when the Yankee-Milwaukee Series was tied at three games each, Arthur Patterson, wrongly characterized by Dick Young as "a third-string club official," read a fifty-two-word statement ending: "The stockholders and directors of the Brooklyn baseball club have today met and unanimously agreed that the necessary steps be taken to draft the Los Angeles territory."

Young wrote, "Following the Giants' defection, New York is left without a National League club for the first time in 67 years."

The United Press telephoned Bob Hope in Palm Springs.

"The Dodgers are going to be very big out here," Hope said. "I can't wait to see Duke Snider in a bare-midriff uniform."

Benny Weinrig, a diffident little fellow who served sandwiches in the Ebbets Field press box, burst into tears that night. "This team," he told his mother, "has been my whole life. What is it now?

"Just a joke . . ."

*

The Era was done. Durocher was gone and Robinson and DiMaggio; Reynolds and Raschi; Roe and Gionfriddo; Bobby Brown and Bobby Thomson; Koslo and Rizzuto; and Charlie Dressen, managing the Washington Senators, got himself fired very early in 1957. Fired in May.

The Era ended when it was time for the Era to end: Stengel defeated in the World Series, the Dodgers and the Giants moving West.

The Era ended when it was time for the Era to end and that, I believe, is everlastingly part of its beauty and its glory.

March 6, 1990–October 31, 1992
Croton-on-Hudson, New York

Afterword

Time is a sort of river of passing events,
and strong is its current; no sooner is a
thing brought to sight than it is swept by and
another takes its place, and this too
will be swept away—
—Marcus Aurelius

Why am I quoting an ancient Roman philosopher and emperor in a baseball book? Because from title to finale *The Era* is not only about baseball, it is also about Marcus Aurelius's "river of passing events." It is about time.

In the decade since I pounded out the final words (on an indestructible Olympia Standard typewriter) many of *The Era*'s notables have left the planet: Roy Campanella (1993), Mickey Mantle (1995), and Joe DiMaggio and Pee Wee Reese, both in 1999. But new things, as Aurelius foretold, have been brought to sight.

The Dodgers, who developed into baseball's most valuable franchise during the lifetime of Walter O'Malley, fell into disorder under O'Malley's son, Peter. For only the second time in a history dating from the nineteenth century, the team finished last in 1992. At this writing, the Dodgers have not won a play-off game since 1988. Late in his not so gay nineties, Peter O'Malley put the club up for sale and Governor George Pataki appointed me to a committee charged with bringing the Dodgers back to Brooklyn. What a nice dream, I thought (and so did Pataki). But quickly we found quite real and serious backing from a mighty utility company, and former New York governor Hugh Carey was designated to call the Dodgers and begin exploratory talks. Could Camelot come again, and, by the way, what would we name the new ball park? O'Malley dismissed Carey as arrogantly as his father had dismissed Brooklyn. Peter already had a deal, he said, and after a while Rupert Murdoch, the Australian media magnate, paid $311 million for the Los Angeles Dodgers. Murdoch is said to have spent his first game as head honcho searching the playing field for wickets.

Peter O'Malley left baseball whimpering that the day of the individual owner was done. Apparently he was unfamiliar with the works of George Michael Steinbrenner III. During the 1990s Steinbrenner restored the New York Yankees to a dominance roughly comparable to that of the old Casey Stengel/George Weiss gang. Steinbrenner calls himself "managing partner." One comment nicely illustrates his individualistic dominance: "Nothing on earth is as limited," an investor told me, "as a limited partner to George Steinbrenner." In his maturity Steinbrenner has created a baseball general staff for the Yankees that includes, among others, Yogi Berra, Reggie Jackson, Don Mattingly, and Al Rosen. They gather with the team at Tampa in spring and meet regularly to discuss, analyze, and suggest. The final word, as you may suspect, belongs to Steinbrenner. But with the Yankees winning three consecutive World Series ('98, '99, '00), his credentials as a baseball executive are approaching the impeccable.

Near the fiftieth anniversary of Bobby Thomson's famous home run, a young *Wall Street Journal* reporter printed a story that said the Giants were stealing signs at the Polo Grounds by posting a spy with binoculars in the centerfield clubhouse. In short, before the fateful pitch, Thomson *knew* Ralph Branca would throw him a fastball. Squeals of outrage followed. You will hear none here. Al Rosen told me that preceding his first major-league at bat, the late Lou Boudreau (then managing Cleveland) told him, "Watch the left side of the scoreboard, kid. If a fist comes through the hole, it's gonna be a curve." Fist did. Rosen doubled. Further, as Joe Black recently pointed out, in game 1 of the 1951 playoff, Thomson also homered off Branca, but this was at Ebbets Field. Nothing was stolen from the Dodgers there; this was just good hitting by Thomson. Two thoughts come to mind. In the majors you do what you have to do to win. At the momentous moment in game 3, Branca should have thrown a breaking ball.

The Yankees are again the Yankees. Murdoch's Dodgers have been treading water. The San Francisco Giants, finally given a bearable ball park, have become a solid team, and in Barry Bonds they have a lineal descendant (at least with the bat) of Willie Mays, who is, incidentally, Bonds's godfather.

What of Brooklyn, nastily booted out of the major leagues so many years ago? Fans of a certain age remain hurt and angry. They supported the O'Malley Dodgers handsomely and were betrayed. Younger fans are interested in the Brooklyn Cyclones, a team that plays in the New York Penn League against such rivals as the Utica Blue Sox. But to old timers, the Cyclones serve only to underscore the wrong that the O'Malley family committed. Old timers say such things as, "Where do they come off making Brooklyn a minor-league town?"

That seems to cover everything except that indestructible Olympia Standard typewriter mentioned earlier. Like almost everyone else, I've switched to a word processor. The Olympia sits very quietly in a corner of my office—except when a visitor says "computer" or "Bill Gates." Then it makes an ominous, growling sound.

Stone Ridge, New York
August 2001

Notes and Comment
on Sources

◆

H ISTORY," Henry Ford once remarked, "is the bunk."
History is neither bunk nor junk, but the more one re-
searches, the more one recognizes that history does become terribly subjective. Important events take place away
from cameras and microphones. Often nobody takes notes.
That forces the researcher to rely on memories, which differ.
When one must rely on something as uncertain as memory,
the bunk factor appears, persists, and tends to spread, like
mushrooms in a wet, ill-tended lawn.

Walter O'Malley liked to boast that the Dodgers were the
only baseball franchise to have won the World Series on both
coasts, once in Brooklyn and many times in Los Angeles. When
I told O'Malley that the Athletics had won the World Series in
Philadelphia and in Oakland, he looked chagrined; not, it developed, at being corrected but at his own mistake.

Arthur E. Patterson told me in 1991 that he was the only
man who had started out as a sportswriter and become president of a major league team (the California Angels). But Wil-

liam Veeck, Sr., father of the famous hustler, was a sportswriter who became president of the Chicago Cubs, sixty-five years earlier.

There was no malice, no willful deception in the statements by O'Malley and by Patterson. Yet each is bunk. Each has been reported in newspaper stories and found its way into files and databases, assuring all that the inaccuracies will appear again in yet more newspaper stories and magazine articles. I consider myself fortunate to have kept these two minor errors out of my own work. I am not so vain as to believe that I have been able to exclude all others. Frank Ryan, the former Cleveland Brown quarterback who earned a Ph.D. in topology, speaks of "zero errors" as an objective. "But that's fairly hard to achieve," Ryan says, "particularly at quarterback." Zero errors has been Ryan's objective in the precise world of theoretical mathematics, and zero errors has been my objective in the less precise world of social history, with sliders.

Zeal is an enemy of reasonable discourse, but zeal appears more often than one would like. Bill James, who writes and edits bestselling books he calls "baseball abstracts," found several mistakes in David Halberstam's popular *Summer of '49*.

> I'm not trying to tell David Halberstam what his standards should be. But hell, I hire a research assistant and Halberstam's a lot bigger name than I am. Why on earth didn't he hire somebody who knows something about baseball to read his book carefully before it came out? . . . Is Halberstam this careless with the facts when he writes about the things he usually writes about? It is frightening to think that Halberstam is this sloppy in writing about war and politics.

In one of the abstracts, James published comment on my own book *The Boys of Summer*. He got the year of publication wrong. Does this mean that James is a careless, sloppy, and frightening reporter? I don't believe he is. This means only that James, or his hired research assistant, made a mistake.

Collegial dialogue is all to the good. Excess frothing, in commentary or in beer, is unfortunate.

The most contentious episodes during the Era played out at the beginning and the end: the Cardinals' racist strike against Jackie Robinson and Walter O'Malley's avaricious abandonment of Brooklyn. Neither story easily gives up its secrets or truths.

Most surviving St. Louis ballplayers say during the 1990s that a strike against Robinson was never discussed in 1947. Stan Musial maintains that "the story was made up." But research informs us that Musial was sick and feverish with raging appendicitis while strike plans developed. He is not deliberately misleading anyone. But in early May 1947, Musial was too ill to know what was taking place; later, when the strike was squashed, his teammates did not seek him out with the obscene particulars of their failed idea.

"Hey," says Joe Garagiola, "I was rootin' for Robinson. Strike? Me try to spike him? Hey. No way. I was tryin' to *avoid* spiking him when I tripped and tore up my shoulder."

However, in the picture *The Sporting News* published in the summer of 1947, Garagiola appears to be challenging Robinson to a fistfight. We may here have a prominent television interviewer rewriting history and his role in it. I prefer to believe that Joe is deceived by his own memory, the recurrent phenomenon of wishful history.

"Stanley Woodward made the whole [strike] story up," Enos Slaughter said. "That son of a bitch kept me out of the Hall of Fame for twenty years."

"Ford Frick never spoke to us about the racial situation," Terry Moore said. "Doc Hyland talked to us. Not Frick."

"Woodward," wrote Bob Broeg, of the *St. Louis Post-Dispatch*, "was practicing barnyard journalism."

Trying to put these versions together, I come up with something like this: The Cardinals never intended to strike against Jackie Robinson. They liked him. They admired him, even when his adventurous play cost them ballgames and money. Woodward made up a barnyard story about a racial strike that was never planned. The Cardinals' team physician told the captain of the team not to proceed with this strike that nobody was planning anyway. *Bunkum americanus.*

As the Giants moved West, most accepted Horace Stoneham's apologia: "I can't stay where I am, pally. If I don't move the team, I go bankrupt. Except for Chub [Feeney], all my relatives would starve."

Starvation was remote from the Brooklyn Family O'Malley. By locating figures O'Malley provided me during the 1950s and adding the television and radio receipts wrung from him by Congress, I provide documentation, I believe for the first time, of the extraordinary profits the Dodgers earned in Brooklyn. But while all the specific figures were not common knowledge during the 1950s, most assumed that O'Malley was making a decent profit in Flatbush. His move was widely and accurately regarded as a matter of greed, not need.

O'Malley's early years in California were bumpier than expected. His subscription television plan did not work out and the Los Angeles city fathers finally deeded him the promised land in Chavez Ravine by a narrow margin. He had to use a football field, the Los Angeles Coliseum, as his home base for a while. "I'll admit," he told me early in the 1970s, "that for a time it looked as if we'd have to play our home games in the middle of Wilshire Boulevard."

The new ballpark, Dodger Stadium, opened on April 10, 1962. O'Malley met the cost, $22 million, with a low-interest (two percent) loan from the Union Oil Company, which in exchange won exclusive rights to advertise within the ballpark. Dodger home attendance began to surpass three million late in the 1970s.

Some find irony in the fact that O'Malley's son, Peter, led opposition to the Giants' moving from San Francisco to St. Petersburg, Florida, after the 1992 season. But the O'Malleys are businesspeople, expedients. It seemed good business for Walter to move West at the end of the Era. It seemed bad business to Peter O'Malley for the Dodgers to lose a profitable intra-California rivalry a generation later.

I suppose every researcher has favorite sources. For the Era, I recommend the *Daily News*, because of Dick Young, and the *New York Post*, because of Jimmy Cannon and Milton Gross. I have never seen an overall sports section as good as the one Stanley Woodward edited at the *Herald Tribune* in the late 1940s.

When the *Tribune* fired Woodward in 1949, the paper took the first step on a road of decline that ended with its death in 1966. To some that was as tragic as the death of two fine New York baseball teams a few years earlier.

A Brief Thanksgiving

◆

T HE AUTHOR'S SON, Gordon J. Kahn, A.I.A., of Som-
ers, New York, was kind enough to check certain details
pertaining to the Flavian Amphitheater, the Coliseum, in
libraries of architecture. My old *Herald Tribune* colleague Harold Rosenthal was particularly generous with his memories, as
were many old traveling companions, including Dr. Robert
"Bobby" Brown, Stan Musial, Harold "Pee Wee" Reese, and
Edwin "Duke" Snider.

Mark Balk provided tireless research assistance, as did Susan
Kilgour. Barbara G. Flanagan copyedited the manuscript with
great care. Karen Sevell Greenbaum punched it into her word
processor. Neil Reshen and Dawn Reshen-Doty, of Benay En-
terprises, run the business side of my writing life and they
performed difficult work skillfully.

One reads today, with some justification, about changes in
publishing, the ascendancy of the M.B.A., and the decline of
the editor and editing. This is something close to my twentieth
book and I have never been privileged to have more careful,

tasteful, and even loving editing than that which John Herman of Ticknor & Fields offered to *The Era*.

My thanks to the following for generous help: Marty Adler; Mel Allen; Emil J. "Buzzie" Bavasi; Yogi Berra; Mildred (Mrs. Bill) Bevens; Ralph Branca; Andrew Bullen, Center for Research Libraries, Chicago; Roy Campanella; Mary Carey, New-York Historical Society Library; Jerry Coleman; Bill Deane, National Baseball Hall of Fame Library; Don Drysdale; Dennis Falcone, WCBS-FM; Edward Falcone, Field Library, Peekskill, N.Y.; Charles S. "Chub" Feeney; David Fischer, Time-Life Library; Edward E. Fitzgerald; Joe Garagiola; Albert Gionfriddo; William J. Guilfoile, National Baseball Hall of Fame; Tommy Henrich; Gene Hermanski; Clem Labine; Al Lightner, Salem, Oregon; Carroll "Whitey" Lockman; Lee MacPhail; Terry Moore; Donald Mueller; Arthur "Red" Patterson; Mark Reese; Arthur Richman; Phil Rizzuto; Emily Rose, Putnam Valley, New York, Library; Albert "Flip" Rosen; Faigi Rosenthal, chief librarian, New York *Daily News;* Steve Saks, New York Public Library; Mike Shannon; George Shuba; Lisa Siclare, SUNY, Purchase; Charlie Silvera; May Stone, New-York Historical Society Library; Robert "Bobby" Thomson; Mariam Touba, New-York Historical Society Library; Gary Van Allen, National Baseball Hall of Fame; Peter Wessley, Field Library; Wesley Westrum; Sal Yvars; and Vic Ziegel.

Bibliography

◆

Adomites, Paul. *October's Game*. Alexandria, V.A.: Redefinition, 1990.

Alexander, Charles C. *Our Game: An American Baseball History*. New York: Holt, 1991.

Allen, Ethan. *Major League Baseball: Technique and Tactics*. New York: Macmillan, 1938.

Allen, Lee. *The World Series: The Story of Baseball's Annual Championships*. New York: Putnam's, 1969.

———. *The Giants and the Dodgers: The Fabulous Story of Baseball's Fiercest Feud*. New York: Putnam's, 1964.

Allen, Maury. Voices of Sport. New York: Grosset and Dunlap, 1971.

———. *You Could Look It Up: The Life of Casey Stengel*. New York: Times Books, 1979.

———. *Damn Yankee: The Billy Martin Story*. New York: Times Books, 1980.

———. *Jackie Robinson: A Life Remembered*. New York: Watts, 1987.

Allen, Mel, with Ed Fitzgerald. *You Can't Beat the Hours: A Long Loving Look at Big League Baseball*. New York: Harper and Row, 1964.

Allen, Mel, with Frank Graham, Jr. *It Takes Heart*. New York: Harper and Row, 1959.

Alston, Walter, with Sy Burick. *Alston and the Dodgers*. Garden City, N.Y.: Doubleday, 1966.

Anderson, Dave, and Harold Rosenthal et al. *The Yankees: The Four Fabulous Eras of Baseball's Most Famous Team*. New York: Random House, 1979.

Barber, Walter ("Red"). *The Rhubarb Patch*. New York: Simon & Schuster, 1954.

———. *The Broadcasters*. New York: Dial, 1970.

———. *1947: When All Hell Broke Loose in Baseball*. Garden City, N.Y.: Doubleday, 1982.

Barber, Walter, and Robert W. Creamer. *Rhubarb in the Catbird Seat*. Garden City, N.Y.: Doubleday, 1968.

Bardolph, Richard. *The Negro Vanguard*. New York: Vintage, 1961.

Berra, Yogi, with Ed Fitzgerald. *Yogi: The Autobiography of a Professional Baseball Player*. Garden City, N.Y.: Doubleday, 1961.

Berra, Yogi, with Tom Horton. *Yogi: It Ain't Over . . .* New York: McGraw-Hill, 1989.

Black, Joe. *Ain't Nobody Better Than You: An Autobiography of Joe Black*. Garden Grove, Calif.: Ironwood Lithographers, 1983.

Borst, Bill. *A Fan's Memoir: The Brooklyn Dodgers, 1953–57*. Glyndon, Md.: Chapter and Cask, 1982.

Borstein, Larry. *Great Moments in Baseball*. New York: Grosset and Dunlap, 1973.

Broeg, Bob, with William Miller, Jr. *Baseball from a Different Angle*. South Bend, Ind.: Diamond Communications, 1988.

Buchanon, Lamont. *The World Series and Highlights of Baseball*. New York: Dutton, 1951.

Campanella, Roy, with Joe Reichler. *It's Good to Be Alive*. Boston, Little, Brown, 1959.

Cannon, Jimmy. *Nobody Asked Me, But . . .* Ed. Jack Cannon and Tom Cannon. New York: Holt, Rinehart and Winston, 1978.

Chandler, Albert B. ("Happy"). *Heroes, Plain Folks and Skunks: The Life and Times of Happy Chandler*. Chicago: Bonus, 1989.

Charlton, James. *The Baseball Chronology: The Complete History of the Most Important Events in the Game of Baseball*. New York: Macmillan, 1991.

Creamer, Robert. *Stengel: His Life and Times*. New York: Simon & Schuster, 1984.

Daley, Arthur. *Sports of the Times: The Arthur Daley Years*. Ed. by James Tuite. New York: Quadrangle, 1975.

Dark, Alvin, with John Underwood. *When in Doubt, Fire the Manager: My Life and Times in Baseball*. New York: Dutton, 1980.

Davenport, John W. *Baseball's Pennant Races: A Graphic View*. Madison, Wis.: First Impressions, 1981.

Day, Laraine, with Kyle Crichton. *Day with the Giants*. Garden City, N.Y.: Doubleday, 1952.

Devaney, John. *Gil Hodges: Baseball Miracle Men*. New York: Putnam's, 1973.

Dexter, Charles. *Don Newcombe: Baseball Hero*. Greenich, Conn.: Fawcett, 1950.

Dickey, Glenn. *The Great No-Hitters*. Radnor, Pa.: Chilton, 1976.

———. *The History of the World Series Since 1903*. New York: Stein and Day, 1984.

DiMaggio, Joe. *Lucky to Be a Yankee*. New York: Rudolph Field, 1946.

Dittmar, Joseph J. *Baseball's Benchmark Boxscores: Summaries of the Record-Setting Games*. Jefferson, N.C.: McFarland, 1990.

Drysdale, Don, with Bob Verdi. *Once a Bum, Always a Dodger*. New York: St. Martin's, 1990.

Duberman, Martin Baum. *Paul Robeson*. New York: Knopf, 1988.

Durocher, Leo, with Ed Linn. *Nice Guys Finish Last*. New York: Simon & Schuster, 1975.

———. *The Dodgers and Me: The Inside Story*. New York: Ziff-Davis, 1948.

Durso, Joseph. *Casey: The Life and Legend of Charles Dillon Stengel*. Englewood Cliffs, N.J.: Prentice-Hall, 1967.

———. *Casey and Mr. McGraw*. St. Louis: Sporting News, 1989.

Einstein, Charles. *Willie Mays: Coast to Coast Hero*. New York: Putnam's, 1963.

———. *Willie's Time*. New York: Lippincott, 1979.

Falkner, David. *The Last Yankee: The Turbulent Life of Billy Martin*. New York: Simon & Schuster, 1992.

Fitzgerald, Ed. *The Story of the Brooklyn Dodgers*. New York: Bantam, 1948.

Ford, Edward C. ("Whitey"), with Joseph Durso and Mickey Mantle. *Whitey and Mickey: A Joint Autobiography of the Yankee Years*. New York: Viking, 1977.

Forker, Dom. *Sweet Seasons: Recollections of the 1955–64 New York Yankees.* Dallas: Taylor, 1990.

Frank, Stanley B. *The Jew In Sports.* New York: Miles, 1936.

Frick, Ford C. *Games, Asterisks, and People: Memoirs of a Lucky Fan.* New York: Crown, 1973.

Frommer, Harvey. *Rickey and Robinson: The Men Who Broke Baseball's Color Line.* New York: Macmillan, 1982.

———. *New York City Baseball: The Last Golden Age, 1947–1957.* San Diego: Harcourt Brace Jovanovich, 1985.

Gallagher, Mark. *Day-by-Day in New York Yankees History.* West Point, N.Y.: Leisure Press, 1983.

———. *Explosion! Mickey Mantle's Legendary Home Runs.* New York: Arbor House, 1987.

Gies, Joseph, and Robert H. Shoemaker. *Stars of the Series: A Complete History of the World Series.* New York: Crowell, 1964.

Gluck, Herb. *Baseball's Great Moments.* New York: Random House, 1975.

Goldstein, Richard. *Superstars and Screwballs: 100 Years of Brooklyn Baseball.* New York: Penguin, 1991.

Golenbock, Peter. *Dynasty: The New York Yankees, 1949–1964.* Englewood Cliffs, N.J.: Prentice-Hall, 1975.

———. *Bums: An Oral History of the Brooklyn Dodgers.* New York: Putnam's, 1984.

Graham, Frank. *The New York Giants: An Informal History.* New York: Putnam's, 1952.

Graham, Frank, Jr. *Casey Stengel: His Half Century in Baseball.* New York: John Day, 1958.

———. *Great Pennant Races of the Major Leagues.* New York: Random House, 1967.

———. *A Farewell to Heroes.* New York: Viking, 1981.

Halberstam, David. *Summer of '49.* New York: Morrow, 1989.

Hamilton, Virginia. *Paul Robeson: The Life and Times of a Free Black Man.* New York: Harper & Row, 1974.

Hano, Arnold. *A Day in the Bleachers.* New York: Crowell, 1955.

———. *Sandy Koufax, Strikeout King.* New York: Putnam's, 1964.

———. *Willie Mays.* New York: Grosset and Dunlap, 1966.

Harwell, Ernie. *Tuned to Baseball.* South Bend, Ind.: Diamond Communications, 1985.

Henrich, Tommy, with Bill Gilbert. *Five o'Clock Lightning: Ruth*

Gehrig, DiMaggio, Mantle, and the Glory Years of the New York Yankees. New York: Carol Publishing Group, 1992.

Hodges, Russell P. ("Russ"), and Al Hirshberg. *My Giants.* Garden City, N.Y.: Doubleday, 1963.

Holmes, Tommy. *Dodger Daze and Knights: Enough of a Ballclub's History to Explain Its Reputation.* New York: McKay, 1953.

Holtzman, Jerome. *No Cheering in the Press Box.* New York: Holt, 1973.

Honig, Donald. *Baseball Between the Lines: Baseball in the 40's and 50's, as Told by the Men Who Played It.* New York: Coward McCann Geoghegan, 1976.

————. *October Heroes: Great World Series Games Remembered by the Men Who Played Them.* New York: Simon & Schuster, 1979.

————. *The Brooklyn Dodgers: An Illustrated History.* New York: St. Martin's, 1981.

————. *Baseball's Ten Greatest Teams.* New York: Macmillan, 1982.

————. *Baseball America: The Heroes of the Game and the Times of Their Glory.* New York: Macmillan, 1985.

————. *Baseball in the Fifties: A Decade of Transition.* New York: Crown, 1987.

————. *The New York Yankees: An Illustrated History.* New York: Crown, 1987.

Horowitz, Harold H., and Ralph Toleris. *Big Time Baseball.* New York: Hart, 1950.

Hynd, Noel. *The Giants of the Polo Grounds: The Glorious Times of Baseball's New York Giants.* New York: Doubleday, 1988.

James, Bill. *The Bill James Historical Baseball Abstract.* New York: Villard, 1988.

Jennison, Christopher. *Wait Till Next Year: The Yankees, Dodgers and Giants, 1947–57.* New York: Norton, 1974.

Kelley, Martin. *Baseball in and Around New York, 1901–51, Viewed Through the Eyes of an Old Timer.* New York: Leaves of Plates, 1991.

Kempton, Murray. *America Comes of Middle Age.* Boston: Little, Brown, 1963.

Kiernan, Thomas. *The Miracle at Coogan's Bluff.* New York: Crowell, 1975.

King, Martin Luther, Jr. *Strength to Love.* New York: Harper & Row, 1963.

Klein, Dave. *Great Moments in Baseball.* New York: Cowles, 1971.

Koppett, Leonard. *A Thinking Man's Guide to Baseball.* New York: Dutton, 1967.

Kuklick, Bruce. *To Every Thing a Season.* Princeton: Princeton University Press, 1991.

Lansche, Jerry. *The Forgotten Championships: Postseason Baseball, 1882–1981.* Jefferson, N.C.: McFarland, 1989.

Lardner, John. *It Beats Working.* Philadelphia: Lippincott, 1947.

———. *Strong Cigars and Lovely Women.* New York: Funk and Wagnalls, 1951.

Linn, Ed. *The Great Rivalry: The Yankees and the Red Sox, 1901–1990.* New York: Ticknor & Fields, 1991.

Lipman, David. *Mr. Baseball: The Story of Branch Rickey.* New York: Putnam's, 1966.

Lowry, Phillip. J. *Green Cathedrals.* New York: Society for American Baseball Research, 1986.

MacDougall, Curtis D. *Gideon's Army.* New York: Marzani and Munsell, 1965.

MacPhail, Lee. *My 9 Innings: An Autobiography of 50 Years in Baseball.* Westport, Conn.: Meckler, 1989.

Mann, Arthur. *Baseball Confidential: Secret History of the War Among Chandler, Durocher, McPhail and Rickey.* New York: McKay, 1951.

———. *Branch Rickey, American in Action.* Boston: Houghton Mifflin, 1957.

Mantle, Mickey, and Phil Pepe. *My Favorite Summer, 1956.* New York: Doubleday, 1991.

Martin, Billy, and Peter Golenbock. *Number One.* New York: Delacorte, 1980.

Mathewson, Christopher. *Pitching in a Pinch, Or, Baseball From the Inside.* New York: Grosset & Dunlap, 1912.

Mays, Willie, and Lou Sahadi. *Say Hey.* New York: Simon & Schuster, 1989.

McGuire, William. *The World Series.* Mankato, Minn.: Creative Education, 1990.

Meany, Tom. *The Artful Dodgers.* New York: Barnes, 1953.

Miller, Douglas T., and Marion Nowak. *The Fifties: The Way We Really Were.* New York: Doubleday, 1977.

Musial, Stan, as told to Bob Broeg. *The Man Stan.* St. Louis: Bethany, 1977.

Neft, David S., and Richard M. Cohen. *The World Series: Complete Play-by-Play of Every Game, 1903–1989.* New York: St. Martin's, 1990.

Obojski, Robert. *Great Moments of the Playoffs and World Series.* New York: Sterling, 1988.

Olsen, Jack. *The Black Athlete: A Shameful Story, the Myth of Integration in American History.* New York: Time-Life Books, 1968.

Parrott, Harold. *The Lords of Baseball.* New York: Praeger, 1976.

Pepe, Phil. *The Wit and Wisdom of Yogi Berra.* New York: Hawthorn, 1974.

Pietruza, David. *Major Leagues: The Formation, Sometimes Absorption, and Mostly Inevitable Demise of 18 Professional Baseball Organizations, 1871 to Present.* Jefferson, N.C.: McFarland, 1991.

Polner, Murray. *Branch Rickey.* New York: Atheneum, 1982.

Rader, Benjamin G. *Baseball: A History of America's Game.* Urbana: University of Illinois Press, 1992.

Reichler, Joseph L., ed. *The Baseball Encyclopedia: The Complete and Official Record of Major League Baseball.* 5th ed. New York: Macmillan, 1982.

Reidenbaugh, Lowell. *Baseball's 50 Greatest Games.* St. Louis: The Sporting News, 1986.

Ribakove, Barbara and Sy. *The Nifty Fifties: The Happy Years.* New York: Award Books, 1974.

Rickey, Branch, and Robert Riger. *The American Diamond: A Documentary of the Game of Baseball.* New York: Simon & Schuster, 1965.

Riley, Dan. *The Dodgers Reader.* Boston: Houghton Mifflin, 1992.

Robinson, Jackie. *Jackie Robinson: My Own Story.* New York: Greenberg Press, 1948.

———, as told to Alfred Duckett. *I Never Had It Made.* New York: Putnam's, 1972.

Robinson, Ray. *The Home Run Heard 'Round the World: The Dramatic Story of the 1951 Giants-Dodgers Pennant Race.* New York: HarperCollins, 1991.

Rosenfeld, Harvey. *The Great Chase: The Dodgers-Giants Pennant Race of 1951.* Jefferson, N.C.: McFarland, 1992

Rosenthal, Harold. *Baseball Is Their Business.* New York: Random House, 1952.

————. *The Ten Best Years in Baseball: An Informal History of the Fifties*. Chicago: Contemporary Books, 1979.

Rowan, Carl T., with Jackie Robinson. *Wait Till Next Year*. New York: Random House, 1960.

Rust, Art, Jr. *Get That Nigger Off the Field*. New York: Delacorte, 1976.

Schoor, Gene. *The Willie Mays Story*. New York: Messner, 1960.

————. *Joe DiMaggio: A Biography*. Garden City, N.Y.: Doubleday, 1980.

————. *The History of the World Series: The Complete Chronology of America's Greatest Sports Tradition*. New York: Morrow, 1990.

Seymour, Harold. *Baseball*. New York: Oxford University Press, 1971.

Shapiro, Milton J. *The Sal Maglie Story*. New York: Messner, 1957.

————. *Mickey Mantle, Yankee Slugger*. New York: Messner, 1962.

————. *The Whitey Ford Story*. New York: Messner, 1962.

————. *The Don Drysdale Story*. New York: Messner, 1964.

————. *The Roy Campanella Story*. New York: Messner, 1968.

Silverman, Al. *Mickey Mantle: Mister Yankee*. New York: Putnam's, 1963.

Siner, Howard. *Sweet Seasons: Baseball's Top Teams Since 1920*. New York: Pharos, 1988.

Smalling, R. J. ("Jack"), and Dennis W. Eckes. *Baseball Address List*. Cleveland: Edgewater, 1990.

Smith, Curt. *Voices of the Game: The Acclaimed Chronicle of Baseball Radio and Television Broadcasting, from 1921 to the Present*. New York: Simon & Schuster, 1992.

Smith, Red. *Out of the Red*. New York: Knopf, 1950.

————. *Views of Sports*. New York: Knopf, 1954.

————. *The Best of Red Smith*. New York: Watts, 1963.

————. *Strawberries in the Wintertime: The Sporting World of Red Smith*. New York: Quadrangle/New York Times, 1974.

————. *To Absent Friends*. New York: Atheneum, 1982.

————. *The Red Smith Reader*. Ed. Dave Anderson. New York: Random House, 1982.

Snider, Duke, and Bill Gilbert. *The Duke of Flatbush*. New York: Zebra, 1988.

Starr, Bill. *Clearing the Bases: Baseball Then and Now*. New York: Michael Kesend, 1989.

Stein, Fred, and Nick Peters. *Giants Diary: A Century of Giants Baseball in New York and San Francisco.* Berkeley: North Atlantic Press, 1987.

Stengel, Casey, as told to Harry T. Paxton. *Casey at the Bat: The Story of My Life in Baseball.* New York: Random House, 1962.

Stone, I. F. *The Haunted Fifties.* New York: Random House, 1963.

Sugar, Bert Randolph. *Baseball's 50 Greatest Games.* New York: Exeter, 1986.

Sullivan, Neil J. *The Dodgers Move West.* New York: Oxford University Press, 1987.

Thomson, Bobby, with Lee Heiman and Bill Gutman. *The Giants Win the Pennant! The Giants Win the Pennant!* New York: Kensington, 1991.

Thompson, Lafayette F. ("Fresco"), with Cy Rice. *Every Diamond Doesn't Sparkle.* New York: McKay, 1964.

Thorn, John. *Baseball's Ten Greatest Games.* New York: Four Winds, 1984.

Trimble, Joe. *Phil Rizzuto: A Bio of the Scooter.* New York: Barnes, 1951.

Tulius, John. *I'd Rather Be a Yankee: An Oral History of America's Most Loved and Most Hated Baseball Team.* New York: Macmillan, 1986.

Tygiel, Jules. *Baseball's Great Experiment: Jackie Robinson and His Legacy.* New York: Oxford University Press, 1983.

Urbano, Carlos. *World Series Baseball.* Evanston: Beisbol, 1989.

Veeck, Bill, with Ed Linn. *Veeck as in Wreck.* New York: Putnam's, 1962.

———. *The Hustler's Handbook.* New York: Simon & Schuster, 1965.

Vescey, George. *The Life Story of Sandy Koufax.* New York: Scholastic, 1968.

Warfield, Don. *The Roaring Redhead: Larry MacPhail, Baseball's Great Innovator.* South Bend: Diamond Communications, 1987.

Weinberger, Miro, and Dan Riley. *The Yankees Reader.* Boston: Houghton Mifflin, 1991.

Woodward, Stanley. *Sports Page.* New York: Simon & Schuster, 1949.

Index

♦